Conservative Counterrevolution

THE WORKING CLASS IN AMERICAN HISTORY

Editorial Advisors
James R. Barrett, Julie Greene, William P. Jones,
Alice Kessler-Harris, and Nelson Lichtenstein

A list of books in the series appears at the end of this book.

Conservative Counterrevolution

Challenging Liberalism in 1950s Milwaukee

TULA A. CONNELL

University of Illinois Press
URBANA, CHICAGO, AND SPRINGFIELD

© 2016 by the Board of Trustees
of the University of Illinois
All rights reserved
1 2 3 4 5 C P 5 4 3 2 1
∞ This book is printed on acid-free paper.

Library of Congress Cataloging-in-Publication Data
Names: Connell, Tula A., 1960–
Title: Conservative counterrevolution : challenging
   liberalism in 1950s Milwaukee / Tula A. Connell.
Description: Urbana : University of Illinois Press, 2016.
   | Series: The working class in American history |
   Includes bibliographical references and index.
Identifiers: LCCN 2015031905 | ISBN 9780252039904
   (hardcover : acid-free paper) | ISBN 9780252081422
   (paperback : acid-free paper) | ISBN 9780252098062
   (e-book)
Subjects: LCSH: Milwaukee (Wis.)—Politics and
   government—20th century. | Conservatism—
   Wisconsin—Milwaukee—History—20th century.
   | Liberalism—Wisconsin—Milwaukee—History—
   20th century. | Social movements—Wisconsin—
   Milwaukee—History—20th century. | Social
   conflict—Wisconsin—Milwaukee—History—20th
   century. | Zeidler, Frank P. | Mayors—Wisconsin—
   Milwaukee—Biography. | Milwaukee (Wis.)—
   Economic conditions—20th century.
Classification: LCC F589.M657 C66 2016 | DDC
   977.5/95—dc23 LC record available at http://lccn.loc.
   gov/2015031905

For John
My brother

Contents

Acknowledgments ix

Introduction 1

1 A Liberal in City Government 14
2 The Media Makes the Message 39
3 Public or Private? The Battle over Channel 10 58
4 Let the People Vote 73
5 Race, Class, Free Enterprise, and Suburbia 96
6 Collective Action and the Threat to Free Enterprise 127
7 Public Interest vs. Public Employees 148

Conclusion 175

Notes 189
Bibliography 219
Index 235

Photographs follow page 126

Acknowledgments

Recognizing that it is impossible to acknowledge by name all those who have provided assistance along the way, I would like to highlight those whose support has been especially indispensable in bringing this project to fruition.

I am most grateful to the scholars who engaged with early and ongoing drafts and who offered detailed, analytical critiques that gave shape and direction to this work. Many, many thanks to Joseph McCartin, Thomas Sugrue, Adam Rothman, Andrew Kersten, Cecili Bucki, and Randi Storch for their incisive and masterly reviews.

I am deeply grateful for the support of my Milwaukee friends, new and old, whose hospitality, warmth, and kindness made a multiyear project like this particularly enjoyable. My deepest gratitude goes to Shelly and Perry Pace, who never failed to open their home to me and who never lost faith that someday, they would read the fruits of my research.

I want to extend my appreciation also to all the dedicated and expert archivists and staff whose assistance has been invaluable throughout this project. Foremost among them is Gayle Ecklund, archivist at the Milwaukee Public Library, who shared her deep knowledge of the library archives, provided ongoing assistance and, not the least, cheered me on throughout the process. Gayle is one of many incredibly knowledgeable Milwaukee Public Library staff to whom I am grateful.

Special thanks to Joanne Ricca, Ken Germanson, and all the dedicated volunteers who maintain the Milwaukee Labor Historical Society. Much gratitude to Anita Zeidler, Phil Blank, Rep. Fred Kessler, Charlotte Bleistein, and the many other Milwaukeeans whose gracious generosity with their time and assistance with this project truly represents the best of the city's welcoming open-door reputation. A big shout out to Patricia Woodhouse and Stephanie Harp, who undertook the monumental task of proofreading, and to John Goltz for his technical assistance.

Also thanks to Kevin Abing, archivist, and Steve Daily, assistant archivist at the Milwaukee County Historical Society; Ellen Engseth, former archivist at the Wisconsin Historical Society; Marge McNinch, Hagley reference archivist; Harvey Parker, Bureau of Labor Statistics economist; and Christine Silvia, researcher at the AFL-CIO. Many of the archives and libraries consulted for this project are public institutions staffed by public employees who once again have demonstrated their commitment to outstanding public service.

Most of all, I am indebted to Joseph McCartin, a mentor without peer, whose intellectual acuity steered the project's scholarly course and whose steadfast support for my work as it evolved provided the solid foundation needed to carry it to completion. Despite many commitments, he generously gave of his time, offering intellectual and practical direction that made this book possible.

Introduction

> We went through a peaceful revolution in this country in 1933. We are now in the counterrevolution.
> —Thomas Stokes, columnist, May 1948

On June 27, 1955, as he sat in his office at Grede Foundries in Milwaukee, Wisconsin, where he oversaw the operation of multiple iron-casting plants, William Grede dictated a letter in response to a fellow Milwaukee businessman, congratulating him on his efforts to promote the philosophy of far-right conservative Clarence Manion among his employees. Such proselytization at factories and colleges was effective, Grede wrote. And it was necessary: at a time when more and more workers were signing up with unions, increasing labor's economic and political strength, and in an environment in which unions and the government were working together to push for broad-based social programs, conservative business leaders needed to take action to reverse the tide. "As someone said to me recently," Grede wrote, "'The revolution of 1933 was possible only because of the revolution that took place among the so-called intelligentsia at the turn of the century.' Our job is to start a revolution in the other direction, like that of the early 1900s and hope that in the next fifty years we can swing it back."[1]

Downtown in the mayor's office, Frank Zeidler embodied much of what Grede rejected. A self-described socialist, Zeidler had won the mayoral election in 1948 at the head of a powerful nonpartisan liberal coalition and was poised to win a third term in 1956. Grede's work in the local Republican Party had failed to make inroads in challenging the city's top office, and Grede faced the threat of more liberal reforms, such as the affordable housing programs Zeidler had pushed early on. Stymied locally, Grede also had little hope of support for his brand of conservatism from national political leaders and was especially disillusioned with the moderate direction of the Republican Party under President Dwight D. Eisenhower. If the threat represented by those like

Zeidler was to be repulsed, Grede believed, it would take courageous action by like-minded businessmen championing an alternative to what they saw as New Deal collectivism. Grede vowed to fight back.

As Grede's words made clear, he knew he was not alone in anticipating a decades-long struggle to overturn the social welfare programs of the New Deal and reshape the sociocultural environment away from one that accepted broad-based government involvement in the economy. When conservative intellectual Frank Chodorov initially defined a "fifty-year project" in 1950, he referred only to the effort to uproot "socialism" from college campuses. But by the end of the decade, Chodorov joined other conservatives in calling the overarching effort to undo "the socialization of the American character" a fifty-year project. This "counterrevolution," recognized at the time by perceptive journalists such as Thomas Stokes, quoted above, was a project William Grede was determined to advance, and Milwaukee was a key battleground in this long war.[2]

At midcentury, cities like Milwaukee were indeed crucial political battlegrounds in the postwar era. They became the locus of intense fights over union power, racial equality, access to housing, taxation, annexation, the control and expansion of government services, and the unionization of public employees. In these metropolitan milieus, the often inchoate yet passionately held postwar ideals of the public good promoted by New Deal liberals ran up against notions of individual rights expressed largely, though not exclusively, through unfettered free enterprise. The struggles that ensued when these ideals were put to the test on the full range of issues confronting cities and their suburbs across the nation would both determine the limits of the New Deal order and help define what would take its place. At times, the interplay between liberalism and conservatism was not clear-cut. Liberal assertions of what constituted the public good were complicated by personal ideology, political expediency, and a failure to grasp the challenges ahead. With such complex visions competing to define the city's future, Milwaukee illustrates both the limits of postwar liberalism and the resurgence of conservatism, a dynamic repeated in cities across the nation.

This book argues that 1950s Milwaukee stood on the fault line of an emerging conflict that would in time come to shape postwar American politics. The growth of unions, the expansion of government, and the rise of those like Frank Zeidler galvanized embattled conservatives such as William Grede, who shared an individualist worldview, fueled by an aggressive, anti-union, free-market-based conservatism. The formula that conservatives developed in Milwaukee effectively contested notions of the common good that had undergirded Franklin D. Roosevelt's New Deal order. In Milwaukee, as elsewhere, this challenge to liberalism represented a reemergence of prewar conservatism and contributed to the anti-liberal resurgence that would sweep much of the nation in the following decades.

Conservatism and Liberalism in the 1950s

Before proceeding, a clarification of terms is in order. Conservatism, like most "-isms," is a notoriously elusive category. Scholars have noted its shifting and temporal character, its lack of logical coherence, and its "often contradictory principles and political interpretations," descriptions that fit other political classifications as well. Political scientist Clinton Rossiter, a self-described "middling" conservative, offers a useful framework for considering conservatism in this study. First formulated in the mid-1950s, Rossiter's analysis benefits from its reflection of the contemporary political environment.[3]

Rossiter divided conservatives into three groups: "liberal," "middling," and "ultracon." Rossiter's criterion for classification was based on the relative willingness of each group to accept the burdens of a "domesticated New Deal" and allow for certain international involvement, such as membership in the United Nations. In Rossiter's schema, liberal conservatives were those who "accept the new dimensions in government with little rancor or regret." Middling conservatives "will consider social legislation that others propose, and though they are likely to react as angrily as ever to any mention of the New Deal, they seem entirely willing to leave the New Deal agencies in operation." Ultracons "not only oppose any further social legislation but call for the scrapping of many agencies and programs."[4]

This study focuses on the conservatives occupying the middle and right portions of Rossiter's 1950s spectrum but uses the less politically charged terms "moderate" and "far right" in place of "middling" and "ultracon." At the same time, this study acknowledges that neither category is clear-cut, and it looks for how the ideologies and tactics of those in these categories often overlapped. This study also focuses on economic conservatism, arguing that the emphasis on free enterprise intrinsic to American conservatism in many instances superseded other aspects of domestic postwar conservatism. This is also in keeping with Rossiter's understanding. If the "notion of a bundle of freedoms is increasingly popular among conservative orators," he wrote, "it should be noted that most sticks in the bundle appear to be economic in character."[5]

A key component of postwar economic conservatism is anti-unionism. Although the U.S. labor movement was at its historic height in the late 1940s and the early 1950s, anti-unionism in these decades was a growing force, even in solidly unionized midwestern cities. Corporations modernized their anti-union tactics from the century's early decades but did not alter their unstinting opposition to workplace-based challenges to their authority. Examining the backlash against the 1935 National Labor Relations Act (NLRA) in a heavily unionized city such as Milwaukee helps highlight how conservatism did not "emerge" in the 1950s or 1960s but rather represented a resurgence of a deep current in America's history in which the New Deal era was a "byproduct of the massive crisis of the Great Depression rather than the linear triumph of the liberal state."[6]

Among moderate free market conservatives, such opposition manifested primarily at the bargaining table, where each side attempted to limit the other's gains. But in its most extreme form, economic conservatism sought to eliminate unions and the laws that made possible the free association of working people. In this vision, any intrusion in undiluted capitalism was a slide into socialism. The proper operation of free enterprise therefore was predicated on businesses and individuals remaining unfettered from government laws and regulations and free from the involvement of third parties who sought to represent a collective group.

Economic conservatism provided much of the foundation for religious and race-based conservatism. For instance, by setting up individual free will in opposition to communist and socialist economics, free enterprise conservatism fed such notions as Christian opposition to "Godless unions," with their roots in collectivism. In community after community, conservative resistance to legislation barring discrimination in housing sales was predicated on the free-enterprise notion of property rights. Although the extent to which such economic assertions took precedence over outright racism generally cannot be ascertained, arguments steeped in language of individual liberty proved powerful tools of popular mobilization against admitting African Americans as neighbors.[7]

Liberalism in this period reflected a belief in, and a desire to, continue or expand federal economic policies established in the 1930s and 1940s. Unlike moderate economic conservatives, liberals backed federal efforts to expand affordable housing and initiate broad healthcare coverage. Scholars such as Alan Brinkley and Lisa McGirr also have pointed to vulnerabilities in postwar liberalism. Liberal intellectuals "cast liberalism as the sole intellectual tradition in American life," writes McGirr. "By failing to take into account the deep-seated conservative ideological traditions on which the Right drew and by refusing to closely examine the ideological universe of conservatives, liberal intellectuals underestimated the resilience and staying power of the Right in American life."[8]

Often complacent after the gains made in the New Deal and during World War II, liberals also did not pursue expansion of programs such as affordable housing with the energy and determination of prior years, leaving a lacuna for the re-emergence of conservatives within domestic policy decision making. Brinkley cogently argues that liberalism in this period also began to redefine its mission. "American liberals . . . detached liberalism from its earlier emphasis on reform—its preoccupation with issues of class, its tendency to equate freedom and democracy with economic autonomy, its hostility to concentrated economic power."[9]

Milwaukee and Our Evolving Understanding of Conservatism's Rise

From LaFollette progressivism to "sewer socialism," Milwaukee's politics have seemingly set it firmly on the side of liberalism. Yet this book complicates our view of Milwaukee's history, shedding light on the challenges facing even the most liberal municipal administrations in one of the nation's most unionized cities. After all, the same area that produced Victor Berger, the nation's first socialist member of Congress, also gave birth to Sen. Joseph McCarthy and George Kennan who, in manifestly different ways, were key figures in creating and shaping Cold War–era politics. In exploring Milwaukee's history in this critical period, this book illuminates numerous issues that have concerned historians in recent years.

One such issue is the relation of city to suburb. Suburban conservatism proved to be a driving force shaping Milwaukee's response to the postwar urban challenges. The rise of the suburban "silent majority" was an expression of modern conservatism, one rooted in the tension between private rights and the collective good. While manifesting most dramatically in the urban–suburban battles over civil rights, housing, and busing, this tension existed wherever the public interest challenged the reassertion of individual rights, as embodied within the context of free enterprise.

The history of suburbanization has greatly expanded since Kenneth Jackson's pioneering study of suburbs reconceptualized spatial politics to incorporate the interconnection of suburbs and urban centers. Following Jackson, scholars such as Matthew Lassiter, Kevin Kruse, and Robert O. Self have explored how the suburbs served as proving grounds for the grassroots conservative racial backlash. In *Suburban Warriors*, Lisa McGirr highlights conservatism as a social movement, with assertions of local control and opposition to federal power central to a distinct southern and western regional identification.[10]

The story told in this book contributes to recent scholarly efforts by historians like Thomas Sugrue to move beyond the suburban enclaves, consider the larger metropolitan perspective, and broaden metropolitan narratives to illuminate the interaction of class and race.[11] While studies of conservatism have addressed race, religion, geography, and a variety of sociocultural issues, much more scholarship on the economic elements fueling urban–suburban power politics must be undertaken to provide a comprehensive understanding of the disputed terrain of the postwar city. Within this framework, a study of the contentious battles between Milwaukee and its suburbs illustrates how racist politics are often inextricably mixed with the politics of class.[12]

This book also challenges narratives that locate the emergence of suburban conservatism in the 1960s. By highlighting the immediate postwar years as formative for metropolitan conservatism, this study rejects the "backlash politics" narrative popularized by Thomas B. and Mary Edsall. As most versions of the backlash narrative see it, white working-class voters embraced conservative politics in response to African American assertions of their rights, the growing militancy of the anti-war movement, the rise of feminism, and other perceived radicalism in the 1960s. This book joins with the work of Joseph Lowndes and Kim Phillips-Fein, who point to the resurgence of conservatism well before the 1960s "backlash" began.[13]

This study also contributes to our ongoing reevaluation of conservatism's history. Since George Nash's now-classic examination of conservative intellectuals, the historiography of postwar conservatism has broadened considerably.[14] Studies in recent years have included histories of conservative organizations,[15] the influence of politics in defining conservatism,[16] and the role of women in the movement.[17] Scholars increasingly are pointing also to conservatism's deep roots in American history, with Jefferson Cowie and Nick Salvatore arguing that the postwar era was a "long exception" to the norm of American politics, and that liberalism never laid the cultural foundation for an alternative to the conservative individualism of earlier decades.[18]

Further, scholarship on postwar conservatism has expanded to include studies of the far right. Until recently, scholars and contemporary analysts writing in the late 1950s and early 1960s were far more likely to take seriously the extreme end of the conservative spectrum. Daniel Bell's 1963 classic *The Radical Right: The New American Right* compiled essays on the topic in the mid-1950s. The Anti-Defamation League in 1964 published Arnold Forester and Benjamin Epstein's *Danger on the Right*, after Anti-Defamation League Director Oscar Cohen recognized that the league's extensive documentation of such activities warranted a book. In 1967, George Thayer chronicled the movement in *The Farther Shores of Politics: The American Political Fringe*

Today. Contemporary observers clearly did not dismiss these individuals and movements and, in fact, pinpointed a trend toward far-right extremism they found deeply disturbing.[19]

Recent biographies have broken through long-accepted narratives that pigeonholed far-right movements as incapable of influencing the national dialogue. Oil magnate H. L. Hunt, news reporter John Flynn, and *Reader's Digest* founders DeWitt and Lila Bell Wallace have come under examination. This study furthers the historiography that takes seriously those dismissed as insignificant fringe elements, while it examines the interconnectedness of the far-right movement with moderate conservatism. By contextualizing "extremist" figures like Grede, this work illustrates the extent to which their ideologies and actions fit comfortably within the broader conservative framework in Milwaukee and the nation.[20]

Further, while other studies have included labor as a target of these actors, this work seeks to emphasize how the economic opportunity that unions afforded the working and middle class was a key aspect of the New Deal–era expansion of marketplace opportunity and therefore directly challenged the prevailing power structure, which drew its strength from economic domination. In this sense, anti-unionism provided an economic underpinning for the later expansion of conservatism into sociocultural and religious areas.

Shaping public opinion was essential to early postwar efforts aimed at chipping away at the foundations of the New Deal. Yet while these newer studies of far-right figures also have begun to challenge the focus by scholars of conservatism on national media publications like William F. Buckley's *National Review* or the works of postwar Austrian School economists, much research remains to demonstrate the inroads conservatism made among the broader public through mass media. Heather Hendershot's study of far-right radio broadcasters during the Cold War cracks open the door onto this influential but largely overlooked segment of postwar conservatism.[21]

By examining the rapidly evolving postwar media, this book broadens the scholarship of far-right conservatism, illustrating how the proliferation of far-right local and national media engaged a larger audience than has been recognized. In Milwaukee as elsewhere, far-right conservatives reached a significant number of people through the media. National periodicals such as *Reader's Digest* and H. L. Hunt's *Facts Forum News*—dismissed as nonintellectual and therefore safely disregarded—touched a wide and populist base—those not likely to peruse the highbrow *National Review* but certain to talk with neighbors and families about what they read and to go to the polls to act on it. With their even vaster reach among Milwaukee area residents, conservative suburban weeklies at times defined the political debate on such key issues as affordable housing and racial tolerance. The expansion of the far-right media took place in an environment that saw a decrease in publications and radio broadcasts focused on the issues of concern to the working class and a marked turn toward economic conservatism by the major national media.

Business contributed to the media's renewed emphasis on free enterprise. Robert Griffith, Wendy Wall, Richard Tedlow, Stuart Ewen, and others have amply demonstrated business's efforts to sell free enterprise through elaborate and well-funded public relations campaigns. Further, their work demonstrates how the corporate postwar public relations push in the 1950s built on similar self-selling efforts in the years before the Depression, part of a corporate playbook opposing an expansion of the social welfare state interrupted by the New Deal.[22]

Recent scholarship has further expanded on the postwar influence of business by examining its opposition to labor and liberalism. Historians such as Kim Phillips-Fein and Elizabeth Tandy Shermer have amplified the early work of Elizabeth Fones-Wolf, which showed how business leaders and smaller employers found that "reorienting workers away from their newfound loyalties to organized labor and government" was essential for reshaping the "ideas, images, and attitudes through which Americans understood . . . their relationships to the corporation and the state." In targeting unions, conservatives shredded the underpinnings of the nation's broad-based economic prosperity and sought to tilt the playing field back toward the corporations and wealthy individuals who significantly funded their endeavors.[23]

This study expands scholarly understandings of how the conservative assault on labor unions was essential to the larger project of delegitimizing government's role in domestic social programs. In doing so, it also points to the mirage-like nature of the celebrated business-labor consensus, illustrating that modern conservatism was not newly generated in the 1950s or 1960s but rather represented a resurgence of a deep current in America's history. By highlighting the role of business, this work also furthers recent labor historiography, which, unlike "new left" histories of previous decades that attempted to recover America's "progressive" past, sees the conservative role of business as crucial to circumscribing worker radicalism.[24]

The Milwaukee story makes it possible to see how business leaders challenged presumptions of labor's legitimacy at the workplace and within the civic arena, even in a heavily unionized and politically liberal environment. Milwaukee workers struggled with employers in sometimes hard-fought contests, challenging the notion of postwar labor–management accord and shedding light on the early genesis of corporate opposition not only to Keynesianism but also to the form of commercial prewar Keynesianism that emerged after World War II. Historian Robert M. Collins characterizes commercial Keynesianism in part as an active monetary policy and a passive fiscal policy, along with reductions in taxation and increases in private spending over increases in public spending. The response of the area's major corporations to labor also opens a door on the day-to-day resistance union members faced from conservative forces in the civic sphere. While Milwaukee is perceived as the prototype of liberalism, where unions had a powerful voice on the job and at the ballot box, lawmakers, the local media, and city administrators sought at times to mute them.[25]

Tracing the Conservative Challenge to Liberalism

Chapter 1 explores the immediate postwar economic, political, and cultural environment of Milwaukee, a city where decades of stasis were compounded by a changing demographic that included suburban flight and an increasingly lower-income urban core. The long municipal governance by socialist Mayor Daniel Hoan (1916–1940) and the city's high levels of unionization had fostered a strong middle class from the early decades of the century through World War II. But far more than most industrialized midwestern cities, Milwaukee had seen little modernization since the 1920s, with brewery industrialists and other business leaders markedly absent from contributing to citywide improvement, unlike their peers in cities such as Pittsburgh. By war's end, the necessity to meet the growing and evolving needs of city residents, and generate a solid financial base to do so, created a crisis atmosphere recognized by political leaders and private-sector actors alike.

At this critical juncture, the 1948 mayoral elections provided Milwaukeeans the opportunity to set the direction for their future, and they chose Frank Zeidler, an avowed socialist who ran for mayor as a liberal. Zeidler's campaign emerged from a coalition of liberals unified under a principle that centered on addressing through public initiative those socioeconomic needs the private sector had not addressed. In the ensuing twelve years as Milwaukee mayor, Zeidler would govern not as a socialist but rather in the liberal tradition set forth by Franklin Roosevelt. Although Zeidler revisited his conception of public governance throughout his life, he maintained a foundational belief that government, rather than the market, was best suited to serve the common interest.

Unlike many elected officials, Zeidler took office with a thoughtfully formulated philosophy of governance, one that this chapter looks at in detail. Zeidler's conception of the "public interest" guided his actions, at times setting him apart from both liberal and socialist expectations. His meticulously defined and clearly stated goals, well within the Rooseveltian model that privileged a large role for the public sector in addressing the collective good, offer a solid foundation for consideration of the challenges to the postwar liberal agenda.

As elsewhere in the postwar years, dwindling media diversity in Milwaukee resulted in diminished coverage of economic issues facing the working class, even as the mainstream media more explicitly beat the drum for unfettered free enterprise. Chapter 2 looks at how the city's fading foreign-language press and financially challenged labor media were offset by a vociferous conservative suburban press. Simultaneously, large mainstream media outlets began a notable ideological shift toward free market triumphalism, while the surge in far-right national broadcast media and print publications began reaching Milwaukee households.

This chapter underlines how the spread of far-right media, far from spontaneous, was generated with the partnership of large corporate interests that privately financed such endeavors even as they publicly espoused support for New Deal principles. Although most corporations publicly remained moderate in their approach to issues such as public provision of social welfare programs and unionization, many joined with "fringe" groups to surreptitiously unravel the postwar New Deal economic order. As such, even businesses that seemingly had bought into commercial Keynesianism played a considerable part in the conservative backlash to the New Deal.

The contested terrain over media control manifested in a divisive battle over creation of a public television channel in Milwaukee—a seemingly innocuous issue that far less liberal cities like Houston addressed without controversy. Chapter 3 examines how moderate conservative activists united with the far-right conservative local media, which sharply opposed the Zeidler administration, to challenge the role of the public sector in providing educational television. The battle over Channel 10 was part of the larger struggle between proponents of an expansive public sector and champions of limited government.

In one of Milwaukee's most defining struggles of the decade, a grassroots conservative movement ran a successful campaign against City Hall's effort to create affordable housing, defying the odds in a city where the majority of residents favored public housing. Chapter 4 details the strategies involved in the 1951 campaign by a coalition of small property owners and anti-tax proponents who sought to halt creation of public housing through a ballot referendum. Leading the coalition, long-time civic activist and savings-and-loan official William Pieplow exemplifies Rossiter's definition of moderate conservative. Pieplow's elevation of individual rights was tempered by a belief in "public virtue"—a willingness to sacrifice private to public interests, a characteristic championed in the early days of the nation's founding as essential for republican government. Although the referendum campaign received some support from the national housing and builder associations, which vehemently opposed the 1949 Housing Act, the movement Pieplow and his cohorts spearheaded was a genuinely grassroots expression, one that sought to defend against the perceived loss of individual rights that would result from the provision of public housing.[26]

Chapter 5 broadens the narrative with its focus on suburban opposition to annexation. Zeidler's attempt to annex land on the city's periphery and provide the territorial expansion and improved tax base necessary for Milwaukee's growing population set the stage for a massive battle with the suburbs. The conflict highlights the interconnections between classist and racialist notions, with the growing socioeconomic needs of the city's inner core of low-income residents pitted against an "iron ring" of suburbs whose inhabitants were equally convinced of the right to define who could be their neighbors. As it did elsewhere, the focus on skin color in the struggles surrounding housing and urban renewal obscured a deeper examination of economic conditions underlying what, in large part, was an unrecognized tension between income classes. Further, the years-long standoff, which gained momentum in the mid-1950s, highlighted the winner-take-all perception involved in the battle between individual rights and the collective good, and further complicates the suburban–urban dialectic that often focuses on busing or white flight.[27]

The chapter also explores how the issue of race was wielded as a political weapon against Zeidler, dividing the city as never before. Although Milwaukee's black population, at 3.4 percent in 1950, was far below that of larger northern cities such as Chicago and Detroit, Zeidler's support for integration—more so than his membership in the Socialist Party at the height of Cold War fear mongering—served as the nexus of political opposition to his 1956 re-election.[28]

Chapter 6 underlines the role of anti-unionism in challenges to the New Deal consensus, further highlighting the influence of economic conservatism in the immediate postwar years. New Deal–era laws increased workers' ability to form unions and set a minimum wage for many workers, fueling an economic prosperity that by the 1950s had created the century's narrowest income gap between the wealthy and middle-income workers. Corporate and conservative interests had challenged these laws from the start, and many, like Grede, emerged from World War II motivated by a renewed determination to slow labor's growing momentum and return workplace economics to the private sector.[29]

Workers faced opposition not only on the job, where employers contested collectivist notions that elevated employees in decision-making contexts, but also when they championed broad-based public programs that would benefit the larger community. The support by Milwaukee workers and their unions for the St. Lawrence Seaway, a project requiring extensive public funding, further heightened tensions with those who, like industrialist Walter Harnischfeger, unfavorably associated both government and unions with diminished personal freedom. In championing the expansion of government's role in the economy, unions became inextricably connected with the New Deal environment, further fueling corporate opposition to labor.

Although as far-right conservatives, Grede and Harnischfeger seemingly operated outside mainstream conservatism, a closer look shows they were influential figures in prominent national organizations, city business associations, and local Republican Party politics. Respected members of the community and national influence makers, they were not outliers in their efforts to delegitimize labor, a project fundamental to remaking a New Deal environment that often privileged the working class and middle class.

Chapter 7 highlights the city's contentious debate over the right of public employees to bargain, strike, and otherwise enjoy the same economic and workplace rights as unionized private-sector workers. The concerted push for public-employee bargaining rights that began in Milwaukee ultimately resulted in Wisconsin becoming the first state to adopt collective bargaining for public employees. Yet municipal workers unexpectedly encountered some of their strongest opposition in City Hall, where the mayor and some liberal members of the Milwaukee Common Council proved unlikely opponents.

Zeidler's strong support for unions, coupled with his opposition to full collective bargaining rights for Milwaukee's municipal employees, highlights the limits of political classification. The militant fight by city workers to achieve bargaining rights late in the decade brought to the surface the inherent tension in Zeidler's philosophy of governance and climaxed in the strongest challenge to his conception of the precedence of the public good over interest-group politics. Zeidler championed worker rights but firmly rejected a pluralistic view of society, one that privileged group-based prerogatives. The dual role of municipal employees as public servants and as workers tested as no other his understanding of a single "public."

Events in postwar Milwaukee help clarify the extent to which notions of individual economic rights were pitted against the vision championed by the Roosevelt administration, a social-welfare state widely presumed to be operative following World War II. A majority of Milwaukeeans popularly supported the New Deal and widely assumed its legacy would be the enduring status quo. Yet beneath the trappings of liberal city leadership, a strong and well-rooted labor movement, and a tradition of liberal politics, Milwaukee, along with the rest of the nation, included a significant segment of those who rejected the New Deal consensus and actively worked to overturn it. Although this increasingly vocal minority represented a small fraction of the American public, their numbers and influence were growing.

Reaction to government's expanded role in public life began even as the U.S. Supreme Court considered New Deal legislation in the 1930s. Conservative resistance simmered in cities like Milwaukee as the nation emerged from World War II and began boiling over by the 1950s. Traditionally perceived as a bastion of liberalism, Milwaukee in these years provided a microcosm of this growing reaction. At the same time, the shifting positions of liberals in city government further complicated efforts to provide meaningful resolution to the city's urban challenges.[30]

Moderate and far-right conservatives in Milwaukee achieved notable success in slowing or blocking key programs championed by the city's liberal coalition. In cohering around contentious issues such as creation of publicly funded housing, suburban annexation, and public television, conservative interests also forged an individual-rights philosophy based on the preeminence of the private sector. Although in the short run moderate and far-right conservatives failed to halt the growth of unions or to hamstring most public-sector programs, they built a base from which to move forward. While developments in the 1970s and 1980s, such as de-industrialization, a growing nonunionized service sector, and increased globalization played a part in circumscribing the role of government and advancing a conservative agenda, the conservatives considered here were key to the progress that conservatives, including those on the far right, had made by the twenty-first century.

Liberalism still held the upper hand as the 1950s came to an end in Milwaukee, but liberalism's great promise—once represented by Frank Zeidler's election—had been contained, its internal contradictions had been exposed, and its opponents were gathering strength. Despite the odds against them, conservatives were beginning to reverse the tide toward their favor. Understanding how they did this in Milwaukee helps illustrate how they would do so elsewhere in the following decades.

1   A Liberal in City Government

> Municipal government is not purely housekeeping. It involves a philosophy of government.
> —Frank Zeidler, *A Liberal in City Government*

Milwaukee emerged from World War II with urban challenges the city could no longer ignore—significant urban decay, including crumbling infrastructure and outmoded technology; limited public amenities; and the housing, education, and employment needs of a rapidly changing population. In the immediate postwar years, the struggle over Milwaukee's future involved a competition between those who espoused an individualist, free-market-based ideology and those who saw government as the foundation for pursuing the collective good. Like similar tensions around the country, the contest took place on an urban battleground defined by economic power, one that often manifested around issues of working people and their unions. As Milwaukee's veterans shed their military uniforms and took their places back at the metal lathes, the iron smelters, and the vast vats of yeast and brewery hops, the nation's return to normalcy removed the constraints of war, opening the way for the reemergence of the conservative challenge to the Rooseveltian landscape. Milwaukee's 1948 municipal elections, which ended a caretaker administration and ushered in an unabashedly liberal mayor, dislodged this latent discord and laid the groundwork for a heated grassroots conservative challenge.

"Plump and Complacent" Postwar Milwaukee

Stretching along the west shore of Lake Michigan, Milwaukee early on was defined less by that vast body of water than by the three rivers slicing through the city, the Menomonee, the Milwaukee, and the Kinnickinnic. Running north to south, the Milwaukee River, which flows through the central city, formed the area's first natural boundary, dividing Juneau Town from Kilbourn Town, two settlements founded in the early to mid-1800s by Solomon Juneau, a fur trader and land speculator, and Byron Kilbourn, a surveyor and railroad executive. By the 1870s, Juneau's east river settlement on bluff land above the lake was largely inhabited by the English or native-born business owners. Kilbourn's west side became home to middle-class German immigrants and their families. The marshland area across the Menominee valley, which ultimately made up Milwaukee's South Side, started out as the area's least pleasant district. Unskilled workers, largely of Polish, Russian-Polish, and Bohemian extraction, settled there and on the limestone bluffs beyond, with the less-desirable land providing lots and housing they could afford. Between the North and South Sides, the Menomonee River valley, cut through with rail yards, stretches 4.5 miles inward from Lake Michigan and long had cradled industrial factories, tanneries, and tool-and-die shops filled with workers pouring in from either side.[1]

By the mid-twentieth century, descendants of German, Austrian, Scottish, and southern European immigrants still inhabited the valley's north side, while those of primarily Polish and Serbian heritage lived on the south side. Overlooking the valley from the north, the central downtown included the Italian and Greek Third Ward, sandwiched between the Milwaukee River and the lake. Farther west and north, African Americans were replacing the once largely Jewish population in the city's Sixth Ward, with 80 percent of Milwaukee's 8,821 African Americans living there after the war. Another 10 percent of the city's small black community lived in the adjacent Tenth Ward. Just west of downtown, Irish families clustered on the edges of Marquette University.[2]

Elsewhere, the city's primarily German population filled a large stock of duplexes, the two-story, two-family homes with living room, dining room, kitchen, and multiple bedrooms that had replaced the cottage as the dominant house form in many working-class neighborhoods. Tenants of a "Milwaukee flat" could achieve a "comfortable quality of life and standard of domesticity without relying on homeownership or the single-family house to achieve it." Such housing, identified in the early twentieth century as the standard domicile for skilled German workers, was unaffordable for most Milwaukee Poles, the city's second-most-numerous ethnic group.[3]

Germans still made up the vast majority of the population in the 1940s, and most were Lutheran, their steepled churches dotting the city landscape. By 1940 the number of foreign-born whites in the urban community had dropped to less than 15 percent, but more than 20 percent of the residents still spoke German. The first large group of Germans had arrived in 1848, refugees from the failed European revolutions. By the end of the 1800s most of Milwaukee's German laborers were skilled or semi-skilled, and the pool of unskilled labor, which floated from one plant gate to another, in good times as well as slack, was made up largely of immigrant newcomers, especially Poles, who began arriving in large numbers in the 1880s and became the second-largest foreign-born group by 1890.[4]

Even in the early decades of the century, when Poles generally held lower-paying jobs, most Polish families owned their own homes, wood-frame houses that filled the city's south-side Fourteenth Ward, some still retaining the "rear alley houses" that had contributed to vast overcrowding in the century's early decades. As throughout the rest of the city, nearly each block was anchored by a tavern or two, some opening their doors at 6 A.M. to accommodate third-shift factory workers. Two towering churches presided over the Polish community, the twin-steepled St. Stanislaus Catholic Church on Mitchell Street, the main South Side artery, and the hulking Basilica of St. Josaphat, the city's largest church. Many poorly paid Polish laborers had taken out second mortgages on their homes to fund the construction of St. Josaphat, which was completed in 1901 and declared a basilica in 1929. Serbian families, although not as numerous, also settled on Milwaukee's South Side. Only after World War II were they joined by Mexican Americans, the city's first Spanish-speaking residents.[5]

Between 1930 and 1940 the number of Polish Milwaukeeans increased slightly, from 18.3 percent to 19.6 percent, while the percentage of those of German heritage fell from 44.9 percent to 40.7 percent. Despite the clear geographic separation between the largely Protestant area north of the Menomonee River valley and the predominantly Catholic South Side, religion in the 1940s and 1950s played little part in municipal politics. But the German mark on the city was unmistakable, not only in the city's preferred cuisine—bratwurst and beer—but also in its dark stone architecture. A New Yorker who moved to Milwaukee in 1949 was struck by how German pronunciation and phrases lingered in the local language. "Burleigh Street was pronounced 'Burl I' as if written in German, not 'Burl-EE' as in England where the name originated; shoppers went not 'to,' but 'by' Schuster's (from the German 'bei')."[6]

In the late nineteenth century, Milwaukee's most prosperous families had moved to the high ground east of the central business district on the Milwaukee River. Distant from the crowded, closely built working-class houses in the city's central core and South Side, the North Shore offered a stunning contrast. There, brewery barons built massive mansions, perched on the cliffs with stunning views of Lake Michigan. Beginning at the northeastern edge of downtown along Prospect Avenue and extending north through the well-appointed villages of Shorewood and Whitefish Bay, their dark stone manses sat heavily behind thick foliage.

The geographic distance was paralleled by a social and cultural separation, as the families of the city's biggest breweries—Pabst, Schlitz, Miller, and Blatz—joined with those of the area's wealthiest industrialists in a closed, mutually reinforcing social circuit. "It has been the way of well-to-do Milwaukee families, both those of German heritage and those out of New England, to build the biggest homes they could afford, and, in a manner of speaking, to wall themselves up inside," a local reporter, Richard Davis, wrote after World War II. Frederick Pabst, owner of Milwaukee's largest brewery, built a large estate in Whitefish Bay that became the premier summer resort for Milwaukee's upper crust of the 1890s and 1900s.[7]

Although many midcentury cities received a boost from their resident rich, Milwaukee's beer barons and iron industrialists had rarely given to charity and had invested little in their city. "The wealth in the city is far greater than outsiders realize, but most of it was hard to come by and apparently is even harder to give away," Davis wrote. Few improvements had been made since the Depression, and after World War II, wrote another contemporary observer, "nearly everyone admitted the town was starting to show its age,"[8] with deteriorating commercial buildings and blighted neighborhoods. Even basic steps toward modernization moved slowly: the city did not retire its last horse-drawn sanitation cart until 1952. "The commercial buildings were old. Neighborhoods of little frame houses on little lots had gone to blight," Davis wrote. He described postwar Milwaukee as sitting "in a complacent shabbiness on the west shore of Lake Michigan like a wealthy old lady in black alpaca taking her ease on the beach."[9]

Downtown Milwaukee was the least pretentious business district in all of urban America. The skyline was nearly the same as it had been in the 1920s and only superficially changed from 1900. Two heavy stone buildings, the Pabst Theater and the elegant Pfister Hotel, anchored the city's core district. Both were built in the late nineteenth century. The few twelve-story brick-and-stone office buildings and the half-dozen movie and live-performance theaters had been erected primarily before the 1920s and were showing their age. As Davis noted: "Numerous cities of half the size are twice as imposing in the height of their office buildings, in the number of their good hotels, in their look of hustle, bustle, and wham."[10]

City Hall, an eight-story, asymmetrical, wedge-shaped building, topped off with a Romanesque–Northern European bell tower, sat on the site where the typewriter was invented in 1868 by a Wisconsin reporter. Facing south, its back to the northern suburbs, the city's most recognizable landmark overlooked the expanse of downtown, from the city's eastern edge along the Lake Michigan shore and miles into its ragged western boundaries. Along Wisconsin Avenue, the city's main thoroughfare, the Pfister and Boston Store, Milwaukee's second-largest department store, perched along its edges, as did the Empire Building, a twelve-story, buff-colored brick-and-stone office building that housed the twenty-four-hundred-seat Riverside Theater, built for vaudeville and movies. Emanating from the dark, heavyset brick breweries farther north and west of the central core, the smell of hops and yeast hung heavily over the city, matched in intensity by the pungent odor from the tanneries in the Menomonee River valley.[11]

Gimbels Department store, an eight-story neoclassical building whose monumental façade curved along the Milwaukee River, was downtown's primary draw. Selling goods that ranged from Limoges china to woolen mittens, the store served as a unique space in Milwaukee, drawing together residents of all income levels. Its vast interior provided a cheery respite from the freezing winter winds and the steel-gray skies that rarely broke for weeks on end. Children and their parents flocked to its Tasty Town restaurant for banana splits and strawberry shortcakes, part of the sixteen hundred orders employees filled each day for sundaes, sodas, and malts. In 1948, Tasty Town customers consumed more than one hundred gallons of ice cream on an average day.[12]

Milwaukee also was distinguished from other midcentury American cities by well-established commercial decentralization that already had begun at the turn of the twentieth century. Major store chains like Schuster's, Milwaukee's popular department store on North Third Street, never had a downtown outlet, and many of the larger plants had followed the European custom of having their business offices next to the production facilities rather than wasting money on the luxury of downtown office space. While Gimbels remained a big draw in central downtown, Milwaukee shoppers had other options. South Siders could patronize stores along Mitchell Street, and West Side residents were close to the clusters of commercial options on upper Third Street; smaller shopping districts along Twelfth Street and Vliet Street offered even more West Side options. All were situated at trolley-line terminations not more than two or three miles from the principal hub of activity, creating early competition with downtown and restricting the growth of the central business district.[13]

Although ethnic and racial enclaves defined Milwaukee's geographic composition and therefore, to a large extent, the social and cultural experiences of its residents, several citywide traditions crossed these boundaries. In addition to baseball and beer—and the corner taverns to drink the Milwaukee beverages—the Friday-night fish fry found families across town lining up each week for beer-battered feasts. Once associated with Catholics who observed Lenten abstinence from meat on Fridays, the all-you-can-eat fish frys became a staple of restaurants as diverse as Italian and Serbian and appealed especially to Milwaukeeans' penchant for penny-pinching. Sausages turned out by the family-run Usinger's in the downtown Third Ward also crossed ethnic culinary lines, with bratwurst and beerwurst becoming staples of corner pubs and family meals. In time for the holidays, the November Folk Fair drew huge numbers to the Milwaukee Auditorium, in 1953 attracting twenty-eight thousand visitors who sampled food and purchased goods produced by the area's many ethnic groups. When the long winters broke, Milwaukeeans joined up for picnics throughout the city's extensive park system, which included miles of green space along the lakefront—fifty-eight landscaped parks in all.[14]

While the city was best known for its breweries, far more factory workers—115,956 out of 177,202—were employed in heavy industry in 1947. Its highly skilled and semiskilled workforce, along with high unionization rates, made it a solidly middle-class city in the mid-twentieth century. Among the twenty-five largest cities in the United States, Milwaukee had the fifth-highest income, according to the 1950 census. Along with major factories such as Allen-Bradley and Allis-Chalmers, a heavy machinery producer with more than ten thousand employees that manufactured turbines for the Hoover Dam, hundreds of small plants dotted the industrial landscape, specializing in die casting, stamping, pattern making, and metal working. Lake Michigan, running north to south along the city's eastern edge, gave Milwaukee a deep-water port sufficient for lakes trade as well as the ability to dock some oceangoing vessels.[15]

Physically atypical compared with cities of similar population and size, Milwaukee's political temperament also set it apart. As another observer at the time wrote, "Chicago and Milwaukee are less than a hundred miles apart geographically. Politically, they are on different planets. In Chicago, small-scale graft causes no more stir than a tip to a hat-check girl; in Milwaukee, a municipal employee discovered accepting a five-dollar bribe would be pilloried on the front page of the [*Milwaukee*] *Journal* and bounced out of city hall." Milwaukee's abhorrence of graft was matched by its longstanding aversion to incurring municipal debt—the city had been out of debt since 1923, a situation that endured even through the Depression. But its decades-long "pay-as-you-go" policy had meant that by war's end, it had millions of dollars in the bank but nothing on the drawing board.[16]

A Shrinking City

The city had decayed to such an extent that after the war, downtown business leaders, spurred to action by embarrassment over the city's failure to celebrate its hundredth anniversary in 1946, formed Milwaukee's first private-sector coalition to undertake large-scale, comprehensive planning. The 1948 Corporation—so named because its members were determined that the same lack of attention would not prevail in the state's 1948 centennial—sought to counter what it saw as a lack of vision in city planning and marked a move away from the city's prewar business elite bankers and German industrialists, who did not take part in civic affairs. In October 1947 the group released a plan for the central area that called for new highway construction and other transportation infrastructure, middle-class housing in the downtown area, a redeveloped civic center, a downtown entertainment center to attract tourists, a new stadium for the Braves baseball team, and a new zoo.

To jump-start the process, the group raised $100,000 and then successfully campaigned for passage of a 1948 referendum enabling the city to incur debt to fund new projects. Ultimately, only a handful of the group's goals were realized—most notably, the county sports stadium, indoor sports arena, and lakefront war memorial—and Milwaukee business leaders generally returned to their traditional remove from city affairs. In picking and choosing unrelated individual development projects to pursue, the 1948 Corporation did not set out to achieve long-term planning goals, and its plans lacked a broad-based vision of the city's future. While formation of the 1948 Corporation helped crystalize the debate in which principles of metropolitan efficiency and productivity were set against the ideals of democratic access and distribution, Milwaukee's contentious postwar environment involved more than competing visions held by working-class residents and the business elite. As across the nation, the struggle over urban revitalization highlighted the resurgence of economic conservatism, an individualist ideology that challenged the prevailing Rooseveltian legacy of the collective good through aggressive grassroots conservatism.[17]

The 150 business professionals who coalesced in this new organization, later renamed the Greater Milwaukee Committee, owned or managed at least a quarter of the business property in the city. The committee also included one of the city's most prominent union leaders, Peter Schoemann, president of the Milwaukee Building and Trades Council. More motivational than financial, the 1948 Corporation sought to persuade Milwaukeeans to abandon their long tradition of funding capital improvements without incurring bonded debt and to support large-scale borrowing through bond issues. Boston Store president Richard Herzfeld hired an econometrics firm to survey the area, and it predicted the current course would lead to a decline in population by 1960, with stagnant or shrinking industrial capacity. But convincing residents to spend money modernizing their city would not be easy. As one reporter put it, the report pointed out that Milwaukeeans "are ultra conservative, ultra complacent and above all ultra thrifty. To spend money like this is absolutely contrary to the ingrained Milwaukee attitude."[18]

The 1948 Corporation offered the first formalized response to the city's deterioration, launching the coming decade's struggle between, on the one hand, corporate and private interests who sought to limit the role of government while pursuing the advancement of their economic interests, and, on the other hand, Milwaukeeans whose vision of urban improvement was rooted in seeking the "public interest" through government-fostered intervention. As in cities across the nation, the need to act was acute. Throughout the 1940s, more and more Milwaukee residents and industries headed to the suburbs. Although nearly 77 percent of county residents lived in the city in 1940, by 1950 that percentage had declined to 73 percent. The econometrics firm reported that land valuations in the suburbs were increasing faster than the City of Milwaukee's valuations, and downtown property valuations were declining rapidly—standing at nearly 53 percent of what they were in the early 1930s.[19]

Zeidler Emerges from the 1948 Mayoral Primaries

Illustrating the demand for a new direction, fifteen contenders packed the 1948 March mayoral primaries in the city's first postwar primary election, including attorneys, a sheriff, an ex-alderman, at least two Communists, and Daniel Hoan, the city's longtime former Socialist Party mayor who ran as a Democrat. Henry Maier, a Republican-turned-Democrat, also was among the contenders, and although he did not make it to the general election, he ultimately was elected mayor in 1960.

Mayor John Bohn's decision not to run for re-election had opened the doors to the large pool of candidates. Bohn had served as mayor through the war years, replacing first-term Mayor Carl Zeidler, who left office to join the war effort after the Japanese attack on Pearl Harbor in 1942. Elected mayor at age thirty-two, Zeidler was a handsome, blond dynamo with a law degree from Marquette University; bright campaign posters featured the name Zeidler boldly stretched across the rays of a giant sun. He had won the hearts of Milwaukeeans with his propensity to break into song on the campaign trail so often, he was said to have sung "God Bless America" more often than singer Kate Smith, whose career was indelibly linked to that anthem. Within weeks after twenty thousand Milwaukeeans crowded around the train station to see him off to war, Carl Zeidler's merchant vessel disappeared in the South Atlantic. His last public photo shows a solemn, uniformed mayor saluting in front of Milwaukee's Romanesque City Hall tower, which bore the message "Good Luck, Lieut. Zeidler."[20]

Bohn, Common Council president at the time he became acting mayor at age seventy-five, went on to be elected mayor in 1944. Although nominally not aligned with a political party, the former South Side alderman with a background in real estate governed as a conservative, as did Carl Zeidler, whose 1940 election as an independent conservative had ended the twenty-four-year administration of Dan Hoan, the city's second Socialist Party mayor.[21]

After the March 1947 primary votes were counted, two candidates remained: Henry Reuss, who was among the first U.S. soldiers to cross a bridge over Germany's Rhine River, and thirty-five-year-old Frank Zeidler, whose weak eyesight and history of heart illness precluded his serving in the war, unlike his older brother and former mayor, Carl Zeidler.

Frank Zeidler was born September 20, 1912, the third son of Michael and Clara Zeidler. Michael's parents immigrated to the United States in the 1860s. Frank was not athletic like his two older brothers, Carl and Clem, but he was a serious student and the salutatorian of his high school class at West Division, where he graduated precociously early at age sixteen—although not all his teachers admired his skills. A grade-school math instructor gave him a zero on a test because Frank completed all the long division problems in his head and did not show the processes on paper.[22]

Together with their sister Dorothy, the Zeidler boys grew up on the northern edge of the Menomonee valley, in the Merrill Park section of the city's Fourth Ward, a mostly Irish area just west of downtown. They started out in a "Milwaukee flat," first on 89 Sixteenth Street and then at 99 Sixteenth Street, with their grandmother and two aunts occupying the floor below them.[23] Their neighbors worked primarily in the railroad yards half a mile to the south as engineers, firemen, car shop employees, and officials. Their father, Michael, operated a barbershop and continued working there until age ninety-one, walking seventeen blocks from his home and back every day, unless it was raining so hard "an umbrella won't do" and he was forced to take a bus. The social setting of the barbershop expanded Frank Zeidler's contact with Milwaukee residents beyond his relatives and immediate neighbors, opening a window onto a wider universe. Frank Zeidler attributed the barbershop environment to bringing his family into contact with many different cultural groups and said such exposure likely gave him openness to the concerns of African Americans, some of whom he encountered there.[24]

Walking from his home to the Sixteenth Street viaduct, five-year-old Frank Zeidler could watch the trains rumble through the industrial valley below, carrying troops on their way to World War I battlegrounds. Even at that age, young Frank was "very much aware" of the atmosphere of war. Relatives remaining in Germany had been killed, and the brutal conflict was the primary topic of conversation among Milwaukee's predominantly German population. After Woodrow Wilson declared war on Germany, Carl came home from school with the news that the city's public schools would no longer teach German at the elementary level. "Germania" was removed from the façade of a building that housed a bank, and many Germans hurriedly began Americanizing their names. A block north of the Zeidler home on Wisconsin Avenue, a giant, upside-down Uncle Sam's hat stood at the center of a war fundraising drive, one of numerous symbols of American nationalism that rattled city residents, many of whom were first- or second-generation immigrants eager to assimilate. Zeidler recalled the German community as "shaken," because "they thought they were accepted as Americans and now felt that they were not accepted."[25]

Although the Zeidler family heritage was Catholic, with their origins in Tachov, a town on the Czech–German border, their mother Clara was Lutheran, and the children followed her religion, accompanying her to church on Sunday. Michael's father, a tavern keeper, was killed by a car possibly driven by a possibly intoxicated driver in 1916, likely influencing Frank Zeidler's abstinence from both alcohol and driving. While at West Division High School, Frank served as secretary of the 35th Street Advancement Association, beginning a lifelong involvement in dozens of civic, political, and religious groups. Michael characterized his son as the kind of person who, "if he's hungry and has 10 cents and is on his way to a lunchroom and somebody says to him, 'Mister, I'm hungry,' that fellow would get a nickel or the whole dime." Michael said that Clara scolded Frank as a child, admonishing him that he should "look out for himself more."[26]

Frank Zeidler enrolled at Marquette University, but a heart ailment forced him to leave; by the time he recovered, the Depression was underway, and his family was unable to afford further college tuition. (Throughout the rest of his life, Zeidler took so many college courses and read so prodigiously, many agreed he could qualify for an undergraduate degree.) It was during these years that Zeidler encountered those who, like J. T. O'Baird, a railroad machinist for the Chicago, Milwaukee, St. Paul, and Pacific Railroad, held fast to a socialist philosophy of a cooperative commonwealth. In the 1930s O'Baird, nicknamed "Cotton Picker" because of his Georgia roots, held meetings on the capitalist underpinnings of the nation's rampant unemployment, which Zeidler attended in his neighborhood of railroad workers. As a child, Zeidler befriended Mayor Dan Hoan's son, a shy boy who sat in front of him in their eighth-grade classroom. Hoan, who arguably governed more in a liberal than socialist tradition, nevertheless held to his party label, inuring most Milwaukeeans to alarmist connotations of the word. All these influences led Zeidler to join the Socialist Party in 1932, and by 1937 he was secretary of the state and county Socialist Party chapters.[27]

Zeidler enumerated the elements of socialist philosophy that registered with him: "One was the brotherhood of people all over the world. Another was its struggle for peace. Another was the equal distribution of economic goods. Another was the idea of cooperation. A fifth was the idea of democratic planning in order to achieve your goals. Those were pretty good ideas." Describing himself from his youth as having a readily aroused sense of justice and fairness, he saw as formative to his values both his family's emphasis on treating people fairly and his Lutheran upbringing. As such, he challenged authority from an early age. Attending Lutheran Bible camps in the summer, Zeidler made it clear to his teacher that he did not interpret Bible narratives literally, causing his pastor to describe some of his stances as heretical.[28]

A visceral horror of war and of its underlying causes—imperialism, jingoism, and the clash for ideological supremacy—also underlay Zeidler's adoption of socialism. Years after World War I ended, Hearst published pictures of dead and wounded soldiers stretched across World War I battlefields, and the images seared into Zeidler's mind at nearly the same time the stock market crash launched the Depression. During those years he read works by socialist icon Norman Thomas, Christian socialist and anti-war activist Kirby Page, and prominent American pacifist and socialist Devere Allen.[29]

Allen, whose sole book, the seven-hundred-page *The Fight for Peace*, was published in 1930, spent much of his life as a journalist and founder of news services devoted to chronicling world affairs and served with Thomas on the Socialist Party's Executive Committee from 1934 to 1939. In *The Fight for Peace* Allen asserted that human nature is not programmed for war, either biologically or psychologically. Yet Allen rejected the peace movement's nonresistance stance for its passivity, arguing for the necessity of actively working to "conquer" war.[30]

Allen's analysis reinforced Zeidler's formative experiences as a child, surrounded as he was by Milwaukee's fearful German community during World War I and further bolstered by his brother Carl's death in World War II. Later, when the trappings of war manifested in nuclear arms, Zeidler began a lifelong crusade against weapons of mass destruction. Already deeply involved in civil-defense planning from the time he was first elected mayor in 1948, Zeidler's apprehension markedly deepened after April 1952, when he was one of two mayors to witness the largest atomic explosion to date at the Mercury Proving Ground in Nevada. "As I said then and as I say now," Zeidler recalled months later, "that burst sealed the doom of the . . . metropolitan community as we know it today." The threat of war and nuclear destruction weighed heavily upon him, fueling an innate seriousness he frequently punctured with his self-deprecating humor.[31]

Zeidler first ran for office at age twenty-six, winning the position of county surveyor. Three years later he was elected to the Milwaukee School Board, where he served with Meta Berger, the wife of the Socialist Party of America's founder and Milwaukee resident, Victor Berger. He was elected to a second term in 1947, from which he stepped down after becoming mayor. Other campaigns for office, including those in 1942 for governor and in 1944 for mayor, were not successful. Zeidler received encouragement from Bridgeport's Socialist mayor Jasper McLevy, who told him, "Losing elections at your age can teach you a lot. It don't hurt you none."[32]

A Socialist City?

Zeidler also identified with the Socialist Party, in part, because of the city's long history of socialist political leaders. The national Socialist Party of America was formed in 1901 by a group of socialists that included Milwaukee's Victor Berger. The Socialist Party in Milwaukee evolved along the lines of Berger's belief that socialist political participation should be evolutionary, not revolutionary. Berger believed socialism would come slowly, "gradually evolving from capitalism as capitalism had evolved from feudalism, not from a cataclysm which would bring forth socialism in a pure and finished form." Later, this willingness of Milwaukee socialists to work within the government, their emphasis on achieving immediate demands rather than fomenting class warfare, and their focus on bread-and-butter issues over municipal ownership of industries led to schisms within the Socialist Party nationally—but proved effective in the re-election of Milwaukee mayors aligned with the party.[33]

Socialism had been "built on the premise that the introduction of public ownership was necessary to the alteration of economic relationships among sectors of society and was in fact the key to transforming the system into one of worker control." Yet even before 1910, Milwaukee socialists already were moving away from that goal, according to scholar Sally Miller, who emphasized they did so "because of what they would term a realistic recognition that there were structural restraints on their abilities, and also no doubt because of an interest in garnering as much public support as they could." Thus, they continually "sought to cast a wide net in their march to office." The 1910–1912 term of Emil Seidel as Milwaukee's first socialist mayor, accompanied by a majority of socialists elected to the Common Council, was the nearest to socialist governance the city experienced, although as one midcentury Milwaukee academic observed, "Typical of the community's conservatism, Milwaukee's socialism produced no socialism."[34]

Seidel's victory spurred Wisconsin lawmakers to make the election of socialists much more difficult. Democrats and Republicans, embarrassed over their loss in 1910, joined forces to create an ethnically balanced ticket to rid Milwaukee of "Red" rule and defeated Seidel in the 1912 elections. (The Republican and Democrat Parties first used the "fusion" slate tactic in 1887 to defeat a coalition of Populists running as the People's Party.) These Milwaukee leaders convinced the state to enact nonpartisan municipal elections for cities "of the first class," that is, those over a certain size, which in this case included only Milwaukee. Practically, the law, which is still in effect, meant that candidates could not be identified on the ballots by party, eliminating the ability of residents to easily cast their votes along party lines. Both Seidel and Hoan, in the 1916–1920 period, also were handicapped by the lack of home rule in the face of an antagonistic state legislature and were weakened by the requirement for a three-quarters majority on the Common Council for the passage of procedural changes.[35]

Daniel Webster Hoan continued Seidel's good government practices. But he lacked a socialist majority on the Common Council throughout nearly all of his twenty-four years in office, and contemporary observers generally agreed that "socialism as an economic doctrine played little part in the reforms of efficient, practical Dan Hoan." Hoan's abhorrence of municipal debt—a principle later championed by Zeidler—resulted in a soundly run but static city. During the Depression, Milwaukee's work-relief program offered an average $50 per month to families, compared with $7.31 in Virginia and $8.18 in Kansas. Hoan nearly doubled the size of the city from twenty-six square miles in 1922 to forty-two square miles in 1929 through annexation of adjacent townships and suburbs, a tactic that became the blueprint for future administrations.[36]

The 1932 elections gave Hoan his only Common Council majority (twelve of twenty-seven aldermen were socialist, and two nonsocialist Polish aldermen sided with Hoan); during that four-year term, he attempted the first move toward public ownership of a large industry. Yet he did not do so by fiat—he put up for a referendum vote the decision of whether the city should run its electric power system. Voters rejected it. By that time, socialism as a third party option was waning in the city. In 1936 the Socialist Party counted three thousand dues-paying members among the city's 578,000 residents.[37]

The environment for supporting a candidate who identified as a socialist had begun to sour. In the 1936 municipal elections, the president of the Lindemann and Hoverston Stove Company threatened to move his $1 million annual payroll out of the city if Hoan was kept in power. Other businesses at the same time also reportedly canceled expansion plans or prepared to move. Not coincidentally, Hoan the year before had enacted the Boncel Ordinance, which empowered the mayor or chief of police to close any strike-bound plant when an employer refused to negotiate with workers. The act sought to maintain public safety at a time when police violence against striking workers frequently occurred in many cities.[38]

In large part because of the Boncel Act and Hoan's attempt at municipal ownership of the electric power industry, Hoan in 1936 for the first time faced a bitter campaign fight. Milwaukee's move away from backing its self-identified socialist mayor in the wake of his support for union strikers echoed the adverse reaction by business leaders across the nation, alarmed by the 1935 enactment of the National Labor Relations Act (NLRA), which gave workers more freedom to form unions. So not only did Hoan confront a stiff challenge to re-election, but, in a precursor of the ideological battles ahead, his share of the votes also dropped, from 62 percent in 1932 to 54 percent, when he faced Milwaukee County Sheriff Joseph Shinners, an Irish Democrat with a family of ten who was backed by both the American Legion and the Nazi Friends of New Germany.[39]

Hoan's loss in 1940, declining support for the Socialist Party, and a business environment increasingly hostile to workers, whose growing workplace strength was made possible in large part by the NLRA, formed the backdrop to Milwaukee's first postwar municipal elections. The diminishing strength of the Socialist Party nationally after the launch of Franklin Roosevelt's New Deal was mirrored in Wisconsin, where leaders of the Wisconsin State Federation of Labor, who once were identified with the Socialist Party, demanded in 1935 that the Socialist Party take its name off the state ballot. Labor leaders sought to unite the Left under the Wisconsin Progressive Party so as to improve chances for electoral victory. The new party had emerged from the Republican Party's Progressive wing, led by Robert LaFollette Jr. and his brother Philip. Because the Republican Party's Progressive wing actively competed with socialists for votes in Milwaukee County, the result often was the election of more conservative Democrats and Republicans. To improve their electoral chances, Wisconsin Progressive Party members, socialists, and leaders from the Wisconsin Federation of Labor and the Milwaukee Federated Trades Council in 1935 formed the Progressive Party, also known as the Farmer-Labor Progressive League. In 1938 Frank Zeidler first ran for office on the Progressive Party ticket for county surveyor.[40]

The Progressive Party formally disbanded in 1946 after Robert became a Republican and lost the senate primary race to Joseph McCarthy, but its fortunes statewide had already plummeted: between 1942 and 1944 the percentage of the vote for the Progressive Party candidates for governor had dropped precipitously from 53 percent to 3 percent. Wisconsin's rejection of left-leaning politics paralleled the national trend. As historian Richard Polenberg has pointed out, "Every opinion poll in 1938 and 1939 indicated much the same thing: between two-thirds and three-quarters of the American people preferred that the Roosevelt administration follow a more conservative course." The Socialist Party returned to its own ticket after the 1940 election, when Hoan was defeated by Carl Zeidler, but its political marriage with the Progressive Party had further eclipsed its viability. Given voters' large-scale migration back to mainstream political parties, it is likely the Socialist Party would not have fared significantly better with its own ticket.[41]

Working within the capitalist system rather than outside it, Hoan was "commonly looked upon by the conservative groups of the city as being one-tenth Socialist and nine-tenths a lawyer and businessman, and a good one," wrote a University of Wisconsin professor after the 1928 elections. Hoan operated much as any farsighted Democrat mayor might. The efforts of Hoan and others to compete in the political mainstream had separated them from East Coast socialists—who were divided between revolutionary militants and a Marxist old guard. Long-term Socialist Party chairman Morris Hillquit derided them as "practical" Socialists who were first concerned with getting into office, asserting: "I do not belong to the Daniel Hoan group to whom Socialism consists of merely providing clean sewers to Milwaukee." The term "Sewer Socialism" quickly became an alliterative appellation referring to those Socialists whose evolutionary socialism involved a focus on providing clean sanitation and other healthy living conditions, rather than on a revolutionary change of government.[42]

Hoan was not alone in governing as a socialist in name only. Socialist mayors in Schenectady, New York; Reading, Pennsylvania; Haverhill, Massachusetts; and Bridgeport, Connecticut, "epitomized progressive municipal reform" more than socialism. Jasper McLevy, Bridgeport's socialist mayor whose twelve terms in part overlapped with the mayorships of Hoan and Frank Zeidler, carried out a laborist agenda when possible, but the city's socialists considered among their greatest accomplishments "the reduction of the city's debt, the reduction of its tax rate, a restoration of Bridgeport's credit rating, and the maintaining of business and industry in the city." Strong labor support was another factor contributing to the elections of McLevy, a trade union member, and other successful socialist mayoral candidates.[43]

Studies of municipal socialism have consistently demonstrated a clear connection between socialist victories at the ballot box and the party's close relationship with the local labor movements. In Milwaukee, that connection was especially strong. From the onset, Milwaukee's Socialist Party worked with union leaders within the Federated Trades Council, which was associated with the American Federation of Labor (AFL). The Austrian-born Victor Berger, who, in the words of a Milwaukee historian, led the Socialist Party "from the thickets of theory and into City Hall," repeatedly referred to labor's "economic arm" and socialism's "political arm" as part of the same body, with neither controlled by the other. Socialists elected to office were overwhelmingly union members, with the majority serving as union leaders such as Berger, who was president of the local Typographical Union.[44]

Winning Office with "Ideals and a Mimeograph Machine"

Frank Zeidler, who was uncertain about another run for office, met with friends and like-minded supporters late in the fall of 1947. By this time, the thirty-six-year-old was married, and he and his wife Agnes had six children. He supported the family with a series of jobs, including land surveyor, in which he plotted one of the New Deal's Greenbelt cities, Greendale, Wisconsin. As he wrote later about his entry into the 1948 race, "With my tiny income, large family and dim prospects of election, I was not keen about the personal sacrifice my family would have to make; but I felt strongly then, as I do at the time of this writing, of the necessity of liberals, few in number, of keeping themselves together on a common program." The result of that meeting was the Municipal Enterprise Committee (MEC), a coalition of labor unions, community activists, and Wisconsin Progressive Party supporters, and the group sought candidates to run on its coalition platform.[45]

In the fractured political environment of the late 1940s, Zeidler did not immediately garner labor's support, but ultimately both the AFL and the Congress of Industrial Organizations (CIO) endorsed him. John Schmitt, a brewery worker at the time who was later elected second president of the merged Wisconsin state AFL-CIO, said union members supported Zeidler because he was "for the working man." Many Milwaukee residents lived in union households, which in election seasons were regularly contacted through the political mobilization campaigns of the AFL and CIO, or by unions not affiliated with the two federations. Along with his official school board duties, where he had fought to increase teacher's pay and funding for new schools, Zeidler actively pursued other issues for the welfare of the city, most recently petitioning the Common Council in a successful effort to hold a hearing on the local gas company's rate increases. As a surveyor in the 1930s, he became a member of Technical Engineers Association Local 54, AFL. He also served as a delegate to the Federated Trades Council in Milwaukee. Like Berger, Zeidler understood the importance of a political alignment with labor. Reuss, on the other hand, did not have working-class roots. Using the German word for money, Schmitt said working people knew Reuss "had all the *gelt*."[46]

The platforms of the two men were nearly identical—except the MEC included the traditional "pay as you go" stance of Milwaukee's socialist mayors. Reuss also did not back the core goal around which the group united: supporting "public initiative and enterprise if the private sector was not meeting public need." With intensive redevelopment essential to shore up the city's decaying infrastructure, the question of whether to break with tradition and turn to bond issues for capital development was among the top issues in the election. Voters ultimately approved referenda that increased debt measures—at the same time they elected a mayor who opposed debt.

Zeidler, who had hoped to make the MEC a viable new political mechanism, ultimately was the only candidate to run on the slate. Shortly after it was formed, the MEC reported only $26.11 in its campaign chest, and the contributions that later filled its coffers typically ranged from a quarter to one dollar. To counter the city's daily newspapers, which supported Reuss, the MEC, which did not even have sufficient funds for billboards, engaged in a massive but low-cost publicity barrage. Volunteers, many of them union members, printed window cards and posted them in hundreds of stores throughout the city and walked door to door to distribute newspapers describing Zeidler's platform.[47]

Fueled only by "ideals and a mimeograph machine," Zeidler issued press releases for each edition of the morning and afternoon newspapers, made frequent radio speeches, and typically spoke at three or more public meetings a day, many involving stumping at plant worksites. Members of the city's labor movement—which included nearly half of Milwaukee's working population—fueled the MEC's grassroots outreach, becoming the bedrock of his success. As the April 6 election day neared, Zeidler's campaign volunteers reported that voters increasingly were responding favorably to their outreach.

Eight years after Carl sang his way into the mayor's office, Frank Zeidler's mayoral campaign offered editorialists the chance to compare the two. "They were alike in their friendliness, their wholesome and instinctive liking of people, but there the similarity ended," opined one reporter. "Carl, the handsome bachelor, was effusive in his friendship and contacts, a gladhander," while Frank, the father of six children, was a "mild, bespectacled, studious sort of person of medium height without any of the dash of his brother." Observed another reporter, "He is no great shakes to look at, cannot sing for sour apples," and overall appears "somewhat frail." With Carl setting the family standard, Frank caught a tough break by comparison. Yet Zeidler's generally serious demeanor was broken up not infrequently by a sparkle in his eyes at the onset of some bit of humor. Seemingly unassertive, his voice emerged unexpectedly strong, with an authoritative delivery that belied his appearance as a quiet intellectual. Reserved but not, as the media would have it, introverted, confident but not arrogant, and by nature a diplomat, Zeidler inhered the same characteristics that helped propel Carl to office, shorn of flamboyance and spectacle.[48]

When not focused on Zeidler's physical demeanor or singing ability, observers were more complimentary. "In sizing up the man, Frank Zeidler, probably his most important characteristics are his friendliness, gentleness and moral integrity or courage," wrote the same reporter who had found him without the "dash" of his brother. A friend noted that Zeidler could talk "off the cuff" on nearly any topic, "from religion to politics to history to astronomy to soil and water." But he never used "his vast knowledge to dominate a conversation or belittle his audience. Rather, he shared his insights in a quiet, gentle, and kind manner. Still, the depth of his learning was encyclopedic, and he was seemingly genuinely interested in nearly everything."[49]

After the polls closed on April 6, the first returns were inconclusive, but Zeidler soon pulled ahead and, around midnight, his victory seemed certain. Before going to Turner Hall to celebrate with supporters, Zeidler characteristically went to several radio stations to publicly renew his pledge for good government and to thank his volunteers. Turner Hall, several blocks from City Hall, served as the locus for progressives and was the bricks-and-mortar vestige of the nineteenth-century Prussian Turnverein movement, which advocated physical fitness and fostered ideas of social liberalism, especially the right of free speech and clean government.[50]

Among those awaiting him were Michael and Clara Zeidler, who, Zeidler noted, "again showed some puzzlement as to how another of their sons had won the mayoralty of the City of Milwaukee." Zeidler also spoke with many volunteers on his campaign, some of whom described the difficulties involved, impressing Zeidler "by the number of people who sacrificed their time and effort for a cause of liberalism, of which I was the current symbol."[51]

Also awaiting him was Agnes, who had taken the rare move to hire a babysitter for their children, a financial luxury the couple seldom enjoyed. Zeidler met Agnes Reinke in the late 1930s at the Socialist Party office. Entering the office one day, he saw a young woman hanging perilously out the window and hurried to "save her from dying." Agnes was at the party office for the first time to attend a meeting for a peace group in which she was active. Unable to endure the office's dirty windows, she had begun cleaning them inside and out. A graduate of Milwaukee Girls Technical High School, her Lithuanian immigrant family could not afford the college where she had won a scholarship—her father did not believe in higher education for girls anyway—and she devoted herself to social justice issues. In the 1940s she managed Zeidler's initial mayoral campaign and became the rock in Zeidler's life, organizing their large family always with "humor" and a "light touch." In 1956 she became the first woman among her peers to get a driver's license so as to assist Zeidler, and she went on to teach all her friends.[52]

In one of his customarily modest comments, Zeidler often attributed his victory to a "series of flukes." More realistically, he saw his success in part because, he being a Zeidler, voters didn't distinguish between him and his war-hero brother. In addition, he recognized the essential support of the union movement, the backing of five colleagues on the Milwaukee school board, longtime friendships with liberals, and a campaign that offered the only platform of any candidate. Zeidler attributed the MEC's platform to helping him gain the first endorsements from unions because it "was something that could be placed in people's hands for them to read and comprehend."[53]

A Liberal in City Government

As Wisconsin celebrated its centennial year of statehood in 1948 and the nation embarked on the Cold War, Zeidler took office ready to put into practice his long-held belief that "municipal government is not purely housekeeping. It involves a philosophy of government." Central to Zeidler's philosophy was serving the public interest, which he saw as a great honor. On his first day in office, Zeidler gathered his immediate staff and told them, "We'll be called upon by people who are in trouble and who want problems solved." Yet while "some will ask in a calm and official way," others "will seem unbearable, but you have to bear with their impatience and the gravity of their problems. Never turn away a person who comes to you in trouble, no matter how trivial or how ridiculous it may sound. Consider yourself very fortunate to be in a position where you can help." His subsequent re-election to two additional terms before retiring from office proved both the success of his electoral tactics and the appeal of his vision in which an honest government looks after the best interests of its citizens, especially those who could least care for themselves.[54]

Whether he was found at home upstairs in his attic looking at the stars through a telescope by a reporter seeking a quote or drafting elaborate plans for the metropolitan form of government that he championed, Zeidler's approach as mayor was both hands-on and visionary. He constantly interacted with Milwaukeeans, making two thousand speeches during his first term in office and regularly walking through neighborhoods. He carried a surveyor's notebook, a remnant from his work in the field, carefully recording the complaints and comments from citizens who encountered him at the trolley or bus stop—his preferred means of transportation to City Hall—the county fair, or the countless evening events he attended. Members of his administration became accustomed to receiving such notes with a request from the mayor that they be promptly addressed. No matter what the concern, said Zeidler's longtime assistant Arthur Saltzstein, "You can be sure the next day some department head got a memo and Mr. Public who raised the question got a response." Zeidler also was set apart from harried urban mayors in his attention to long-term goals. Even when running for his third term, he handed voters a forty-eight-page platform he developed along with the MEC.[55]

Yet Zeidler's election was implausible, both because his persona defied that of the typical Milwaukeean and because, by the late 1940s, a socialist ideology no longer held sway, even in the city that gave birth to the Socialist Party. In a town with multiple breweries, several taverns per block, and a population that in 1945 drank a barrel of beer per person, Zeidler did not drink alcohol. Where baseball was the major sport, he attended "as few games as convention permits." He spurned "Wisconsin's fine hunting and fishing," did not smoke, and detested cocktail parties. His idea of a fun night was to "stroll to nearby Garfield Park with his family to study the heavens." He played bridge "infrequently, but superbly" and dabbled in gardening, cooking, mathematics, and poetry.[56]

When his eldest daughter, Clara, had trouble understanding Shakespeare, Zeidler translated *Macbeth* into colloquial English, careful to retain the iambic pentameter and the bard's most famous lines. His version of *Macbeth* enjoyed a six-night run in Milwaukee, a rare feat for a sitting mayor. He went on to provide similar treatments of *A Midsummer Night's Dream*, *Julius Caesar*, and *Hamlet*.[57] As the *New York Times* described him in a profile during his last year in office, "He puts in long hours on his job but finds time for a lot of reading, over his lunch of sandwich and milk and far into the night. He dotes upon the heavy tomes of the scientists, theologians, and philosophers. And he is an avowed socialist in a city where the once-thriving Socialist movement is dead."[58]

Ideologically, temperamentally, and personally a socialist, Zeidler nevertheless governed as he described himself in his self-titled autobiography, *A Liberal in City Government*. Zeidler said he did not call the work *A Socialist in City Government* because, as he explained, "The people that I was associated with were all liberals. Socialists were some, liberal Democrats were some, Progressives were there and labor guys. What label can you put? They weren't all socialists."[59]

The notion of aspirational rather than de facto socialist governance is central to the argument by many scholars that Milwaukee, under mayors Hoan and Zeidler, was a socialist-run city. These scholars believe that by merely holding socialist ideals, the two mayors made Milwaukee a socialist-run city, regardless of dependent factors such as the composition of the Common Council.

With no socialists on the Common Council at any point in his three terms, and with a governing platform created by a broad mix of interests, Zeidler reconciled his socialist views with the reality of municipal governance and the national political environment of the 1950s. He infused his administration with a personalist approach that melded common goals of socialism and New Deal–era liberalism, such as support for working people and the poor, and sought to reach those objectives through means similar to those of liberal mayors elsewhere.

Creation of public housing offers one such example. Even as affordable housing was a major thrust of his administration, occasionally garnering accusations of communism and socialism from his political opponents, cities across the nation took advantage of funding provided through the 1949 federal Housing Act to push for the same objectives. As Zeidler put it during his first campaign, he did not seek to socialize "the corner grocery store." Nor did his goals encompass municipal public ownership beyond that which transpired under Democratic leadership in Pittsburgh, Seattle, or New Orleans.[60]

In a city where members of various branches of the Communist Party regularly ran for office and took part in civic affairs, Zeidler made it a point to dissociate himself from them. Although it is likely that Zeidler, in part, sought to avoid the taint of Communism because of the dangers such affiliation posed in an era of national Communist witch hunts, "a real hard divide" existed in the city between the communists and the socialists, said Fred Kessler, an attorney and Democratic Wisconsin state representative. Comparing Zeidler to United Auto Workers (UAW) leader Walter Reuther, a Democratic socialist who put the Communist-led union at Milwaukee's Allis-Chalmers into the equivalent of a trusteeship, Kessler said 1940s and 1950s Milwaukee saw "a real battle between the socialists and the communists in terms of controlling political power."[61]

Despite the city's long familiarity with municipal lawmakers who were members of the Socialist Party, Zeidler believed Milwaukee "never was fully receptive to socialist leadership." A "big chunk" of Milwaukee's working class "would, on occasion, vote for a socialist, but the socialists were always a very small number of people, and in Milwaukee there was a lot of resistance to socialism, especially among deeply religious people who thought all socialists were anarchists or freethinkers." More Milwaukeeans cast a vote for Zeidler's coalition platform than for socialism, and throughout his administration he met regularly with members of the MEC, who informed his governance and helped craft the goals of his three mayoral campaigns.[62]

Zeidler fought to secure the liberal label in the 1948 elections. When one opponent asserted that "liberal" as a political category is relevant only in national politics, Zeidler maintained that liberalism had a place in municipal elections, defining liberalism as a "willingness to accept new ideas" and "sympathy with the many rather than the special interests." In doing so, he sought not only to win the vote of those who did not subscribe to socialism but also to place himself firmly in the liberal camp.[63]

The future mayor understood that his objectives for the city were the essence of a liberal agenda. Recounting his response to an editorial in the 1948 campaign that attacked his socialism and his platform, Zeidler made a speech decrying that "socialist doctrines had been pinned on those who favored a liberal municipal program." Instead, he "asked the other candidates not to abandon proposals for housing, blight removal, parking, a public food terminal and transportation development because they were in danger of being called socialist." His opposition to undertaking debt to finance city programs was the only position that distinguished his platform from the liberal stance. Yet, even there, Zeidler described his approach to municipal debt as the "real liberalism" on the issue. Later, his opposition to collective bargaining rights for city employees at the end of the 1950s set him apart from the liberals of the decade, but not in a direction toward socialism.[64]

Even more, Zeidler saw his brand of socialism as a part of liberalism. In mid-1947, months before the MEC formed with Zeidler on the ticket, Zeidler met with Reuss to ascertain if the lawyer would run as part of a liberal slate.

When Reuss rejected the overture, Zeidler felt that Reuss "did not want to be too closely identified with my kind of liberalism." And when he was elected, he attributed his victory, above all, to the MEC and his supporters who "had ideals and the philosophy of liberalism which made the fight for the people against the special interests in the nature of a crusade for better government and a better city."[65]

Zeidler's liberalism fit easily within the broader postwar domestic liberal agenda, which was based in large measure on support for expansion of New Deal initiatives such as extension of affordable housing and the introduction of nationally funded healthcare coverage and which included strong support for workers and their unions. But some liberals, often complacent after the gains made in the New Deal and during World War II, did not seek such goals or oppose legislative rollbacks to New Deal–era programs with the energy and determination of prior years. Others, by embracing a liberal consensus through burgeoning partnerships with business, had already begun to move away from the Rooseveltian image of the collective good. In contrast, Zeidler actively pursued publicly funded housing, improved public transportation, and other such measures, an activist stance found more frequently among municipal-based liberal lawmakers than those at the national level.[66]

Rooted in socialist ideals and carried out through liberal policymaking, Zeidler's political philosophy found firm foundation in his conception of good governance. Zeidler's overriding ideology was one grounded in the notion of clean, well-managed government serving the people so capably that form and function—citizens and government—were indistinguishable. His philosophy of public service exceeded that of the early-twentieth-century Progressives, for whom ending graft and streamlining services often was an end in itself. Its objectives drew from the same wells as socialism and liberalism but transcended either dogma when the public good was perceived to be at risk. Throughout his three administrations, Zeidler's attempts to serve the public interest and stand up for everyday citizens and working people was put to the test more than once when union members asserted their rights.

Mutual Distrust

The Milwaukee Common Council in midcentury was made up of liberal Republicans and conservative Democrats—although they were never identified as such because of the city's requirement that all candidates for public office run as nonpartisan. Often opposed to civil rights and expansion of social programs that would benefit low-income residents, conservative Democrats on the Common Council resembled Southern Democrats of the era. The council's liberal Republicans were ideologically closer to Zeidler and far more likely to vote with him than were the conservative Democrats, although their support was not guaranteed. As a result, Zeidler "felt quite isolated except for the three or four councilmen who were once [LaFollette] Progressives." Well through the 1950s Milwaukee's city and county politics were dominated by Democrats whose opposition to such issues as affordable public housing, civil rights, and municipally supported public television placed them to the right of their more liberal Republican counterparts, an alignment that had existed since before the turn of the century, although liberal Democrats tried to work through the Democrat Party.[67]

Milwaukee's strong-council–weak-mayor form of government suited his personal inclination toward cooperative rather than authoritative governance. He championed the leading role of the Common Council and purposely took a back seat during much of his administration, abjuring an overriding concentration of power in a single individual. As a result, the council acted as a further restraint on his administration, opposing and stifling many of his key proposals. It was not a given that the Milwaukee Common Council maintained its dominance—Zeidler's successor, Henry Maier, toppled the order through steps carefully crafted to position the mayor's office as the power center.[68]

Zeidler's decision to affiliate with the MEC was the first dexterous step in a political career that combined personal idealism and professional pragmatism. Although Zeidler identified with the Socialist Party for the rest of his life, in his twelve years in office he governed in the manner of contemporaneous mayors like David Lawrence in Pittsburgh, DeLesseps Morrison in New Orleans, and William Berry Hartsfield in Atlanta. But unlike those city officials, he received no support from industrial and business leaders, instead battling their often-outright hostility, circumstances that ultimately limited his ability to enact the far-reaching reforms he sought.

The mutual aversion between the mayor's office and the local corporate elites was fueled on one side by the hardline stance of business leaders who generally refused to work with a self-described socialist, an approach reinforced by the city's traditional lack of public-private partnerships. But had some Milwaukee business officials been willing to ally with the city, they would not have been welcome. Zeidler's blanket distrust of for-profit enterprises and those who led them was unconditional. If there was one way Zeidler governed as a socialist, it was by allowing his rejection of capitalism to dictate his uncompromising stance against the bankers, insurance executives, and factory owners who had not only the financial resources to support city improvements but also the political power to influence the Common

Council, which over the years opposed some of Zeidler's biggest and most dearly held aspirations for the city.

Zeidler's municipal governance set high standards for the time. Acclaimed by *Fortune* magazine, cited with approbation by political scientist Edward Banfield, and providing the model for a federal government official's detailed 1956 text, *American Local Government and Administration*,[69] his administration accomplished much in twelve years. Concrete achievements included more than doubling Milwaukee's geographic base from forty-six square miles to ninety-eight square miles; instituting a model civil defense program; creating a public television station and securing funds through a referendum to create a museum—despite strong conservative opposition in both instances; establishing the Milwaukee branch of the University of Wisconsin system; expanding the public library; completing the civic center; paving hundreds of miles of streets; adding dozens of miles of street lighting, gutters, curbs and sidewalks; and widening and repaving dowdy Wisconsin Avenue to again make it the downtown's "Magnificent Mile." Many of these improvements were made without incurring debt, a feat aided in part by studies the city commissioned, at his urging, to determine how revenue streams could be bolstered and unnecessary costs trimmed.

By aiming to improve the collective welfare of Milwaukee residents through broad-reaching government programs, the twelve-year Frank Zeidler administration represented an attempt to further the New Deal's expansive notion of the public good and its capacious conception of rights. But in postwar Milwaukee, as elsewhere around the country, the challenge to free-enterprise-based individual rights was met by aggressive grassroots opposition, one fueled in large part by economic conservatism.

To advance a conservative agenda, it was necessary to reshape public opinion and steer it away from presumptions of expansive government. In Milwaukee, a public that once had absorbed the Rooseveltian mission through radio fireside chats encountered an increasingly corporatized media focused on furthering a free-enterprise agenda. The "mainstream" media was increasingly supplemented with extremely conservative and highly vocal elements of the local and national press that sought to discredit government, labor, and the economically marginalized as part of their assault on the New Deal order.

2 The Media Makes the Message

> Public sentiment is everything. . . . He who molds public sentiment goes deeper than he who enacts statutes or pronounces decisions. He makes statutes and decisions possible or impossible to be executed.
> —Standard Oil executive, 1946

Midcentury Milwaukee, like much of the nation, saw an increasing consolidation of major media and a decline in alternative foreign-language and labor press. At the same time, business renewed its campaign to sell free enterprise to a public it feared had become brainwashed to depend on government over the private sector for economic growth and stability. Even as mainstream media outlets like the *Milwaukee Journal* became part of a nationwide turn toward corporate involvement in shaping public opinion, far-right economic conservative media outlets, both local and national, captured an increasing share of the Milwaukee audience.

When a Newspaper Manipulates the News

After the large field of candidates for Milwaukee mayor in March 1948 was winnowed to two contenders, Democrat Henry Reuss and Frank Zeidler, the Zeidler camp noticed something unusual in the *Milwaukee Journal*'s coverage of the campaign. In each news article, Reuss's name was invariably placed first and he was described as the "nonpartisan" candidate. Although Zeidler was running on a platform backed by the Municipal Enterprise Committee, a progressive–labor coalition, the *Journal* consistently referred to Zeidler as the socialist candidate. Further, there was talk that the *Journal* had allowed staff to write press releases for the Reuss campaign. Zeidler was among those publicly questioning whether the *Journal*'s "editorial writers knew of the protests of their own staff for interference with impartial handling and writing of news stories."[1]

At the time, such conjectures seemed mere rumor or the typical grumblings of campaign politics. The *Milwaukee Journal* boasted a nationwide reputation for its high-quality journalism and, over the decades, had been repeatedly singled out for its relentless coverage of the most minute instances of political graft or conflict of interest, a point of amusement for pols in other large cities but of high concern to Milwaukeeans who lived up to their squeaky-clean reputation. The *Journal* also earned the admiration of its high-placed peers, with a 1950 poll of newspaper editors and publishers ranking it the third-best newspaper in the nation, behind only the *New York Times* and *Christian Science Monitor*. The *Journal* amassed profits that reflected its influence in the community and its standing as Milwaukee's conscience. In 1949 the *Journal* took in $20 million, making $2 million in profit after taxes. By 1950 the *Journal* led all U.S. newspapers in advertising linage for the first eight months of 1950, ahead of the second-place *Chicago Tribune* by 750,000 lines.[2]

The *Journal*'s daily morning counterpart, the Hearst-owned *Milwaukee Sentinel*, was well-known for its rabid anti-Red slant, and while painful for Zeidler, the vicious, communist-baiting attacks against his candidacy that seeped out of its editorial pages and into news columns were not out of character. So, decades later, when the *Journal* admitted that it had, in fact, issued a directive to reporters that Reuss's name be placed first in all news coverage, that Reuss be referred to as "nonpartisan" and Zeidler as "Socialist," and that the newspaper's management not only approved of *Journal* reporter Dick Davisk's writing Reuss press releases but directed staff to reprint them verbatim—a practice no self-respecting journalist would engage in—the revelation was more than a black eye for the revered daily.[3]

However minimal such journalistic transgressions may appear decades later, by extending its editorial opinion to the intentional, if subtle, distortion of the news, the actions of the *Milwaukee Journal* were part of a broader turn, nationwide, toward direct involvement of corporate-owned media in shaping public opinion, with the ultimate goal of influencing the legislative climate. While discussing the paper's support of Reuss, *Journal* board of directors' chairman Harry Grant told chief editorial writer Will Conrad, "If you back this guy, elect him." Later, when the managing editor refused to issue the directive to staff regarding name placement and identification of the candidates, he was told he would be fired. He then quickly complied.[4]

Ironically, the *Journal* unintentionally made a big contribution to Zeidler's election when, in March 1948, it published a photo of Frank and Agnes Zeidler toting their six small children bundled against the cold as they made their way down a city sidewalk. That photo, said Zeidler, helped "dispel the newspaper's attempt to portray me as a kind of political demon," with the charge that he was a "menace to democracy" evaporating "in the minds of those who saw the photograph."[5]

Like most local newspapers, the *Journal*'s authoritative editorial stances had long made it a key influence-shaper, and editorializing is within the purview of any media. But the *Journal*'s actions in 1947–48 went beyond opinion writing to intentionally manipulating information. For the *Journal*, at least, such active participation in shaping public opinion built on a history of "exposés" or other reportage that, while ostensibly objective, served to advance the newspaper company's goals. In fact, the *Journal* had won a Pulitzer Prize in 1919 for its role as a standard-bearer for the American Way after it remorselessly attacked the pro-Kaiser sentiments displayed by the city's German ethnic majority during World War I. As part of that effort, the *Journal* successfully campaigned to remove compulsory foreign-language instruction from the elementary schools, arguing that in such a "melting pot of races" as Milwaukee, children should "imbibe Americanism and only Americanism." Between 1916 and 1918, pupils studying German in elementary school dropped from thirty thousand to four hundred and the number of German-language teachers from two hundred to one. In June 1919, German was completely discontinued from elementary schools.[6]

The *Journal* also had long done its part to eradicate socialist influence in municipal governance, beginning with Seidel's term, when it actively pushed for "nonpartisan" elections and held a straw poll asking readers to submit names of nonpartisan candidates they wanted to see run, as well as suggestions for the campaign slogan. But the direct order to distort coverage in the 1948 campaign crossed a line—one that newspapers with fewer scruples would do far more regularly and with no retrospective self-reflection documenting their actions.[7]

In one campaign piece aimed at the *Journal*, Zeidler foreshadowed the urban–suburban battles in the coming decade when he wrote that "fundamentally what was at stake was not who should be mayor but whether the judgment of six men on an editorial board, five of whom did not live in the city, should be substituted for the collective judgment of the people."[8]

Although Zeidler felt, as he said, that "the deep division between myself and the *Milwaukee Journal* editors over this campaign never fully mended," the *Journal* went on to support or oppose his administration's proposals and actions on a case-by-case basis throughout his twelve years in office. By 1952 the newspaper backed his second run for office, an endorsement it repeated in the 1956 municipal elections.[9]

Business Recaptures Lost Ground through the Media

While the *Journal*'s direct involvement in shaping the 1947 race was especially errant, the noted midcentury journalist A. J. Liebling, a keen observer of the media environment, recognized that in 1950 media coverage in general less often challenged authority than in the past. "[N]ewspapers as a group have shifted to the right since the Harding days," Liebling noted. "The good fighting Democratic paper, the *New York World*, disappeared in the pre-Roosevelt depression." Presciently, Liebling pinpointed one of the factors behind this direction: media consolidation. "[T]here has been a steady reduction in the number of newspapers, until cities like Minneapolis and Omaha are one-newspaper towns, and a colossus like Philadelphia has, to all practical intents, two newspapers, one morning and one evening, and both are on the same side of the economic and political fence."[10]

Liebling wasn't the only one in the newspaper business to see this trend. Dick Strout, Washington correspondent for the *Christian Science Monitor*, observed, "The publishers keep talking about a two-party system, but they have made a one-party press." In 1948, Washington columnist Thomas Stokes attributed the shift in tone and coverage to the resurgence of corporations. A veteran reporter of politics and the influences that shape the political system, Stokes said it was much easier to do his job in the past. Now, "You are aware of vague pressures against too frank exposition of economic matters and powerful interests that are at work in them. That has disturbed me. . . . We now have back in Washington, back at the battle again, the big economic interests that were restrained somewhat." The result was that "we see the utilities pecking away on various fronts to check the further expansion of public power. Social Security is being attacked from several directions. . . . The battle rages along the whole front."[11]

Indeed, the shift toward economic conservatism in the mainstream press was no accident. Accelerated attacks on fundamental social welfare programs and the growing uniformity of the media's message reflected an increasing corporate influence. Corporate leaders fretted that business was not successfully conveying its "story" to the public, a public it feared had become brainwashed during the Depression to depend on government over the private sector for economic growth and stability. Leaders of American business "entered the post–World War II era shaken to a degree not generally appreciated by the economic and political upheavals of the 1930s and apprehensive that the continued popularity of the New Deal at home and the spread of socialism abroad foreshadowed drastic and undesirable changes in the American economic system."[12]

Corporations in the wake of World War II re-energized the free-enterprise campaign they ran in the 1930s to burnish capitalism's soiled reputation and made a conscious effort to sell themselves as well. The rise in corporate public relations after the war was exponential: public-relations advertising rose by 56 percent in 1948, according to an Opinion Research Corporation survey of industries. *Fortune* magazine estimated that nearly half of the contents of the best newspapers was derived from publicity releases, while nearly all the contents of smaller papers were directly or indirectly the work of public-relations departments.[13]

By one estimate, the corporate free-enterprise campaign accounted for at least $100 million of industry's annual advertising, public-relations, and employee-relations expenditures by the early 1950s as it showed people the benefits of the American private-enterprise system and the potential damage of "swapping this system for government ownership and control."[14]

The view of business that it needed to "tell its story" to the American public was not new. Foreshadowing its later efforts to sell free enterprise, business in the 1920s sought to uphold the canon of laissez-faire capitalism, "reduce the volume of legislation that interferes with business and industry . . . minimize and counteract political regulation of business . . . [and] discourage radicalism by labor organizations."[15]

Then, as later, the corporate sales job of capitalism was inextricably tied to reducing or destroying the influence of unions. In one of the more infamous examples, Ivey Lee, a founder of modern public relations, produced a series of circulars that blamed union-hired agitants for the 1914 Ludlow massacre in Colorado in which nineteen people, including women and children, were killed by the Colorado National Guard after it fired on their tent colony. Before and after World War II, business saw unions as a direct challenge to managerial power, and many business leaders viewed as threatening labor's strides in economically empowering working people at the workplace and through government legislation.[16]

If unions were often the engine driving broad economic opportunity, government was the vehicle through which major national socioeconomic programs were established—and the American people looked to the public sector to do so. A Roper survey conducted for business late in World War II found that the public believed government would help create jobs and generate such economic boosts as minimum-wage increases. To regain the economic influence they enjoyed before the Depression, free-enterprise champions took two tracks. Publicly, large corporations waged large-scale ad campaigns touting private-sector initiative and tying it to individual freedom and Americanism. Less overtly, some of these same corporate entities funded radical economic conservative organizations and media, which directly assailed unions and government and increasingly tied both to the Red threat.[17]

The corporate world achieved its goal in partnership with liberal support. Historian Wendy Wall attributes the 1950s veneer of "consensus and civility" to the concerted effort by corporations in tandem with "corporate liberals" who engaged in a conscious project to unify the nation around a "distinctive American Way." In joining the corporate campaign, writes Wall, many liberals, "increasingly concerned that internal divisions of any sort might tear a democracy apart," abandoned "the language of progressive struggle." Essentially, they bought into the spin within the spin, partnering with business as it sought to clothe its "defense of American-style capitalism in the language of tolerance, pluralism, and national unity."[18]

The result, according to Elizabeth Fones-Wolf, who literally wrote the book on *Selling Free Enterprise*, was a smashing success for corporations: "In January 1960," she writes, "National Industrial Conference Board President John S. Sinclair concluded that as a result of [its public relations efforts], business had probably 'never enjoyed a more favorable climate of public opinion.'" To this degree, at least, the "businessman's intellectual reconquest of America" succeeded.[19]

Fewer Media Voices

As Liebling observed, the increasing corporate consolidation of the printed press meant readers came in contact with fewer views. In Milwaukee, those other voices had primarily existed in the form of foreign-language newspapers and, especially, in this quintessentially Teutonic city, the German-language press. As one scholar noted: "The importance and diversity of the press was apparent almost from the birth of the city. The first German journal appeared in 1844 and half of the new papers issued in the 1850s—fifteen of thirty—were in German, including several radical ones." German dominated among the non–English-language press. From roughly 1880 to the turn of the century, at least two-thirds of all foreign-language newspapers in the country were in German. As a comparison, there were more than one thousand German newspapers published in the United States in 1890, and only 278 other foreign-language papers (eighty-four of which were Scandinavian).[20]

The influence of political immigrant radicals was especially present in the German-language press, with three identifiable phases: the refugees of the failed 1848 revolution; the socialists and anarchists expelled under the German antisocialist law between 1878 and 1890, who gave the press a distinctly radical tone; and the émigré opponents of Nazi rule, who offered an antifascist and anticommunist focus with little attention to labor issues.[21] As the number of German immigrants decreased, so did the demand for such papers. While nearly 20 percent of Milwaukee's population in 1900 was born in German lands, the percentage had shrunk to 5 percent in 1940, although more than 20 percent of the residents still spoke German, including Zeidler.[22]

Even though there was some overlap with non–English-language press, vibrant labor communication also offered a contrasting perspective. Labor expert John R. Commons estimated that nearly 120 daily, weekly, and monthly journals of labor reform were published between 1863 and 1873. To reach the country's largely immigrant working class, unions had long issued papers in scores of languages, and workers' newspapers became an integral part of the communities and movements they served. Even as non–English-language papers decreased, the labor press remained vibrant through the 1950s, with one labor journalist putting the gross circulation of the labor press at 32 million or more, an average of two per member. At the start of the decade, several paid services catered to the labor press: Labor Press Associated, the International Labor News Services, and the Federated Press. The Federated Press, the oldest of such services, came under fire as communist-dominated and lost ground to Labor Press Associated, which operated as a nonprofit cooperative with a governing board elected by member-subscribers and composed of six representatives from the AFL, six from the CIO, and two from independent unions.[23]

In Milwaukee, labor and socialist views had until 1938 been represented in the longest-lived and most successful such paper in the nation, the daily *Milwaukee Leader*. Founded by Victor Berger in 1911, the *Leader* was "a labor paper in the sense it was for working people, the general public, and not an organ of an official trade union." Published six days a week, the *Leader* included comics, sports coverage, something for the whole family—part of Berger's goal to reach the native middle class. The Socialist Party in Milwaukee also aired its views on a local radio station in the early 1930s on *The Socialist Quarter Hour*.[24]

In the 1940s and 1950s, Milwaukee's black press presence was minimal, especially when compared with the black press in other midwestern cities, such as those in Ohio and Michigan. In large part, the lack of a native black press reflected the city's small African American community. But the strong competition of the *Chicago Defender* ninety miles to the south, as well as the repeated efforts by the *Defender* and others to invade the area for crucial subscription dollars, added to the funding difficulties of those who tried to publish. At least six black newspapers failed in Milwaukee in the 1940s and 1950s, with the longest-lived, the *Milwaukee Defender*, part of the Chicago chain.[25]

With the decline of the non–English-language press, Milwaukee's remaining labor newspapers in the 1950s offered the rare alternative to corporate-run media. Among the labor periodicals reaching Milwaukee area residents, the *CIO News* and the AFL-published *Milwaukee Labor Press* were the largest.

Each was sent weekly to members until the 1958 Wisconsin merger of the AFL and CIO created one publication. The *Labor Press* had replaced the *Milwaukee Post*, the 1938 incarnation of the *Socialist Leader*. The Federated Trades Council ran the *Post* as an afternoon daily for working people rather than as an AFL organ. But it ceased publication in 1942, with the trades council unable to sustain it as a broad-readership publication. The advertising subsidies that supported labor's capitalist competitors were, by and large, unavailable, and most labor papers rejected a paid subscription model, both a throwback to the days when working-class readers could not afford to purchase such a paper and a recognition that union members should get as much as possible for their dues.[26]

Far from remaining wedded solely to ink and newsprint, labor at the national and local levels early on recognized the potential that radio offered for communicating with and organizing among its membership and beyond. Before corporations latched onto radio as a profit maker, successfully pushing for governmental regulations that would severely restrict access to the airwaves, unionists urged the labor movement to explore this new medium.[27]

Unlike some cities, such as Detroit, Cleveland, and Los Angeles, where labor had its own radio stations after the war, or in New York City and Chicago, which had worker-run stations, Milwaukee did not have a dedicated labor radio station. Yet residents still had access to a worker viewpoint through occasional locally produced labor radio programs. Also, through the first half of the 1950s, all the major networks provided the AFL and CIO with free time for weekly public-service radio programs, most often featuring panel discussions or debates between representatives of labor and management.[28]

In their radio talks, unionists appealed for public support by emphasizing organized labor's commitment to building a better America for everyone. Drawing on a Keynesian interpretation of the economy, they argued that the collective bargaining process boosted wages and thus raised the purchasing power of the masses. Job security, another key goal, also increased the consumption of goods. As UAW Secretary-Treasurer George Addes asserted in a Detroit broadcast, "The auto worker comes home with more money to spend at the grocery and meat market, and with his dentist and doctor, and with the movie houses and the clothing and department stores." In other words, strong unions make strong communities.[29]

Through its more expansive reach, radio, more than labor's printed press, served as a key mechanism by which unions could more broadly challenge the business agenda often espoused by corporate-owned media and offer a critical alternative voice on political and social issues. While vibrant in the 1950s, labor radio and other noncommercial broadcasting never shared the same access to the airwaves as did corporate media. The Communications Act of 1934, which established the Federal Communications Commission (FCC), and its predecessor, the Radio Act of 1927, "for the most part, provided public assistance to privately owned, profit-based commercial radio." Despite commercial broadcasters' control of radio, unions found they could make far greater use of radio than the new medium that spread through America's households after the war—television.[30]

More Conservative Media Voices

The scope of labor media, which achieved its apogee in midcentury, masks the extent to which its visibility began to be contested by well-funded and nationally distributed conservative print and broadcast media as well as local media that more often reflected the interests of the business elite over those of the working class. As supporters of the status quo, and as profit-making enterprises, local and national media had never been consistent champions of those who, like labor, challenged the normative order on behalf of the economically disenfranchised. But in the years after the war, the public's exposure to diverse opinions became more and more circumscribed as the growing consolidation of local newspapers and the diminishing non–English-language press amplified the reach of the more mainstream media and its increasingly economically conservative bias.

Milwaukee's two daily heavyweights, the *Milwaukee Journal*, which published in the late afternoon, and the city's morning paper, the *Milwaukee Sentinel*, helped shape the city's political bifurcation. With only two English-language dailies, Milwaukeeans' newspaper options had shrunk by 50 percent from the late 1920s. Through a paternal and authoritative voice, the *Journal* championed a form of corporate liberalism, one tempered by its existence in a working-class city with a long tradition of left-leaning politics. *Journal* executives were closely tied in with the local business community, and in fact the Greater Milwaukee Committee got its start when Irwin Maier, on his way to becoming Journal Company chairman, called a meeting in the 1930s with half a dozen Rotary Club members. He suggested Rotarians become more active in improving the city, but their plans were put on hold until after the war, when they reconstituted the committee as the 1948 Corporation. The *Journal*'s editorial focus on clean government had meshed well with the anti-graft efforts of the Seidel and Hoan administrations and reflected the ethically conservative public. Yet in keeping with Liebling's observation that the midcentury media increasingly deferred to the political elite, the *Journal* purposely sidestepped opportunities to challenge the authority of mainstream public- and private-sector actors. For instance, *Journal* reporters knew Sen. Joe McCarthy was a heavy drinker—a not-insignificant element that may have called into question the judgment of someone whose actions damaged many lives and livelihoods—but his flagrant abuse of alcohol in their presence did not make it into print.[31]

The *Journal*'s extensive coverage of local news, sports, and topics like fashion and homemaking geared toward women helped ensure its circulation well surpassed that of the *Sentinel*. But each day, many Milwaukeeans woke up with the *Sentinel* at their doorstep, imbibing its unbridled, far-right conservatism along with their eggs and sausage. While its reporters generally maintained journalistic standards, the *Sentinel*'s editorials and columnists made regular use of the words "Reds" and "Commies" in headlines and text, with the overall tone of such opinion pieces one of intolerance fueled by a sense of outrage. The design of its editorial section set the stage for its content. The opening page was adorned at top left with a magnified headshot of William Randolph Hearst and accompanied by one of his quotes ("A newspaper must be conscientious in its service to the community"). A large-typeface quote from the Bible, changed daily, faced Hearst across the top of the editorial page. One of its most influential columnists, William Norris, routinely engaged in Red-baiting and later became a voice for the suburbs in the city's suburban annexation battle.

If the *Journal* represented the midcentury corporate media mainstream, the *Sentinel*—and Milwaukee's Hearst-owned radio outlet, WISN—were rooted both in the mainstream and in the extreme-right media worlds. The reporting staff of the *Sentinel* and the broadcasters at WISN were, of necessity, not beholden to Hearst's Manichean worldview: as a major, profit-driven daily, the *Sentinel* needed to reach a broad audience, as did WISN. But editorially extreme rhetoric situated the *Sentinel* and WISN in the universe inhabited by more far-right broadcast and print outlets. And Milwaukeeans had multiple access to such mouthpieces, both locally and nationally produced.

Locally, the multiple weekly suburban newspapers and the South Side's weekly *Milwaukee Times* consistently expounded economic conservatism, routinely championing business and individual rights—especially those of homeowners—over the collective public welfare. The more sophisticated weeklies hammered home the benefits of small government, while elevating individualism and attacking an expansive view of public service, but several engaged in sharp, over-the-top rhetoric. The *Milwaukee Times*, for instance, combined advocacy for unfettered free enterprise and a conservative interpretation of the Constitution with outright racism and bigotry. Its extremist language was only outdone by the *West Allis Star*, which represented a largely industrial suburb west of the city and whose name reflected the influence of its largest employer, the heavy-industry plant Allis-Chalmers.

Business leaders had a deep interest in maintaining a conservative press. In 1955, local industrialist and far-right economic conservative William Grede and his brother Arthur purchased a firm that published weekly newspapers in the Milwaukee suburbs of Wauwatosa, Brookfield, and Elm Grove, seeking to maintain a conservative voice in the area. Grede hired as editor Carl Colby, who had earned his extreme conservative credentials while working on the advertising staff of the *Milwaukee Sentinel* and as an aide to Wisconsin Republican Representative Glenn Davis. Under Grede's ownership, one of the papers, the *Wauwatosa News-Times*, focused on attacking unions, inevitably connecting its opprobrium to labor practices with its support for democracy, free enterprise, and individualism. When a committee of the Milwaukee County Board of Supervisors recommended that Kohler products be boycotted in county buildings to show support for the striking UAW members at the Kohler factory in Sheboygan, the *News-Times* was outraged. It called the proposal "one of the most brazen and undemocratic resolutions ever to come before that body." More than a singular incident, the boycott recommendation justified suburban opposition to consolidation with surrounding jurisdictions, which was then under discussion, and exemplified the dictatorship of "labor bosses." As the *News-Times* wrote, "The display of a willingness by the county supervisors committee to surrender to labor bosses is one of the reasons why these suburbs are unwilling to relinquish their independent governments and join a county-wide administration that might be subject to dominance by pressure groups not interested in the welfare of all citizens."[32]

The paper backed the city's opposition to calls by Wauwatosa's city employees to strike over wages, and it opposed the union's attempts to secure dues checkoff, a process in which the city would automatically deduct union dues from workers' paychecks. The *News-Times* also expended much ink on the congressional McClellan Committee hearings, using the federal-level investigations into organized crime in labor unions as a convenient springboard for slamming unions. The paper supplemented its own editorials excoriating labor with reprints of articles similarly attacking the union movement and strategically sought to sow division among union members. In pointing out that unionized teachers with graduate degrees earned $4,300 a year, compared with a "water boy," whose unskilled labor got him $5,086 a year, the *News-Times* offered this as proof of "what might happen to 'white-collar' workers and the intelligentsia should men like Walter Reuther ever grab complete control of the American government and set up a Socialist pattern of union labor control over the county." The paper then touted the ability of suburban county supervisors as the only bulwark against "union pressure."[33]

The *Milwaukee Times* also portrayed the union movement as the enemy of the free enterprise system, utilizing the smallest opportunity to ram home that point. When Milwaukee unions urged firefighters to stop taking part-time construction jobs because it further limited the pool of work available for jobless construction workers, the *Times* saw in the request nothing less than the demise of free enterprise. "We need no longer worry about the future of free enterprise in this country," the paper asserted. "Free enterprise is going down the drain if the very people who depend upon it to keep them at work go into competition with established business. If one element or segment is going to take over, or dictate every facet of American life as the pattern indicates now—then dictatorship, or worse, is already shaping up for this nation."[34]

Harold Towell, the paper's publisher in the 1950s, was continuing the family newspaper begun by his father Henry, who launched the *Milwaukee Times* on the city's South Side in 1888 after emigrating from Lincolnshire, England. The politically conservative family provided a forum for anti-housing advocate William Pieplow, printing his speeches in full and giving him space for a semi-regular column. While the *Times* addressed issues involving the city's minorities with bald-faced racism—describing calls for better jobs and housing for black residents as nothing but "coddling the minorities"—the *Wauwatosa News-Times* was slightly more circumspect.[35]

The Grede-owned *Wauwatosa News-Times* led the charge in defending the reputations of business leaders, in this case those of industrialists of whom, not coincidentally, Grede was one. "In more recent times, it seems that an effort has been made by some to make 'industrialist' a bad word in our language," the *News-Times* opined. Reflecting the national-level corporate public relations message, the *News-Times* pointed out that one of every twenty Americans was a stockholder—implicitly identifying its middle-class readers with the owner class and separating them from the working class. Three years before Robert Welch founded the John Birch Society, the *News-Times* described him as a "staunch friend of the free-enterprise system in America." In fact, Grede was close to Welch and was among the Birch Society founders, along with Milwaukee architect Fitzhugh Scott Jr. and Fred Koch, founder of Koch Industries.[36]

Conservative Media: Nationwide Reach with Mainstream Funding

Milwaukeeans' exposure to increasingly conservative local media was further heightened by the expansion of conservative media with a nationwide reach. One such publication had been arriving monthly in the homes of millions of subscribers since its inception in 1922 as the quixotic brainchild of DeWitt Wallace: *Reader's Digest*. Slanted to reflect Wallace's conservative worldview, the *Digest*'s circulation soared from five thousand copies in its initial mailing—labeled and shipped off by a combination of volunteers from a community club and patrons at a speakeasy above Wallace's New York City storeroom—to a subscriber base of 290,000 in 1929, bringing in $900,000 a year.[37]

By the 1940s the *Digest*'s popular conservative outreach was helping fuel fears of British-style nationalization crossing the pond. "Never! Never! Never!" screamed one such headline denouncing British socialized medicine. Assaults on the federal government had always been present, but the number of such articles increased at the start of the 1950s and focused on government incompetency, corruption, Big Brother–style intrusion into the lives of individuals, and the extent to which increased taxation indicated a growing, collectivist state.[38]

Young Milwaukeeans like Phil Blank regularly paged through *Reader's Digest* as they grew up, feeding on the magazine's steady diet of Cold War warnings mixed with "aw shucks" stories. Blank, who started out politically conservative before becoming involved in the effort by the city's public employees to win collective-bargaining rights, said as a young man he was antagonistic toward socialism and backed the concept of running government like a business. Like other Milwaukeeans who were unfamiliar with union and noncorporate presses, Blank did not recognize the magazine's agenda. Sandwiched between homespun advice ("Goodbye to Faucet Drip"), profiles ("Every Dog Should Own a Man"), and content targeted to women ("What Became of the Man I Married?"), the *Digest* provided readers with an incessant stream of alarmist content over the direction of the nation, the external communist threat, and the internal move toward "big government." As in all such *Digest* articles, the authors dutifully spelled out for readers the lessons to be learned. "If government took all the wealth of corporations, it wouldn't put the country on a sound financial keel. But it would put the corporations out of business and workers out of jobs."[39]

The *Digest* whittled away at the credibility of the labor movement in the same manner as it took on the federal government—by highlighting narratives of "corruption," intrusion into the lives of individuals, and financial waste (taxes in the case of government, members' dues for labor). In laying the groundwork for widespread distrust of government and labor, the *Digest* played an outsized role in delegitimizing the notion of a shared society, the fundamental premise of the New Deal. By 1951, *Reader's Digest* reached a total U.S. circulation of more than 9.5 million. In comparison, thirty-eight magazines had a circulation of more than 1 million each in 1947. Fifty years earlier, no magazine reached one million readers, highlighting another critical shift in midcentury communications: the increasing market saturation of national media. The *Digest*'s readership suggested a far-reaching appeal to the nation's influence makers. In 1952, the *Digest* claimed that 45 percent of all business executives and "professional men" read it regularly. Its audience was composed of 51 percent upper-income and 43 percent middle-income readers. More than half of those with college degrees read *Reader's Digest*, a total audience reach that made it a formidable force in the ideological battle to overturn the New Deal order.[40]

While no other conservative publication could claim the *Digest*'s range in the 1950s, the decade saw a surge of such publications and, increasingly, radio broadcasts. Facts Forum combined both. Bankrolled by, and the brain child of, Haroldson Lafayette (H. L.) Hunt, Facts Forum was set up in 1951 to organize "small discussion groups devoted to the study of the art of living, social advancement, the science of government, and agriculture." A self-made millionaire after years of oil speculation in the United States and abroad, Hunt settled in a Dallas home that was a replica of Mount Vernon—only bigger. By World War II, Hunt had more oil reserves than the Axis nations combined, with an estimated fortune of $600 million. As did other postwar corporate leaders, Hunt urged his cohorts to counteract the public's less-than-rosy opinion of the private sector. In Hunt's view, "the businessman has been propagandized into a false conception that he must take the public as he finds it" rather than see that it was possible to mold public opinion.[41]

Rarely appearing in public and secretive about his personal life, which included two simultaneous marriages, Hunt in 1951 spelled out his philosophy in a rare public speech, describing the world as locked in a Manichean struggle to the death between two divergent groups—the far left and far right. Communists and New Dealers were equally menacing, in Hunt's view, because the threat they posed was largely and directly economic.[42]

Within a year of its launch, Facts Forum saw outside contributions "pouring in at rate of nearly $1 million annually." Hunt initiated ambitious television programs and other special projects and hired more staff. The staff star, Dan Smoot, a former university English professor and FBI agent, resigned from the bureau to work for Hunt. As a member of the FBI Communist Squad, Smoot said he wondered why "those who oppose Communism were vilified and slandered," before learning the reason. "It was because people were blindly following the philosophy of the New Deal, which stands for the total transfer of power from the individual to the Federal Government under the claim of using the power beneficently. . . . It is also the basic philosophy of Communism, Fascism and Nazism." Smoot was in great demand as a speaker—even at his per speech rate of $750.[43]

Federal communication laws required Hunt's publication and broadcasts to present both sides of an issue to keep the organization's tax-exempt status. Smoot's job was to weigh the pros and cons of a key topic, but his neutral presentation on liberal issues was counterpoised with his sense of urgency in conveying conservative concerns. The federal government and labor were frequent topics among the "even-sided" discussions Smoot moderated and, as with *Reader's Digest* and other conservative media outreach, Facts Forum found that appealing to consumers' pocketbooks was the surest way to erode the public's confidence in the federal government.[44]

In less than two years, Facts Forum claimed a network of 125,000 active participants, and regular listening and viewing audiences of at least five million more, with much of the broadcast content reprinted in its sixty-six-page newsletter. Facts Forum "provided an entire lifestyle and an instant society for those who felt displaced and disaffected by mainstream society. The model Facts Forum 'participant' would be a member of a neighborhood 'discussion group'" who would have television programs to watch, radio programs to listen to, books to read, and letters to the editor to write. In short, Facts Forum "gave those who felt they could do nothing to change the world things to do." Hunt ensured wide distribution of the newsletter, sending subscriptions free to educational organizations such as the Milwaukee School of Engineering.[45]

The broadcasts and publication offered the audience a means to interact with Facts Forum and each other. Long before online interactivity helped spur virtual communities, and decades before it became common practice to use multimedia messaging to target and engage an audience, Hunt had created an ingenious device by which to connect Americans alienated by the post–New Deal milieu. Monthly polling questions also engaged the audience, with such queries as "Is Social Security a fraud?" (56 percent said yes).[46]

Facts Forum encouraged its audience to go beyond the pages of its publication to connect in real time with family and neighbors by forming Facts Forum groups. In Milwaukee, Howard Reap looked for advice on forming one in his city, heartened to see that "at last, an effectual counterattack has been launched against the political and social trends that have been in the ascendancy in this country for the past twenty years." At the instigation of Facts Forum, many readers and listeners wrote letters to the editor and contacted their congressional representatives. One House member registered astonishment at "the flood of mail coming to newspapers and Congress from listeners in support of the side which Facts Forum supports." Gerda Koch was among readers submitting a letter to the editor, winning a cash prize from Facts Forum after the *Milwaukee Journal* printed her missive decrying taxpayer money going to "help Red plans and propaganda."[47]

Reap and Koch could join Edna Goss and other Milwaukeeans in listening to Facts Forum broadcasts on the popular, Hearst-owned local radio station, WISN, Mondays at 9:45 P.M. The geographic and cultural chasm between Dallas and Milwaukee notwithstanding, Goss said she had succeeded in getting "many of my friends to listen . . . all comments have been favorable." More than 550 affiliates on the Mutual Radio Network aired *Facts Forum State of the Nation*, and 50 television and 138 radio stations carried *Answers for Americans*, which featured discussions of questions submitted by readers of *Facts Forum News*. Smoot's thirty-minute weekly television debates ran on 80 television stations and in fifteen-minute segments on 265 radio stations.[48]

Facts Forum appealed to a wide and mainstream audience. Many in prominent positions agreed with Hunt's ideology. Governors of Texas, Oklahoma, and Pennsylvania, as well as senators from Texas and Nevada, took time to send Hunt congratulatory letters on his endeavors with Facts Forum. A *Facts Forum News* survey in 1956 revealed the majority of its readers were solidly middle- to high-middle-income, with 42 percent falling into the average annual salary range of $5,000 to $10,000, and 20 percent in the $10,000 to $20,000 annual income bracket. Seventy percent were homeowners. The survey also indicated a uniformly broad age appeal, with the percentage of readers in each of five age groups nearly identical. Questions determining the extent to which readers might influence others found that 19 percent held public office and 70 percent belonged to organizations. *Facts Forum News* readers were dedicated: they spent, on average, nearly four hours reading each issue, and 25 percent said they read it cover to cover.[49]

Such national exposure required deep pockets. Of the $4 million per year required to keep the radio and TV programs on the air, $3 million came from radio stations that carried the programs, along with some thirty commercial sponsors. The rest came from Hunt and an estimated two thousand contributors.[50]

Facts Forum broadcasts were part of a surge in growth of right-wing radio, which "picked up tremendous momentum between 1955 and 1966," a trend attributable in part to "an informal national network of manufacturers" who funded these endeavors. Listeners generally were unaware of the special interests behind the programs—and corporations were careful the public did not find out. When anti–New Deal reporter John Flynn in the late 1940s tried to get funding for a weekly, fifteen-minute commentary on the radio news show, *Behind the Headlines*, corporate sponsors—including Milwaukee's Allis-Chalmers and Schlitz brewery—who otherwise donated to his projects, supported his effort but did not want to be seen publicly as donors. Executives told Flynn's agent that their sponsorship "might stimulate their New Deal friends to make some labor trouble." So Flynn changed tactics and in 1948 set up a nonprofit corporation to provide sponsorship for the show, enabling business to quietly support the program without their corporations becoming official sponsors.[51]

Conservative radio continued its expansion into television throughout the 1950s with the assistance of deep-pocket backers. Clarence Manion's radio program made the big step up to television when it received the financial backing of Dallas Bedford Lewis, the millionaire president of Lewis Food Company, which manufactured Skippy brand pet foods. Lewis, whom *Fortune* called "vehemently anti-union," was president of the Organization to Repeal Federal Income Taxes. After Smoot struck out on his own and launched the *Dan Smoot Reports* radio program in 1956, he also received Lewis's patronage, enabling him to produce a television program as well. With access to millions of dollars, Hunt, Manion, and Smoot were among right-wing broadcast messengers making significant inroads into the world's newest medium, reaching millions of Americans with their televised message. In 1965, Group Research, a liberal monitoring organization, reported to the Democratic National Committee that in 1950 there were two nationally syndicated TV or radio programs produced by "radical right" spokesmen. By 1965, the number had grown to sixteen.[52]

The Corporate–Far-Right Partnership

Corporations in midcentury advanced their agenda through the twin pillars of mainstream free-enterprise marketing and covert funding for far-right media ventures. Far-right conservatives who hawked their messages nationwide would not have been able to do so without the type of funding only corporations and the very wealthiest individuals could provide. Not only was such a dual approach not mutually exclusive, it was a necessity. With public support for government at an all-time high in the immediate postwar years, a nationwide corporate publicity campaign taking its playbook from Facts Forum would not have been saleable.

In a public-relations version of good cop–bad cop, U.S. businesses publicly advanced the benefits of capitalism and free enterprise—along with their individual brands—and implicitly indicated a willingness to work with government and labor to meet the needs of the nation. Simultaneously, many of these same corporations filled the labor-bashing, government-attacking publicity coffers of far-right conservative organizations, their deep-pocketed funding enabling far-right propagandists to spread their message across the airwaves. In softening up a general public—one that bought into the New Deal society—with visions of an individualist-centered American Dream generated by the private sector, this corporate publicity push created the illusion of consensus, one that some liberals at the time also bought into in their eagerness to work across party lines for a common goal.

Corporations' massive overt and covert midcentury publicity outreach intersected with the beginning tremors of what ultimately would prove to be a tectonic shift in media: the increase in newspaper consolidation, a decrease in alternative foreign-language and labor media, and the emergence of television as an unaffordable venue for noncorporate voices. Just beneath the surface of the liberal consensus, the far-right conservative media voices continued to penetrate, reaching a reading, listening, and, increasingly, viewing public. Their breathless hyperbole has long been comfortably dismissed by scholars.

In 1955 the *Milwaukee Times* editorialized that the United States "is on the brink of dictatorship" because the impending merger of the AFL and CIO meant the usurpation of free government. The consolidation of labor, the weekly wrote, advanced the "boring from within" by "segments of the American people who are destroying freedom and democracy from within" more swiftly than "the Russian or Chinese Soviets ever could."[53]

Such rhetoric, despite its frequency in local and national media, seems easily disregarded. Yet for decades the *Milwaukee Times* reached a loyal audience among the 220,000 South Siders, many Polish Catholic, shaping their views with images of a less benevolent, more threatening government and hardening their opinions against socially progressive legislation such as affordable housing and civil rights. Dismissed by many scholars as extremists with little impact on the political center, editorialists such as the *Milwaukee Times*'s Towell family, suburban weekly publishers like Grede, eccentric millionaires such as Hunt, and renegades like Manion and Smoot chipped away at the foundation laid by the New Deal, likely well aware, as was Grede, that theirs was "a fifty-year project."

Even as the variety of media voices dimmed in Milwaukee, indirectly amplifying the views of the growing numbers of print and broadcast outlets that expounded far-right economic conservatism, the city was torn by a public-private struggle over ownership of a new television channel, newly made available by the federal government. Corporate interests argued that the private sector was best positioned to operate the channel, and they were supported by grassroots champions of small government, ideologically opposed to municipal involvement in broadcasting. In contesting the privatization of publicly available airwaves, a coalition of groups representing labor, women's, and religious and educational organizations sought to claim the channel as a public space, arguing it should serve the community interest through educational and informative programming. The clash highlights both the ambition of mainstream corporate interests to further enlarge their media platform and the growing tension between champions of a New Deal–era collective good and those seeking to halt further expansion of government.

3 Public or Private? The Battle over Channel 10

> BE IT RESOLVED that the members of the Milwaukee County Property Owners' Association are opposed to any organ of government possessing ownership of an instrument of mass communication, such as TV.
> —Alma Bartell, association secretary, in a letter to Frank Zeidler, November 26, 1951

Unlike radio, access to television for public-relations purposes was nearly prohibitive for labor and other nonprofit groups. Far more expensive, with accessibility even more tightly limited than radio, the new "cool" corporate-controlled medium from the beginning systematically excluded alternative voices. Not that unions, community groups, and educators did not try to secure entry from television's earliest days. The challenges for local nonprofits to gain access to television airwaves in communities across the nation were exemplified in Milwaukee, where media outlets fought the city's attempt to operate an educational television channel. Working with the Common Council and supportive community groups, commercial broadcast interests turned what could have been a simple process of accepting federal provision of airspace for nonprofit use into a years-long ideological struggle between supporters of publicly funded services and their opponents.

Public TV: In the Public Interest

Back in 1941, when the FCC had authorized commercial television broadcasting to begin, the Milwaukee Journal Company became the first in the city and the state to receive permission to launch a television station—a monopoly it would enjoy for five years after it began broadcasting on WTMJ in 1947. WTMJ remained the sole station for years after the war because the FCC in 1948 froze all pending applications for television permits while it sorted out issues of bandwidth interference.[1]

As the FCC prepared to lift the freeze early in 1951, it also let it be known that it planned to make available high-frequency channels for use as educational television by cities that demonstrated an interest in reserving one. Milwaukee's labor and community organizations quickly joined forces to secure a place on the bandwidth. Tony Weinlein, director of research and education for the Building Service Employees International Union (BSEIU), was the first to urge the mayor to act to secure the channel. As had happened throughout the nation, television viewership had spread rapidly in Milwaukee. At the start of 1948, city residents boasted 781 television sets—a number that skyrocketed to 397,853 a mere five years later.[2]

The Milwaukee Common Council also took action. Less than two weeks before the March 24, 1951, FCC announcement, five members of the Finance Committee introduced a resolution directing the council's Special Committee on Radio to study the prospect of a municipally owned television transmitter available for use by any qualified nonprofit. While the committee studied the issue, the FCC announced it was releasing only one channel for commercial use in Milwaukee, while opening up the other as an educational station. To reserve channel 10 for municipal operation, the council needed to file a statement of interest by May 7, 1952. Even though a unanimous council ultimately adopted such a resolution, the action did not definitively commit the city to its operation, although Zeidler urged the council to pass a resolution to do so.[3]

The council's refusal to commit the city to operating a public television channel indicated the division among aldermen over the issue, and provided valuable time for opponents of a municipal television station to wage a broad-based campaign. Three Milwaukee radio stations, WEMP, WFOX, and WISN, led the charge against public funding for channel 10. Each had previously applied for television broadcasting permits and were eager to get on the air after the three-year freeze on channel allocation. Huge profits were at stake for the broadcast corporations. In the first year of its operation, WTMJ had generated advertising revenue totaling 25 percent of the Journal Company's broadcasting budget, with the remaining 75 percent coming from its radio station. By the next year, the ratio was switched. WTMJ-TV continued to generate a profit every year. FCC Commissioner Frieda Hennock estimated channel 10 would be worth $5 million.[4]

The split on the council played out through much of the debate. On one hand, when the council appointed the committee to study the issue, it named members of labor, including Peter Schoemann in his role as School Board president—but no media representatives, to the outrage of the commercial broadcasters. At the same time, as two of the three radio stations seeking television permits filed comments with the FCC opposing a publicly run channel, an alderman introduced a resolution to give the educational station to commercial interests.[5]

In May 1951, four city officials, including the mayor, traveled to Washington, D.C., to determine the viability of the FCC's proposal to create noncommercial stations. After meeting Hennock, Frank Zeidler, like others, saw her as "the recognized leader of the movement to establish 500 outlets for educational television." In fact, Hennock nearly singlehandedly set the stage for educational television. The first female commission member, Hennock was nominated by President Truman, whom she said had made it clear he wanted educational television because he saw it as analogous to the land-grant colleges. Hennock embarked on a letter-writing campaign in which she encouraged educators to testify on educational television to the FCC. As a result, the national Joint Committee on Educational Television was formally organized in April 1951 and made up of seven educational organizations, including the National Education Association and the American Council on Education. The Joint Committee was partially funded by the Ford Foundation.[6]

FCC chairman Wayne Coy also strongly backed creation of public television. As Coy saw it, "Television frequencies constitute an important and large part of a great national resource, the radio spectrum. It is essential that such a resource be utilized in the public interest." When the FCC held hearings on the matter during 1950 and 1951, seventy-six witnesses from the education field testified, and more than eight hundred sworn statements and exhibits were filed with the commission indicating interest in television channels for education. Because of the public's input, the FCC voted to reserve 10 percent of TV channels for noncommercial educational use, with Hennock in dissent because she wanted 25 percent.[7]

In creating one VHF channel for immediate commercial use and one for public operation in Milwaukee, the FCC also set aside three of the newer, higher-frequency UHF channels—but they were not yet available. Hearst-owned WISN, which had previously applied to the FCC for channel 10, and the other two broadcast outlets seeking commercial television stations argued that setting aside a special channel for public education was unnecessary because they would donate 15 percent of their telecasting time to public service. Zeidler was not impressed. He called the commercial stations' assurance they would reserve space for educational broadcasting "a mere bagatelle of a promise," which "is neither enforceable nor practicable." The mayor's characterization pained WFOX President Charles Lanphier. "The phrase, 'a mere bagatelle of a promise,'" Lanphier wrote Zeidler, "appears to be a most uncomplimentary reflection upon the sincere and honest statements of three reputable Milwaukee radio stations."[8]

In response, Zeidler noted that if the commercial stations gave time for public service broadcasting, "it is almost a foregone conclusion that the educational features will be allocated awkward hours." But at stake was more than just bandwidth. "The attempts of potential commercial operators of TV stations to take from the educators a precious television channel is not at all in the public interest." As he often did, Zeidler appealed to a sense of broader community well-being. "This issue is an extension of the century-old struggle to establish free public education; if viewed from that point, I am sure that you would clearly see it to your interest to bow to the larger public good." Zeidler saw the battle as going even beyond the local issue of community welfare. "But more than that: The fundamental right to use these natural channels of communication rests with public groups, doesn't it, and for educational groups to settle for something less than their full heritage is to not keep faith with the principles of democratic American education."[9]

A 1950 FCC study confirmed fears that public programming would be severely limited on commercial stations. The study found that in a "composite week" that year, only 3 percent of all commercial programs were of an "educational type." Connecticut Senator William Benton, a congressional champion of public television, sought to develop educational programs on radio networks as vice president of the University of Chicago. There he found that in a comparison of educational radio, networks "were doing a far poorer job" in 1940 than in 1930 and 1950. Benton said both studies showed that "the commercial pressure toward trivialization in radio has proved irresistible." He asserted that "commercial television, if it is allowed to mushroom along the lines of commercial radio, without guidance from Congress or from organized public opinion, will never remotely do the great and urgent educational and public service job required by the time." As Hennock put it, "Inadequate provision for educational television primarily penalizes, not the educators, but rather the American people, who own these airwaves."[10]

At the request of the city's Vocational and Adult Schools, which sought to run channel 10 as an educational outlet, community leaders who supported a publicly run channel in 1951 formed a formal coalition, the Milwaukee Educators' Committee on Television. Committee members included the mayor; Vocational Schools director William Rasche; the superintendent of Milwaukee Public Schools; the president of Wisconsin State College; and the director of the University of Wisconsin, Milwaukee Extension Division. An informal, broad-based committee of public-television supporters included the UAW/CIO, with its twenty thousand Milwaukee members; the UAW/AFL, also representing twenty thousand members; the Catholic Archdiocese of Milwaukee, which included one hundred schools, forty-five thousand students, and fifteen hundred teachers; the Milwaukee County Council of Churches, made up of twelve denominations in one hundred congregations and forty thousand congregants; and the eleven-hundred-member Protestant Business Women's Council.[11]

To ensure channel 10 remained available for educational use, the Milwaukee Educators' Committee on Television submitted to the FCC a ninety-five page study on the administration, programming, and cost of educational television, as well as evidence of available educational resources and citizen support. In its testimony before the Common Council, the committee asserted that sufficient volume of educational program material existed in tax-supported agencies in Milwaukee for full-time, noncommercial educational television.

With five private colleges, a branch of the state university, and numerous schools of art, business, and engineering in the area, the committee concluded the high quality and variety of material available "will reach in some part and in some way the whole television audience of the community . . . and thus assist in raising the general cultural level of the community." Labor organizations like the local machinists union passed supportive resolutions, as did groups such as the Business and Professional Women's Club of Milwaukee. On the Milwaukee School Board, labor leader Anthony King led the fight for a vote to reserve channel 10, with the board members voting unanimously in support of the measure.[12]

Despite the broad representation of the groups supporting a city-run channel, proponents still needed to sell the issue to the public. But in framing public television as one benefiting the educational needs of Milwaukeeans, they opted for a public-relations campaign that was rejected by educational television proponents elsewhere, who avoided such terms as "educational TV" or "educational programming." A Milwaukee publicist critiqued the city's discussion over public television as "unexciting and academic." He suggested the city compile a tentative schedule of interesting programs, based on the vast resources of the city's libraries, museum, and colleges, to whet the public's appetite for such programming. Similarly, Dr. Harold Wigren, director of audiovisual education for public schools of Houston, which was the first locality in the nation to broadcast educational programming, highlighted the need to counter the stereotype of educational television as the visual equivalent of wheat bran.[13]

While commercial radio interests sought channel 10 primarily as part of a larger drive to increase profits, Hearst-owned WISN also used the issue to advance an economic conservative ideology. In doing so, Hearst exemplified how it straddled both the mainstream corporate media orbit—one that exhibited a conservatism driven more often by profit motive than ideology—and the universe inhabited by more extreme, far-right broadcast and print outlets. Utilizing the *Milwaukee Sentinel* as its mouthpiece, Hearst published an ostensibly objective reporting series on the issue, mixing facts and opinion to argue against public television based on its cost to taxpayers. The Vocational School's independent taxing powers drew much of its ire. The Vocational School Board had earmarked $250,000 for construction, planning, and funding to purchase a site and build the station, which led the FCC to open up channel 10 as public. Not only had taxpayer money convinced the FCC to offer the channel to the city, but WISN had been the first to bid for channel 10 before the FCC's decision to open up the airwaves. To broaden distribution of its argument beyond the newspaper's pages, Hearst reprinted and distributed the series as a pamphlet.[14]

The media corporations were supported in their opposition to public television by members of the city's largest and most active anti-tax organization, the Affiliated Taxpayers' Committee. The longstanding organization had deep roots in the community and was amply funded by local realtor associations and other business entities. The group drew a hard ideological line against taxation. In the 1920s, Affiliated Taxpayers had opposed the city's Depression-era toy loan program, launched to combat juvenile delinquency. Modeled after the library loan system with staff who took time to help troubled children, the program was supported by the city's most prominent juvenile justice and child experts. Its popularity forced Affiliated Taxpayers to privately oppose the program while publicly calling for drastic reductions in all welfare budgets.[15]

With publicly funded television a possibility, members of Affiliated Taxpayers testified against it before a Common Council committee, where the organization opposed even the council's move to evaluate the issue. "You don't need a study, and you don't need a city station, and you could vote today to stay out of that business," the Affiliated Taxpayers' counsel testified. "It's just too deep for you. It's a field in which you can't adequately qualify. Let the people who know the business take care of it."[16]

Another staunchly economically conservative organization, the Milwaukee County Property Owners' Association, opposed "any organ of government possessing ownership of an instrument of mass communication, such as TV." Like Hearst, the organizations waved the red flag of higher taxes when urging the public to oppose a city-run television station. When the struggle later moved to the state level, the *Milwaukee Times* argued that educational television "indiscriminately pushed out over the airwaves is, to our way of thinking, another waste of taxpayers' cash." But while the potential for tax increases was a legitimate concern and served as a potent public rallying point, opposition to public television was rooted in a deeper, underlying antagonism to government expansion, one that fueled the ideological battle against public television throughout the multiyear confrontation over channel 10.[17]

Public TV: A Radical Idea

The issue gained steam as Zeidler emerged fresh from his April 1, 1952, re-election victory for mayor, in which he carried all but one ward, defeating a South Side lawyer and auto dealer by a whopping 152,658 to 58,590 vote. That same month, Milwaukee marked a milestone in modernization of its municipal services: the city retired its last horse-drawn sanitation trucks—or, as a *Milwaukee Journal* headline phrased it, "At Last, Milwaukee's a None-Horse Town." But there was nothing parochial about the controversy brewing over whether the city should accept federal funding for a nonprofit educational station. The previous fall, the Common Council reacted to the FCC announcement by passing a resolution opposing public funds for educational television. Zeidler vetoed the resolution and the council sustained it.[18]

On the Common Council, council president Milton McGuire, working with Hearst, found another avenue of attack: hamstringing the Milwaukee Vocational School, the only likely operator of the channel, by preventing it from using its funds to set up an educational television station. (The vocational school had been founded early in the century by Emil Seidel.) It is likely that McGuire, who regularly took the side of the realty industry, was acting on behalf of the County Property Owners' Association and Affiliated Taxpayers when he succeeded in pushing a resolution through the Common Council in May 1952 that questioned the right of the vocational school to spend a portion of its budget to construct an educational television station. The council unanimously adopted the resolution, Zeidler vetoed it, and the council overrode the veto by a 20–7 vote. Passage of the resolution effectively put the council on record as opposing local funding for educational television, a move Zeidler felt was superseded by the council's vote the previous fall that sustained his veto on a similar resolution. Zeidler not only saw the council's vote as inappropriate but also attacked the manner in which it was taken: in a nonpublic session. Zeidler issued a stinging rebuke over the council's behind-closed-doors process.[19]

"I desire to voice my regrets at the manner in which this resolution was passed," Zeidler wrote in his veto message. "It originated in caucus, without aldermen delving into facts and circumstances, and was approved by the

Common Council without a hearing by a committee or public discussion. Surely this undemocratic manner is not the way to treat a subject of such vital importance to Milwaukee and its future generations." Zeidler admonished the council to instead consider televising "its own proceedings or a portion of these proceedings," to "bring to the people of Milwaukee an actual and forthright view of their city government in action."[20]

Following the vote, the superintendent of schools for the Milwaukee Catholic Archdiocese conveyed to the council that it is "difficult to understand how representative Milwaukee can reject channel 10 for educational television. Have we reached the point where all education in our community must be serviced over commercial channels?" Many members of the council answered in the affirmative. The council's Public Utilities Committee, charged with studying the issue, had early on in the process recommended channel 10 be given to corporate broadcasting interests, whose public opposition to the education channel and behind-the-scenes lobbying clearly influenced the council's decision to block public television. The Common Council's opposition grew, despite vocal public support for an educational television channel. One alderman suggested a referendum on the issue "before anything so radical as this is undertaken."[21]

The council passed a resolution asking the city attorney to furnish a legal opinion about whether the Milwaukee Vocational School, which was in the best financial and technical position to run an educational television station, had spending powers for the "construction, maintenance, or operation of an educational television station." A few days later, the city attorney's office provided a detailed response that concluded "the operation of a television station under the supervision of the Federal Communications Commission by an educational entity such as the Vocational School could conceivably be construed as appropriately within the educational program circumference of such an entity."[22]

As the debate raged, Hearst shifted tactics, with executives from its New York headquarters traveling to Milwaukee to see the mayor shortly after his re-election. The cordial, nonconfrontational meeting strongly contrasted with the ideological battle Hearst had waged through the *Sentinel*. But the parent company needed the revenue channel 10 would generate because the *Sentinel* recently had begun to lose money. The paper had been profitable in the years immediately after World War II, largely because the Hearst Corporation had subsidized scarce newsprint for its publication at a time when the *Journal* cut back circulation and advertising due to paper shortages. (Hearst continued subsidizing the *Sentinel*'s losses through the remainder of the decade, costing the company roughly $1 million a year.)[23]

Hearst officials argued that it would host educational programming on channel 10, offering as example the corporation's handling of educational television through Hearst's Baltimore affiliate, WBAL. Their discussions with Zeidler centered on the inability of local organizations to provide educational programming in Baltimore, with Hearst stepping in to provide the needed resources and expertise. But in providing details about the live educational programs WBAL hosted, Hearst executives also inadvertently demonstrated why proponents of publicly run channels did not trust commercial media: two of three WBAL education programs ran at 10 P.M. or later, times inaccessible for many.[24]

In October 1952 the Milwaukee Board of Vocational and Adult Education adopted four resolutions enabling the vocational school to take steps toward preparing to host a public television station, one of which approved $131,055 for the school to set up a closed-circuit television lab. In response, Affiliated Taxpayers' Committee chairman Edwin Zeidler filed a lawsuit against the vocational school as a private citizen. A Milwaukee County Circuit Court judge issued a temporary restraining order against the school, requiring it to show why a permanent order preventing it from applying to the FCC or spending tax monies on a television station should not be issued. The taxpayers group claimed that because the station's signal would reach beyond the Milwaukee city limits, residents should not be required to fund a facility that would benefit nonresidents. Without the taxpayer suit, FCC commissioner Hennock said Milwaukee could have had an educational television in a few months. Meanwhile, the race for commercial television superiority manifested literally in WTMJ's construction of a new television tower which, when it reached 420 feet, was the tallest in the state and exceeded the height of Milwaukee's landmark City Hall tower.[25]

That same month, the council again acted on the issue—this time, in a manner even more suspect than during its May closed vote—an action that caught the attention of the press. Council members unanimously passed a resolution requesting the city attorney "oppose any action or actions of the Board of Vocational and Adult Education for the construction of a television station, and matters pertaining thereto." But the council passed the resolution under suspension of the rules, without discussion or debate, and without members of the press aware it was up for a vote. Further, the resolution, introduced by McGuire and his First Ward ally Alderman Alfred Hass, bore the unusual tally number of 197.5, although half-numbers had never been used to list council resolutions, and reporters said they had not seen it in the public records before the vote.[26]

Zeidler was outraged and issued what the *Milwaukee Journal* called his "most sharply worded message" to the council. Zeidler began with a tempered response, giving the council the benefit of the doubt, noting that "it is possible that the resolution was indistinctly read, inadvertently omitted, unintentionally omitted, or not included at all but put into the file of resolutions purportedly passed—which would be borne out by the unusual tally number of 197–1/2." Because the resolution had been signed by the city clerk, Zeidler said he must act on it. He then castigated the manner in which the council conducted its proceedings, saying, "Its dignity and integrity has been impaired by the manner in which this resolution has purportedly been passed." Zeidler went on to ask, "Is it the function of the Common Council of the City of Milwaukee to liquidate or destroy the educational assets of the city? Is it the function of the Common Council to prevent education from reaching the television viewers of Milwaukee unless it is endorsed by some commercial sponsor?" The council's move seemed to bolster the mayor's resolve. "The struggle for a free and untrammeled opportunity for education has been a long one and it is apparently by no means over. The right of educational systems to radio and television must now be established."[27]

Possibly shamed by its action, or more likely fearful of voter backlash, the council in November failed to override Zeidler's veto. At the same time, the court lifted part of the restraining order against the school, enabling it to apply for a television license but prohibiting it from entering into any contracts or beginning actual operations until the matter was tried. The FCC dismissed Hearst's application for channel 10 in the same month, and two days later the Affiliated Taxpayers' Committee and the city attorney made public an agreement to dismiss the lawsuit that sought to prevent the vocational school from constructing and operating a television station. Edwin Zedler's attorney said they still believed the suit was sound but that it appeared the 1953 state legislature would pass new laws giving vocational schools the right to operate such stations. In addition, the school already had $250,000 in its budget for such a station, and its proposed agreement with WEMP to locate a television transmitter at the station's facilities and an antenna on its tower would not require the school to spend significant taxpayer money.[28]

Milwaukee's contentious debate over public television was repeated across the country as corporate interests attacked publicly funded education nationwide. Although the FCC had granted nine construction permits, with action on five other applications pending by late 1952, the handful of cities that had given the go-ahead to educational television were few in light of the fact that the FCC had set aside 242 television channels for noncommercial education use. Hennock pointed to powerful forces throughout the United States attempting to overturn the FCC order, saying, "The commercial radio interests are fighting us everywhere," even as "the people are almost 100 percent behind educational television."[29]

Nationally, the 1952 fall elections were in full swing, with Milwaukee getting set to re-elect Senator Joseph McCarthy and vote for General Dwight Eisenhower over Democratic candidate Adlai Stevenson. Speaking in Salt Lake City on the campaign trail, Eisenhower advocated a "middle way" to government, labor and management problems, and national defense as a defense against communist subversion. He told the crowd, "We want to go forward—not to the right or to the left, but straight forward. We want to get rid of extremes and extremists and back on the middle way." Previewing his consensus approach to governance, Eisenhower said some extremists think the more government the better, while others deny "the obligation of government to intervene on behalf of the people even when the complexities of modern life demand it." Both are wrong, he said, but in the middle way lies the answer to the strengthening of liberty and security.[30]

When the FCC first made channels available for public use, Zeidler submitted to the council a letter from Pittsburgh mayor David Lawrence to bolster his position in support of a municipally run station. Lawrence, who at the time was the president of the U.S. Conference of Mayors, pointed out that if cities did not immediately claim channels assigned for educational use, the channels "will be forever lost to education."[31] But even less liberal public figures found reason to support publicly provided programming. Walter Lippmann, among the more vocal of those in the postwar era sounding the alarm over collectivist incursions by the federal government, called for an adequately financed noncommercial network to provide an alternative to commercial broadcast.[32]

> We should not, I believe, shrink from the idea that such a network would have to be subsidized and endowed.... Why should it not be subsidized and endowed as are the universities and the public schools and the exploration of space and modern medical research, and indeed the churches—and so many other institutions which are essential to a good society, yet cannot be operated for profit?[33]

In this instance, Lippmann, like Eisenhower reflected a moderate conservative vision that allowed for some government involvement in providing for the broader common good. But in Milwaukee and other cities debate over issues such as public television represented a deep and growing division about what constituted the public interest and how it was to be achieved.

Corporate Media's Temporary Setback

Ultimately, channel 10 was licensed through the Milwaukee Vocational School in 1956 and broadcast its first program on October 28, 1957, as WMVS-TV.

But in the years after the city-level debate over public television, a majority of aldermen took their fight against public television to the state. Twenty-two of twenty-seven aldermen signed and submitted a petition to the state assembly opposing an educational television station run by the vocational school. Later, the Common Council Judiciary Committee voted unanimously to recommend to the council that it pass a resolution opposing two bills in the state legislature, one that would have broadened the powers of vocational schools to run educational television stations and another that would have created a state educational television network. Zeidler vetoed it in May, and the council overrode it.[34] The Wisconsin Republican Party also weighed in, voting for a resolution at its 1954 convention opposing state-operated educational television and "urging liquidation of the state FM radio network." As late as January 1956, Affiliated Taxpayers tried to get the council to put a referendum on the spring ballot opposing the Vocational School's continued preparation for hosting channel 10 in face of a 1954 statewide vote rejecting tax-supported educational television.[35]

Hearst also had not given up. Through WISN radio and the *Milwaukee Sentinel*, Hearst supported McCarthy in the 1952 general election. After his re-election, McCarthy announced on November 29 that the FCC would come under the scrutiny of his U.S. Senate investigating subcommittee in the new Congress, at the suggestion of three unnamed senators who suggested he look into the commission's "wastefulness" and "favoritism" in granting new licenses to radio and television stations. Hearst petitioned the FCC for a new hearing. In January 1953 McCarthy was named chairman of the Senate investigating committee and, the following day, he announced he was doubling its investigating staff. (Simultaneously, McCarthy notified the FCC that he opposed the request by Badger Television for a television application. Badger was the parent company of the daily Madison *Capital Times*, which routinely attacked him.) In late January the FCC granted Hearst a new hearing and set a precedent in allowing first-ever oral arguments.

The Milwaukee Board of Vocational and Adult Education filed a statement with the FCC supporting the reservation of channel 10 for educational use and asked for dismissal of Hearst's petition for a rehearing. In February 1953 McCarthy and his Wisconsin counterparts, Republican Senator Alexander Wiley, Republican Representatives Lawrence Smith and Charles Kersten, and Democratic Representative Clement Zablocki, wrote to the FCC saying the commission should make channel 10 commercial because commercial stations would make plenty of educational time available. In March, the FCC denied Hearst's petition for a rehearing and dismissed its application for channel 10. By the mid-1950s, eleven public television stations went on air, potentially reaching 20 million viewers. Twelve more were under construction, and action was taken in more than one hundred other communities to reserve local stations for public television.[36]

At the same time that proponents of public television spent years struggling to obtain a local educational television channel, the National Association of Manufacturers easily directed millions of dollars into creating a series of programs based on what for NAM was a new strategy: the soft sell. In late 1950, NAM launched a series of self-produced weekly television shorts, *Industry on Parade*, and offered the package free of charge to television stations. Even if the station sold the program to a local advertiser, NAM took no funding, adding a profit incentive to the deal. Each newsreel contained four or five stories, two minutes to four minutes long. The format and story treatment resembled an orthodox newsreel, but the material was not dated. Focusing on how products are made, each reel included at least one story taking the viewer through American industrial plant gates and behind the scenes in the development and manufacture of products consumers used every day. Enveloped inside these films of "American industry, business ingenuity, and enterprise," two forty-second segments, "A Message from Industry to You," called attention to "the superiority of the United States economic system, the dangers of inflation, the benefits of research, the need for employment of the physically handicapped, the importance of voting, and the conservation of our material resources."[37]

With television stations hungry for content to feed this new medium, few turned away the chance at free programming. Of the sixty-three market areas that received a sample reel, forty-six stations immediately accepted the series, with nine signing later. The programs were a huge hit in Milwaukee: residents there gave *Industry on Parade* a higher ranking than the news program *Meet the Press*, which was aired in the same Sunday afternoon time segments. Reports of other audience measurements showed the series ranked high in viewer program preferences, in many cases holding its own against strong competition by high-budget television shows. The newsreels received a second and third life as NAM encouraged stations to turn the reels over to schools after they were aired or distribute them to community groups.[38]

NAM's soft-sell campaign, even less confrontational than Hunt's broadcasts, enabled the organization to reach a broad audience, with the newsreels marketing both the NAM "brand" and the superiority of unbridled free enterprise. Unlike the poorly funded groups in Milwaukee seeking a television outlet for programming that would never generate a profit, the deep-pocketed NAM easily generated content and ensured its nationwide distribution. Across the country, large corporations repeated this ideological battle in the media and, like NAM, increasingly employed a marketing device that had gained steam in the 1930s: public-interest advertising. Writing in the 1950s, social scientist James Prothro warned of the growth of this trend. "Perhaps the most serious result of such an attempt to sell an American way of life to the American people lies in the fact that it abets a polarization of attitudes that is extremely dangerous to a democratic society."[39]

A Brave New World

Although a direct correlation cannot be established, union membership as a percentage of the total U.S. workforce peaked immediately before television viewership skyrocketed. Many factors fueled unions' declining numbers, yet rarely mentioned is the potential connection between dwindling union membership and the loss of vibrant communication once provided by the early labor newspapers and midcentury radio outreach. Unions never stopped communicating with their members, but the union movement's opportunity for mass outreach among the general public ended with the creation of television media giants and the public's turn away from radio for their news and entertainment.

The growth in television viewership was exponential. In 1946, seven thousand television sets were scattered around the nation. In 1960, there were more than 50 million. By 1956, Americans for the first time were spending more hours watching TV than working for pay, despite the costliness of the purchase. In Milwaukee, a brand-new Zenith in a twenty-one-inch console sold for $309.95 with tax in 1955—a considerable sum out of the pockets of middle-income earners, with the majority making between $4,000 a year and $7,000 a year. Television also made it prohibitive for candidates without as much funding, like those in third parties, to use it as a campaign medium. For labor, the transition into commercial media oblivion did not happen all at once. Up into the early 1960s, AFL-CIO president George Meany regularly appeared on NBC's Sunday *Meet the Press*—an event nearly unimaginable in later decades.[40]

Control of channel 10 was about far more than competition for scarce airwaves. In the mid-1950s, Milwaukee opponents of public television and radio carried their battle to the state legislature—a time when more channels were available for commercial use than during the earlier part of the decade. Clearly, the struggle was no longer over limited bandwidth. So why did opponents persist?

Speaking at a 1954 conference on unemployment and education, longtime Milwaukee trade union leader J. F. Friedrick summed up the contest over public services in Milwaukee and around the nation.

> Throughout the history of this nation there have been two opposing theories of government. One, that government is a necessary evil and that, therefore,

governmental functions should be held to the very minimum, and the other that government as the agency of the people should be used to promote the welfare and the interests of the people. Those holding the view that the government is an evil are largely the big business and propertied interests who want to restrict the operation of government to the protection of their property rights and who decry any social legislation as socialistic and welfare statism.[41]

The ideological war against government paralleled efforts to delegitimize the U.S. labor movement. Yet a "parade of books" and popular magazine articles portrayed the New Deal not under attack but thriving. Following Eisenhower's re-election, *Time* magazine hailed the reign of the "New Conservatives," national corporate leaders who put in practice a business plan in which "the progress of the corporation is inextricably linked with the progress of the community at large." In this brave new world, business leaders who once had "fought a long delaying action against the growth of labor unions, against government intervention in economic affairs, against social legislation," were now among the majority who "realize that welfare programs help store up purchasing power in the hands of the consumer."[42]

With the mainstream press relentlessly proselytizing this new breed of benevolent conservatism, and bolstered by the decade's influential sociological studies that played down conflict and emphasized the harmonious and enduring nature of American democratic values, interpreters of the era have amplified this vision of liberal consensus as the decade's defining feature. Yet a few prominent voices at the time challenged this prevailing view. Arthur Schlesinger Jr., whom *Time* had dubbed the nation's "New Dealing Historian," described the spate of media hype over benevolent conservatism as "a romantic nostalgia" for the feudal class system.[43]

Milwaukee proponents of publicly run educational television worried that if corporate interests dominated this new medium, they would offer the public a diet of unedifying pablum inimical to educational development. But in contemplating the longer-term perspective, they also understood that at stake in the battleground over this powerful new medium was the outcome of competing visions of the nation's future, one that championed a collective path to the public good and the other that elevated an individual-rights-based solution.

Just as the battle over channel 10 was about much more than whether a single television station would be set aside for educational programs, a simultaneous contest over affordable housing in Milwaukee had, at its core, ideologically opposed conceptions of the public good. When Milwaukeeans cast their ballots in a 1951 referendum vote on the future of public housing, they weighed in also on the extent to which the city would privilege an expansive government role in the road forward.

4 Let the People Vote

> "When the people grasp the true concept of the effect of socialized housing in a community, the old-time American spirit makes itself felt and in most cases through referendum vote it down."
> —William Pieplow, civic activist, 1949

In city after city, attempts to address the nation's postwar housing shortage resulted in an ideological clash between proponents of the public good and those espousing individual liberty rooted in free enterprise. In Milwaukee, that struggle emerged in a 1950–51 referendum battle in which economic conservatives sought passage of a municipal law that would effectively obstruct construction of public-housing projects. Although the campaign received support from the nation's powerful real estate and building industries, the effort to halt government expansion in the city's housing market was home grown, spurred by small-property owners and economic conservatives who saw free enterprise and public service as mutually exclusive.

Ninety Thousand Housing Units Short

Milwaukee's postwar housing crisis was formidable. Living units constructed in the previous forty years were nearly ninety thousand behind the number of new families in the city, with its population hovering just above six hundred thousand by the end of the 1940s. Housing starts had lagged through the 1930s, when the city's Common Council, dominated by conservative extremists, refused to establish a housing authority to build public housing with federal aid. By 1944 a group of women concerned with housing issues succeeded in getting the council to create a housing authority, but the first units of the low-income Hillside Terrace complex in the blighted Sixth Ward north of downtown Milwaukee did not open until December 30, 1948.[1]

War veterans returning to Milwaukee bore the brunt of the city's housing shortage. In November 1948, 19 percent of married veterans in Milwaukee

County were doubled up with other families or living in rented individual rooms or private trailers, and the thirty-three hundred temporary veterans' housing units in Milwaukee County were filled. The Red Cross Housing Bureau reported being unable to place more than seventeen thousand veterans' families. Quonset huts filled the city's downtown McArthur Square, where veterans lived with their families, unable to find permanent housing.[2]

The crisis was exacerbated by substandard housing conditions. A survey of the inner core by the Milwaukee Housing Authority in 1949 found two-thirds of housing units were dilapidated, meaning they did not have one of the following: electric lighting, hot and cold running water, a stove, a flush toilet, or bath and shower. One-fourth of the families in these dilapidated units were headed up by war veterans.[3]

An average of fifty to sixty appeals for housing per day poured into the mayor's office in the months after the 1948 election, while the Red Cross Housing Bureau received between 350 and 450 requests per month for rental housing. Many were unable to find suitable living space for their families, such as the mother of four and her husband who lived in a three-room attic with no fire escape. Ordered to move by the fire inspector, the family had nowhere to go. As did many others, Theresa Buller placed her children in an orphan's home because no one would rent to so large a family.[4]

The housing crisis persisted into the new decade, with up to 250 children filling the County Home for Dependent Children at taxpayer expense in late 1951, some living there for five or six years. Even before Hillside opened its doors in fall 1949, the Housing Authority received thousands of applications for the 232 units in the city's new public housing complex. The municipal eviction court was packed, leading one tenant, surrounded by others losing their homes like him, to wonder, "If the elected officials of our community, state, or nation do not take immediate action on this problem, then all we can say is: 'Where do we do go from here?'"[5]

William Pieplow, Civic Activist

Many in Milwaukee saw creation of affordable housing as the solution to the city's crisis. In January 1949 the Milwaukee Housing Authority announced a proposal to create 7,260 units primarily for low-rent residents. But local builders "violently opposed the plan," even though the Housing Authority estimated it would cost the city only $325,000 of the $90 million project.[6]

A little over a year after Milwaukee's municipal elections, the national dynamics seemed to shift in favor of public housing proponents with passage of the 1949 Housing Act, which amended the Housing Act of 1937. The slim five-vote margin reflected a strong ideological bifurcation, with passage resulting in part from the mobilization of housing-reform proponents, who had maintained the public's attention on the issue through the war with a steady stream of articles in daily newspapers, popular magazines, and professional housing journals.[7]

The federal housing act had made local consensus on public housing central to the process—and in doing so, created multiple hurdles for states and localities to overcome before they could qualify for federal housing funds. Among them, states had to pass legislation enabling municipalities to set up local housing authorities, the city council was required to vote to apply for public housing loans, and the local housing authority needed official approval so it could exempt the land from taxation. At each step, a community's efforts to achieve affordable housing could be derailed—and that is what the real estate industry sought to do, seeing the local planning stage as the most effective time to act. The real estate industry built on the formidable national lobbying campaign it honed in fighting the bill to mobilize its members in cities and towns across the nation for an all-out war on the development of public housing. But slowing or halting the creation of publicly funded housing in communities such as Milwaukee was achieved in large part through the self-motivated foot soldiers who shared the industry's ideological outlook.

William Pieplow, who emerged as leader of the effort to block public housing in Milwaukee, had long been active in his South Side Milwaukee community. Well into his seventies by the time he engaged the public-housing battle, Pieplow's life experience and ideology of individualism prepared him to take the leading role in defending the free-enterprise ideal. Although prone to a winner-take-all stance that brooked no compromise on issues such as publicly funded housing, Pieplow's world view fell well within mainstream conservatism, one that allowed for government involvement, albeit circumscribed, in providing services, and one that trumpeted civic participation as a key duty of individual citizens. In contrast, far-right conservatives like William Grede championed the total elimination of government involvement in social services and many other spheres.[8]

Pieplow headed up the city's oldest civic organization, the South Division Civic Association, and wrote regularly for the conservative *Milwaukee Times*, but early on, his civic interests extended beyond the northern boundary of the Menomonee River. In 1902 he was elected to the Milwaukee School Board at age twenty-six, launching a twenty-year career as a board member, complemented by his role as a trustee for the Milwaukee Public Library and a member of the Milwaukee Museum Board.[9]

William George Bruce, one of the founders of the 1948 Corporation, described Pieplow as a man whose "interests center wherever the welfare of the community is under consideration, and no plan or project for public benefit seeks his aid in vain." Further, Bruce effused, Pieplow's broad societal vision placed him in "that class of men whose definite purpose and intelligently directed effort constitutes an element in public progress and general advancement as well as in individual success."[10]

Pieplow developed and refined his views on the role of citizenship, individual enterprise, and government in large part through his long involvement with the U.S. Savings and Loan League. When the Milwaukee Security Savings and Loan Association was incorporated in 1913, Pieplow became its first president. By the time he took on the challenge of defeating public housing, he was president of the Wisconsin Building and Loan League and had written a history of savings and loan associations, celebrating the industry for cultivating the value of thrift. For Pieplow, inculcating thrift in individuals through saving money was closely tied with—and preferably the trigger for—amassing sufficient savings to afford a house.[11]

In fact, much of his savings-and-loan history focused on the virtues of home ownership. "The building of a home is the dream of all right-minded persons," Pieplow wrote. "It plays a chief role in the development of morale of the people. . . . It stimulates self-reliance." More than merely a means of self-development, Pieplow saw the home as "the foundation of American life. . . . The founders of the American Nation were home owners. . . . Ownership of home stimulates love of country." If private home ownership was the American way, government involvement in housing meant the nation was "headed for statism," in which the government "subordinates the people to an all-powerful state," Pieplow argued. "The set-up is to have the government support the people rather than the people the government."[12]

By 1946 there were 150 savings and loan associations in Wisconsin, with assets totaling nearly $175 million. Fifty-three of those were in Milwaukee, and they engaged in more than half of the city's home mortgage business. Like the real estate industry, the U.S. Savings and Loan League had forcefully opposed the 1949 Housing Act, and when it came to lobbying and political connections, the league was "comparable in power and effectiveness to [the National Association of Real Estate Boards] NAREB." When the Housing Act passed, the more than twenty-five thousand boards of directors of its member institutions foretold of impending socialism, asserting, "We are closer to having in this country a managed, socialistic economy than most businessmen may realize."[13]

Similarly, Pieplow argued the bill's passage was just the beginning of state involvement in all aspects of life. Government-funded housing would embolden the "Marxists," who soon will be "clamoring for nationalized automobiles, for public food, for public clothing. . . . The same arguments now being used for housing can be invoked for cars, steaks and decent dress."[14]

Milwaukee's Battle over Public Housing Begins

In 1948 voters had approved bonds for veteran housing and slum clearance, defying the city's long pay-as-you-go tradition and paving the way for municipal construction of affordable housing. The Milwaukee Common Council then gave the go-ahead for public housing in early 1950, shortly before the federal deadline to apply for funding. In response, housing opponents pushed the council to consider a bill that effectively would derail further construction of public housing. That fall, the council debated the bill, which would make each proposed housing project subject to approval by voter referendum. The bill's backers included the Affiliated Taxpayers' Committee, whose members included Pieplow, an active participant since the organization had opposed the city's Depression-era toy loan program.

The council debate drew up to five hundred residents in a crowd evenly divided between proponents and opponents of the bill. Opponents argued that municipal housing generated a paucity of tax revenues and that the nation's housing crisis could more efficiently be addressed through private-sector solutions. Although many aldermen opposed public housing in principle, they feared that if it was killed by a voter referendum, slum clearance would not take place—and without slum clearance, black residents, whose presence was increasing in the city, would move into their wards.[15]

When Pieplow saw the aldermen were not inclined to approve it, he engaged in a heated debate on the council floor, vilifying municipal housing as "nothing but Communism" and asserting it was "immoral" to move people into public housing who never had saved a dollar. Pieplow, who described himself as generally a "pleasant fellow," also noted he had been tutored early in his career by his employer at a small manufacturing operation "who was known throughout the city as a man of vigorous, strong, and biting speech." Pieplow had taken his employer's training to heart.[16]

As the city followed the Byzantine and bureaucratic route required by Congress to qualify for federal housing funds, Pieplow and others on the Affiliated Taxpayers' Committee, rebuffed in their efforts to move the bill through the council, shifted tactics. They prepared to derail creation of public housing through a voter referendum, the real estate industry's most proven mechanism for slowing or stopping the momentum for public housing. The voter referendum aimed to accomplish the same goal as the bill the council rejected: to make each proposed housing project subject to approval by voter referendum.

With its official motto, "Watching Your Taxes," Affiliated Taxpayers included three delegates each from the Milwaukee Association of Commerce, the Milwaukee Board of Realtors, the Milwaukee Building Association, the

Building Owners and Managers Association, and the Milwaukee Savings and Loan institutions. Each organization paid $600 in annual dues. Early in the referendum effort, the Milwaukee Association of Commerce withdrew its support from the group. The move followed a letter it received from the mayor questioning its stance on the referendum, with the Milwaukee Association of Commerce board of directors agreeing they did not want to be aligned with a single-issue organization. The association took a more considered approach to public housing than did Affiliated Taxpayers. While vehemently opposing public housing in general, the association had backed the $3.5 million bond issue in 1948 to fund veterans' housing.[17]

On November 2, 1950, the Affiliated Taxpayers formed the Public Housing Referendum Committee, which served as a vehicle to secure signatures to qualify the initiative for the spring 1951 ballot and to campaign for its passage. Pieplow, the Milwaukee Savings and Loan representative on the Affiliated Taxpayers' Committee, undoubtedly received the U.S. Savings and Loan League kit of anti-public-housing materials, which included ready-to-use ads and editorials tailored to appeal to specific consumers, with some emphasizing emotions and others statistics or logic. The Savings and Loan League urged members to emphasize that public housing meant "paying someone else's rent"—a message the Milwaukee Referendum Committee frequently employed.[18]

Pieplow served as Referendum Committee chairman. Other officers included Milwaukee Builders Association president Elton Schultz as vice chairman and Edwin Zedler as treasurer. Zedler, chairman of the Affiliated Taxpayers' Committee, had long been a public-housing foe, arguing in 1945 that "Milwaukee does not want public housing and the resultant drain upon taxpayers for the purpose of benefiting a pitifully small percentage of Milwaukee's citizens." H. Ellis Saxton, public relations director for the Milwaukee Board of Realtors, held the public-relations spot on the committee. The group's attorney, Lewis Stocking, expressed the sentiment of local realtors and property owners, opposing creation of housing even for America's war veterans. Stocking asserted that such housing would not generate taxes, and he disparagingly equated government-funded housing for war vets with giving them $20 bills. Stocking, like most of the builders and realtors, lived in Milwaukee's wealthy northern suburbs.[19]

Following passage of the federal Housing Act, Pieplow had predicted that "when the people grasp the true concept of the effect of socialized housing in a community, the old-time American spirit makes itself felt and in most cases through referendum vote it down." Pieplow and the Taxpayers' Committee had already achieved success through the referendum process. When the group originally formed in 1932 as the Taxpayers' Advisory Council, it had sought to decrease municipal spending by 25 percent through lobbying and the courts. After those tactics failed, the Advisory Council placed on the ballot a measure to drastically cut spending through 1937. Even as Milwaukee voters elected to office a Socialist Party slate, they also strongly passed the tax-cutting initiative and went on to vote down a measure Socialists later placed on the ballot to repeal the mandate. Following passage of the 1949 Housing Act, the Savings and Loan League, with Pieplow an active member, approved a measure urging Congress to amend the act by requiring a referendum on each proposed project. So the real estate industry's push for referenda to defeat local housing initiatives was not a new tactic for Pieplow and the Taxpayers' Committee.[20]

The day after it was formed, the Referendum Committee began mobilizing volunteers to secure the 32,513 signatures needed to qualify—10 percent of Milwaukee's registered voters. Standing outside shops and public offices in the bitter Milwaukee winter, where temperatures averaged a high of 21 degrees in January, these volunteers surpassed the goal in less than three months, filing 38,328 signatures on February 6. Thirty-five volunteers, most over age sixty and many members of the Milwaukee County Property Owners Association, made up the committee's activist core. This "Captains' Group" met in the evenings, up to three times a week, with the Referendum Committee providing additional "material, guidance, and the enthusiasm necessary to combat growing resistance by opposition groups as well as wind and weather." Team captains and members received memos from the committee detailing strategies for obtaining their quota of names for petitions, whom to ask for signatures, and where to carry the petition for signing. Those who signed up to volunteer received an enthusiastic welcome letter from Referendum Committee chairman Pieplow congratulating them on enlisting in the fight and exhorting them to "exert every effort to get your quota of signatures and send them to headquarters, or your *team captain*, IMMEDIATELY!"[21]

Some volunteers saw their best chance of garnering signatures as portraying the measure as a pro-public-housing ballot initiative—and, in fact, its wording offered a variety of interpretations:

> That unless the electors of the City of Milwaukee shall give their approval by referendum, the City of Milwaukee shall not construct any additional housing projects which are not subject to general property taxes at the same rate as privately owned property and shall not authorize the Milwaukee Housing Authority of the City of Milwaukee to do so.[22]

Walter Kirchuebel was one Milwaukee resident taken in by those portraying it as a pro-housing measure. After reading a newspaper report about the sham, Kirchuebel reported that "a lady contacted me . . . asking me if I'm in favor of public housing. I told her I am, that I own a home, but others aren't so lucky to have a place to live. 'Then please sign this, as we are for public housing, too,' she said." Regretting that "somebody got the best of me through lies," Kirchuebel asked that his name be taken off the petition. In fact, voters who supported public housing needed to vote "No" on the referendum.[23]

The petition campaign reached a crescendo—and, in the view of the Referendum Committee, a turning point in public support—after an incident at city hall on January 9. As three women and an elderly man sought signatures in the lobby of the city's stone-towered municipal building, some ten CIO members and union leaders appeared, carrying signs such as "This Petition is Misleading—DON'T SIGN YOUR NAME." CIO secretary-treasurer Fred Erchul, alerted by a union member that petition solicitors were at city hall, immediately mobilized a group in response, creating picket signs before heading over. The elderly man in the petition group, John Marx, called Erchul a communist, to which Erchul replied, "You are the ones who are breeding communism, because you want to keep slums and bad living conditions. That's what causes communism, and you want to perpetuate it."[24]

Upstairs in the mayor's office, Zeidler accused the petition circulators of creating a disturbance, and police escorted both groups from the building. The Referendum Committee responded by placing blame on the CIO members. When Marx died of a heart attack a few days later, the Referendum Committee moved quickly to capitalize on the tragedy, portraying housing supporters as thugs bent on repressing the freedom to vote, emphasizing that "condemnation of the referendum by the Socialist Party, the CIO Goon Squad and other persons and groups frequently associated with Socialistic proposals, was a clear threat to the people's fundamental right to vote on highly controversial issues."[25]

While the proposed ballot initiative threatened Milwaukee's long-term ability to create public housing, also at stake was the city's immediate goal to meet a federal funding deadline for the proposed Hillside Terrace addition. Calling the ballot initiative's language "weasel-worded," and seeking to flush out the identity of the organizations and the funding behind the group, the mayor demanded the Referendum Committee observe the spirit of the state's Corrupt Practices Act by registering with the City of Milwaukee Election Committee. The statute required any organization advertising for or against governmental action or policy to provide details on its operation, including income sources. But the Referendum Committee successfully fought efforts requiring it to divulge its funding.[26]

After the Referendum Committee submitted petition signatures in February, the mayor hired a handwriting expert to examine them. The Captains'

Group then hit the streets again, obtaining several thousand more as backup. Although supporters of public housing contended many names on the petition were forged and launched a legal challenge, a Milwaukee County District Court ultimately upheld the petition as valid.[27]

Green Space, Red Herrings

Community members, including long-time affordable-housing proponent Genevieve Hambley, a coalition of women activists, and the union movement, led by the formidable Milwaukee Building Trades Council president Peter Schoemann, worked to oppose the referendum. The AFL-affiliated Federated Trades Council of Milwaukee urged its union members not to sign the petition, saying it falsely gave the impression that it supported public housing. When the Common Council indicated its support for the petition, the Women's Trade Union League and other organizations denounced the move. The League of Women Voters took another tack, urging the Common Council's Joint Committee on Housing and Finance to approve funds for voter education on the referendum battle. The committee turned down the request.[28]

The Joint Action Committee for Better Housing and the Public Enterprise Committee (the newly renamed Municipal Enterprise Committee) held a public meeting at the Wisconsin Hotel and invited property owners, realtors, and builders. When realtors asserted the projects would pay much more if they had been done privately, Milwaukee Housing Authority director Richard Perrin replied that private builders would not have put up the projects in the first place, and, if they had, low-income people would not have afforded them. Perrin, named director prior to Zeidler's election, provided crucial support for housing proposals throughout the 1950s, and the mayor supported his recommendations.[29]

Affordable-housing backers had repeatedly argued that private builders were unable or unwilling to fill the city's housing needs. Testifying in Congress a year earlier, Milwaukee Alderman Alfred Hass, chairman of the Common Council's Housing Committee, said the extent of the need—nearly one-quarter of the city's housing supply was substandard—meant "we have no reason to believe that its replacement can ever be contemplated in terms of the usual process of private house building." The mayor also met privately with builders, pointing out that the city's costly efforts to annex additional land, which benefited builders, might need to be "revised" if they opposed slum clearance. The builders remained unconvinced.[30]

Attacks on government-funded public housing were red herrings, Zeidler believed. He challenged the hypocrisy of property investors for supporting aspects of the federal housing law from which they would benefit while opposing municipal housing. Local builders' association representative Roland Teske had said the group opposed public housing, "but that doesn't apply to slum clearance features of the new federal law"—a stance Zeidler said showed that builders saw where they "could profit under 'socialism' and were looking out for federal aid for themselves."[31]

Zeidler, who had set creation of ten thousand new units of affordable housing as a goal of his new administration, made achieving that promise a priority. He came to the issue from deeply personal experience as well as intellectual exposure to visionary housing philosophies. With five children in the mid-1940s, Frank and Agnes Zeidler had been unable to find housing they could afford, and so they moved frequently, even renting a home as far away as Watertown—forcing Zeidler to commute more than seventy miles one way to Milwaukee for his duties as Milwaukee Public School Board member. They returned to the city only after Frank's father purchased a home in 1946 for the family—which ultimately included six children—and never again moved.[32]

Zeidler's firsthand experience intersected with his philosophical vision, one informed both by the turn-of-the-twentieth-century British Garden City movement initiated by English housing planner Ebenezer Howard, and the farsighted Milwaukee public parks system planned and undertaken in the 1920s by socialist Park Commissioner Charles B. Whitnall. Howard, whose Garden City projects in the United Kingdom were replicated on a smaller scale in the United States as the federally sponsored Greenbelt suburbs built in the Depression, aimed for far-reaching goals, such as ending urban sprawl by establishing economically self-sufficient towns and solving housing affordability problems through nonspeculative forms of real estate ownership. The Garden City concept was rooted in public ownership of the land or in a community-held trust, a goal sought as well by agricultural economist Rexford Tugwell in his role as head of Franklin Roosevelt's Resettlement Administration and strongly supported by FDR.[33]

Tugwell's Greenbelt New Town program established the nation's first federally planned communities—Greenbelt, Maryland; Greenhills, Ohio; and Greendale, Wisconsin—before opposition to publicly funded housing projects mired the fourth, planned for New Jersey, in litigation. In 1936 a young Frank Zeidler was among those helping turn 3,411 acres of land southwest of Milwaukee into the Town of Greendale. Working as a survey rodman on a surveying crew and struggling to support his family, Zeidler later attributed his work in Greendale to helping shape his philosophy of urban housing, one in which affordable and approachable low-rise buildings and ample green space with playgrounds for children defined affordable living environments.[34]

Milwaukee offered another lesson in green urban planning—its more than one thousand acres of parks, crowned by eighty-four miles of green space along the county's watercourses, including the three-mile city parkway skirting the city's eastern edge along Lake Michigan. Whitnall, the visionary of Milwaukee County's far-reaching parks system, was a city treasurer on Seidel's socialist slate in 1910 and went on to become a leader of the city's Public Land Commission and the county's Park Commission. His 1923 master plan for a coherent system of parks and parkways designed to preserve the influence of nature became, with little revision, the official guide for all local land-use planning. In 1927 Milwaukee County formalized its approach and adopted the nation's first county zoning ordinance.[35]

A Grassroots or Canned Campaign?

Housing supporters in Milwaukee and across the nation recognized that the real estate industry's campaign did not die with the Housing Act's passage. In setting the act's blueprint, Congress had made private enterprise a main player, with the preamble's first goal stating that "private enterprise shall be encouraged to serve as large a part of the total need as it can." Yet corporate forces lined up against the act, portraying it as nothing less than a federal government takeover.[36]

The real estate industry understood that defeating public housing required a massive effort. Public-opinion polling in May 1950 showed that a large majority of Americans, 69 percent, backed congressional funding for slum clearance and low-rent housing. Only 21 percent did not. Those polled demonstrated they knew who would foot the bill—and most were willing to pay more taxes to do so, with 46 percent saying they would pay higher taxes to aid with publicly funded housing and 40 percent saying they would not.[37]

The real estate industry and other corporate stakeholders were well equipped to challenge public housing initiatives after the act's passage. The tactics they had honed during the federal legislative debate over the Housing Act—including the creation of mass messaging such as sample editorials and radio spots for local member organizations—enabled them to quickly roll out a campaign to slow or block the efforts of local housing activists. Shortly after passage of the act, the National Association of Home Builders (NAHB) distributed a "Dear Fellow Home Builder" letter signed by its president, Rodney Lockwood, accompanied by a detailed guide for defeating public housing. "Public Housing on the Community Level" explained the mechanics of the public housing law and furnished arguments for combating and preventing its creation in local communities. NAHB, with 16,350 individual members, spent $28,168 on public relations in 1948, a figure it boosted to an annual $250,000 by 1950.[38]

The Home Builders sent the booklet to every association, board of directors, president, and secretary of all its local affiliates. Central to the guide was a checklist detailing how the builder could derail the local process. Among those, the initiative and referendum ballot process became the most widely used, with the fastest and ultimately most successful route involving a vote on whether a public housing project should be approved. The seemingly spontaneous formation of anti-public-housing groups often occurred at the behest of local real estate interests. Congressional hearings on lobbying in 1950 uncovered the industry's far-reaching network of members on tap to carry out well-orchestrated actions at the local and national levels.[39]

While the campaign to stop public-housing construction in Milwaukee benefited from its connections with the national real estate and Savings and Loan associations, the effort was fundamentally homegrown, driven by a private enterprise activist whose lifelong philosophy was premised on the belief that homeownership was the basis for individual economic freedom and personal responsibility. Participation in the campaign paralleled that of the labor movement, where local union leaders rallied members for campaigns supported by the AFL or CIO. Another industry tactic involved sending national-level real estate officials to cities and towns around the nation to drum up support for anti-housing measures. Frank Cortright, NAHB executive vice president, spent considerable time in Madison, Wisconsin, trying to force a referendum, but there is no evidence Cortright or other such figures came to Milwaukee.[40]

Zeidler described members of the Milwaukee County Property Owners Association, whose members included many referendum activists, as primarily older residents dependent on the income they garnered from their one or two rental properties. In noting that association members "had a militancy which exceeded all others," Zeidler attributed the group's stridency to their dependence on their income from the rental property and their fear that "this [was] income the city was threatening to take away from them—or so they thought." The ground troops who made up the Referendum Committee's grassroots outreach were individuals driven by similar personal beliefs, some of whom thought they stood to lose financially if the city and federal government helped fund housing. Not that local real estate interests didn't try the tactics used elsewhere: the Milwaukee Board of Realtors sought to create a false-front "Citizens' Committee" to fight public housing, but the Referendum Committee's momentum proved it unnecessary.[41]

Anti-Housing Referendum: A Slim Chance for Passage

For Pieplow and the Housing Referendum Committee, obtaining sufficient signatures to qualify the referendum was the easy part. The group's analysis of the city's past voting patterns on housing issues showed the near impossibility of passing a ballot initiative that threatened affordable housing. In April 1948 all twenty-seven wards voted for a bond issue to finance public housing projects for veterans. The large turnout, spurred by the Zeidler-Reuss mayoral race, showed a clear majority in favor of the bonds in every ward, with some wards voting in favor of the measure by four to one. In the same election, another bond issue asking for $2.5 million for blight elimination also carried by a wide majority but was close in many wards and disapproved in the Eleventh, Twelfth, Fourteenth, and Twenty-Fourth Wards. All four wards were on the city's more conservative South Side.

Further, an April 1949 referendum on state-supported veteran housing was favored in every ward except the Twenty-Sixth, which disapproved it by eighty-nine votes. "From a purely political standpoint," the Referendum Committee concluded, it "was clear that we had no strength to speak of anywhere in the community and it was obvious, in fact, that the odds were greatly against us." Based on these data, the Referendum Committee strategically focused on eighteen of the city's twenty-seven wards and depended on newspapers and radio to sell the argument to the remaining nine wards, "so that the majority against us in those wards would not be overwhelming."[42]

The Referendum Committee's high-profile public relations and advertising campaign, launched even as signature petitions were being circulated, helped drive momentum. A January 1951 21 full-page ad in the two dailies, the *Milwaukee Journal* and *Milwaukee Sentinel*, ran on a Sunday, the largest circulation day, and urged readers to sign and tear off the petition and mail it in. The ad took the stance that Milwaukee voters deserved a chance to cast their ballots on the issue. From the start, the Referendum Committee framed the initiative as a right-to-vote issue—its letterhead depicted a hand inserting a ballot into a box with the slogan: "To vote is a privilege, a duty, the American way."[43]

The public relations campaign moved into high gear after the signatures were submitted to the city, with Referendum Committee members distributing fliers in their targeted wards, such as the one depicting a caricature of Perrin as a king sitting atop a pile of money with the caption, "Monarch of all he Surveys." The accompanying text asserted the Housing Authority controlled nearly $27 million worth of "socialized public housing" with plans for $85 million more and "no limit in sight." Playing on taxpayers' fears overshadowed the Housing Authority's attempts to convey the message that residents benefited from increased tax revenues as a result of public housing. In 1950 the Housing

Authority published a study showing that tenants of Hillside, which opened in 1948, paid more in taxes when living in public housing than they did in rundown areas.[44]

With the new effort underway, members of the Captains' Group rechanneled their petition efforts and increased their numbers. Volunteers now went door to door, and phone bankers were given scripts to read as they called residents to urge them to vote "Yes" on the referendum. Milwaukee residents also received postcards urging them to support it. The Property Owners' Association provided critical funding for mailing letters and printed pieces in addition to its own efforts to pass the measure. The association devoted an entire issue of its monthly newspaper, *The Property Owner*, to the referendum. Leaders of the Property Owners included Zedler, chairman of the Affiliated Taxpayers' Committee, and Edward Plantz.[45]

The Referendum Committee began one-on-one outreach to influential community members as early as the first week of December, with a letter directed to members of Building-Savings and Loan Associations and a generic version aimed at leaders of community organizations. Both included packets of petitions and pitches urging the leaders to secure signatures from their members. Later, organizations received a sample resolution in support of the referendum and were urged by the committee to present it to their membership for passage. Recognizing the potential influence of religious leaders, the committee contacted all clergymen in the county, both during the petition drive and while campaigning for the referendum, reassuring them that if there is "a demand for future housing projects, voters will, under the provisions of this referendum," have the choice.[46]

Perrin argued that public housing opponents could say the referendum would put voters in command of deciding housing issues because the committee had created a "very slyly" worded ballot measure. It sounded reasonable because it was not asking voters if they supported or rejected public funding for housing. But by establishing a time-consuming requirement for voter approval of individual proposals, Perrin argued the referendum's passage would destroy the city's chances for securing federal housing funds because Milwaukee would then miss federal financial assistance deadlines, and the money would be "diverted to such other communities which are progressive enough to utilize them in a manner which bespeaks sincerity in carrying out the program." Perrin also pointed out that it was "extremely improbable" anyone would suggest a referendum vote be required for any other issues considered by the Common Council. "Yet, in the case of housing and redevelopment, it is desired that the Common Council abdicate and deny its competency to judge the question."[47]

After the American Legion came out against the referendum, the Referendum Committee addressed its potentially most formidable foe by organizing a Veterans Against Public Housing committee made up of American Legion members. In announcing the new organization, Guy Laubach, chairman of the group and member of the Bay View Post of the American Legion, said "self-styled spokesmen" of the Legion who were urging defeat of the anti-public-housing referendum were "speaking without the authority of the entire membership." More than thirty years before such groups were derogatorily labeled "Astroturf" for their role as false fronts, the Referendum Committee went on to set up several more, including the American Citizens League and the Women's Civic Group, with the latter countering the strong League of Women Voters.[48]

The committee sought to maximize free publicity throughout, meeting with newspaper editorial staffs, especially the *Milwaukee Journal*, and submitting "suggested editorials" for publication. Referendum backers also gained free media coverage by responding to Zeidler's attacks on their efforts, ultimately getting what committee members saw as an "even break" in news coverage because of their aggressive response.

Although the Referendum Committee avoided Red-baiting in its ads and fliers, Pieplow frequently threw down the socialist gauntlet in his more intemperate remarks—even inserting one in an early press release in which he called opponents of the referendum "radical pressure groups working for state socialism" who attacked the proposal "because they fear it is an important roadblock against socialistic planning."[49]

Beginning in late March, as the April 3 election date neared, the Referendum Committee unleashed a full media blitz in print and on radio. The weekend before the Tuesday election, the Referendum Committee ran a three-quarter-page ad in the *Journal* and *Sentinel* and in a Polish-language daily that combined the main messages used throughout the campaign: housing supporters do not want the public to vote on the issue and therefore have something to hide by opposing the referendum, and public housing will raise taxes. Radio spots for foreign-language programs misleadingly alarmed listeners that their search for "opportunity and personal freedom" was threatened unless they supported the referendum and saved their homes.[50]

Dueling Referenda

To counter the referendum drive, organizations such as the Democratic Organizing Committee, the American Legion, the League of Women Voters, and representatives from labor and faith groups created a committee in 1950 headed by 1948 mayoral aspirant Henry Maier. Along with the Public Enterprise Committee, they actively fought the referendum and convinced the Common Council to place a second housing referendum on the ballot which read: "Shall slum clearance housing projects be built with federal funds under the 1949 Federal Housing Act irrespective of any other resolution or act?"[51]

Although Milwaukee's labor movement was divided among the AFL, the CIO, and independent unions, it worked jointly on issues, and its unified position helped turn out union members to vote. At the national level, the AFL, which had supported progressive housing legislation since 1935, passed a resolution condemning actions by the national real estate industry and others to defeat public-housing legislation and asked every local union to actively support public housing and join with other groups to conduct an education campaign "to make clear the issues involved in the real estate lobby's fight against public housing." The Milwaukee AFL, like other pro-housing groups, hammered on the misleading wording of the referendum and challenged the Referendum Committee's assertion that its foes sought to deprive the public of expressing its views on housing.[52]

Milwaukee's labor movement was a powerful force in the city, with several aldermen who opposed public housing voting for it because they feared losing the vote of union members. Schoemann, among the city's most influential union leaders, had over the years doggedly pursued municipal housing. As chairman of the city's Housing Authority, he faced down a Common Council so recalcitrant in pursuing public funds to build affordable housing that some of its members even opposed plans to create housing for the city's returning war veterans. By the time he became Housing Authority chairman, Schoemann already was a significant presence within the city as well as the nation. He joined the Milwaukee School Board in 1932 and was there at the same time as Zeidler, who received the School Board's key endorsement for his 1948 bid for mayor. In 1947 Schoemann was appointed by President Truman as an adviser to the U.S. delegation to the International Labor Organization (ILO) in Geneva and was a member of the Labor-Management Committee of the War Manpower Commission. Schoemann eventually went on to become president of the national plumbers union, turning down calls along the way to run for mayor.[53]

Even as the Referendum Committee sought public support for its measure, Schoemann continued to push for approval of a plan by the Housing Authority to build 520 additional veterans' housing units. While Schoemann's members who were in the building and construction trades stood to gain by any publicly funded housing projects, it is likely he did not engage in the multiyear fight solely to build union membership. Although sometimes accused by socialists of being a "capitalist business agent"—he was among the founding members of the 1948 Corporation—Schoemann's sentiments are highlighted in an action he took as acting president of the national Plumbers Union. Writing in an editorial in the union's *Journal*, Schoemann touched off national outrage when he accused the Eisenhower administration of engaging in "give-aways to big business."[54]

Schoemann was on the 1951 ballot for school board, and union leaders anticipated he would deliver the union votes of all fifty thousand AFL-affiliated building-trades members in opposition to the anti-public-housing referendum. But as the Referendum Committee gleefully noted after the election, the total vote against the referendum was some sixty-six hundred less than the votes for Schoemann, leading the committee to conclude that "obviously the labor vote as well as the veterans and the rank-and-file members of other organizations are not following blindly the dictates of their 'bosses.'"[55]

The CIO's grassroots efforts were channeled through the Citizens' Anti-Slum Committee, a group it created from its political action committee funds, and one that the Referendum Committee described as a "formidable foe." The Milwaukee CIO repeatedly requested union affiliates donate to the fund, with many locals giving $500 apiece. Headed by Henry Nunn, a retired industrialist, the Anti-Slum Committee included union leaders, community members, and clergy, such as W. J. G. McLin, pastor of the African American St. Matthew CME Church. The Anti-Slum Committee produced and distributed mass voting materials, including one hundred thousand copies of a four-page, full-sized newspaper it mailed to voters and a smaller "Voter's Guide." The Referendum Committee complained internally that the Anti-Slum Committee made it difficult for the group's speakers' bureau to get slots, and asserted CIO members left behind in voting booths small cards that reproduced the referendum questions with marks indicating how to vote.[56]

Meanwhile, the mayor's office requested numerous reports from the Housing Authority that illuminated Milwaukee's housing shortage, investigations by the city's building inspector on the deteriorating safety and health of existing housing, and studies determining the extent of blight in densely packed areas such as the city's downtown Third and Sixth Wards. Less than a month before the election, a fire in an old structure built to house two families killed one resident and sent a second to the hospital—and revealed that thirty-eight people were living in the unit.[57]

Despite the odds, the Referendum Committee's ballot measure passed by 45,178 to 43,338, carrying fourteen of the twenty-seven wards in the city—all of which had been selected by the Referendum Committee for its ground effort. The CIO attributed passage of the referendum to a lack of political mobilization by its members, while the AFL pointed to the measure's wording as the culprit.[58]

Yet voters also passed the referendum pushed by the labor movement and pro-housing groups, effectively contradicting themselves. Only four wards cast their ballots against the measure—one by a mere fourteen votes. Zeidler interpreted the conflicting result to mean that voters wanted public housing because the council's referendum was worded "straightforwardly," unlike the property owners' referendum. Zeidler pointed to low voter turnout, typical in a year without city officers up for election, and noted that the wards where people needed housing the most cast the lowest percentage of the vote."[59]

Nationwide, a Hard Fight for Public Housing

The struggle for federal funding in the wake of the mixed referendum results and continued opposition by builders and realtors, as well as battles over slum clearance, delayed the creation of public housing, including housing for veterans. But those projects approved prior to the 1951 referendum vote eventually were completed, and Zeidler's administration ultimately created thirty-two hundred new housing units. While far short of the ten thousand units Zeidler had set as his goal during his 1948 campaign, it is probable that significantly less public housing would have been constructed between 1948 and 1960 had not Zeidler pressed for its creation.[60]

Although other mayors had more success in creating public housing, they also faced tough opposition. Pittsburgh Mayor David Lawrence, who took office in 1946, promised to join with Zeidler in his fight against the real estate lobby. Lawrence had a striking advantage over Zeidler in repelling the power of the real estate industry: the might of the Mellons and other wealthy industrialists who backed creation of affordable housing. Millionaire financier Richard Mellon threw his influence behind the formation of a committee, the Allegheny Conference on Community Development, whose forty key members or sponsors included U.S. Steel president H. J. Heinz. Lawrence's partnership with Republicans pushed the Pittsburgh package of enabling bills through the state legislature in Harrisburg, permitting the mayor and city council to create an urban redevelopment authority, a public parking authority, a public auditorium authority, and the Allegheny County Sanitary Authority.[61]

In New Orleans, populist Mayor DeLesseps Morrison also encountered opposition from the building industry and other foes of public housing, plus the increased demands of a growing urban population. Still, New Orleans was "successful in the construction of architecturally unimaginative, but functional low-rent housing." A referendum to derail public housing in Chicago at the same time as in Milwaukee never was put to a vote, because supporters failed to obtain sufficient signatures to place it on the ballot.[62]

But by June 1951 public housing elsewhere was voted down in twenty-five of thirty-eight local referenda, plus one state referendum in California. As many as four hundred thousand public housing units could have been built by that time under the Housing Act of 1949; three months after Milwaukee voters went to the polls, only 1,480 family dwellings had been completed and occupied nationwide under the law. The increased activity by anti-housing forces paralleled the waning momentum of housing proponents. By the end of 1957, *Fortune* magazine could write: "Today, public-housing people are searching for a new rationale and their fervor is gone; the movement today is so weak that most real estate groups hardly bother to attack it any more."[63]

The outcome of Milwaukee's 1952 municipal elections further undermined the drive for public housing, with conservative gains in the Common Council augmenting the power of council president—and 1956 mayoral candidate—Milton McGuire. Endorsed by Milwaukee's real estate interests, McGuire assembled a majority coalition of Republicans and conservative Democrats who opposed public housing and later received backing from the real estate industry to challenge Zeidler for mayor. Symbolically, McGuire changed the name of the council committee that oversaw housing issues, removing the word "housing," because he said the city should not be in the housing business. With Zeidler opting not to run for reelection in 1960, large-scale public housing effectively came to an end in the 1950s. His successor, Henry Maier—who in the 1948 elections was among mayoral candidates backing public housing—took the politically safe route throughout his six terms in office by focusing on new units for the elderly.[64]

Pieplow and Zeidler: Shared Roots, Divergent Visions

The 1949 Housing Act, Pieplow believed, made it the responsibility of the federal government to guarantee a decent home and suitable living environment for every American family. But Pieplow did not see this as a laudable goal. Instead, such security reversed "the American idea of responsibility of individual thrift and initiative to achieve home ownership." Zeidler held that the Housing Act was critically needed because without federal aid, cities would be unable to ameliorate their dire housing shortage. For Zeidler, "the hopes of many hundreds of thousands of Americans for decent homes" were dependent on congressional passage of the federal Housing Act.[65]

Both Milwaukee natives with strong family ties and deep roots in their communities, the men shared much in common. Although Zeidler lived on the North Side, he retained his membership in the South Division Civic Association, of which Pieplow had been president and where he remained an active member. Both opposed the 1947 bond referendum allowing the city to go into debt, and both strongly opposed attempts by the suburbs to retain city-provided services while rejecting annexation by the city. Each also made time for the arts—Pieplow was president of the South Side Milwaukee Handel Choir and vice president of the citywide A Capella Choir, while Zeidler wrote poetry and translated German literature.[66]

A Republican and active supporter of Republican Governor Walter Kohler, Pieplow ran on a slate with Kohler's father when the senior Kohler made an unsuccessful bid for governor in the 1930s. Far from an Ayn Randist, Pieplow championed a view of individual liberty operating not in isolation but within a broader civic sphere. Even his beloved Savings and Loan League was gauged by that measure, with Pieplow stating that, while the savings and loan industry must pursue "enlightened selfishness," it also should "cling to the idea that it must be in the interest of the general public."[67]

Both lifelong Lutherans active in their congregations, Pieplow and Zeidler drew much of their inspiration and strength from their religious identities, with firm beliefs in aiding their fellow citizens. Pieplow, who asserted he voted for Zeidler in 1948, attributed that act to his surety that Zeidler's "Christian bringing-up" would be an inspiration to youth. But while Pieplow's vision of achieving societal improvements rested on a notion of citizenship dependent on individuals carrying out their obligations to improve living conditions, Zeidler saw members of a shared community joining together to achieve the common good, aided when necessary by impartial and high-minded leaders in government.[68]

In Zeidler's view, government was the instrument for benefiting society; for Pieplow, government was an obstacle that required constant challenging. Government's involvement in providing low-income housing would require homeowners to pay the taxes that enabled people to live in houses provided by government, an "unjust situation" that "cannot be tolerated." Such government-mandated dispersion of funds to benefit struggling members of society was an unfair burden to prop up those who did not pay their fair share, and even far more unacceptable than higher taxes.[69]

Zeidler believed government, through its public servants, was charged with a moral imperative: "We participate in local government in order that by our participation there may emerge nobler beings with enlarged concepts of liberty, truth, justice, cooperation, peace, and righteousness. This should be our objective, and this we should not forget." Pieplow saw government as sapping individual initiative and coddling freeloaders. Zeidler saw public service as a heroic enterprise: "As we recount the services of local government, we come to realize a present basic reason for cities and their governments: We build cities to build men."[70]

Pieplow rejected "a system of government which subordinates the people to an all-powerful state." The government, in Pieplow's view, was the outsider, pursuing a statist doctrine that "maintains that the ownership of property, especially land and homes, should reside in the community as a whole or in the state as the designated agent of the people." Zeidler envisioned government not as an impersonal machine but as a living entity made up of individuals, each of whom ideally would be dedicated to carrying out the solemn duties of helping fellow citizens. Zeidler embodied his vision of government leadership, which especially at the local level he saw as having one purpose: the public welfare.[71]

Pieplow embodied a synthesis of republicanism and liberalism, setting aside self-interest on behalf of the common good with the desire to pursue marketplace ambitions, the Adam Smith/David Hume belief that commerce has the capacity to promote rather than destroy virtue because it encouraged the development of disciplined and energetic individuals. Zeidler sought to redress the imbalance of market capitalism through his conception of the public interest, which he viewed through the role of the public servant. Public service, he stated, must "lead to the ennoblement and enrichment of the cultural heritage of mankind in the struggle against ignorance, squalor, want, disease and death."[72]

Milwaukee's Next Steps

The direct influence of the national real estate and building industries was not as manifest in Milwaukee's referendum battle because it was not necessary: Pieplow's Referendum Committee generated a grassroots effort fueled by guidance from national organizations but built from a core of committed local anti-housing activists. Within weeks, they succeeded in creating a force that could challenge the much-longer-standing organizational capacity of the CIO's well-funded PAC and the union movement's formidable on-the-ground political mobilization experience. The expertise of Pieplow and others in adapting the real estate industry's message to appeal to the distinct experiences of Milwaukeeans, the misleadingly worded ballot initiative, and the committee's strategic targeting of resources to maximize votes in wards most likely to support the referendum turned an improbable venture into a stunning success.

The battle for affordable housing prefigured the struggles of the 1960s and hinted at the greater social and economic polarization to come. Three weeks before the referendum election, the issue of race publicly emerged, with rumors spread to suggest that Zeidler's across-the-board support for equal opportunity underpinned his strong stance in favor of public housing. This race-baiting, never touched on in Referendum Committee ads or campaign messaging, connected the creation of public housing with an increase in Milwaukee's black population and "infected the people like a fever," according to Zeidler, who battled race-based attacks throughout his next two terms as mayor.[73]

The degree to which race spurred the efforts of the cadre of Referendum Committee volunteers and the voters who supported them was at the time inseparable from the Referendum Committee's economic conservatism. Some aldermen feared expanding the geographic base of black residents, but their opposition to creation of public housing was checked by the large pool of union voters on whom they depended for support. Yet as more African Americans moved to Milwaukee, expanding the residential needs of the black community, the issue of race increasingly played a central role, both in the availability of adequate housing for black residents and in the city's struggle to expand through suburban annexation.

Over on Milwaukee's South Side, Pieplow continued his duties at the Savings and Loan Association through much of the decade, visible in his office window on busy National Avenue well into his eighties. "Friendliness is the key to Pieplow's personality," an observer wrote. "A visitor to his office feels it, in the warmth of the reception given everyone who comes through the door. Even school children who pass by the office window feel that Pieplow is their friend. They exchange waves with him. If his back is turned while he is busy with a caller, the children knock on the window to attract his attention." Fulfilling their promise to take action at the state level, leaders of the Referendum Committee transformed the group into the Citizens' Free Enterprise Committee and nearly won passage of a bill that would have set a statewide voting approval requirement for creation of public housing, as did its Milwaukee referendum.[74]

Across town, in the shadow of the City Hall tower, Zeidler's successful 1952 bid for re-election included his call for the council to move quickly on slum clearance and an offer, ultimately rejected, for the real estate industry to join with the city in addressing the ongoing housing shortage through public-private partnerships like those in Pittsburgh and Chicago. Turned away by private interests and frustrated in the drive to create sufficient public housing, City Hall sought to expand Milwaukee through suburban annexation to relieve the crowded inner core and provide space for additional tax-generating industries.

The city's contest with the suburban "iron ring" proved even more contentious than the fight over affordable housing. Milwaukee's challenge to the concept of suburbanization set off a debate over the extent to which individual rights, as embodied in the suburban assertion of autonomy, superseded efforts by municipal leaders to secure the public good through annexation. These dueling visions of the public good were further complicated by notions of race and class, with white, higher-income suburbanites rejecting the city's bid for an expanded tax base to serve the larger collective good. As tensions escalated in the struggle over city-suburban boundaries, the clash over the role of government highlighted the extent to which suburban conservatism did not emerge full blown in the upheaval of the 1960s but had its roots in the strong opposition to New Deal liberalism that emerged from the end of World War II.

5 Race, Class, Free Enterprise, and Suburbia

> We, who live in the North, are not aware of the deep-rooted feelings of the South where the Negro problem is concerned. We have been tolerant from the start.
> —*West Allis Star*, April 5, 1956

Stymied in its ability to create more affordable housing to alleviate congested neighborhoods and provide decent living space for low-income residents, Milwaukee by 1952 faced a burgeoning crisis. The city's growing African American population, prevented by discriminatory practices from purchasing housing, lived in increasingly crowded neighborhoods. At the same time, the city's financial future was imperiled by a diminishing geographic base unable to provide space for tax-generating industry. Milwaukee's solution to these twin problems centered on annexing adjacent land—a move that sparked a suburban backlash, one premised on economic conservatism and racial prejudice. And when the 1956 municipal elections brought racial issues to the fore, the alarm over the expansion of a minority population was in part based on conservative opposition to broadening an inclusive public social service structure.

Black Middle-Class Milwaukee

In June 1954, Milwaukee business leaders gathered in the rathskeller of Schlitz Brewing Company for a premiere of a movie whose cast included Commerce Secretary Sinclair Weeks and an array of black actors. The film, *The Secret of Selling the Negro*, was on its way to being presented to business leaders across the country to "drive home the point" that black consumers represented a huge and profitable market. Census Bureau figures showed African Americans' income had quadrupled since 1940, making this group an estimated $15-billion-a-year market—a figure that was nearly as large as the national income of Canada and more than the value of all U.S. export trade. Already, some 374 radio stations nationwide broadcast special programs to sell to African American listeners, and a New York City marketing firm had on board a special consultant on the African American market who in two years increased its accounts from two to forty. As *Time* magazine noted, "Such figures are making businessmen everywhere sit up and take notice. They are paying more and more attention to the long-ignored Negro customer."[1]

Unless, that is, that black customer was in the market for a house. In Milwaukee, as elsewhere throughout the northern United States, it was far easier for an African American family to purchase a new car than to buy or rent a home. Notre Dame president Theodore Hesburgh, a member of the six-person Civil Rights Commission formed in 1957, was "startled to find more residential segregation in the North than in the South." As historian Thomas Sugrue demonstrated in his pioneering work on the struggle for civil rights in the North, "Racial inequality took different forms on each side of the Mason-Dixon Line in the twentieth century.... Northern blacks lived as second-class citizens, unencumbered by the most blatant of southern-style Jim Crow laws but still trapped in an economic, political, and legal regime that seldom recognized them as equals."[2]

In 1950, 15 percent of nonwhite families nationwide were living doubled up with other families, nearly three times the number of white families in such conditions. Given the "buying power" of African Americans, much more was behind their lack of suitable housing than ability to afford it. A 1952 government housing report found that "higher proportions of nonwhite than white families in the relatively high income and rent groups were occupying housing that was deficient in various respects."[3]

In part, the lack of quality housing was exacerbated by the large-scale postwar migration of African Americans from the South to the North. Between 1940 and 1960, the nonwhite population more than doubled in thirty metropolitan areas in the Northwest, North Central, and West, increasing by nearly 2 million. This migration combined with the return of war veterans and the onset of the baby boom to create an unprecedented population surge, with cities like Milwaukee, where new housing had not been built since before the Depression, scrambling to provide enough shelter. But for African Americans the shortage also masked the underlying racial exclusion from quality housing practiced throughout the North.[4]

Milwaukee attorney Bruno Bitker, who chaired the city's Human Rights Commission, described housing segregation as greater there than in any other northern city. In 1952 black residents occupied nearly half of substandard housing in Milwaukee although they made up only 3.6 percent of the population. Compared with other midwestern cities, such as Chicago and Detroit, Milwaukee's black population was not large in the early 1950s, but the rapid increase in the number of black residents during and after the war, as a percentage of the city's population, contrasted sharply with previous decades. The African American population grew from 0.2 percent of the city's total population in 1910 to 1.6 percent in 1945, putting the size of Milwaukee's wartime black population nearly at the bottom of the nation's twenty-five largest cities. From 1950 to 1960, Milwaukee's black population grew from 21,772 to 62,458, a 187 percent increase that alarmed many white residents and provided fuel for a race-baiting mayoral campaign against Zeidler in 1956.[5]

A few dozen black leaders anchored Milwaukee's small African American middle class, which had solidified in the 1920s. Among them were Wilbur and Ardie Halyard, who founded the Columbia Building and Loan Association in 1925 in part, Ardie recalled, because "it was almost impossible for Negroes in Milwaukee to obtain [mortgage] loans prior to the formation of Columbia." They opened their first office in a room inside an undertaking parlor, with Ardie staying up at night to balance the accounts after her job at Goodwill, where she was ultimately promoted to personnel director. Ardie, a Georgia native, was one of twelve children and helped take care of her siblings after her mother died. In 1950 she reactivated the dormant Milwaukee chapter of the NAACP and served as its president. Wilbur, who grew up in South Carolina, recalled he was inspired after hearing Booker T. Washington speak. "I came away from that meeting with the idea of improving myself."[6]

Like nearly all of Milwaukee's black population, the Halyards operated their business and lived in an area dubbed Bronzeville, located on the city's near North Side. After 1915, "through a mixture of choice, economic necessity, restrictive housing covenants, discriminatory real estate and loan practices, and overt racism, an identifiable thirty-five-block 'black district'" emerged. By 1940, Bronzeville, increasingly called the "inner core," expanded to seventy-five blocks and housed more than 90 percent of Milwaukee's black population. The postwar influx of African Americans from the South expanded the area north and west, with residents unable to move east because of the Milwaukee River and downtown's Third Street shopping district, nor south because of the commercial strip along Wisconsin Avenue, the city's main corridor. Further south, across the Menomonee River valley and its heavy industrial plants, the South Side remained primarily Polish and nearly all white.[7]

For many years, Bronzeville remained a mix of the original German, Jewish, and Eastern Orthodox settlers, along with the newer African American residents. As whites left the area, their large homes were subdivided into rooming houses or one- and two-bedroom apartments. By the 1950s, Milwaukee's Tenth and Twelfth Wards, which covered large portions of the inner core, had become a safe seat for Democrats and African Americans in the state assembly. Isaac Coggs, owner of the popular tavern 700 Tap and the Rendezvous and Cross Town taverns and president of the Near Northside Businessmen's Association, served six terms in the state assembly before being elected to the county board of supervisors.[8]

The tightly knit Bronzeville community watched over its neighborhood children, Chuck Holton remembers. "Your deportment and manners were overseen by the entire community." White Milwaukeeans mingled with black residents at black-and-tan clubs such as the Metropole, with its blend of jazz and blues. Between seventy-five and one hundred social clubs, such as Le Mesdames and La Pal, each with ten to fifteen members, rented the clubs on Sunday afternoons for matinees, providing entertainment that ranged from amateur hour to nationally known acts. From 1940 to 1950, the number of black-owned businesses nearly doubled, growing from 109 to 210. The 1950–1951 *Negro Business Directory of the State of Wisconsin* listed more than 150 licensed rooming houses, thirty-five taverns, dozens of restaurants and eating establishments, and twenty-one dry cleaners, along with eight attorneys, seven doctors, and six dentists. A 1957 survey found that, on a per-capita basis, Milwaukee's black residents owned and operated more businesses than in any other large metropolitan area.[9]

Segregation, Northern Style

Although owning a business was the best way for black Milwaukeeans to be assured of employment, many did not have the means for such an option, especially the increasing numbers of black migrants from the South. In 1952, 4,786 black workers were employed by 167 firms in the city, primarily in manufacturing. Many worked at A. O. Smith, a major producer of bombs in World War II. But until the federal Fair Employment Practices Commission (FEPC) intervened, the heavy-industrial plant refused to hire black workers. In January 1942, FEPC public hearings revealed A. O. Smith had not hired a single black worker. "After several days of public castigation and behind-the-scenes negotiations, A. O. Smith relented." By the war's peak, the company employed more than 800 black workers, 5 percent of its workforce.[10]

Without federal enforcement, other Milwaukee employers did not readily employ African Americans. The first black brewery worker had only been hired in 1950. Some large industrial plants, like those operated by Walter Harnischfeger, made minimal attempts to hire nonwhite workers. In 1955 the giant

Allen-Bradley industrial controls and electrical components company, with more than ten thousand workers on the payroll, employed one black worker.[11]

A 1952 Milwaukee Urban League sample found that black workers were hired at 75 percent of the places where they applied for work. The Urban League's emphasis on employment clearly had an effect, through its efforts to address reported discrimination and because it actively worked to create a climate in which white employers felt comfortable hiring black workers. The Urban League had recourse in the 1945 Wisconsin Fair Employment Practices Law and the state's Fair Employment division, which investigated reports of job discrimination and took part in scores of speaking engagements, conferences, and radio and television programs.[12]

The city's union movement provided little succor for African American job seekers. As elsewhere, local building and construction trade unions, which had been a key part of the AFL since its founding in the late 1800s, were a driving force of political conservatism. The trades were set apart structurally from other unions by their apprenticeship training. To qualify for a unionized trades job, then as now, workers first go through apprentice training programs, meaning unions, not employers, determine which workers are accepted. Essentially acting as employers, building-trades unions often replicated the exclusion of minority workers prevalent throughout the private-employment sector. Black workers understood they were not wanted in the white brotherhood, and most did not apply for membership.

While Milwaukee's top union leaders generally espoused support for the plight of black job seekers, they made little effort to work with the Urban League, despite the League's outreach. African Americans had better success with the Milwaukee Vocational School, which was out front in addressing black employment immediately after the war. It helped train white supervisors and offered skills training for black workers.[13]

African Americans had had access to jobs as public elementary school teachers since 1939, when Urban League President William Kelley brokered an agreement in which the Milwaukee school board would hire black teachers, with the understanding that the board would assign them only to predominantly black elementary schools, a practice that lasted through the 1950s. After the Supreme Court in 1953 ruled in *Brown v. Board of Education* that schools could not be segregated, African Americans began a multipronged push to end discrimination among students and teachers alike. By the mid-1950s several elementary schools were 90 percent black, and the trend toward segregation was increasing. Further, black leaders argued that the education system was preparing black children for low-wage work only, and the students were not encouraged to prepare for college. Although *Brown v. Board of Edu-*

cation did not address teacher hiring, Kelley sought to build on the ruling to further the employment of black teachers at high schools and throughout the public school system.[14]

Milwaukee's de facto segregation in education, as with housing and jobs, was on a par with most areas north of the Mason-Dixon Line, where the practice had generally been banned since the late nineteenth century. As the numbers of black migrants moving to Milwaukee grew through the decade, discrimination limited the jobs they could find, if they found any at all, and circumscribed their children's chances to get ahead. The experience of African Americans, prevented from obtaining housing outside the city's increasingly decaying inner core, was emblematic of the barriers they faced in 1950s Milwaukee.

Subtle and Not-So-Subtle Housing Discrimination

Well into the 1950s Bronzeville residents remained apart from the rest of the city, with racially mixed interactions occurring primarily at the workplace or occasionally at a black-and-tan club. In 1944 there were intimations of the clashes to come as black and white residents increasingly jostled for living space in the city's rapidly diminishing geographic terrain. That year, eighteen black families who sought to purchase land in the city's far northwest to build new homes obtained the property only after a white man fronted for them. White residents sought to block their occupancy and convinced an alderman to sponsor a resolution to set aside the land for a playground. Ultimately, the resolution was rescinded after a counter-campaign from black residents and their white allies.[15]

In another instance, a white mob tried to intimidate a black Navy veteran and his family from moving into a trailer to which they were assigned on the city's West Side. Sheriff's deputies made it clear they would protect the family and, after the story became public, a coalition of groups, including the Mayor's Commission on Human Rights, the NAACP, the Catholic Church, and labor, offered support. A few days after the event, eight leaders of the hostile residents appeared in the district attorney's office to apologize.[16]

Both highly publicized incidents, they drew public outrage and sparked groups to coalesce around positive action. But far more subtle housing discrimination tactics in private-sector housing were not so easily recognized and remained long unchallenged. One such gambit involved "sundown towns"—towns and suburbs that passed laws prohibiting African Americans from being in public spaces after certain evening hours. An estimated 90 percent of Milwaukee subdivisions contained restrictive covenants prohibiting sale of housing to African Americans since 1910, in addition to "gentlemen's agreements" to sell no property to African Americans outside the borders of central downtown. Until the civil rights era, some Milwaukee suburbs such as Greendale "enforced laws that forbade blacks to buy homes in their communities or to walk the streets after 10 P.M."[17]

Another tactic, blockbusting, became an issue in Milwaukee in 1952, well after its appearance in cities elsewhere. The practice, in which real estate sellers canvassed neighborhoods to frighten homeowners into selling their property at cut-rate prices, typically involved white and black "border" neighborhoods. Real estate representatives sometimes hired a black woman to walk her baby carriage along a white residential street, or they spread rumors that a black family was moving in the neighborhood. In Milwaukee the real estate industry distributed fliers that asked homeowners if they were selling *and* implicitly signaled to them the possibility that black families were moving in. One such flier, "Thinking of Selling . . . Your Property?" directed at white residents in the racially mixed North Side suggested that "cash buyers" (African Americans unable to get credit) were lined up to move there.[18]

When African Americans were able to purchase property, they often did so at grossly inflated rates. At the end of the 1950s a Milwaukee League of Women Voters' report found records in the Milwaukee County Courthouse showing that real estate agents purchased properties in or surrounding the inner core at prices far below market value. The properties were then sold within days or months to African Americans, sometimes at twice the price paid by the original owner. The report noted, "No building permits are on record for these properties, so no additions or alterations could have been effected."[19]

While the city's Human Rights Commission sought to investigate price gouging, blockbusting, and other practices, the commission often faced outright hostility from the Common Council, which was not eager to fund it. Like many such municipal human rights commissions, it was formed in 1944 following Detroit's racial unrest and included thirty-two members from a range of community organizations. Zeidler had defied the council to support expansion of the human rights commission, ignoring the real estate industry's complaints that none of its members was appointed, saying he refused to name anyone "who believed in racial discrimination."[20]

The issue of inflated housing prices for African Americas emerged before the Common Council late in 1952 and throughout 1953. At one council hearing, a black resident pointed out that a real estate agent "had boosted the price of a house from $12,500 to $14,500 when he saw the prospective buyer was black." George Brawley, a black attorney, then told the council that black residents were not permitted to rent flats or apartments in many areas, although the dwellings had been vacant for as long as a year. Yet many aldermen expressed doubt that the real estate industry would engage in such actions. The council also repeatedly refused Bitker's request for $2,000 for the Human Rights Commission to investigate blockbusting practices, despite evidence showing it was on the rise and the testimony of one of their own members about the frequency of the practice. Fred Meyers, longtime alderman for the city's racially mixed Sixth Ward, described white resentment against blacks moving in. "Those real estate birds went around from house to house saying the Negroes are coming," Meyers related. "People called me up and said the real estate men had frightened them to death. I told them that there's a Constitution in this country and people have a right to move and that it's the owner's right to sell the house or keep it and not to get excited." Meyers was an exceptional voice on the Common Council, many of whose members a few years earlier had expressed their opposition to relocating black residents displaced by slum clearance to a primarily white housing project.[21]

Blighted, Crowded Areas "Breeding Evil"

In November 1952 Josephine Prasser, secretary of the Sixth Ward Better Housing League, presented a petition to the Common Council with thirteen hundred names supporting immediate and large-scale slum clearance. Prasser told the Common Council's buildings-and-grounds committee that the city was "breeding evil by allowing thousands of people to live in houses that are unfit for human habitation." She went on to admonish the aldermen that it was their duty to "see that all races are treated the same." Prasser's comment elicited a rebuke from Alderman Matt Gromacki, who had just lost his fight against funding the Human Rights Commission. "You're supposed to be talking about housing, but now you're talking about human rights. Why don't you go to the Human Rights Commission?"[22]

Addressing overcrowding by tearing down residences was not sufficient. Those displaced, many of whom were low-income residents, needed to relocate to affordable housing. Yet new national housing regulations had severed the ties between public housing and redevelopment, giving developers the go-ahead to engage in urban renewal without responsibility for assisting those left homeless.[23]

Fresh from its 1951 housing referendum victory, the real estate industry targeted Zeidler. Agents involved in blockbusting visited North Side homes and sought to scare owners into selling by telling them, "Mayor Zeidler is going to move Negroes into your block." Even Zeidler's elderly uncle, also named Frank, ill and suffering from injuries incurred in an industrial accident, asked Zeidler, "What is this my neighbors say you're leading blacks in our neighborhood?" A rumor that began in the 1948 campaign took fire again, in which Zeidler, who lived until his death in the North Side home, was said to be building a house in far-off suburb to avoid the influx of black residents.[24]

A series of crimes on the lower North Side late in 1952, including the murder of three people in a dry cleaners by a mentally ill black man, generated broad public outcry, and the mayor pressed city officials to take action. The three murders contributed to a near doubling of the city's annual homicide rate that year, from fourteen in 1951 to twenty-six. At the same time, the two Milwaukee dailies were quick to label race in crime incidents, making "racial friction" worse and impairing good relations, according to Milwaukee Urban League activist Bernard Toliver. Seeing crime in part as an outgrowth of crowded living conditions, Zeidler requested the Housing Authority expedite its housing and slum clearance work. In a message to city residents, Zeidler acknowledged their alarm but also pointed out their own role in creating tensions, fueled, as he saw it, by mounting housing pressure. At bottom, Zeidler believed that crime was caused by poverty. "Much of our crime is directly or indirectly traceable to involuntary poverty with its overcrowding, its lack of proper means of expression, its ignorance, the inability to obtain the necessities of life, and the resulting desire to secure some of the 'swag' so patently displayed by the aristocracy of wealth."[25]

Prior to the crimes, "there had been a great deal of animosity on the part of white residents of the area over the influx of Negro residents into areas which had heretofore been all white," Zeidler said. "I feel that a part of the problem is that we were blocked in our efforts at slum clearance by the property owners." Or, as Meyers phrased it, the fault lies with "the landlord who wants to get rich on nothing by overcrowding dwellings and the courts that frustrate attempts to enforce building and health regulations by granting continuances." A report from a countywide crime commission, formed in response to the events, recommended legislation to curb excessive rents, called for private, low-rent homes, and asked for increased staffing for city planning and slum clearance offices as well as strict enforcement of housing codes.[26]

In this atmosphere of malicious rumors, public unrest and city hearings over racial tension, crime, and blockbusting, the mayor publicly challenged the real estate industry. After learning that the National Association of Real Estate Boards president called for an end to all federal government involvement in housing, including slum clearance, Zeidler demanded to know the

Milwaukee Board of Realtors' stance on urban renewal. In response, John Roache, executive vice president, charged Zeidler with fueling racial tension with his "irresponsible and inflammable statements," denied the industry bore any responsibility for discriminatory housing policies, and went on to blame Zeidler implicitly for the increase in the black population.[27]

While Roache dismissed accusations that his members engaged in blockbusting—even as Zeidler asked him to come to City Hall and read files filled with letters residents had sent the mayor demonstrating otherwise—the industry had long officially advanced segregationist practices. Beginning in 1913, the NAREB instructed its members not to contribute to residential race mixing, and in the 1920s it adopted racial criteria for appraising property. Although NAREB in 1950 eliminated racial bias from its Code of Ethics, many local realtor ethics codes did not.[28]

The federal government's housing policies had set the direction for housing discrimination in both its publicly administered programs and private mortgage loans. The Federal Housing Administration (FHA) home mortgage loan program used racial restrictions to determine the actuarial soundness of a neighborhood and, in Milwaukee, the local FHA office, "adhering to established procedures, excluded blacks from new housing, advancing loans to blacks for repair on old buildings only."[29]

A 1948 Supreme Court decision ruled racial covenants illegal, but in practice the move to prohibit FHA loans with racial covenants did little to increase mortgage loans to black residents. It took two more years before the Housing and Home Finance Agency (HHFA) announced the FHA would no longer insure a mortgage if the contract had a written restrictive covenant. But realtors soon learned the new policy on mortgages applied only to the construction of new homes, and FHA underwriters did not protest unwritten "gentleman's agreements." The Supreme Court also did not prevent white homeowners from selecting buyers based on race. By 1958 a Milwaukee NAACP survey found only sixty-eight black families, exclusive of those in low-cost housing, moved outside the inner core and transitional areas, in sharp contrast with the numbers of wealthier black families in Chicago and Detroit who increasingly moved out of the inner city.[30]

By the end of the decade, a committee Zeidler established to study inner-core problems and recommend solutions found that residents of that area still could not obtain home financing. "As a result of this lack of mortgage financing, the active transfer of property in the core area is financed principally by land contracts bearing high interest rates, highly inflated sales prices, short terms, and 'balloon'" notes with all the inherent risks to the home buyer that the pre-Depression property owners faced prior to government intervention and aid brought into being through programs of recovery." Such policies resulted in living conditions like those *Milwaukee Journal* reporters encountered in 1960. Unable to obtain decent housing despite a good income, a black couple with a child and another on way lived in a basement flat with two closet-sized bedrooms, broken windows and water dripping through the ceiling when the upstairs tenants took a shower. As the reporters noted, "A white family making $80 a week wouldn't be in the market for a country estate, or a ranch house in . . . Whitefish Bay. But they wouldn't be living under conditions like these, either."[31]

In addition to preventing African Americans from obtaining home mortgage loans, federal policies reinforced segregated living in other ways as well. The ease with which white city residents could obtain FHA mortgages accelerated the pace of new housing construction in the suburbs, creating white enclaves surrounding urban centers that increasingly housed low-income black residents. Zeidler noted that middle-income white residents who obtained such financing did not recognize that they, like those who lived in public housing, were being subsidized by the government.[32]

Milwaukee's inner-core living conditions were rapidly deteriorating at the same time the area was becoming more segregated. The 1950 Census showed that 55 percent of Milwaukee's black residents lived in less than 2 percent of the city's census tracts. Nationally, *Time* magazine pointed to the inability of cities to reverse the increase in blight, in part because the real estate industry "repeatedly raised cries of socialism against Government housing projects that often accompany slum-clearance projects." In 1954, the city estimated that four thousand buildings in Milwaukee were "so dilapidated, insanitary [sic], or structurally unsound they would qualify for razing under the condemnation statute," but because of limited personnel only 578 buildings had been razed from 1948 to 1953. Zeidler calculated the rate the city's housing stock was becoming obsolete at approximately sixty blocks per year. The Housing Authority's efforts to build public housing were stalled between the 1951 referendum and 1953, when the Common Council adopted a resolution effectively removing the requirements of the ballot initiative in an effort to move on an approved city housing project, the Hillside Terrace Addition.[33]

Milwaukee voters in 1953 approved $750,000 in city bonds for slum clearance. But the city could not qualify for federal funding until the statutes were upheld by the courts. A city housing supporter purchased land as a test case to meet the federal government's requirement. Late in 1954 the Wisconsin Supreme Court upheld a lower-court ruling that the city had the power to clear blight, freeing up the Housing Authority to take action.[34]

Redevelopment was costly. Estimates ranged up to $22 million for Milwaukee to furnish a square mile of new development with a population between twelve thousand and fifteen thousand people. Despite some sentiment not to engage in expansion because of the cost, the mayor and most Common Council members recognized that if the city did not incorporate additional urban areas in its own boundaries, new suburbs would form that would find a way to force the city to pay expansion costs anyway, without the city getting the benefit of the new tax base thus formed.[35]

Scapegoating Minority Migrants

If the real estate industry, Common Council, Mayor Zeidler, progressive housing supporters, the city's two daily newspapers, and the area's founding black community did not find common ground on the solutions for the inner core, they all agreed on the cause of the crisis: black migrants from the South. The northern migration of blacks occurred much later in Milwaukee than in other midwestern manufacturing cities such as Detroit, Cleveland, and Chicago, which experienced their influx during World War I. Much of the city's increase in the black population between 1940 and 1950 stemmed from in-migration from the South. When crime beset the city's inner core, nearly all the city's residents attributed it to these new residents.[36]

The "difficulties in the Negro area are not caused by the Negro citizens of Milwaukee but by newcomers from the South," asserted local real estate leader John Roache. Discussing the inner core, Zeidler said, "What makes this problem difficult to manage is the cultural difference that exists between the southern people—both white and non-white—and the northern people—both white and non-white. As the new migrants come into the community they bring with them standards of living which are not acceptable to their newly established neighborhoods." *Milwaukee Journal* articles repeated the claim without question, and the South Side voice of far-right conservatism, the *Milwaukee Times*, editorialized that the "Johnny-come-latelies from the undernourished cotton fields of the south" brought to the state "on promises of jobs and easy money, should be sent home by the people who brought them if, within the year, the rash promises fade."[37]

The city's black press acknowledged that the sentiment was widespread even in the African American community when it chided its readers for their stance on newcomers. "We must help our brothers . . . [and] join with our legions of white friends in helping the immigrant Negro to become oriented to a new and strange though better way of life. We should not and must not resent his coming lest our already limited freedom be destroyed." Certainly there were exceptions within the black community—W. J. G. McLin, pastor of St. Matthew Colored Methodist Episcopal Church, said he was sick of the claim that newcomers were at fault, and he attributed crime and delinquency to "old-timers" who have "laid a foundation to exploit newcomers"—but the attitude prevailing among the small business owners and other solidly middle-class residents of the inner core paralleled that of the city's white leadership.[38]

In his study of black Milwaukee through 1945, historian Joe Trotter found a "fundamental division of the black population . . . between the expanding urban industrial and domestic worker class and small black bourgeoisie." Class divisions sharpened in the 1950s as large numbers of generally low-income southern African Americans moved into the city's black working- and middle-class neighborhoods. Such a divide paralleled that in other cities.[39]

Many in Milwaukee pointed to the rural roots of the new migrants and the cultural practices they brought with them. As the *Milwaukee Journal* put it, "In the South, they sweep the yards, they don't mow them." Although differences in "cultures" were attributed to the assimilation challenges of these newcomers, "culture" easily substituted for "class," a term so fraught since the founding of the nation, it was avoided by even the mayor who identified with socialism. The committee charged by Zeidler late in the decade to examine the inner core wrote in its report that "we must recognize the existence of at least three different cultural systems in the inner core"—and then went on to distinguish these "cultural" groups by class: "the middle class, the laboring and industrial class systems, and the culture pattern of the people newly migrated from the deep South." Continuing to muddle "culture" with "class," the report went on to note that "in the past, a large portion of the area had a middle class, and so leisure and social-welfare services were geared to that group. In the current shift in population, these families are being replaced by people with a different cultural background who do not respond to the traditional agency services." The solution then was to reorient municipal services "from middle-class values to the habits and concepts of the people living there."[40]

Yet the divergence between middle- and low-income residents, whether white or African American, underlay the tension over Milwaukee's migrant community. Vel Rogers Phillips, who became the first female and first black Common Council member in 1956, recalls her childhood as one in which she and her sisters were raised with strict rules of deportment and urged by their parents to achieve a college education. The Rogers girls were not allowed to chew gum on the first floor of their spacious house, which was cleaned by a maid, because "ladies did not chew gum." They were taught the polite way to get in and out of a car. When black families from the South moved in down the block, Phillips says her mother Thelma was appalled by their behavior, unaccustomed to neighbors shouting outside to each other, and Phillips recalls her mother commenting, "They are so crude and they have no class." Her mother, Vel said, "was very class conscious."[41]

Mary Ellen Shadd, who after the war compiled the annual *Negro Business Directory of the State of Wisconsin*, went on to found the *Milwaukee Defender* in 1956 in an effort to redress the lack of a black press in the city, where a series of such publications had quickly come and gone. As a leader in the community, Shadd sought to exhort her peers out of complacency. In an editorial looking at the future of the city's black residents, Shadd wrote that "the Negro in this city is not taking advantage of the excellent opportunities for a first-class education . . . he is not yet alive to the tremendous power in politics for his protection and well-being [and] we have yet to produce and follow dynamic leadership." The "true leaders of this area" had yet to come forth, Shadd said, and the black community "is divided and thus conquered." The *Defender* echoed themes from *The Globe*, an African American paper published in Milwaukee in the immediate postwar years that leaned Republican and emphasized personal responsibility over collective solutions, along the lines of Booker T. Washington.[42]

Like Shadd, Phillips, who went on to play a pivotal role in the fight for fair housing in the 1960s, straddled two worlds: the city's politically alienated but established black community, one that had long been willing to accept incremental improvements and that was at times disdainful of new residents outside their middle-class milieu, and a new generation of black leaders who were impatient with driblets of change and who demanded full rights as they led the city's civil rights movement.

Most Milwaukee Common Council members were resistant to improving the civil rights of the city's African Americans. Those who supported such change, like most white municipal leadership elsewhere, reflected a lack of connection with the city's black community. Although the mayor appointed black leaders to such positions as the Human Rights Commission and Housing Commission and, like council members such as Meyers, recognized housing discrimination, sympathetic city officials never fully embraced the black community as they did the labor movement or religious groups.

Shorn of strong support from nearly every quarter of the city, migrants, specifically minority migrants, became an easy target for lawmakers. The Common Council approved a resolution in December 1951 backing a law passed by the Milwaukee County Board of Supervisors restricting public housing eligibility to those with several years' residence. Zeidler returned the resolution to the council unsigned, with a note stating, "The action of the County Board was apparently taken in contemplation of preventing migrant people of southern origin from getting Milwaukee County aid easily."[43]

The residency issue was not confined to African Americans. On the South Side, where few African Americans lived, newcomers were primarily Latino. When discussion arose in 1959 to lift the residency law, the South Side *Milwaukee Times* opposed such a move on the grounds that it would be "an open invitation to all of the flotsam and jetsam of the nation to hustle to Wisconsin for a free ride on the taxpayers." The *Times* went on to acknowledge the "pitiful Mexican family's plight," with the caveat that their troubles were "their own fault, to a degree." The William Grede-owned *Wauwatosa News-Times* pointed out that its support of residency requirements was not un-Christian: "The Good Samaritan gave temporary help; he didn't become his brother's keeper for life."[44]

Some churches and activists in the black community held fundraising drives and solicited other means of support to aid the often-jobless new arrivals. But as late as 1957, the Milwaukee Urban League was discussing whether the organization should discourage African Americans from the South from moving to the city. The Urban League's longtime president William Kelley believed that, in the midst of a tight labor market, "we continuously have Negroes coming into the city with no special skills, and when unable to find jobs or when laid off from jobs find it impossible to receive relief, and this is creating a great problem." While noting he was not suggesting the league urge new residents to return to the South, Kelley said that "it has reached the point where when they run out of money, they live with relatives rather than go back South, then things also get very hard for the relatives."[45]

Kelley, a Nashville native with a degree from Fisk University in sociology, had led the Milwaukee Urban League since 1928, shaping its outreach to focus primarily on economic opportunity and social advancement. Under Kelley, the Urban League was highly centralized, with official policies formed at the top. Kelley and other board members pushed back on a suggestion by a community organizer that the league get the cooperation of ministers to tell their congregations to discourage members of their families from coming to Milwaukee unless they have a trade or skill.[46]

Cecil Brown Jr., a political columnist for the *Defender*, called for the formation of an independent voting league to mobilize minority members for elections. In Wisconsin, 12,500 black residents in 1957 were registered to vote out of 20,750 eligible, with 90 percent of the black population living in Milwaukee. Brown noted he would be "very much surprised if such a group was formed without the opposition from Uncle Toms." In fact, his column drew a lot of mail, some supporting his proposal but most against it. Yet Brown persisted. Recognizing that individuals, not groups, should form the leadership of a voting league, he invited forty black ministers to a tea to discuss their roles in making arrangements for an upcoming visit by Rev. Martin Luther King Jr. to Milwaukee. Out of the forty invited, twelve said they would come. Eight showed up.

"Once there," Brown noted, "they came up with no plans and the only positive suggestion was that the ministers meet with King before his speech. And even that suggestion failed. Only one minister was on the platform with Martin Luther King when he spoke." Black religious leadership in civil rights issues was notably absent in Milwaukee during this period. "The closed doors of some of our churches are mute testimony to the fact that some of our local churches have not met our needs," wrote Shadd.[47]

The "urban adjustment" archetype, in which rural migrants were perceived as "being unprepared in general for urban life," worked for the majority of city residents both because it was more politically palatable to scapegoat an outside group and because that group, as an "other," could more easily be marginalized by city residents who did not identify with them. Further, this "Grapes of Wrath picture of migrants" as the dispossessed had a tight grip on the American imagination. In fact, not all black migrants to Milwaukee were rural. "Milwaukee's black migrants, like those of Chicago, Cleveland, and Detroit, were a combination of agrarian and semi-skilled workers," according to scholar Paul Geib. Nor did migrants move to Milwaukee or other northern cities because of public services. Studies showed that a focus on migrants masked systemic inequities "faced by members of racial minorities wherever they are in America, difficulties that migration simply transplants and concentrates in cities."[48]

Not all cities reacted defensively. In contrast with Milwaukee, Chicago created a Migration Services Department to ease the adaptation of migrants to the city. The agency also assisted community organizations in areas of racial transition that "are recognizing the futility of trying to preserve the quality of their neighborhoods simply by excluding minority groups." Still, Chicago, like most cities and states, had no laws prohibiting housing discrimination.[49]

City's Tax Base Moves to the Suburbs

Even as city officials grappled with elements of urban renewal such as blight removal and undertook endeavors like crime prevention, they saw Milwaukee's urban crisis as fundamentally stemming from a lack of geographic space, one that limited their ability to increase the city's tax base and open up options for residential expansion. The issue united the mayor and nearly the entire Common Council, and throughout the mid-1950s they centered their efforts on expanding the city through suburban annexation. By seeking to decrease urban congestion and expand to the periphery, Milwaukee went against the grain of the New Urbanism planners, who saw dense cities as community building, and toward the mayor's vision of "the city beautiful," the garden-city model of Ebenezer Howard. This approach built on the city's long emphasis on annexation, beginning with Hoan, who in turn reflected the influence of Progressive-era reformers' emphasis on city beautification.[50]

The Milwaukee area mirrored the nation's shifting demographics. Nationally, between 1950 and 1970 the suburban population doubled from 36 million to 74 million, with 83 percent of U.S. population growth taking place in the suburbs. By 1960 more whites in the North lived in the suburbs than in central cities. In Milwaukee the number of suburbs rapidly increased in the 1950s, with seven new cities or villages springing up in the metropolitan area between 1951 and 1955. In contrast, Milwaukee's seven previous suburbs had formed over a span of nearly fifty years. The 1950 U.S. Census showed that without its recent annexations, the city would have lost population.[51]

Using municipal services as both carrot and stick, Zeidler, supported by the Common Council, continued the Hoan administration's policy of refusing to extend its water service beyond city boundaries, requiring those who wanted such service to consolidate with Milwaukee. In his twenty-four years in office, Hoan expanded the city from twenty-five to forty-six square miles through annexation. By the 1950s the fight over water services had shifted from a prosaic jurisdictional struggle to a contest between those who envisioned public service providing for the common good and those who supported an individualism conditional on race and income level.

The suburban "iron ring" and its political vehicle, the League of Milwaukee County Municipalities, grew stronger throughout the decade. The league found a receptive audience in the Wisconsin State Legislature, which time and again ruled against Milwaukee in its efforts to expand. In 1955 the legislature voted in favor of the request by a southern suburb, Oak Creek, to change its status from township to fourth-class city, a move that would prevent Milwaukee from annexing that territory. The ruling gave unprecedented leeway to towns, enabling them to bypass various levels of lower-level municipal status to one that laws protected from being annexed.[52]

Prior to the "Oak Creek Law," Milwaukee undertook twenty-nine annexations, increasing its area from just over sixty-seven square miles to seventy-two, and adding more than 8,880 residents. But passage of the bill resulted in a domino effect, with the townships of Franklin and Greenfield, both southwest of Milwaukee; New Berlin, west of the city; and Mequon in the northwest each incorporating, closing the iron ring tighter around the central city. With the annexation routes to the direct north, southeast, and south shut off, Milwaukee looked to annex areas in the southwest, the northwest, and an area between West Allis and Wauwatosa.[53]

The pattern of suburban resistance to incorporation with its urban center was repeated across the nation and with the same results. The 1959 Commission on Civil Rights reported that "with the suburbs forming a practically impenetrable ring around the city, the expanding lower-income city population is trapped." Further, the report noted that the pattern of dispersion experienced by immigrants was not occurring with African Americans. But as in so many instances, racial bias became inextricably linked with class prejudice, as new suburbanites sought out low taxes that often supported little beyond the basic services required by higher-income residents.[54]

Appeals to class-consciousness formed the basis for early suburbanization. As early as 1905, the Central Railroad of New Jersey published a magazine to entice city-dwellers toward the periphery. "One of the most encouraging features of suburban growth is the high class of population that the suburb draws to itself," a typical article gushed. Similarly, Milwaukee's wealthy northshore suburbs sought from the start to zone their land to prevent low-income residents from moving in. Shorewood even banned all apartment buildings in the early 1920s. By enacting zoning restrictions that mandated residences be built on large parcels of land, suburbs not only kept out middle- and lower-income families, many of whom were minorities, they also avoided extensive fiscal outlays for sewers, water lines, schools, and other public services, thus minimizing government.[55]

In Milwaukee as elsewhere, the loss of higher-income groups meant rising taxes for those who remained in the city, a vicious downward spiral for urban solvency. By annexing the suburbs, Milwaukee could benefit from a residential tax base grounded in larger residential incomes, expand land resources to draw in new industry, and prevent the loss of valuable commercial taxpayers that suburbs would lure from the central city, in part, with promises of low-cost, city-provided water.

The Battle of Green Bay

Milwaukee's hard line against providing water to the suburbs unless they consolidated with the city sparked outrage among suburban politicians. In 1953, the urban-suburban battle reached such a boiling point that the County

Board of Supervisors appointed a Committee of 21 to study and recommend solutions. Zeidler saw creation of the committee, made up of seven officials each from the county, city, and suburbs, as a backdoor maneuver by the suburbs to circumvent a state-level investigation that the suburbs could not control. County Supervisor Bert Busby chaired the Committee of 21 and was the brother of State Senator Allen Busby, who represented West Milwaukee, by far the most muscular suburb, with its enormous tax base, few residents, and low taxes.[56]

While the issue engaged several suburbs, Milwaukee's confrontation with two, Wauwatosa and West Allis, grew especially contentious. It became clear early on that the urban-suburban divide was also ideological, based on competing views of the role of government. The West Allis Common Council summed up the broadly held suburban perspective in a resolution assailing amalgamation with Milwaukee, saying its opposition was "predicated on an aversion to big city government, its undue concentration of political power, and other inherent infirmities."[57]

Abutting the city's western edge, Wauwatosa incorporated in 1897, making it one of the oldest suburbs. It had acted quickly in 1946 to establish its municipal status, thereby staving off annexation to Milwaukee after the city revived its annexation department that year. Unlike the majority of suburbs, Wauwatosa was landlocked, with no portion of its territory abutting Lake Michigan, the area's water supply, a vulnerability that made it an appealing target for the city's especially aggressive tactics. The situation grew particularly dire in the early 1950s, when it became clear that the area's water table was receding by seven feet each year, threatening the eight wells that supplied Wauwatosa with water.[58]

South of Wauwatosa, West Allis, although also landlocked, was bolstered by a vibrant tax base because of its large number of heavy-industrial plants, putting it in a strong position to challenge Milwaukee. Incorporated in 1906, West Allis had been created in part as a tax haven for industries, and it had attracted so many that it levied no property taxes throughout the first half of the twentieth century. The mayors and the majority of Common Council members of each suburb were staunch political conservatives and fiercely determined to retain jurisdictional separation from Milwaukee, a struggle they saw in terms no less fraught than that of the original battle for American independence.[59]

Wauwatosa itself was annexing adjoining territory and became increasingly desperate for a steady water supply. Even as residents were forced to stop watering lawns in the summers and others complained of little or no water access, Wauwatosa annexed eight-and-a-half square miles in 1954, doubling its territory in a move that helped boost its population from 45,000 to 51,500 in one year. The Committee of 21 adjourned with no action, leaving Wauwatosa without access to water and Milwaukee unwilling to accede to its demands for water. A special committee set up by the governor to study the urban-suburban dispute delayed reaching any recommendations. It was then, in 1956, that Wauwatosa's city attorney found a 1908 law stipulating that Wauwatosa could tap Milwaukee water mains.[60]

"Wauwatosa will get Milwaukee city water only over my dead body," declared Alderman Matt Schimenz, chairman of the Milwaukee Common Council Public Utilities Committee, as the suburb brought up the 1908 law. "Wauwatosa is the only suburb adjacent to Milwaukee which that city has refused to serve with water," the suburb correctly countered and then proceeded to petition the Wisconsin Public Service Commission to order Milwaukee to supply Lake Michigan water.[61]

West Allis had sufficient funding to contract with an engineering firm in 1956 to construct a reservoir and pumping station to supplement the city's million-gallon storage tank that was filled with water purchased from Milwaukee. But until it was built, the suburb bitterly attacked the city over the water shortages that beset it along with the entire area and, like the other suburbs, fought Milwaukee's attempt to increase water rates.[62]

The city and suburbs went head to head that October in Green Bay at the annual meeting of the League of Wisconsin Municipalities. Schimenz introduced a resolution asking for a statewide study by the legislature of problems confronting metropolitan areas, a move the suburbs strongly opposed. Oak Creek City Attorney Anthony Basile, who authored the bill enabling that township to qualify as a city, called the resolution an attempt by Milwaukee to obtain complete amalgamation of all municipalities in Milwaukee County. To ensure it was voted down, suburban officials packed the room with delegates, no matter how far flung: Oak Creek corralled a member of its city cemetery commission and an advertising manager of the local newspaper to take part in the vote. Amid shouts and cheers, the crowd defeated the proposal by more than two to one. The slap in the face to Milwaukee was well deserved, a *West Allis Star* editorial crowed. "Is it hard to understand why the enmity between Milwaukee and the suburbs is growing? Who holds water as a club for annexation? Who labels suburbanites as 'parasites?' Who will accept only complete dissolution of the suburbs as the practical answer to countywide problems?"[63]

Although Zeidler knew the suburbs were purposely packing the meeting in Green Bay, he refused to do the same because he saw such action as unethical. The "Battle of Green Bay" reaffirmed his view that the suburbs "were willing to sit down with the city of Milwaukee to see how the city could furnish the suburbs' water supply, sewers and incinerators, but they would not talk about unequal tax burdens, slum clearance or problems that the city had."[64]

"Negroes from the South Have Clocked to this County"

The suburbs' high-pitched struggle to attain water service from Milwaukee had always masked much deeper issues involving economic conservatism interwoven with racial and class prejudice. But the issues underlying suburban antipathy to Milwaukee emerged more clearly after Zeidler began publicly discussing metropolitan consolidation along the lines of efforts by Dade County, Florida. The area was in the process of creating a governing body for Miami and its suburbs, made up of city and county elected officials. With the possibility of annexing entire suburbs slipping away, consolidation was another way to engage in the intelligent planning necessary for cities to remain uncongested workshops, where people gather to "produce efficiently the world's goods and to raise the standards of human life and enjoyment," as the original MEC platform phrased it. Supporters of consolidation also cited a 1946 Council of State Governments report endorsing single local government entities with sufficient population to permit effective public services at low cost.[65]

The Milwaukee Common Council backed such a move and, in July 1956, passed a resolution inviting suburbs to consolidate with the city, an action that predictably met with rejection. In repudiating the invitation with a resolution of its own, the West Allis Common Council obliquely referenced racial and class issues when it decried the city's "other inherent infirmities." Throughout the 1950s the suburbs never overtly stated their opposition to gaining black neighbors. In fact, the suburbs prided themselves, as part of the North, on not harboring the "deep-rooted feelings of the South where the Negro problem is concerned," as *Star* editors put it. "We have been tolerant from the start." Tellingly, the editorial pointed to racial segregation as a moral issue, not one that should be addressed through legislation.[66]

In Milwaukee suburbs, racial animus was camouflaged in language attacking urban crime, poverty, or the city's social safety net. As the *Star* opined, Milwaukee "has a goodly number of problems—which it would like to unload on more people—hence consolidation." *Wauwatosa News-Times* editors applauded Milwaukee County for cracking down on welfare applicants, asserting that the county's reputation as a "'soft-touch' for those who prefer relief to work" is the reason "Negroes from the South have clocked to this county." Issues of race and class were also inextricably associated with suburban hostility to expansive government. Decrying public-assistance programs, editors at the *News-Times* called out the "vicious cycle" in which "dependence on government has encouraged the inevitable human inertia that saps the people's initiative" and results in more government dependence.[67]

Extensive government programs, in turn, were a defining characteristic of urban living. "The suburbs believe that there should not be created in Milwaukee County a huge municipal creation to spawn the big-city evils so repugnant to the tradition of Wisconsin," a delegation of West Allis officials told Zeidler in 1953. The officials contrasted their suburban lifestyle as "offering a high degree of participation by citizens, strong civic and community spirit, low crime rates and other 'small town' virtues." As elsewhere around the country, Milwaukee suburbanites' small-town ideal was predicated on a homogenous socioeconomic demographic, one that excluded those with low incomes or dark skin. Venting frustration, Sol Ackerman, the city's first urban housing director, said, "If the city of Milwaukee is to be completely hemmed in by suburban communities, then these suburban communities must be prepared to take their share of families who are not of the highest income class but who can purchase their own homes whether such homes are new or used."[68]

Wrapped in individualism, suburbanites' economic conservatism evoked the freedom to choose where to live and which government to support. In this view, nothing less was at stake than the original independence fought for by the American colonists. The fight against consolidation, the *Star* opined, "will demand the wholehearted support of every person in the suburbs who believes that our freedom of speech, religion and the press also includes the determination to live under the kind of government which we choose."[69]

Suburban residents' hostility to public service was deep—many joined the call by the Affiliated Taxpayers' Committee to vote against a $7.5 million bond issue to create a county museum—but apparently not deep enough for the *Wauwatosa News-Times*. Editor Jack Cory took residents to task for their demands that the suburb establish a bus service to "haul their youngsters a few blocks to school," seeing such dependence upon government as nothing less than socialism. "When the body politic becomes pregnant with socialism, it seems you can't have a little bit of socialism. It grows and grows." If school buses manifested socialism, there was little room in this view for maintaining social services.[70]

In 1958 the state Public Services Commission ruled that Milwaukee had to provide water to Wauwatosa based on the 1908 agreement. Although the Milwaukee Common Council voted to fight the ruling in court, Zeidler vetoed the measure. Wauwatosa had threatened that if Milwaukee sued, it would work through the state legislature for creation of a metropolitan water commission, effectively taking away the city's control of the water supply. With those alternatives, Zeidler believed providing water to Wauwatosa was "the least evil of the prospects facing us."[71]

The suburbs' growing confidence was reflected earlier that year at an annual dinner meeting of local officials, where the Wauwatosa paper crowed, "Suburbia polished up the iron ring . . . and found that all the rivets were firmly clinched, indicating that Milwaukee may be unable to crush her neighbors for another year." The 1958 conference theme of the League of Milwaukee County Municipalities summarized the growing suburban and exurban solidarity: "We all have to stick together or get annexed separately by Milwaukee."[72]

The Public Services Commission ruling effectively ended the city's expansion, but not before the city doubled its geographic base and broadened its tax base to meet the needs of an increasingly low-income population. Milwaukee went from thirteenth in size in the nation in 1950 to eleventh in 1960, and it temporarily counteracted the inner-city decay by providing new lands for expansion.[73]

"The Shame of Milwaukee"

Throughout the 1951 referendum vote and in suburban resistance to annexation, the issue of race often had been the implicit thread weaving through the background of public discourse. But the 1956 mayoral race burst the bounds of tensions long unspoken as Zeidler's main challenger, Alderman Milton McGuire, centered his campaign on opposition to the rising number of African Americans in the city.

McGuire represented the city's downtown East Side Third Ward and had been Common Council president since 1948. His campaign fueled a rumor circulating since the 1951 referendum fight that Zeidler posted billboards throughout southern states to attract African Americans to Milwaukee, luring them with promises of low-cost public housing. The rumor was so threatening to Zeidler's 1956 re-election, the local AFL asked central labor councils throughout the South to report on whether the billboards existed. From High Point, North Carolina, to Meridian, Mississippi, union leaders avowed they never had seen such billboards from the mayor of Milwaukee. But union leaders did find one solicitation urging African Americans from the South to come to Milwaukee—from the Wisconsin Employers' Association looking for summer agricultural workers.[74]

Although Zeidler supporters forced McGuire to publicly come out against the billboard rumors, McGuire's campaign repertoire included the slogan

"Milwaukee needs an honest white man for mayor," and it was reported that "McGuire aides have sneered at Zeidler workers for associating with a 'nigger lover.'" The alderman also used more subtle appeals. At a meeting of Milwaukee's Certified Rental Operators, a group "especially exercised over the race issue," he promised that, as mayor, he would keep Milwaukee free of "southern migrants," a euphemism for African Americans.[75]

Playing on white voters' fears that large numbers of low-income African Americans were moving to Milwaukee worked in tandem with the McGuire campaign's false accusations that the city's crime was escalating out of control because of gang violence. Police Chief John Polcyn took after McGuire, following a campaign ad that declared marijuana- and liquor-crazed "hoodlum mobs" ranged the city "with wolf-pack viciousness." Calling it "the most infamous falsehood ever perpetrated against the citizens of Milwaukee," the outraged chief, supported by other law enforcement officials, succeeded in getting McGuire to repudiate the "wolf pack" ad, which McGuire attributed to an outside ad agency that created it without showing it to him in advance.[76]

Always in fragile health—although he ultimately lived to age 93—Zeidler approached the 1956 mayoral election determined not to run. But as his political opponents ratcheted up the issue of race, he decided he had to meet the challenge. Zeidler was "determined to fight" those who charged he was "being too friendly to Negroes"—even if that meant alienating allies. A union official called Zeidler one night and "laid it on the wood" about how disturbed union members were over "black gambling, drugs and property standards." Church leaders, who demonstrated a lack of support for civil rights, could not be counted on. Nor did Zeidler feel he had the backing of black or Hispanic leaders, "for they feel, almost universally, that all the white attitudes are wrong. These leaders continually stress the duty of the white citizens to them, and overlook their own shortcomings." Even some liberals in Milwaukee complained "bitterly" to Zeidler when blacks moved in their neighborhoods.[77]

McGuire, who received campaign funding from suburban residents and realtor groups, returned to the issue of Zeidler's socialism as a way to attack the mayor's urban policies while championing his own support for unfettered free enterprise. He also sought to separate himself from labor interests, but his campaign was likely behind the formation of a small "Labor for McGuire" group, knowing that in union-dense Milwaukee, no politician could get elected without the backing of union members.[78]

While McGuire gained a superficial veneer of labor support, he received real backing from the brand-new local chapter of "For America." At the national level, the committee led by Clarence Manion was seeking to throw the

1956 presidential elections to the House of Representatives as a way to both stymie a Democratic win and unseat Eisenhower, in the belief that the two parties were tainted with "international socialism." In Milwaukee, the group campaigned for McGuire by mailing brochures to area business leaders and asked them to form a "chain" by ordering copies and distributing them to family and friends. Milwaukee's Woerfel Corporation was among those to oblige, with its head, J. J. Woerfel, writing to his employees and urging them to read the "Think, Milwaukee Voters!" brochure. Woerfel assured them that if they kept the letter chain alive, they would get a better Milwaukee "led by a man who firmly believes in the American free-enterprise system." Zeidler, appalled at the extremism of For America, whose platform opposed the income tax, asked McGuire to denounce the group's support of his campaign.[79]

McGuire instead threw his support behind Milwaukee For America, saying he had "checked out" its pamphlet and "it tells the truth." His attacks on both black migrants and expansive government programs advanced a message that resonated with many voters. A handwritten letter from "a disappointed taxpayer" to Zeidler illustrated the muddling of race and economic conservatism. "Whites just don't want to live with the blacks in any district and integration won't work here any more than in the South. . . . The New Deal, the Truman administration were not Democrats [sic]—they were Socialists like you are. Are you with the whites or against us?"[80]

McGuire's Red-baiting alone would not have reshaped the mayoral race in a city where voters took for granted that Socialist Party mayors had governed longer in the twentieth century than any other party. Even the *Journal* asserted, as it did in the 1952 election, that its fears of socialism under a Zeidler administration had not been realized. But by combining race-baiting and Red-baiting, McGuire hit on a powerful combination that appealed to many residents angered by the collective embrace of the New Deal and looking for a scapegoat to target. Conversely, Zeidler's 1956 victory, as in previous years, could not be attributed to the Socialist Party. The voting pattern of the 1956 election "bore little resemblance to the patterns in the heyday of the Milwaukee Socialist Party." Zeidler carried all the wards in the city except his opponent's home ward and the solidly Republican Eighteenth Ward located along the city's tony north lakeshore, suggesting more "a split between Democrats and Republicans than between socialists and anti-socialists" and also pointing to the lack of religion as a factor in any of his mayoral races, with voters on the Catholic South Side wards in 1956 not throwing their support behind one of their own in sufficient numbers to swing the race.[81]

In stark contrast with its stance in the 1948 municipal campaign, the *Milwaukee Journal* not only strongly supported Zeidler but relentlessly attacked

McGuire, pointing out, as did Zeidler, the number of times the alderman had held closed-door Common Council sessions away from the public—including those involving the debate over educational television. The paper's editorialists countered McGuire's charges of inaction under Zeidler, pointing to the city's strong-council–weak-mayor form of government and asserting that, as president of the Common Council, McGuire had been more powerful than the mayor. "It has been in the Council, where McGuire was leader, that the civic development, off-street parking, consolidation of rubbish and garbage collection, and other things have 'bogged down,'" the paper wrote.[82]

In fact, a year after McGuire sought to make an issue of the city's poor management and its "bad reputation" outside Wisconsin, a *Fortune* magazine series on cities ranked Milwaukee as the second-best-run city in the nation and profiled Zeidler as one of the most outstanding mayors in the country. "St. Louis, Cincinnati, and Milwaukee, all with long traditions of honest government, have a remarkable trio of mayors: each wears a distinctively scholarly air and is a pretty good politician to boot." *Fortune* assembled scientific and opinion data for the twenty-three largest cities, from which it highlighted the top eight. Cincinnati and Milwaukee received the highest number of good marks for municipal services such as fire protection, public health, and recreational facilities. Milwaukee was only one of three cities given triple-A bond ratings by Moody's. Back in 1948, the Junior Chamber of Commerce had named Zeidler as one of the nation's most outstanding young men.[83]

The race-baiting campaign had unleashed vicious personal attacks directed at the Zeidler family, who received "vile letters" and late-night phone calls. Following the election, the attacks took a more dangerous turn. Because the campaign had generated such national publicity, Zeidler and his family began receiving out-of-state threats that Zeidler considered so serious, he contacted the FBI. After the FBI refused to investigate, saying the matter was outside its jurisdiction, Zeidler asked for police protection and, throughout the summer of 1956, two Milwaukee police officers were stationed at his house, one in front and one in back. The Zeidler's five daughters and one son, mostly grade-school age, thought the officers were new playmates, until their mother Agnes told them they had to leave them alone to do their job. The Zeidlers explained to the children that the police were there to protect them from people who wanted to harm Zeidler and his family, but they did not learn the details until they were adults.[84]

In highlighting the campaign's race component before the election, *Time* described it as "The Shame of Milwaukee." When Zeidler won by twenty-three thousand votes, the slimmest margin of his three mayoral races, periodicals across the nation extolled the victory against racism. "The people of Milwaukee appear to have chosen well," declared the *Toledo Blade*. The *Washington Post and Times Herald* applauded his reelection, decrying the "bigots" who "waged an especially despicable campaign against the mayor through appeals to racial prejudice." *Time* declared the achievement "The Smear That Failed."[85]

Milwaukee Elects Its First Black Female Council Member

While Milwaukee's 1956 mayoral election became nationally known for its unbridled verbal attacks on African Americans, the municipal elections that year provided an ironic twist: the city elected its first African American and woman to the Common Council, Vel Phillips. Over the years, other African Americans had run for council in the largely black Second Ward Phillips sought to represent, so the issue of race did not generate animosity in the campaign as it did in the mayoral race. But Phillips recognized her other "handicap"—that of being a woman—likely would be the biggest barrier.

After graduating from the University of Wisconsin law school, Phillips and her husband Dale had moved to Bronzeville, taking an apartment above a drugstore on the busy commercial Walnut Street. When Phillips could not convince Dale to run for office, she did so herself, reading up on campaign strategies in books at the public library. Phillips made good use of her gender-neutral first name (shortened from Velvalea), instructing campaign volunteers to stump for "Vel Phillips, an attorney" as they handed out literature that intentionally did not include her photo so as not to reveal her gender. Phillips recruited volunteers from black congregations like the Tabernacle Baptist Church and from groups like the League of Women Voters, dispatching white and black volunteers to talk with voters in neighborhoods made up of their own races.

Phillips received the most votes in an eight-person primary, despite being the last name listed on the ballot, coming ahead of Leroy Simmons, the first African American member of the Wisconsin Assembly. No woman had ever previously survived a primary election for alderman—but it was clear many did not know they cast their ballots for a woman. On the general election day, she and Dale continued getting out the vote, checking the large notices posted on telephone poles by the Milwaukee Election Commission that listed people who had voted. Updated throughout the day, the lists enabled candidates and campaign volunteers to visit homes where residents had not cast their ballots. At one such home, the Phillips drove a couple and their child to the polls.

On the way, Phillips gave a rundown of whom they should vote for, starting with Frank and saving herself for last so her name was freshest in their minds. When she got to her recommendation for alderman, the woman told Phillips they had already picked a candidate—Vel Phillips. "So I turned around to thank her," Phillips said, "but before I could thank her, the man said, 'Yes, we think he's a great guy. He's a lawyer, and . . . he graduated from law school, and all that.' [M]y husband didn't miss a beat. He said, 'Oh, great, we think he is too.'" Fifty years later, Phillips said she still "ruffles feathers" when she asserts it is harder to be a woman than an African American in American society.[86]

Only 10 percent of black voters turned out in 1956, compared with 25 percent of white voters in the Second Ward that Phillips would represent. Some told Phillips they had not registered because they had not been allowed to vote in the South. But the overall lack of political involvement by African Americans in the Second Ward was representative of the lack of black political involvement throughout the city, which in turn translated into far less influence in municipal governance. Re-elected for three more terms, Phillips went on to become a fair-housing champion, introducing such legislation four times between 1962 and 1966. Council members shot down each of the proposals—which merely mirrored state law—eighteen to one.[87]

By the end of the decade, the fatal shooting of a twenty-two-year-old black man, Daniel Bell, as he ran from white officers, and other episodes escalated racial tensions. A few years earlier, Milwaukee Police had rounded up 260 African American men for questioning after the rape of a white women, a dragnet that furthered the black community's distrust of city law enforcement. Similar incidents on a much smaller scale throughout the decade prompted an explosion of pent-up frustrations after Bell's death, with some in the black community staging protests. Others, such as Phillips and other middle-class African Americans, joined Zeidler in opposing the gatherings out of fear they would escalate into violence.[88]

But the tragic event proved a turning point for the city, shifting the sociopolitical dynamics between the black community and the city's municipal leadership and galvanizing some long-time African American Milwaukeeans like Isaac Coggs. Just a few years earlier, Coggs had backed the Near Northside Businessmen's Association's efforts encouraging black migrants to cooperate with Milwaukee police. After the Bell shooting, Coggs publicly denounced the police and equated their actions with the murder of Emmett Till in Mississippi. Twenty years later, one of the police involved confessed that he and his partner had planted a knife in Bell's hand after shooting him to provide them with an excuse for the unprovoked murder.[89]

The city responded by setting up a Study Committee on Social Problems in the Inner Core Area of the City, and the committee released its report as Zeidler left office in April 1960. The largest-ever study of the city's black community, its recommendations included employment training and youth outreach. Yet, as critics have pointed out, the report did not go far enough—for instance, by not advocating fair housing legislation but proposing a "Covenant of Open Occupancy," a remedy that urged support for those who "refuse to conform to racial discrimination in housing with friendship, mutual aid and cooperative action."[90]

Calling it short on practical solutions, Maier, who followed Zeidler into office, shelved it immediately after his election. Maier, a one-time Republican who joined the Democratic Party in 1948, then put a two-year freeze on public-housing construction to "review" the situation. Those actions meant that when 14,219 inner-core housing units were razed between 1960 and 1967 to create Interstate Highways 43 and 94, low-income residents had few affordable alternatives. More than half of those displaced were black. In 1963 Maier warned his community-relations commission to go slow on civil rights and refused to push the council to pass fair housing legislation, telling Phillips the South Side would never re-elect him if he advocated fair housing.[91]

Maier, whose response to the city's race riots in 1967, was widely seen as exacerbating the city's racial tensions. He left "a community divided along racial lines," the *Milwaukee Journal* editorialized after Maier's exit in 1988 after twenty-eight years in office. "If asked about segregation in the city, he would point to segregation in the suburbs. He would be right, of course, that a metropolitan answer was needed. But his response did not address what the city itself could do." In 2002, data showed Milwaukee was the most segregated city in the nation.[92]

Speaking to reporters before the 1956 election, Zeidler presciently noted, "If my opponent leaves any heritage to Milwaukee, whether he wins or loses, it will be racial tension where none existed before." One journalist reflected that "the 1956 election taught Milwaukee politicians the dangers of being friendly to African Americans." While Zeidler ultimately won, politicians such as Maier learned the political peril involved in championing civil rights.[93]

Race, Class, and Opposition to Expanding Government

Amid the city's rapidly changing demographics, some white Milwaukeeans gave qualified support for racial equality, while many others, in part because they believed their economic interests were threatened, demonstrated stiff resistance. Meanwhile, Milwaukee's black community remained internally divided on methods for achieving full civil rights. Although Zeidler was proud that his was a rare voice for racial equality among municipal leaders, he rued that it was difficult to make headway on civil rights. Many of his administration's proactive measures to address inequality—increasing the stock of affordable housing and poverty alleviation predicated in large part on expansion of city limits—were stymied by economic conservatives threatened by a challenge to individual rights and the expansion of services to racial minorities. Other efforts, such as the Human Rights Commission's attempt to address blockbusting, were thwarted by a shortsighted Common Council that included members antagonistic to the needs of the city's African American residents. Aldermen's opposition to relatively small measures explicitly tied to addressing racial disparity left little hope for passage of expansive legislation, such as fair housing, if championed by the administration.[94]

Reacting to outrage over racial profiling and disparate treatment by police, the administration responded with community meetings that, while a necessary step, ultimately resulted in few substantive measures. The administration shared with community leaders on the Inner Core report committee the belief that such practices were undertaken by only a few bad actors on the force, which, under John Polycn's leadership, had in the early 1950s instituted a program to promote better race relations.

Although Zeidler could have appointed more African Americans to public committees, until the late 1950s members of the black middle class taking part in municipal politics reflected more the city's liberal consensus that blamed "newcomers" than the interests of those economically and politically marginalized. The mayor's support of the 1960 report mirrored the views of the racially mixed group of one hundred community members involved in the project. The Inner Core report's lack of concrete prescriptions for addressing such issues as job discrimination, school desegregation, or fair housing manifested the perspective of Milwaukee's liberal middle class, one that saw eye to eye with suburban conservatives in believing that racial injustice cannot be "legislated away."

Middle-class Milwaukeeans were not alone among residents of northern cities in their lack of understanding of the depth of racial discrimination. At the same time as the Inner Core report was released, a six-person Commission on Civil Rights established by Congress in 1957 issued its findings after investigating constitutional violations of civil rights in the North and South. Many Southern members registered bitter dissent to the recommendations. In response, Chairman John Hannah, a former assistant secretary of defense, reminded the public that racial discrimination was a problem "that is native to neither North nor South. It is, rather, a dilemma that concerns all Americans."[95]

That dilemma also was tied into an economic conservatism that appealed to the mainstream middle class but often was propagated by activists on the political fringe. McGuire's embrace of both racism and the far-right economic conservatism embodied in groups like America First offers a prism for understanding the interplay among race, class, and opposition to a collective notion of the public good. By tying the city's growing minority population to expanded public services, McGuire broadened his electoral appeal to those voters whose primary fear was unbridled dispersion of their taxpayer dollars. There is no doubt that numerous McGuire supporters held white supremacist or racist views; for others, however, issues of poverty, race, and expanded social services were so intermixed that their inchoate resentment found an easy target in African Americans.

Just as Milwaukee's suburban conservatism had its roots in strong opposition to New Deal liberalism, the ideological divide in the city's 1956 elections highlighted how appeals against munificent taxpayer outlays wrapped in racial prejudice could undermine a climate generally supportive of progressive politics and generate antagonism against low-income recipients of public services. Racism and economic conservatism mutually reinforced each other and, as McGuire nearly demonstrated, offered opponents of economic populism a winning ticket. While playing out at different times in other urban areas, similar issues of race and fears of big government intertwined in the immediate decade after the war, with opponents of public-service expansion finding that race-baiting could be used to slow or block progress that would assist the economically marginalized.

Few areas showcase economic conservative opposition to the New Deal vision of broad economic empowerment more clearly than the interplay between union members, as they sought to exercise their workplace freedoms, and the employers and their supporters, who saw such collective action not only as challenging corporate authority but also as imperiling the nation's individual-driven free enterprise system. Even in Milwaukee, where a long and strong union tradition bred a comfortable familiarity with the labor movement, workers faced sharp attacks when seeking more control in their work lives even as some employers, attempting to hinder class-based action, sought to portray the labor movement as antithetical to free enterprise and the American way.

Gimbels department store served as a space that drew residents of all income levels in postwar Milwaukee, its aging downtown bisected by the Milwaukee River. Milwaukee Journal © 2009 Journal Sentinel, Inc., reproduced with permission

After three months on the picket lines in 1958 at a plant owned by industrialist Walter Harnischfeger, a union leader described him as "an adamant, reactionary, calloused and biased employer who refuses to accept the philosophy that labor unions are today an integral part of our national economy." Milwaukee Journal, 1958 © 2009 Journal Sentinel, Inc., reproduced with permission

After the *Milwaukee Journal* published this now iconic image of Frank Zeidler and his family during the 1948 elections, Zeidler said the charge that he was a "menace to democracy" evaporated "in the minds of those who saw the photograph." Milwaukee Journal, 1948 © 2009 Journal Sentinel, Inc., reproduced with permission

Milwaukee industrialist William Grede tirelessly campaigned for a range of conservative economic issues, speaking here before three thousand industrialists at a 1956 NAM convention in New York. The previous year, Grede traveled some eighty-five thousand miles, making 273 U.S. appearances, including thirty-three press conferences and fifty-two live and recorded radio programs. Milwaukee Journal, 1956 © 2009 Journal Sentinel, Inc., reproduced with permission

Employing roughly ten thousand workers after the war, the heavy-industry manufacturer A. O. Smith company used its bully pulpit to proselytize "free enterprise" in mandatory "employee economic education" sessions. Milwaukee Journal, 1950 © 2009 Journal Sentinel, Inc., reproduced with permission

Mayor Frank Zeidler and William Pieplow shake hands during what likely was the April 1958 anniversary celebration for Pieplow's years of service with the South Division Civic Association. Although Pieplow led a successful attack on Zeidler's most cherished project, expansion of affordable housing, Zeidler spoke in Pieplow's honor at the event. Courtesy of the Milwaukee County Historical Society

In 1956, Vel Phillips (seated next to Mayor Frank Zeidler) became the first woman and first African American elected to the Milwaukee Common Council. Milwaukee Journal, 1956 © 2009 Journal Sentinel, Inc., reproduced with permission

As part of its 1951 campaign to derail public housing, the Public Housing Referendum Committee conducted an extensive media campaign, which included ads such as this in Milwaukee newspapers.

6 Collective Action and the Threat to Free Enterprise

> Unfortunately, after the second World War . . . the government did not return to free enterprise. It aided and abetted the unions in a monopolistic control of the labor market. . . .
> —William Grede, in a letter to E. J. Ellis, March 27, 1952

With their attempts to confront labor largely interrupted during the war years, economic conservatives like William Grede emerged from World War II fueled by a renewed determination to slow labor's growing momentum, a stance strengthened by a national political climate increasingly favorable to corporate interests. By charging unions with circumscribing personal freedom, interfering in the private sector, and breeding Communism, conservatives framed their opposition in fundamentally the same terms they utilized in maligning government expansion. In contesting collectivist notions that elevated workers in economic decision making, and in challenging labor's support for broad-based public programs, Grede and other union opponents sought not only short-term gains. They saw the de-legitimization of labor as a key part of a long-range effort at remaking a New Deal environment that often privileged the working and middle classes.

"Union Membership Not Required"

Nearly five months into a strike at Smith Steel, where workers in 1946 sought a collective-bargaining contract with their employer, the *Milwaukee Journal* carried a display ad from the plant's owner, William Grede. "A strike is still in progress at the Smith Steel Division," the ad began. "Experienced steel foundrymen will find a number of good openings on the day shift . . . Inexperienced help! We will train you on the job. Earn good wages while you learn." The ad went on to describe Grede Foundries as a good place to work, with such advantages as "the dignity of the individual" and "freedom from domination by any group" in an environment where "union membership is not required."[1]

Within a week of the ad series, coordinated by Morison Advertising Agency in Milwaukee, the company hired twenty-nine new production workers. Advertising magazines highlighted the ad campaign "as an example of the effectiveness of the print media to sell anything, including ideology." Grede supplemented this public outreach with a series of semi-public daily letters to his employees at Smith and at another striking plant, Milwaukee Steel, urging them to shun what he described as the communist-backed CIO, with which the steelworkers union was affiliated. Despite federal War Labor Board hearings on the impasse and the involvement of national steelworkers officers, Smith Steel and Milwaukee Steel workers, like all other employees who waged strikes at Grede plants in the Milwaukee area, returned to their jobs without a union contract. Grede's biographer described the outcome: "The failure of the steel strikes in Milwaukee and the relative success of Grede's position in attracting public sympathy was a harbinger of a substantial change in the national climate of opinion regarding labor."[2]

A fervent opponent of the changes wrought by the New Deal, Grede saw his role as not only holding the line against such incursions as unionism in his foundries but also carrying out a personal crusade to proselytize to his workers and the broader public about the benefits of free enterprise unencumbered by union intervention. Born in 1897 on Milwaukee's East Side, Grede was the grandson of a German immigrant and son of Henry, a carriage blacksmith and partner in a manufacturing firm, George Grede & Bro. Grede dropped out of the University of Wisconsin when his father, who never thought much of college, offered him a "whale of a lot of money" to become secretary, bookkeeper, and handyman at a gray iron foundry Henry acquired. Within a few years, William Grede owned his first operation, Liberty Foundry.[3]

By the 1940s, Grede acquired two more, merging all three into Grede Foundries, Incorporated. When he purchased Smith Steel in 1942, he refused to recognize the union and, after closing the plant, forced the workers to re-apply for their jobs under new "open shop" working conditions. At Liberty, he unilaterally changed job descriptions and made it a point to pay by productivity, snubbing the traditional seniority system of a unionized workplace. When confronted with a walkout, he kept the plant open with supervisory staff and, on more than one occasion, contacted local police to simultaneously request protection and threaten that he would hold the police department liable for any damages. Acting as sole negotiator with union representatives, Grede utilized divide-and-conquer tactics, playing on workers' ethnic and gender prejudices, and skillfully employed Socratic debate techniques to guide union representatives to his desired outcome.[4]

Yet clearly Grede found it necessary for his foundries to remain competitive with unionized plants so as to secure the skilled labor required for producing the metal castings for airplanes and, during the war, for the secret bomb project. He paid competitive wages and instituted shorter working hours on the plant floor—not, as he insisted, "out of consideration for the men or for humanitarian reasons," but rather "because it was the most efficient way to operate." In 1947 he began offering a pension plan as well.

To Grede, "the very phrase 'collective agreement' was an outrage, as was the idea that a majority vote could so thoroughly bind the minority." Following the passage of the National Labor Relations Act (NLRA) in 1935, he began speaking openly against unions to his employees and attached NAM "education" pamphlets to workers' paychecks. Nor did Grede want to "do his part" to back the New Deal's National Recovery Act. Unlike many other employers, he refused to display the Blue Eagle at his foundries, which would have indicated his approval for voluntary price and wage controls.[5]

During World War II Grede was among the corporate voices shaping the nation's wartime economic policy. He served on the Tripartite War Labor Board panel, where he represented the Milwaukee Employers' Association and gained recognition from employers such as Allis-Chalmers and other corporations whose cases came before him. In his first case, which involved the Madison, Wisconsin–based battery producer Ray-O-Vac, Grede balked at an agreement reached by the company and the union before the case came to a formal finding because of his "inherent objection to the closed shop" (workplaces in which the employer agrees to hire only union labor). He would accept the agreement only if his dissent was attached explaining why he consented to approve of "so un-American a proposal" as one reached through negotiations. In this period, Grede was also elected a Class B director of the Federal Reserve Bank in Chicago and became a regular counterfoil for debates with labor leaders at public meetings and on radio programs.[6]

For local industries bent on bucking the area's high unionization rates, Grede was their man. In 1953 he joined the board of Racine-based J. I. Case farm equipment maker at the request of the new president, John Brown, who told him that "Case needed an expert on labor negotiations to assist in dealing with the union." Brown came to Case after leaving as vice president of manufacturing for the Chain Belt Company in Milwaukee, partly because Chain Belt preferred accepting a union at its firm over risking a strike. Brown was not the only Case board member to share Grede's views. Frederick Nymeyer's correspondence with Brown and Grede "was as likely to be on the subject of the economic views of [far-right conservative economist Ludwig] von Mises or the mistakes of the English Fabians as on the vagueness of tractor marketing."[7]

Postwar Consensus: Business Opposition to Labor

Grede's success in preventing his employees from joining unions was rare in Milwaukee. But his opposition to the collective-bargaining process was shared by the vast majority of employers across the political spectrum. The massive unionization of the nation's workers was made possible in large part by passage of the NLRA, which offered the nation's first comprehensive legislation protecting those seeking to form unions. By 1946 nearly 70 percent of workers in manufacturing were covered by union contracts.[8]

Their collective power in the industry enabled them to go beyond wage and seniority issues to fundamentally challenge management's right to initiate and implement change by insisting on the consent of both company and union. At Milwaukee's Allis-Chalmers, members of UAW Local 248 requested that shop rules governing seniority, transfers, promotions and demotions, apprenticeship, levels of absence, and vacations be jointly determined and applied only when union and management were in agreement. Despite the local union's history of radicalism—workers had long fought for union recognition and protection, and its leadership supported Communism—its strategy was "more in line with that of the rest of the labor movement than its extremist tactics and rhetoric would suggest."[9]

The more than ten thousand workers at Allis-Chalmers, a producer of heavy machinery, joined the national strike wave in April 1946 in a walkout that lasted nearly a year. The increasing duration of strikes throughout the city paralleled a similar development across the nation. Already alarmed by the turn of political events in Britain, where social-welfare policies had taken hold, and the continued postwar involvement by the U.S. government in price controls, corporate leaders viewed the more than 5 million working men and women who went on strike for weeks and months in the year or so after the war as a major threat to the gains they had made during World War II.[10]

Business had opposed the nation's new labor laws from the start. In 1939 a *Fortune* poll of executives showed strong opposition to the New Deal cornerstone: only 3.7 percent said they were willing to keep the NLRA as it was, with 41.9 percent in favor of its modification and 40.9 percent for repeal. The reconversion strike wave helped to create a political climate in the country for a major curtailment of the NLRA. As the end of wage and price controls heralded a return to normalcy, many business leaders resumed their full-fledged opposition to the NLRA.[11]

Business viewpoints were not monolithic, ranging from NAM's vitriolic opposition to New Deal–era programs to the circumscribed support of the Committee for Economic Development (CED). "NAM propaganda encouraged a receptive public to believe that industrial conflict, shortages and inflation were the fault of . . . labor and of the federal government's economic mismanagement." The CED, founded in 1942 as a business-led nonprofit policy organization, found common ground with other business leaders and neo–New Deal liberals around "commercial Keynesianism," supporting neither tax hikes nor spending cuts but opposing publicly funded programs.[12]

If Roosevelt's expansion of government involvement was an economic Rubicon, the NLRA was the nucleus of the invading army. Undermining the legitimacy and power of labor was an essential part of business's efforts to discredit the ideological underpinnings of New Deal liberalism. Unions provided working people with the strongest counterpoint to corporate dominance of the economic sphere. By shifting the sociopolitical climate to better reflect the participation of the working class and middle class, the New Deal had fundamentally challenged the status quo of corporate preeminence and threatened to weaken business's long-held power bases at the workplace and in the greater policymaking arena.

It is here, at the nexus of business and labor, where it becomes especially clear that, as some scholars have recently argued, the fundamental distinction between conservative and progressive movements is the signal role of business in the conservative movement—business in the United States has not been merely one interest group among many but has played a role more akin to that of a dominant class or power elite and so "possesses a degree of influence that invariably exceeds that of any other class or interest group."[13]

Given the opposition by even moderate business leaders to the premise of the New Deal, most did not share Eisenhower's belief in the "mediatory role of the government," and this was especially the case at the workplace. The postwar consensus that existed centered primarily among business leaders who united around opposition to the fundamental ideals of the New Deal rather than in support of its maintenance as a permanent economic structure. Business leaders knew that greater numbers of unionized workers also meant unions would have the strength to "claim a voice in the management process far beyond the limited field of personnel policy and to challenge business in political action." Time and again, business leaders rebuffed national union leaders' efforts to partner with them to achieve a corporatist vision in which labor would have a voice in the production goals, investment decisions, and employment patterns of the nation's core industries. At the same time, workers at the factory level often challenged such a collaborative stance, waging an average of 352 major work stoppages per year in the 1950s, compared with 285 annually throughout the next two decades.[14]

Undermining union strength meant first and foremost weakening or eliminating the legal protections that had enabled workers to challenge management prerogative. Business leaders had sought to overturn or amend the NLRA as soon as it passed, and they ramped up their efforts to do so as the war wound down. Corporate actors from across the political spectrum lobbied hard for passage of the Taft-Hartley Act. Passed in 1947 and drafted in large part by NAM and the Chamber of Commerce, it ended secondary strikes, prohibited supervisory staff from joining unions, outlawed closed shops, and gave employers nearly free rein to oppose workers' efforts to unionize. It was no accident that the first significant rollback of a New Deal cornerstone involved weakening workers' ability to collectively challenge individualist assertions of rights inherent in unfettered free enterprise. Economic conservatives across the political spectrum understood that the greatest challenge to their vision of unfettered free enterprise lay in the collective strength of workers.

Big City Support for Unions

Unions derived their power in part from government support for collective bargaining rights, and like many Democratic mayors of Northern urban centers, Zeidler worked closely with labor. Zeidler also went out of his way not only to enforce laws upholding workers' rights on the job but also to personally assist unions and their members—always while balancing the needs of the public.

Unions consistently supplied key support in his elections, and several union leaders were integral to his first campaign. Anthony King, who started out as a business representative for Plumbers and Gasfitters Local 75 and later became vice president of the Milwaukee Building and Construction Trades Council, served as Zeidler's secretary of labor for his 1948 campaign, and Zeidler appointed him to several committees throughout his three terms. King, the youngest of twelve children, also became Zeidler's lifelong friend and advisor.[15]

One of the first letters Zeidler wrote as mayor was to UAW President Walter Reuther, expressing his "anxiety and grief" over the April 1948 assassination attempt that hospitalized the well-known labor leader.[16] Union leaders whose members were affected by strikes regularly appealed to Zeidler to help them find temporary jobs or unblock bureaucracies that seemingly stood in the way of securing employment. Invariably, he asked his staff or other city officials to follow up on such requests, and although he often could not provide material assistance, he always responded at minimum with ideas for alleviating workers' plight.[17]

Like Hoan, Zeidler intervened on behalf of union strikers to prevent violence on the picket line. In 1949, when City Attorney Walter Mattison asked Zeidler to ask the police chief to take the names and addresses of strikers who were stopping streetcars in violation of an injunction, Zeidler amended Mattison's hard line. He told the police chief he did not "want to have any altercations on the street, but if he took the license numbers that would be sufficient." Yet Zeidler always was mindful of his larger obligation to public welfare. During the streetcar strike, Zeidler also told the police chief to "tell the union men that if they wanted to talk to the men operators they should talk to the men at the end of the line rather than to dump the passengers unceremoniously out in the middle of the street."[18]

Despite union strength in Milwaukee, the Common Council often pushed back against labor. Zeidler appointed to public committees a range of union representatives along with other civil leaders. Yet even for less-than-high-profile committees, he faced opposition in his efforts to ensure union members a place in city government. One such union leader, Richard Block, faced heavy pressure against his appointment by Zeidler to the Fire and Police Commission in 1949. Some Common Council members charged that Block could not provide unbiased decisions—although as the *Milwaukee Labor Press* pointed out, "Apparently industrialists, professional men, or attorneys (even if engaged by employers) could do so." Block's appointment squeaked by the Common Council Public Utilities Committee by a 3–2 vote.[19]

As in all other aspects of his municipal oversight, no request was too small for Zeidler to consider. When Cigar Makers Local 25 expressed concern that no union-made stogies were sold at the cigar stand in City Hall, Zeidler dispatched his assistant, Stanley Budny, to check out the matter. Budny reported that he talked with the cigar-stand owner, who said he carried five union brands when he opened up but no one bought any—but he was willing to give it another try.[20]

Discredit Unions, Chip Away at the New Deal

At the federal level, government support of unions had been severely weakened with passage of the 1947 Taft-Hartley Act. While not providing business with immediate benefits, Taft-Hartley nevertheless offered a significant psychological boost; its "most important immediate value to the business community was as a source of reassurance, a sign that the social and political 'revolutions' of the New Deal years were well and truly burnt out." Despite this game-changing victory, the corporate world knew it had much work ahead. A February 1949 Gallup survey found that 62 percent of U.S. voters said they approved of labor unions, with only 22 percent disapproving and the rest offering no opinion. It was therefore necessary to realign public opinion against unions, which business carried out through the relentless sale of free enterprise and the American Way, counterpoising against both what they portrayed as the anti-individualism of unions and their "unnatural" interference in the free market—the same charges they levied against government expansion. But it was also essential to directly face down workers and their unions.[21]

Milwaukee industrialist Walter Harnischfeger was among employers willing to do so. Starting out at age sixteen as a ten-cent-an-hour apprentice at his father's industrial equipment plant, Harnischfeger, the son of a German-born industrialist, presided over a corporation that in 1953 saw $68 million in net sales, with a $3.1-million net income. A company booklet described him as "an avid champion of and believer in the rights and dignity of the individual," not unlike his friend William Grede, who believed that Jesus and Adam Smith both pointed to "the revolutionary impact of respect for individual conscience."[22]

As an active member of the Association of Commerce and chairman of its National Affairs Committee, Harnischfeger testified before Congress on domestic labor issues. When labor sought to repeal all or part of Taft-Hartley, he used his position on the Association of Commerce to call on its members to actively oppose such legislation.[23]

Unlike Grede, Harnischfeger was not successful in blocking unionization at his plants. But he strongly challenged unions' right to represent workers. When the United Steelworkers went on strike at a Harnischfeger plant in September 1958, primarily for nonwage contract improvements such as voluntary union dues checkoff and improved health coverage, they already had held twenty-two bargaining sessions in two months with Harnischfeger, to no avail. Workers still were on strike with no settlement as the walkout entered its third month when George Haberman, president of the Wisconsin AFL-CIO, summed up labor's view of the situation in an update to affiliated unions: "Nearly 1,800 men and women are now on strike because of an adamant, reactionary, calloused and biased employer who refuses to accept the philosophy that labor unions are today an integral part of our national economy."[24]

Among Taft-Hartley's many provisions, the "free speech" clause, which allowed employers to propagate anti-union messages to their employees, proved among the most effective. Many did so by hiring anti-union consultants, whose tactics in the 1950s were refined versions of the clubs and brickbats of the robber-baron generation and followed "roughly the same playbook that an earlier generation of employers used"—one interrupted by the pre–Taft-Hartley NLRA and World War II. Following Taft-Hartley, the number of "labor relations experts" skyrocketed. Nathaniel Shefferman, one of the most successful and well-known anti-union consultants, remarked that his fellow practitioners were "springing out of the ground by the dozens, scores, and soon by the hundreds."[25]

Taft-Hartley's free-speech provision was expanded by a series of National Labor Relations Board (NLRB) rulings in the 1950s enabling employers to give captive-audience speeches without allowing the union equal time and permitting them to assert that voting for a union might result in a plant being moved. The NLRB also held that an employer's threat to answer a pro-union vote with lengthy legal proceedings instead of bargaining was "merely an expression of the employer's legal position." NAM crowed that the Republican commissioners, who dominated the NLRB for the first time since its creation, gave the NLRA "a new and almost anti-labor meaning." Five years after the first Eisenhower-appointed NLRB and ten years after the Taft-Hartley Act, economist Joseph Shister "judged the act's free speech amendment to have had a 'dampening effect on new union growth.'"[26]

While business leaders held compulsory, closed-door sessions to deter workers from forming unions, they also proselytized free enterprise. Nationwide, the fear of the free market's erosion reflected a preoccupation by leaders of businesses large and small. A survey of U.S. business journals published between September 1951 and February 1952 revealed widespread distrust of government, portraying the state as intrinsically evil and government intervention in economic affairs as downright dangerous.[27]

Business leaders' moves to confront the expanding roles of both government and unions united at the workplace. At Milwaukee's Allis-Chalmers, where UAW Local 248 had repeatedly flexed its communist-influenced militancy, the company's anti–New Deal managers held a series of compulsory closed-door lectures on "Americanism," compelling its more than ten thousand workers to listen silently to a series of lectures in late 1949. Anyone who asked a question or sought a discussion was sent to see a supervisor. The lectures were prepared by George Benson, a one-time missionary who had produced films emphasizing that the free enterprise system and the "big heartedness of employers" were behind workers' high living standards.

Benson in 1946 had been a star speaker at a rally by protofascist radio personality Father Charles Coughlin and taught at the far-right Harding College in Arkansas. One such lecture on Americanism indirectly attacked the New Deal because its programs involved government in housing, Social Security, and all other socialistic and communistic measures that inserted government in free enterprise. The lectures also emphasized that "unions are not in any way responsible for the great progress that American labor has made in its stride for a better and higher standard of living."[28]

Militant workers were not the only targets of such programs. As early as 1951, business-sponsored movies, from company promotions to highly produced antisocialist films, reached an audience of 20 million people every week, more than one-third of the nation's weekly attendance at commercial movies, a 500 percent increase since 1946.[29]

Employers' anti-union messaging went hand in hand with force-fed efforts to champion free enterprise. For business, the collective process inherent in unions could not co-exist with the type of unrestricted free enterprise they envisioned. In 1952, Milwaukee's A. O. Smith created *Our Way of Living*, a two-hour "employee economic education" film it showed to ten thousand of its employees. The Association of Commerce also actively promoted the film to its members—efforts that included excerpts of it for small groups of company presidents—and estimated that forty companies carried it in the weeks leading up to the 1956 presidential elections.[30]

The Association of Commerce also pushed Milwaukee employers to utilize resources available through the U.S. Chamber of Commerce "American Opportunity Program." The chamber project, which aimed at "building greater confidence" in the U.S. economic system and "correct[ing] misconceptions about it," was carried out through letters to employees, company bulletin boards, annual reports, plant tours, and radio programs. The chamber was among dozens of organizations supplying employers with such "educational" material. NAM was among the most prolific, tapping into such internationally known experts as Ludwig von Mises for its output.[31]

The Wisconsin Manufacturers' Association, although not affiliated with NAM, similarly waged free-enterprise campaigns. The association, which counted a quarter of the state's businesses as members, was directed by a board that included Harnischfeger and Grede. Grede, who served as president in the mid-1940s, was credited by the nearly one-thousand-member group with reorganizing its structure so as to launch an "aggressive program of representation for industry in Wisconsin." Under Grede's leadership Wisconsin newspapers in one month carried more than eight hundred column inches of association-provided news, while its public-relations program encouraged participation by association representatives to speak on radio about industry and its role in the economy. The association frequently sounded the alarm over the impending threat of socialism and communism.[32]

The continued corporate resistance to federal recognition of unions as legitimate players, and their determination to challenge workers' assertions of workplace rights, signaled business's renewed determination to reverse it. Many, like Grede, who had testified in favor of Taft-Hartley after becoming a NAM board member in 1946, did not find comfort in its passage. Nor did Harnischfeger, who agreed with Grede that after the war the "government did not return to free enterprise. It aided and abetted the unions in a monopolistic control of the labor market."[33]

Grede and Harnischfeger shared with business leaders across the political spectrum the goal of limiting, if not abolishing, unions to establish a staunchly individualist free enterprise that had no room for workers acting collectively. Business in the postwar era had, in fact, begun to chip away successfully at the strength of unions and workers' notions of collective action. In 1950, unions experienced a nearly 75 percent win rate in elections supervised by the NLRB. By 1960 such victories had dropped to 63 percent. Union membership peaked in 1954—when nearly 35 percent of U.S. workers were union members—before beginning a steady and seemingly irreversible decline. Labor's numbers, union members' militancy, and the union movement's overall visibility in the 1950s masked these early stages of decline.[34]

The "Clay Boat" Incident

Milwaukee's role in turning away two ships carrying supplies for the Kohler plant in upstate Sheboygan generated some of the city's most high-profile controversies around workers' challenge to free enterprise. In 1956, Kohler employees were in the midst of an ultimately seven-year walkout after management, led by Herbert Kohler, refused to recognize their vote to join the UAW. Kohler workers lived in a company-owned village, were given five-minute lunch breaks, and were required to toil in an enamel plant with enormously high temperatures.[35]

The last time Kohler workers had gone on strike to push Kohler into recognizing a union, workers lost their lives. Walter Kohler Sr. had overseen the Kohler plant during the 1934 strike in which Kohler guards shot and killed two strikers and wounded forty-seven others after the workers threw rocks at the company building, breaking windows. During the 1950s Kohler strike, Walter Sr.'s son, Governor Walter Kohler Jr., urged his uncle, Herbert, to accept mediation with the UAW, which repeatedly offered to enter into binding arbitration. But Herbert Kohler, a longtime fundraiser for the Manion Forum and contributor to the New York Conservative Party, rejected his nephew's request.[36]

The Norwegian ships carrying tons of English ball clay crucial to producing bathtubs and other ceramic hardware had been turned away from docking at Sheboygan by the city's socialist mayor. When the *M.S. Fossum* and, days later, its partner ship, the *M.S. Divina*, arrived at the Milwaukee Harbor, they were met by crowds of union members gathered on the docks to support city employees' refusal to unload cargo headed to a strike-bound plant. As John Schmitt, recording secretary of the CIO Brewery Workers Local 9 colorfully put it, "How can anyone who takes a bath in a scab-made tub ever expect to feel clean?"[37]

Over the next few days, Zeidler ordered the *Fossum* not be unloaded until he met with leaders of the AFL and CIO, who also joined in Common Council emergency sessions and in meetings with the cargo's owner and his attorney. Members of both labor organizations planned a citywide strike if ordered to unload the ship, a move that under city law was illegal because they were civil servants ineligible to strike or bargain collectively. Seeking to avert penalties against port workers—which included job loss—and always mindful of preventing violence and strife, Zeidler appealed to labor leaders to wait until the situation was worked out. They agreed, but by then the *Fossum* had sailed out of the harbor. As the *Divina* approached, Zeidler worked with AFL and CIO leaders who agreed to let the *Divina* discharge its cargo. After the Common Council voted in favor of barring the *Divina*, Zeidler vetoed the measure.[38]

Yet before the *Divina* reached Milwaukee, its owners diverted the ship to Montreal. Many Milwaukeeans were outraged the city had not forced workers to unload the cargo, most commonly charging the city had "caved in to unions." Writing to the ships' owner, an otherwise unidentified "group of Milwaukee taxpayers" "urgently urged" the company to sue Milwaukee for its loss because "Americans have fought wars and died for just such freedom across the waters and yet it is tolerated inside our borders and we resent it to no end. DOWN WITH THE UNIONS!"[39]

Such anti-union rhetoric paralleled sentiments expressed against the public sector, which opponents perceived as interfering with private commerce and individual property rights. Later, during Milwaukee Harbor Commission hearings on the "clay boat incident," Milwaukee union leader Friedrick noted that elsewhere, other ships with cargo for strike-bound plants had been unloaded and the goods put into storage. But he believed a big deal was made about this case because the ship was turned away in Sheboygan by union workers. Friedrick's claim expressed a deep understanding of the extent to which the collective strength of unions and the solidarity of workers challenged a free-enterprise-based system predicated on the exercise of individual rights. The incident cost Milwaukee $43,039 in damages to the importing company and $19,000 to the ship owner.[40]

Ideology Trumps Profit

As the first full decade to benefit from the New Deal era reforms without the aberration of war, the 1950s offered staggering prosperity and a standard of living that leap-frogged ahead each year. In Milwaukee, which ranked seventh in size among the twenty largest metropolitan areas, average income far exceeded the national norm. By 1957, 33 percent of Milwaukeeans were in the highest two income brackets, with nearly 40 percent solidly in the middle. *Time* magazine summed up the abundance: In 1953, Americans "slipped behind the wheels" of six million new cars and drove over forty-six thousand miles of new roads worth $3 billion. They "put their feet into 500 million pairs of new shoes [and] walked into 1.1 million new houses." Milwaukee's Miller Brewing Company celebrated production of its three-millionth barrel of beer, boosting the company from sixth- to fifth-largest among brewers and ratcheting up sales by 275 percent. The following year offered an unparalleled continuation of plenty, with *Time* estimating that even if General Motors' sales dropped by as much as 37 percent in 1954, the automaker could still end up with net profits on par with 1953.[41]

The most crucial economic indicator was not in the number of new shoes slipped on or cars purchased. Fundamental to the 1950s as the era of affluence was its unprecedented lack of income inequality. Between the two World Wars, the richest fifth garnered a little over 28 percent of the total national income after taxes. By 1945, their slice had been narrowed to 17 percent after taxes. Between 1941 and 1950, average family income skyrocketed, rising by 42 percent after taxes for those in the bottom fifth of the income bracket. For the highest 5 percent, income decreased by 2 percent. Unionized operations were essential in lessening income disparity—the list of products *Time* cited as illustrative of consumer plenty were nearly all union made. At bottom, the "consensus" that cemented together disparate parts of American society as never before or after was the historically small income gap, the outcome of Depression-era policies that limited vast accumulation of corporate wealth and supported creation of unions.[42]

Unions were more than just a means by which their members could prosper. The purchasing power of unionized workers bolstered local economies and opened up avenues of higher education for the next generation. Unions also provided a crucial underpinning of support for publicly funded programs that would benefit the larger community. In championing the expansion of government's role in the economy, unions became inextricably connected with the New Deal environment, further fueling corporate opposition to labor.

In Milwaukee, the interests of unions and government intersected in the city's fight to save the St. Lawrence Seaway, a federally funded venture that would open the city's port to oceangoing vessels. The project was vehemently opposed by many area industrialists, as it was by NAM, because of the public expense involved. Although the seaway would afford local industrialists a new avenue for transporting iron ore—which could be shipped more cheaply on ocean vessels than across land from the Mesabi iron range, thereby increasing manufacturing revenue—their opposition illustrates the extent to which an anti–New Deal ideology trumped sound business judgment.[43]

The city had sought expansion of the St. Lawrence Seaway since the 1920s. But the project came to a standstill several times due to congressional opposition by lawmakers in coal-producing states and Eastern port cities who stood to lose as a result of the competition created by the seaway and power project. When the issue resurfaced in Congress in the late 1940s, the proposal included developing 2.2 million units of hydropower electric energy, expanding the seaway's 250-foot locks to 800 feet, and increasing the channel's depth from fourteen feet to twenty-seven feet to accommodate ocean carriers.[44]

As Congress debated the issue into the early 1950s, it became clear that Wisconsin would not appear on Capitol Hill with a united voice in favor of the $800 million project, whose passage was far from certain. The Association of Commerce and industrialists like Harnischfeger opposed it, while some influential manufacturers like Allis-Chalmers, which could have provided crucial support, purposely took no position. Zeidler, who strongly championed the project, seeing in it a vital new avenue to spur the city's production and commerce, worked closely with local labor leaders to press for its passage. He also called for national AFL support, but he did not convince the federation, which opposed the project because of likely job loss for railway and members in related industries on the East Coast.[45]

Milwaukee's seaway proponents sparred with industrialists through House and Senate committee hearings. Testifying before the House Public Works Committee as the representative of the Association of Commerce, Harnischfeger admitted the project would benefit his corporation, which since 1884 had produced overhead traveling cranes, excavating equipment welders, diesel engines, and road stabilizers. All of Harnischfeger's plants—three in Milwaukee, two in Port Washington, Wisconsin, and two in Escanaba, Michigan—were located on the Great Lakes. But ideology—opposition to creation of a federally funded, large-scale project with nationwide reach—trumped the bottom line. As Harnischfeger told the House Public Works Committee, "I believe it is desirable to defer it until such time when manpower and materials are in greater supply, or in other words, this type of project should be deferred and be a recession project."[46]

Labor's support for the seaway, and the likelihood that union jobs would expand with the project, provided another reason for Harnischfeger to oppose it. "The comparison that has been made of the stimulating effect that the Panama Canal has had on intercoastal shipping is questionable," he testified. "The facts of the matter are that the unions have practically destroyed our intercostal shipping."[47]

Outraged that Harnischfeger would plan for the future "with a recession bias," the state AFL wondered "what kind of Association business is this anyway, arguing against a project that will sustain the area for hundreds of miles around the very city in which the Association thrives and for whose benefit it claims the right to live?"[48]

Haberman, president of the Wisconsin State Federation of Labor, told the House committee that the proposed Seaway would open up vast new foreign markets to the Midwest, stimulate the area's industrial efficiency, and raise the standard of living. The basic requirements for American mass production are centered in the Great Lakes district, Haberman said, but the stability and future growth of the nation's industrial arsenal in the Midwest are endangered by the depletion of domestic ore supplies. Without access to cheap ore, the steel supply of the Lake States would be depleted and jobs seriously and drastically reduced.[49]

The stance of local industrialists, although in line with NAM and with far-right economic conservatives, such as those expressed in Hunt's *Facts Forum News*, contradicted that of national Republican leadership, with President Eisenhower calling passage of the bill in 1954 a "historic victory." Without approval for the seaway project, Eisenhower feared Canada would build it and leave the United States "without a clear right to a voice in the seaway's construction, control, operation, and tolls in time of either peace or national emergency." The project ultimately garnered the key support of Senator John Kennedy, who became the first Massachusetts lawmaker to vote in favor of expanding the St. Lawrence Seaway, and construction began in 1954.[50]

Chipping Away at Labor

Many efforts by conservatives to rein in the role of unions did not get far in the 1950s. But at minimum, these attempts served as trial balloons, while chipping away at the union movement's legal rights and moral authority. In Wisconsin as elsewhere, an expanding union membership greatly enlarged the pool of politically active union members, a trend conservative opponents of unions increasingly recognized and acted to restrain. In 1955, Wisconsin Republicans made their first effort to limit unions' political clout, passing state legislation, the Caitlin Act, that prohibited unions from contributing to political parties, committees, or candidates for state and local office.

The role of union money in funding Democratic candidates statewide had gone unnoticed until 1954, when Democrat William Proxmire came within 36,000 votes of unseating Republican governor Walter Kohler Jr. Conservatives chafed at the realization that half of Proxmire's campaign funding came from unions. In the 1956 elections, the first after passage of Caitlin, labor contributions fell dramatically, amounting to only 7.4 percent of the funds raised by Democrats, compared with 36.2 percent in 1954. Proxmire believed the lack of funding cost him the 1956 gubernatorial election. Labor subsequently succeeded in getting the law repealed in 1959, after Governor Gaylord Nelson, a Democrat, took office.[51]

Statewide efforts to circumscribe unions continued. In 1958, even as Wisconsin public employees were moving toward passage of state legislation that would legalize collective bargaining, Republicans were pushing a statewide referendum for right-to-work legislation, a campaign strongly supported by city officials in Milwaukee suburbs such as Wauwatosa. Under federal labor laws, unions must represent all workers in a bargaining unit, even if they choose not to join a union. Right-to-work laws prevent unions from charging non-union members a share of the cost of representing them. That enables those workers to pay no union dues but get the benefits of union membership. Although proponents did not think the effort stood a chance—the measure had only lukewarm financial support from backers, who also were unwilling to spend the time in Madison to lobby for its passage—conservatives elsewhere had made real gains. By 1958 eighteen states had passed right-to-work laws. Eleven states passed these laws immediately after passage of Taft-Hartley, which paved the way for such legislation.[52]

At the national level, labor experienced its severest blow when the 1957–1960 Senate McClellan hearings turned the tide of public opinion against labor. The Select Committee on Improper Activities in the Labor or Management Field, commonly known by the name of its chairman, Arkansas

Democrat John McClellan, began by examining financial corruption and other malfeasance of unions. The committee's most notorious investigations involved the Teamsters, with thirty-four of the fifty-eight volumes of the hearings devoted to that union. But led by its conservative members, the committee early on became overtly political. As committee member Democratic Senator Patrick McNamara noted, "Particularly after the first year, the committee's work was being used to blacken the name of labor as a whole."[53]

The McClellan Committee's hearings on the ongoing Kohler strike and ostensible corruption by the UAW offered those like Herbert Kohler and Senator Barry Goldwater a public stage to denounce unions as bastions of socialism. Goldwater had started out his political career by mobilizing retailers to pass Arizona's 1948 right-to-work law as part of a local group that defined a union shop as the creation of "despotic little labor racketeers" and "would-be Hitlers." After he learned that Reuther's spotless financial management included paying for his own dry cleaning when staying in hotels on union business, Goldwater declared, "I would rather have [Teamster's President Jimmy] Hoffa stealing my money than Reuther stealing my freedom."[54]

By the end of the Kohler hearings, which found no wrongdoing, Goldwater admitted they never should have taken place. But in dragging Reuther before the committee, its conservative members hoped to identify his support for collective workplace action with Teamsters leaders and union corruption—and in doing so, smear the entire union movement.

Unions had previously been defended as vehicles through which workers achieved "some measure of independence and dignity" in the workplace and some protection against arbitrary management decisions. But after the hearings, the "public began to think that unions also were instruments of labor bosses . . . who exploited the workers and lived in ill-gotten luxury from union funds." In a Gallup poll taken before the hearings, 76 percent of the public held a favorable view of unions; by the mid-1960s, that support plummeted to 50 percent. As AFL-CIO president George Meany succinctly noted, the events of the McClellan findings had the "net effect" of indicting "the entire labor movement for the sins of a few."[55]

"Organized Labor—The Dwindling Minority?"

The article in *Business Week* put it bluntly: "Industrial unions seem to be at the end of a line, their membership is falling and probably will continue to drop as more and more plants are automated. Craft unions have more room for growth but employment in their areas is growing only slowly."[56]

The magazine's assessment, familiar to readers in the 1980s, appeared in March 1959, a time looked back upon as epitomizing the nation's industrial apex. But manufacturing employment hit a postwar high of 17.2 million in 1953 and barely five years later had decreased to 15.4 million. Similarly, although the sheer size and strength of the U.S. union movement in the private sector appeared formidable in the 1950s, a 1958 *Fortune* article was tellingly titled, "Organized Labor—The Dwindling Minority?"[57]

The trend already had begun in Milwaukee, where manufacturing accounted for 42 percent of total employment in the county in 1957. Several factors were at play, as well, in eating away at the city's and county's industrial base. In 1959 the lower Milwaukee River was closed to navigation, a clear blow to the city's industrial production. By 1953, 10 percent of the state's industry was relocating elsewhere, beginning the journey first to the southern United States, then to Mexico, Central America, and Asian nations on which many U.S. firms embarked in search of lower costs. Milwaukee County's largest losses were in leather, apparel, and textile, which were crafted in factories whose operations were far easier to relocate than heavy machinery or electrical manufacturing. By 1959 its percentage of industrial growth was smaller in comparison with similar cites, and Milwaukee ranked far down the list when compared with Cleveland and Indianapolis.[58]

In the late 1950s the Association of Commerce kept up a steady drumbeat about the level of state taxes, which it asserted was the impetus behind industrial plant relocation. An anti-tax campaign briefly flared in 1957, with the Milwaukee County Property Owners' Association distributing thousands of leaflets calling for a "tax revolt" and circulating petitions to gather signatures supporting lower taxes. The petition, provocatively titled "Will You Have a Job a Year from Now?" urged residents to join in the tax revolt because "high taxes are causing industry to leave Milwaukee." Zeidler countered by pointing out the inaccuracies of the groups' claims, including the one that taxes had increased without accounting for the equalized tax rate, which had dropped from $32.64 in 1948 to $26.56 in 1957. The Affiliated Taxpayer Committee joined in the anti-tax campaign with a detailed list of twenty-five suggestions for cutting taxes, mostly targeting city services such as libraries.[59]

The combination of postwar national legislative and regulatory actions that weakened federal labor law, aggressive grassroots anti-unionism, the shift away from industrialization, and the fallout from the McClellan Committee meant that even when the labor movement seemed its strongest, its underlying structure was being eaten away. The same forces that had made such strides in delegitimizing private-sector unions had simultaneously weakened the underpinnings of the New Deal's elevation of public service.

"Nothing More Autocratic than Majority Rule"

The fragility of the New Deal order, highlighted in day-to-day contests on the shop floor, in high-profile confrontations such as the Kohler strike, and throughout legislative challenges, did not represent the resurgence of the conservative, free-enterprise right but instead its ongoing resolution to challenge the postwar consensus. Beneath the trappings of liberal city leadership, a strong and well-rooted labor movement, and a tradition of progressive politics, Milwaukee, as in the rest of the nation, included a significant segment of those who rejected the New Deal consensus and actively worked to overturn it. They did so by challenging the premise of the collective good championed both by unions and the public sector.

Influential business leaders like Grede and grassroots activists such as Pieplow had never stopped challenging what they saw as the usurpation by government of individual liberty. Although Pieplow's worldview was seemingly apart from Grede's brand of extremism, Grede was no libertarian seeking the abolition of government. Their ideologies united over limiting government and expanding individual rights. Grede took this philosophy to its logical extension when he expressed a desire to write a book titled *The Virtue of Selfishness*. "This selfish, competitive process has produced in America the highest economic and cultural development in the world—and yet there are enemies of freedom who would destroy it," he wrote.[60]

Grede and Harnischfeger were among a core of staunchly anti-union industrialists in Milwaukee, far-right economic conservatives who, like their counterparts around the country, directed their wealth toward funding like-minded organizations and media endeavors. Further, their high-level positions on national and local platforms provided them the authority to shape and steer legislative and policy decisions. A friend of President Herbert Hoover, Harnischfeger directed eight overseas plants, which led him to increasingly channel his concerns over government influence into public speeches on international trends and U.S fiscal policy. In 1951 Grede was elected president of both NAM and the YMCA. From his national podiums, Grede pursued his crusade to convince the public to take action and oppose what he saw as a tidal wave of government involvement, one inevitably leading to socialism.[61]

Grede's passion for his mission translated into an unprecedented speaking schedule. In his one-year term as NAM president, Grede traveled approximately eighty-five thousand miles within the United States, making 273 appearances, which included thirty-three press conferences and fifty-two live and recorded radio programs. His audiences were made up of congressional lawmakers, college students, and members of forty-five non-NAM-related groups. NAM not only paid him for his travel on behalf of the organization but also agreed he should combine his speaking engagements with those he gave in his role as YMCA president. Grede, a Congregationalist, "convinced both organizations that there was no conflict between the message of free enterprise and that of Christian character-building."[62]

Like the Republican Party in Milwaukee, Grede was not openly involved in municipal politics, but both worked behind the scenes. The Republican Party "controlled through friendship and campaign contributions a block of aldermen, including Democratic alderman," according to Zeidler, a bloc he saw as determined to defeat him in the 1956 mayoral elections. Grede played powerbroker behind the scenes: Milwaukee County Republican Party Chairman Arthur Agostini, who announced that the party sought to unseat Zeidler in 1956, was an employee of Grede Foundries and "generally regarded as the political spokesman for William Grede."[63]

By the early 1960s, Grede was among 250 top individual contributors to the far right, whose numbers, as estimated by the Anti-Defamation League, belied the notion of a pervasive liberal consensus. Classifying 20 percent of the population as "radical right extremists" or "extreme conservatives," the Anti-Defamation League in 1964 asserted that between 20 percent and 25 percent of the U.S. public strongly opposed such extremists, with "the remaining 50 percent or 55 percent of American citizens the prize to be won."[64]

Grede created a foundation through Grede Industries to channel his donations. Like most of the foundations, corporations, and public utilities behind such funding, Grede's goal in feeding far-right organizations was not to create a new party but "to change the political climate in the United States to turn the winds slowly their way." Both he and Harnischfeger contributed to the Manion Forum, and both helped launch Americans for Constitutional Action, which set out to combat socialism and offset the influence of Americans for Democratic Action, the nation's first political advocacy organization set up by Eleanor Roosevelt, Walter Reuther, and other prominent liberals.[65]

Grede had a fundraising finger in nearly every organization that challenged perceived encroachments on free enterprise, including the National Association of Businessmen, an organization dedicated to fulfilling General Electric president Charles Wilson's call to "buy out the government" by getting government out of private enterprise. Grede also sought to reach the next generation. Describing to his corporate board members the rationale for his extensive contributions, Grede singled out the need to reach America's youth. "It seems to me that we would be derelict in our duty, if we did not, in the interests of our stockholders and our Corporation, help in this field of education and propaganda for the preservation of our free, competitive enterprise business-system and our republican form of government."[66]

He backed his words with action, pouring money into the Freedom School, opened by Robert LeFevre in 1957, which provided short-term courses steeped in economic conservatism and offered Grede the opportunity to cultivate the change he sought in his hometown. Working through the Employers' Association of Milwaukee, Grede raised scholarship funds to send Milwaukee-area college students to the Freedom School, planting critical seeds among the upcoming generation. The list of Freedom School instructors encompassed a who's who of top conservative intellectuals, including economists Milton Friedman and Ludwig von Mises, who taught college students as well as executives, such as the president of Milwaukee's Falk Corporation and other top leaders of influential Milwaukee operations.[67]

Despite his energetic activity on behalf of far-right organizations, Grede was not a fringe figure. The man who asserted, "There is nothing more autocratic than majority rule . . . majority rule would destroy our society . . ." was also the finance chairman of both the Wisconsin Republican Party and the Milwaukee County Republican Party. Nor was Harnischfeger a rogue element. His opposition to the St. Lawrence Seaway represented the views of Milwaukee's most influential employers' group and echoed the stance of NAM, whose twenty thousand members nationwide contributed to its $12 million annual budget. Although the views of such far-right economic conservatives were not yet in the mainstream, they operated from a strong foundation of financial and ideological support that enabled them over the decades to expand their influence in Milwaukee and throughout the nation.[68]

In the late 1950s, Milwaukee unions' assertions of worker rights and the collective good culminated in an ideological showdown when city employees sought bargaining rights. For economic conservatives who saw unions as the most threatening element of an expansive government, the move to gain workplace rights by public-sector employees confirmed the integral connection between the growth of the public sector and the union movement. When Milwaukee municipal workers proved to be the spark that resulted in Wisconsin becoming the first state in the nation to pass statewide public-sector bargaining rights, the subsequent spread of public-employee unionization generated a conservative backlash essential to an understanding of the motivations fueling conservatism in the ensuing decades.

7 Public Interest vs. Public Employees

> One of the great frontiers for organized labor is in organizing government workers.... It is shocking to think that some officials in City Hall do not appreciate this fact.
> —*Wisconsin CIO News*, November 15, 1957

As the numbers of public employees increased throughout the decade, both blue- and white-collar city workers increasingly asserted their rights. Their efforts, led by the fast-growing public-sector union AFSCME, raised questions anew about the role of government and the extent to which workers should have control over their working conditions. Against expectations, Mayor Frank Zeidler emerged as one of the main opponents of public-sector bargaining, a stance that flew against his long support of unions and remained out of step with many contemporary liberal assumptions.

City Employees Set the Stage for Bargaining Rights

Even in Milwaukee, a city with one of the nation's strongest trade union traditions, where a majority of residents lived in union households, the more than twenty-eight hundred workers who packed a union hall in early December 1958 set a record. Not only was it the city's largest-ever union meeting, but the workers who took part made up more than four-fifths of the total union membership of municipal employees represented by District Council 48 of the American Federation of State, County, and Municipal Employees (AFSCME). Street sweepers, office clerks, sanitation workers, and librarians gathered to vote on whether to accept the Common Council's 2 percent wage increase for the coming fiscal year, short of the 3.5 percent they sought.

But more than that, they were debating whether to strike over exclusive union representation, widely perceived as a prelude to union demands for collective-bargaining rights. Although Milwaukee's municipal workers long had been members of unions, they operated under a "meet and confer" arrangement with the Common Council and, like nearly all public employees in the country, had no legally binding contract with their employer—collective-bargaining rights. Before the end of the meeting, they voted overwhelmingly to authorize Council 48 to call a strike if their demands were not "substantially" met.[1]

Zeidler, in Boston attending an American Municipal Association conference, was outraged. "I will not support any settlement the Common Council makes while the strike threat is on. It is time that we finally get it resolved whether a union can strike against a government." Zeidler, who, as the *Milwaukee Journal* noted in an editorial approving his stance, was "no hard-nosed foe of labor," saw the strike threat as "an attack against the people's government." By taking action now, Zeidler said, the city "would leave the implication that we gave in because of the threat of a strike." Distressed, he discussed the situation with conference attendees and took an informal survey among mayors of the largest U.S. cities, most of whom told Zeidler they opposed written contracts between cities and unions representing city employees. "These mayors also deplore a growing national trend toward strikes by employees to obtain their objectives," Zeidler said to a reporter. In noting that the municipal leaders with whom he spoke felt they could do little to reach a resolution, Zeidler likely described his own sentiments when he said, "Many mayors feel helpless in the face of this trend."[2]

On the financial side, AFSCME sought a cost-of-living increase effective July 1, in addition to a 3.5 percent pay raise, four weeks of paid vacation after twenty years' service, and additional city contributions toward "hospitalization insurance" for employees' families, all of which would add $375,000 to the city's 1959 budget. The Common Council, in a 15–5 vote, had rejected the 3.5 percent increase in November. Alderman James Mortier, chairman of the council's Finance Committee, which approved city salaries, spoke for the majority on the Common Council in his response to the union's wage and benefit requests, saying, "We have strung our budget to the absolute minimum in order to give a raise consistent with those granted by outside industry."[3]

"The city has extended itself as far as it can go—financially and legally," Zeidler said from Boston. "It is extremely unfair of the union, which has received better treatment from the city than from any other unit of government, to threaten to strike because it thinks we are weak. John Zinos has led the union to a hole from which he cannot extricate it. Zinos will not permit us to help him out."[4]

Zinos, the dynamic and dogged executive director of AFSCME Council 48, had been relentless over the years in his pursuit to empower city employees.

A lawyer who worked his way through the University of Wisconsin–Madison, at one point holding four part-time jobs, Zinos was the son of a Greek immigrant who had traveled in steerage to New York. After moving to Milwaukee, the elder Zinos became an assembly worker at a Ford plant, which closed during the Depression, throwing one thousand workers out with no severance pay, an action that infused the younger Zinos with a determination to ensure working people got a fair shake.[5]

Every November as budget hearings began, recalled a reporter for the *Milwaukee Sentinel* at the time, Zinos "would come in and fill the Council chambers with garbage collectors and truck drivers . . . and threaten a strike." Both Zinos and Zeidler shared a key insight into municipal governance. As Zeidler summarized it, "The world may be on fire, war and strife may be occurring in the remote parts of the globe; but to the people at home, the uncollected garbage in the alley . . . and the trouble on the school playground are more important facts of life. The people are interested in what the local authorities are doing about problems like these."[6]

Zinos and the municipal employees AFSCME represented wanted more than pecuniary gain. The agreement they sought—the city's exclusive recognition of AFSCME as the representative of city employees—went well beyond the union's annual budget skirmish with the Common Council. AFSCME already enjoyed dues checkoff, an arrangement in which the public employer agrees to deduct union dues automatically from the paychecks of workers who belonged to a union. Milwaukee was one of few such cities in the 1950s granting checkoff to public employees. Speaking from Boston, Zeidler asserted that the dues checkoff system, approved by the Common Council in 1955 and in effect since 1956, constituted union recognition, noting that checkoff underpinned AFSCME's financial strength to "threaten the city."[7]

As the city endured its worst cold wave since 1876 with temperatures plummeting to minus ten degrees, union leaders, members of the council's Finance Committee, and Zeidler, now back in Milwaukee, met throughout December for talks assisted by the disputes committee of the Federated Trades Council. Zeidler moderated his approach, ultimately working with the council and the union to reach an agreement despite the vote to authorize a strike. He also refined his stance on union recognition, asserting he did not oppose a recognition statement—as long as the union did not ask for "exclusive recognition," saying, "This I am not willing to grant." As if to add insult to injury in the view of the city's union leaders, in the midst of discussions with city leaders, NAM awarded Hebert Kohler its Man of the Year Award for his multiyear lockout of Kohler employees.[8]

AFSCME's Strategy Makes Broad Inroads

By the end of December, AFSCME Council 48 backed off exclusive recognition, instead agreeing that signed representation cards would indicate relative union strength. The move was part of Zinos's thrust-and-parry approach, a strategy he—and AFSCME—had long employed, and one that had enabled the public-employee union to make significant inroads nationwide in representing a segment of workers who were omitted from the National Labor Relations Act (NLRA) and who increasingly sought the same workplace rights as unionized workers in the private sector.[9]

In his institutional history of AFSCME, Leo Kramer, who in the 1960s was a top assistant to the union's founding president Arnold Zander, describes AFSCME's strategy during the 1950s as seeking the best terms it could win at the bargaining table without resorting to the courts. Judicial rulings were uniformly hostile to the concept of granting public employee bargaining rights or expanding them beyond the scope of civil-service coverage. Court rulings fell into two broad categories, the first in which courts held that legislatures delegated power over employment to local public officials and that judges should therefore defer decisions of bargaining rights to local officials. The courts also held that public employers could not confer any power to a private body such as a union. Delegating to labor the power to bargain, or to arbitrators the power to bind governments, would violate constitutional nondelegation documents and, ostensibly, threaten democracy. In both cases, judges "promoted a state structure in which they uniformly deferred to the restrictive rules of local public officials—the direct employers of labor—because such power had been delegated to them." In 1947, for instance, the Missouri Supreme Court ruled that the legislature cannot delegate its legislative powers, and any attempted delegation would be void: "If such powers cannot be delegated, they surely cannot be contracted or bargained away."[10]

So rather than challenge a municipality in court, if a collective-bargaining agreement was more than a city official would accept, the union would seek the same wages and conditions signed in a memorandum of agreement or exchange of letters. If no signed agreement was possible, the union accepted confirmation of negotiations by incorporation of negotiated terms into civil service rules, regulations, ordinances or legislative resolutions, and so on. By adopting an "industrial union" approach, in which public unions pooled their legislative strength with employees' unions in the private sector, AFSCME by the early 1940s succeeded in achieving recognition for city and county employees without formal legislation. In 1941, AFSCME had organized 295 local unions. Barely five years later, it represented 1,025 local unions.[11]

AFSCME, which got its start in Wisconsin in 1932, was chartered by the AFL in 1936, a year after the CIO formed. Zander, who led AFSCME from 1936 to 1964, described AFSCME's creation as an effort to save the state's civil service. The nonpartisan system was threatened after Democrats swept elections in 1932 and sought to eliminate civil service to make room for party faithful in need of jobs. Zander, then employed in the Wisconsin Bureau of Personnel and part of the struggle, went on to steer the union into becoming one of the largest in the AFL-CIO. Recollecting the union's origin, Zander said, "We've never ceased to believe that partisan politicians ought to keep their cotton pickin' fingers out of the administrative mechanism."[12]

From the beginning, AFSCME necessarily focused on extending civil-service rights, with collective bargaining a distant goal. At AFSCME's 1954 convention, the two approaches merged when the union's traditional call for extension of civil service became part of a resolution to seek "job security and union representation for all state and local government employees ... for the establishment of civil-service boards that are truly impartial and do not just represent the administration."[13]

AFSCME also simultaneously pressed for expansion of public employees' rights at both local and state levels. By 1946 collective-bargaining legislation was introduced but not signed into law in Illinois, Indiana, Minnesota, New York, Oregon, Utah, and Washington. In 1947 AFSCME and the Wisconsin union movement successfully pushed for a collective-bargaining law in the state legislature, but Republican governor Walter Kohler Jr.—whose terms in office extended through the onset of the Kohler strike—vetoed the measure.[14]

Even as Zinos and city leaders met in Milwaukee, 150 delegates from AFSCME locals in Wisconsin gathered for a state legislative conference in Madison, where they laid plans to introduce a bill in the state legislature that would allow employees in cities and counties to collectively bargain. The proposed legislation, which excluded law enforcement officers, also would prohibit interference with bargaining rights and give the Wisconsin Employment Relations Board the authority to aid in settling disputes between public employers and unions. The proposals ultimately formed the nucleus of legislation enacted in 1959 and signed by Governor Gaylord Nelson, who took office in 1958 as Wisconsin's first Democratic governor in twenty years.

Its passage made Wisconsin the first state to pass a law granting collective-bargaining rights for city and county employees and the first law of any kind that granted teachers the right to organize into unions. It gave local government employees, except police, the right to be represented by unions in "conferences and negotiations" over wages, hours, and working conditions. Because the law was confusingly worded—for instance, the term "negotiation" was not defined—the law was revised in 1961, and in 1965 it was expanded to include state employees.[15]

Delegates also approved a resolution affirming support for the Milwaukee locals and backed a strike, if necessary. The position of public officials and the press in seeking to deny city and county employees the right to strike was "unfair and impractical," delegates asserted. The resolution noted that the city already recognized the right of city employees to organize. And the right to organize implies the right to strike, the resolution said, because organizing suggests use of the union as "an economic vehicle to achieve the goals." Or, as Zinos put it during an appearance at the conference, "You join a union to bargain on wages, hours and working conditions, and not as a social function."[16]

Milwaukee's long history of ensuring municipal-employee rights began before the Progressive era. City employees had won the eight-hour day with the same pay as a ten-hour day before Milwaukee enacted a Civil Service Law in 1895 and went on to form a variety of municipal unions. Beginning in August 1919, Milwaukee City Hall employees, in some cases representing entire departments, met to create the first such organization. At that initial gathering, workers discussed salary increases that would have totaled between $1 million and $1.5 million. City firefighters organized that same year and, by early 1920, 50 percent of the 585 men in the force were part of the union. In creating the organization, the firefighters' union secretary, W. E. Brown, asserted, "We positively are a non-strike organization. We are organized for educational purposes and naturally to obtain better conditions for firemen." Brown felt it important to note also that the union was nonpolitical. By the 1930s, Milwaukee public employees moved rapidly to form unions and associations, and was the only large city in the region with unions or associations representing public employees.[17]

In the mid-1950s many of the city's 14,585 employees were members of several representation organizations. The City and County Public Service Employees Union, the descendent of Milwaukee City Hall employees, was the oldest. The union had left the AFL in 1922 and remained independent until it joined the CIO in 1937 after the AFL had sought to divide it up into small craft divisions. The Milwaukee Government Service League, formed in 1933, vociferously insisted it was not a union and was the largest city organization to represent municipal workers before AFSCME organized. When AFSCME District Council 48 formed in January 1937, it gained an immediate membership boost from workers who belonged to the recently disbanded AFL Federal Labor Union, which represented city laborers. From the outset, AFSCME reported a membership of two thousand city workers, which, if accurate, would have represented nearly a quarter of the union's membership nationwide.[18]

Desperate to End City Strikes

Although the city had long working relationships with organizations representing municipal employees, one that by the 1950s advanced into a quasi-bargaining arrangement, when it came to strikes by public employees, Milwaukee leaders, as those across the nation, opposed such action. The city had become especially sensitized to municipal walkouts after seven months of periodic strikes and strike threats in 1943 by a variety of AFL, CIO, and independent union members. The walkouts spread after a two-week sanitation workers' strike in which Mayor John Bohn and the Common Council, in a desperate move to end the strike, agreed to pay the workers for their time on the picket line. City laborers and truck drivers followed with strike threats; sanitation workers staged work slowdowns and, by November, another walkout. This time, as 787 garbage workers neared their third day on the picket line, Bohn said he intended to enforce a civil-service rule, making municipal employees liable to be discharged after any three-day absence for failing to obtain leave or to give notice of their intention to return to work.

In sending the discharge notice to the striking workers, Walter Swietlik, commissioner of public works, quoted from a letter by Franklin Roosevelt in which the president came out against collective bargaining for public employees. Roosevelt's statement, cited extensively by opponents of collective-bargaining rights for public employees as the debate intensified in the 1950s—including in legal briefs for court cases on the issue—also blasted public-employee strikes as an unthinkable and intolerable action because they threatened "paralysis of government by those who have sworn to support it." The postwar strike wave later in the decade, which drew national attention and media commentary because of the vast number of workers on the picket lines, further reinforced in the public's mind the seemingly inextricable connection between unionization and disruptive strikes. As the CIO's *Economic Outlook* described the situation in 1945, "[S]trikes are crowding all other news off the front pages. The public is being warned of all the great social cost of this and that strike. You don't see the same treatment accorded to unemployment."[19]

A 1919 strike by Boston police had so alarmed the public and lawmakers, in the opinion of some scholars, that public employees' attempts to unionize were stymied for years. Bills were introduced in Congress to limit the freedom of federal employees to organize, and in 1920 both the Republican and Democrat Parties included planks in their platforms proposing to deny the right of government employees to strike. As governor in Massachusetts at the time, Calvin Coolidge issued what likely is his most famous statement: "There is no right to strike against the public safety by anybody, anywhere, at any time." His stance propelled him to become a national hero. Beginning in the early 1940s, the growing number of strikes, an outward manifestation of newly assertive city and county workers, generated a national backlash against collective-bargaining rights for public employees.[20]

Calls to prohibit public-sector bargaining grew as public employees increased their efforts to form unions in the 1930s. Some, such as the National Institute of Municipal Law Officers, asserted that collective bargaining for public employees was illegal because public employees were not included in the National Labor Relations Act. AFSCME denounced such an interpretation, with AFSCME economist Joseph Mire pointing out that the NLRA did not legalize collective bargaining but protected workers against unfair labor practices. AFL-CIO president George Meany called the omission of public employees and agricultural workers from the NLRA "one of the most grievous acts" in the field of labor relations. "By that action," Meany asserted, "Congress trampled on the principle of equal justice under law. It relegated large numbers of free and equal human beings to a category of second-class citizenship." In 1947, strikes by public school teachers in part prompted the American Municipal Association to pass a resolution advocating legislation to prohibit public employee strikes.[21]

Yet the numbers of public employees joining unions continued to rise. An International City Managers' Association survey of personnel practices of cities with populations over ten thousand showed that in 1949, 322 cities had one or more local unions affiliated with national AFL or CIO public employees' unions. Among them were eighty-nine of the ninety-two cities with populations over one hundred thousand. Nineteen cities said their municipal employees were forbidden to unionize. AFSCME in 1946 claimed a membership of seventy-three thousand, up ten thousand from ten years earlier.[22]

Empowering Workers through Strikes

As public employees asserted their rights in larger numbers, states began enacting laws prohibiting collective action by public employees. In 1947 Wisconsin banned strikes in public utilities after the state legislature considered, but did not pass, two bills that would have made it possible to terminate city or county employees who went on strike. Public employees were jubilant when, four years later, the U.S. Supreme Court ruled the public-utilities law unconstitutional and in violation of federal labor law.[23]

Zinos saw the strike not only as a tool by which the union could leverage workplace improvements but as a means by which to empower workers. A reporter covering Milwaukee City Hall at the time described Zinos as using "his militancy . . . to always threaten these strikes . . . 'cause what he was trying to do was to get public employees off of their belief that if they knew the alderman they could call up the alderman and get a favor, or if they supported the mayor politically they'd get things done." Civil-service reforms had eradicated much favoritism in government but were powerless to address this lingering manifestation of the spoils system. "What John wanted to instill in the ranks of the municipal employees, the public employees, was the fact that they had the power through strikes and other things to enforce what they want, or to give you some equal bargaining power." But for many opponents of expanding collective bargaining to public employees, the strike was the fundamental reason for not doing so.[24]

The issue muddied the political divide. Some aldermen, such as Alfred Hass, whose positions were generally supportive of liberal legislation, opposed granting further rights to municipal employees. Referring to unemployed Milwaukeeans, Hass said, "They didn't have the nice Christmases our city employees had," and he suggested that taxpayers should be asked about pay raises. Alderman Fred Meyers, who had backed the city's efforts to expand affordable housing and was one of the rare voices on the Common Council who acknowledged that black residents faced racial discrimination when trying to rent or own a home, also opposed expanding rights for city employees. He feared a "further breaking down" of government powers into citizens groups.[25]

In the 1958 standoff between the city and AFSCME, Alderman John Budzien, who served on the Finance Committee, asked for an opinion by City Attorney Walter Mattison on the legality of municipal workers going out on strike. During the 1943 city strike wave, Mattison had said that while there was no law prohibiting public employees to strike, the word "strike" meant only the absence from work or a work stoppage, and striking public employees did not have the same rights as unions in private industry regarding collective bargaining and picketing. Mattison ruled that the city had the power to discharge employees who were "neglecting their duties [while] exercising the empty right to strike."

In 1958 Mattison revisited his original ruling and found it still valid—a determination AFSCME general counsel John Lawton blasted as one relying on semantics. While it was true there was "no compulsion in state and federal labor relations laws" that officials had to sit down and bargain with a union, neither was there specific prohibition contained in the laws against collective bargaining between governments and their employees, Lawton said, adding a barbed comment directed at Milwaukee city leaders: when governmental officials had had the "proper attitude," unions had been able to enter into collective-bargaining agreements with them.[26]

Zeidler approached municipal-employee strikes and collective-bargaining demands as he did all other issues: by putting the larger public interest above those of specific workers. His years in office had not altered his views on the role of public servants. In 1951, when garbage workers, represented by the CIO's Civic and Government Employees Union (CGEU) walked off the job, Zeidler requested Commissioner of Public Works Walter Swietlik to cease negotiations with them unless they returned to work. If they did not, Zeidler told Swietlik, in an action identical to that of Bohn in 1943, "You are further requested to invoke, where necessary, city ordinances and civil service rules and regulations which provide for dismissal of employees who do not report to their employment after three days without adequate cause."

The sanitation workers remained on the picket lines, and Swietlik then recommended three workday suspensions for all garbage collectors who were members of CGEU District 600 and District 700 and a thirty-day calendar suspension for CIO Local president Harvey Gau "for restraining garbage collectors who reported for work during work cessation." He also urged a thirty-day calendar suspension for CIO Executive Board member Harry D'Angelo "for restraining by the use of threat various garbage collectors who reported for work during the work cessation period." Zeidler approved the move, knowing that the 1944 mayoral campaign centered in large part on the attitude of each candidate toward the unionization of the city's employees.[27]

City and Suburbs Unite

When it came to public employee strikes, the city and suburbs were in rare agreement. Editorializing against the potential 1958 walkout, the *Milwaukee Times* asserted that "in our book, persons who take positions with a governmental agency have accepted, probably unwittingly, a loyalty to the public at large." In doing so, the far-right Towell family could have been speaking for Zeidler. Both agreed, as the editorial went on to say, that such "loyalty or duty is not comparable in any degree with the work done by employees in private industry." But the *Milwaukee Times* then went on to shape the discussion as one of a pecuniary relationship. "Anyone accepting a governmental job, be it mayor or street sweeper, accepts an obligation—to serve the taxpayers who are his DIRECT employers."[28]

While Zeidler, always thrift-conscious and attentive to eliminating wasteful government expenditures, would not disagree with the goal of providing city residents with the most for their money, his stance was substantively antithetical to the *Times*'s ideological formulation. Public employees who went on strike did not do so as much against *taxpayers* as against the public interest. In seeing taxpayers' concerns as making up only a part of the public interest, Zeidler rejected the growing influence of a pluralist approach to governance, that is, one that recognizes a variety of interest-based factions. For Zeidler, there was only one constituency—an undivided public.

When Zeidler asserted that Council 48's vote to authorize a strike attacked the "people's government," he underlined his fundamental understanding of government. Whether local, state, or federal, government is not an outside entity. It *is* the people. He maintained that such coherence meant public employees did not act against the interest of the people and therefore did not take action in opposition to the government. "If a government permits a right to strike," Zeidler stated, "it permits a challenge to its authority. This means that the power of government passes from the people to the leaders of the employees." The "people's government" was essential to Zeidler's conception of democracy, which he saw as based in a unified concept of citizenship, with the public simultaneously the government and the governed.[29]

During the fraught discussions with Council 48 that bitter December, Zeidler was comforted by a letter from attorney Paul Gauer, who, in supporting Zeidler's position, quoted Victor Berger as saying, "We are a labor party and as such we must support the legitimate demands of labor, but when such demands conflict with the public interest, we must be for the public." Whether Berger ever wrote or spoke those words, the quote represents the essence of Zeidler's philosophy. As Zeidler wrote to Gauer, "I was especially glad to get your quotations from Victor Berger.... A great many labor leaders have criticized me, but I do not think that there is such a thing as a right to strike against the public health and safety."[30]

Many supporters of public employee unionization at the time almost uniformly supported extending such rights only without the ability to strike. "I see no reason why municipal employees should not organize for their own improvement," stated Detroit Mayor Edward Jeffries Jr. in 1947. "On the other hand, I feel that it is a violation of our whole philosophy of government for them to exercise force through strikes. They have so many channels open to them for peaceful settlement of their problems that are not available to employees in private business."[31]

Local union leaders such as Zinos notwithstanding, national-level AFSCME leaders publicly disapproved of the use of strikes. But they also opposed making them illegal. "The outright prohibition of the right to strike by public employees is a denial of a fundamental and inherent right," AFSCME president Zander asserted, noting that to "outlaw strikes will not eliminate them."[32]

Allies of public employees who opposed strikes recognized the necessity of providing workers with an alternative. Former Milwaukee personnel director Herbert Cornell outlined this view when he cited a 1955 American Bar Association report: "Government which denies to its employees the right to strike against the people, no matter how just might be the grievances, owes to its public servants an obligation to provide working conditions and standards of management-employee relationships which would make unnecessary and unwarranted any need for such employees to resort to stoppage of public business." In short, "It is too idealistic to depend solely on a hoped-for beneficent attitude of public administrators." Similarly, Arvid Anderson with the Wisconsin Employment Relations Board, said that "those who seek absolute guarantees against strikes in the public service will find a 'Yes' answer in a police state. What can be done, what should be done, is to develop procedures which make strikes unnecessary and which provide effective means of dealing with those which occur."[33]

More concretely, many saw arbitration as an alternative to strikes. The question then became whether an arbitrator's decision should be advisory or binding, and even whether arbitration should be compulsory or voluntary. AFSCME and the union movement as a whole advocated voluntary arbitration. AFL-CIO president George Meany described compulsory arbitration as unworkable "because it is an abrogation of freedom. The crucial difference between voluntary and compulsory arbitration is the difference between freedom and its denial." But union leaders wanted the arbitrator's decision to be binding, a process ultimately opposed by all the major representatives of state, county, and municipal officials: the National League of Cities, the U.S. Conference of Mayors, the National Governors' Conference, and the National Association of County Officials.[34]

Zeidler sided with Meany in opposition to compulsory arbitration, but from his vantage as government leader. Under compulsory arbitration, Zeidler said, "the ultimate sovereign power of government rests with the arbitrator, and arbitrators will begin to introduce a kind of common law shaping the manner of controlling management-employee relations." He also entertained a more prosaic reason for opposing compulsory arbitration. As he wrote to AFSCME economist Mire in the early 1950s when faced with a potential strike by waterworks employees, "Any attempts at compulsory arbitration simply do not seem to work when the men are angry enough to leave their jobs, so that our principal task must be to keep relations at all times as harmonious as possible."[35]

But it was not only compulsory arbitration Zeidler opposed. Arbitration in general, he believed, involved the "theory as to whether the government is supreme or not." Writing to Milwaukee American Civil Liberties Union (ACLU) president Richard Humphreys in 1959, Zeidler put it this way:

> When the decisions of the government cannot stand by themselves but are subject to arbitration, then the government is no longer the government. Instead, the arbitration board becomes the government. . . . In other words, the duly elected representatives of the people are not supreme under this arrangement but can be successfully challenged by a group of people whom they employ.[36]

Teachers Lead the Way

On a separate but parallel track, teachers had long been in the forefront of expanding their workplace rights, through local and state groups as well as with the two largest national organizations, the National Education Association (NEA) and the American Federation of Teachers (AFT). While the NEA adamantly refused to be considered a union, AFT, like AFSCME, embraced collective bargaining for public employees by the 1950s. NEA opposed bargaining rights and "warned that if teachers behaved like trade unionists, they would lose all respect and status in the community." But more than that, "collective bargaining . . . fundamentally challenged the association's long-cherished concepts of professionalism . . . [I]t was anathema to the association to engage in collective bargaining because the term itself was embedded in unionism." In contrast, AFT pointed out that teachers would gain respect because "at last their salaries would be commensurate with their preparation." As a result, the NEA often had the support of administrators, who urged new employees to join the professional organization.[37]

Newly hired mathematics teacher Phil Blank was among those at the Milwaukee Area Technical College (MATC) joining the NEA at the behest of college administrators who said it would be a good career move. Blank soon felt NEA's approach to its members insulted his intelligence—during an NEA conference, a leader forced participants to sing songs about Sputnik—and he instead signed up with AFT Local 212.

"The MATC administration was very much in favor of the company union, which was the NEA at the time," Blank stated. An "eager union person" even though he was "still on the right" at the time, Blank quickly moved up the union ranks, eventually becoming Local 212 president. In the process, he also became a firm believer in collective bargaining for public employees. The chasm between NEA and AFT in Wisconsin further widened as AFT members debated whether to embrace collective bargaining in the wake of the 1959 state legislation that included teachers. Blank said AFT "really forced" the NEA into supporting bargaining because "prior to that they were absolutely against collective bargaining." The Wisconsin NEA "depicted us as blue-collar workers, carrying lunch buckets and so forth," said Blank, while it emphasized that collective bargaining led to strikes. "Of course they talked about professional sanctions . . . they realized they had to have something." NEA affiliates throughout the nation also typically declared a "professional day" when teachers would call in sick for one day, the equivalent of a strike without using the word.[38]

AFT Local 212 voted for collective bargaining at the end of the school year in 1962, timing it so "NEA wouldn't find out," said Blank, who by that time was local president. "After that, NEA brought in [Washington] D.C. staff to declare themselves a labor union." The vote followed a massive teacher strike in New York City, when twenty thousand walked out of the classrooms that April. As AFT members sought to exercise their collective-bargaining rights, MATC also faced Zinos, who sought collective-bargaining rights for the college's custodial employees. Whether MATC administrators shifted positions in the wake of teacher activism or whether they learned from the city's experience with the AFSCME leader, Zinos "came in and just requested bargaining for what is Local 587, and it was promptly granted to them," Blank said. The custodians "didn't have an election or anything else. Zinos asked for it, and they got it." Inclusion of teachers in the state's 1959 collective-bargaining bill may have come about accidentally, with conservative lawmakers who opposed collective-bargaining rights for public employees adding teachers to convince moderates to vote against it, but the exact circumstances are unclear.[39]

Who Speaks for City Employees?

Public employees' efforts to unionize were boosted with the 1955 merger of the AFL and CIO. The move sparked the eventual consolidation of the federations' public employee unions, with city and county workers uniting under AFSCME, vastly expanding its membership base and increasing its legislative muscle. Although the Wisconsin AFL and CIO branches did not merge until 1958, the CIO's Civic and Government Employees Union and the AFL's AFSCME joined forces in early 1956, with plans to sign up eighty-four hundred members in Milwaukee by 1958, an ambitious organizing drive that would have more than doubled membership. The union's aggressive organizing efforts paralleled its legislative agenda, with the Wisconsin State Federation of Labor strongly supporting AFSCME's move to reintroduce a bill in the 1957 legislative session to legalize collective bargaining.[40]

Already by 1955, fifteen cities and villages in Wisconsin had established bargaining procedures with some employee organizations. In twenty-eight cities, wage determination involved union participation on an informal basis. Most were members of AFSCME, except for firefighters, who were part of the International Association of Firefighters (IAFF). No city denied employees, with the exception of police, the right to join unions.[41]

In this increasingly favorable climate for the expansion of public-employee rights, Zinos in 1955 became AFSCME District 48 executive director. He immediately ramped up the union's pressure on the Common Council, with his main demand exclusive representation for AFSCME. Such recognition would be the first step toward achieving a collective-bargaining contract, and Zinos framed the issue as one in which city employees, a majority of whom were represented by AFSCME in fifteen departments, "deserved the dignity, rights and responsibilities of having a written contract with the city." As Stanley Joers, the union's disputes committee chairman, said to council members in similar discussions two years later, "You, in a word, say we have a right to come here and discuss the rights of the employees. If it's good enough to say, why isn't it good enough to put into writing?"[42]

The depth of passion on both sides of the issue emerged during a 1957 Finance Committee meeting when Zinos, confronted with council members hostile to exclusive representation, stormed out amid heckling and threatened to take garbage workers out on strike. Describing the environment as anarchy, the Wisconsin CIO faulted the disorderly hearing on "city fathers who have let nature take its course." Ultimately, Zinos and council president Martin Schreiber, who replaced McGuire when he left office to run for mayor, agreed to press for a labor advisory committee, with Schreiber remaining a firm champion of city workers throughout.[43]

Although District Council 48 did not win exclusive representation that year, two key cities did, adding further momentum to AFSCME's efforts in Milwaukee. AFSCME Council 33 achieved exclusive recognition for Philadelphia city employees and in 1958 went on to become the first to achieve collective bargaining rights. The contract covered eighteen thousand municipal employees, eleven thousand of whom were union members, and prohibited strikes and work stoppages. Cincinnati in 1957 also gave AFSCME exclusive recognition.[44]

In pushing for exclusive recognition, Zinos ran into opposition not only from city leaders but also from unions and associations independent of the

AFL and the CIO. While other unions did not question the right of collective bargaining for public employees, they did oppose AFSCME as the sole bargaining agent. First, there was the matter of the other public employee organizations that preceded AFSCME as representatives of city employees and who still represented a sizable number of members. Among them, the City and County Public Service Employees, which had more than once been left out of discussions with council members and city hall officials who gravitated toward the larger CIO and AFL organizations. When Zinos in 1956 first proposed exclusive bargaining rights for AFSCME, Robert Gunnis, counsel for the City and County Union, pointed out that fewer than 50 percent of city employees belonged to any organized group and said Zinos was "attempting to preempt the right to speak for all labor organizations." Gunnis understood that under an exclusive contract, Zinos would be the sole bargaining agent for most city employees.[45]

The far larger Milwaukee Government Service League had been an active champion for public employees. Founded in 1935, the league by the following year represented sixty-four hundred dues-paying members in every branch of municipal government, including the fire department, where all eligible members joined. Early on, the league fought off a proposed tax measure that would have limited public services and sought, through radio appearances, news releases, and a speakers' bureau, to resist attacks on government while "improving community appreciation of the workings of the municipal corporation." Seeing itself as fitting in squarely within the civil service system, the league worked to extend retirement provisions and secure other improvements for public employees outside a collective-bargaining process.[46]

When AFSCME brought up the issue of exclusive bargaining rights in 1958, it upped the ante by submitting for passage a prepared resolution to the Common Council. The resolution declared that the city recognized unions as proper agents in wages, hours, and working conditions and that unions and their representatives would be granted "official recognition" as long as they represented a majority of employees in a department or division. It also made an official "finding" that AFSCME District Council 48 represented the employees in the Department of Public Works, the Health Department, the Tax Assessor's office, the library, and the museum, except for those groups represented by the building-trades crafts unions and the Brotherhood of Firemen and Oilers Local 125-B.

The Government Service League countered with a substitute resolution, which it described as recognizing all unions and employee groups and which it said "does not favor any particular union of employee groups." The league's resolution asserted that "city employees may choose to belong to unions or other employee groups or refrain from such affiliation" and offered protection for employees not members of unions or other employee groups so that they might receive all rules and regulations regarding such issues as wages so as to represent themselves. The league told the council that adoption of AFSCME's resolution would mean "complete capitulation" by the city to bargain exclusively with a union. But the league, whose membership numbers had remained between five thousand and six thousand into the 1950s, would back the resolution if its additional language proposal was included.[47]

AFSCME's decision to carve out building-trades members from the exclusive recognition proposal followed a bitter internal battle between it and the building trades, one that reached the Common Council in 1956 when John Zancanaro, president of the Building and Construction Trades, told the aldermen his organization was "utterly opposed" to granting exclusive bargaining rights, arguing that such a contract would infringe upon the jurisdiction of craft and other unions and "would cause no end of trouble." Unlike other union members, those such as bricklayers and carpenters who belonged to skilled trades unions bargained through the well-established prevailing-wage system and had no impetus for abandoning it for a still-undetermined process.[48]

The relationship between the two entities had been contentious since AFSCME's founding, with the building trades objecting to AFSCME's request to be chartered as a union within the AFL, which then delayed AFSCME's charter, making it first a "department" within the federation before granting it full membership. AFSCME also appeased the AFL's Firemen and Oilers Local 125-B by excluding the union from the resolution. The two unions in the past had sparred over the representation of sanitation workers, whom Zinos had accused Local 125-B of "stealing" from AFSCME in violation of the AFL-CIO's prohibition against raiding. But the Firefighters union, which had been a member of the AFL since 1918 and which had organized members in Milwaukee a year later, came out publicly against AFSCME's resolution, saying if any organization should be given sole recognition, it should be the IAFF if its union members were the majority in any department.[49]

After discussions with AFSCME, the Common Council in February 1959 passed a resolution substantially similar to the one Zinos proposed, but Zeidler held off signing it until he received a determination from the city attorney on whether it excluded other employee organizations in its recognition language. After Deputy City Attorney Harry Slater ruled that the term "labor organization" in the final resolution did not exclude other unions, Zeidler signed the bill into law, satisfied that it was "amply broad enough to cover all of the rights of employees to present their petition through the Common Council."[50]

When District Council 48 had gone on strike in 1957 over exclusive representation, Zeidler told Zinos he "would not be party to such a situation" since "many of the other unions were formed long before District 48." In a rhetorical question, Zeidler asked, "Who is more democratic—a government which permits its employees to join any association the employee desires, or a union which says that an employee can only join one association?" Arriving at a formula for representation was among the most difficult questions surrounding public-employee relations, he believed, because "a very basic question concerns the right of the individual employee not to join an employee organization but still be heard in the process of wage setting when there is exclusive union representation." Exclusive representation would "abridge the right of free speech of an individual or group of citizens before local government." Here, Zeidler's argument melded with that of conservative opponents of labor for whom individual rights could not co-exist within the collective process inherent in unionization. Yet Zeidler's otherwise strong support for unions set him apart from conventional definitions of conservative and liberal. Efforts by public employees to have a say at their workplaces challenged traditional notions of public service, worker rights, public interest, and the role of government.[51]

Special Treatment for Public Employees?

The substantive debate over public employee bargaining rights evolved around several key areas: the role of the civil service, the employer-employee relationship in the private and public sectors, and the concept of sovereignty.

The civil service system offered opponents of extending collective bargaining to public employees the easiest argument. In holding up the civil service system as a well-functioning structure that over the years had eliminated the spoils system, they argued it gave public workers recourse to a merit-based process not provided to private-sector employees. Countering that argument, Cornell, who as former city personnel director for Milwaukee had a hands-on perspective of the civil-service system, pointed out the system's limited scope. Most civil-service laws related primarily, if not exclusively, "to the manner of appointment, promotion, discharge and change in status," and so it was a "fallacy to assume that the usual so-called 'merit system' laws governing the civil services are so comprehensive that employees have no proper basis for complaint as to their working conditions or that their grievances are all superficial." Rather, "laws governing employee relationships are usually less flexible in the public service than is generally the rule in private employment."[52]

As AFSCME economist Mire noted, "even under civil service rules and regulations, arbitrary and discriminatory dismissals, fines, suspensions without pay or disciplinary transfers and promotions are by no means exceptional." Further, the assumption that all public employees were covered by civil service was erroneous. In 1947 fewer than half of all public employees were covered by civil service and retirement plans. A city such as St. Louis, with seventy-five hundred employees on its payroll, had no retirement system, and employees had no recourse to Social Security because, like all public employees, they were excluded from the federal act. As a result, the city in August 1945 had on its payroll 144 employees between the ages of 75 and 90.[53]

Although Zeidler did not argue outright that the civil-service system was a sufficient stand-in for unionization, he strongly supported the process because it furthered clean government, the hallmark of Milwaukee's "sewer socialism." He also felt a kinship with the origins of civil service. In a speech to the National Civil Service Assembly, Zeidler also noted with pride that fellow German Carl Schurz, the "father of civil service," was among the "Forty-eighters" who came to Milwaukee. Schurz's efforts helped create a Civil Service Commission in 1871. In 1883, Congress passed the Pendleton Act, setting up the first Civil Service Commission.[54]

A corollary argument to the sufficiency of civil-service protection, and one more popularly citied, was the view that public workers knowingly made some employment sacrifices in return for greater benefits and job security. Or, as Allan Weisenfeld, the secretary of the New Jersey State Board of Mediation handily summarized it, "The popular shibboleths associated with public employment were . . . few hours, excellent working conditions and damn little work."[55]

Collective-bargaining proponents argued that job security for public employees was a myth, one based on a Depression-era view in which regular employment of any kind was a desirable and envied status. Harry Rains, professor of industrial relations at Hofstra College in 1957, argued that, given the clearly obsolete nature of such a formulation, it is "no longer a rational justification for retarded wage scales and other terms and conditions of employment."[56]

Further, as proponents charged, the assumption that in return for inferior pay, public employees have greater security had been disproved by the experience of federal civil-service employees who, although termed "permanent," found themselves summarily out of jobs after their departments were defunded. John Kenneth Galbraith found that the advantage of job security for public employees compared with private-sector workers had diminished because of economic security in general. In short, said Weisenfeld, public employees' salaries had not kept up with the general movement of wages, their once-superior benefits had been attained or exceeded by those in the private sector, and the security that "was supposed to be the *sine qua non* of public employment was a snare and a delusion."[57]

Opponents of public-employee bargaining also asserted a qualitative difference existed between private and public employers. The argument centered on the government as a not-for-profit employer and so theoretically not subject to private greed or competitive market forces. Mire would have none of it. Describing local governments as operating on a "master-servant" relationship, the economist blasted the notion that the government was immune to exploitation of its employees.

"Conditions of pay and work in some public institutions are disgraceful. . . . In some areas, they are paid less than the minimum which their own Department of Welfare allows for needy families." Further, collective-bargaining proponents noted that "the pressure of powerful groups to reduce taxes and government expenditures furnishes as effective an impetus as do considerations of profit to the resistance of employee demands for higher wages and improved working conditions." Whether in the executive or legislative branch, elected officials "are acutely aware that tax increases, induced by unmanaged increases in labor costs, are fatal to their continuing survival," wrote Jesse Simons, director of the American Arbitration Association's Labor Management Institute.[58]

"The electorate, on whose judgment the survival of an office holder is dependent, zealously protects its pocketbook, peers vigilantly at budget and tax policy, holds accountable the executive or legislative representatives and blithely tosses them out of office, in marked contrast to the cautious and restrained actions of stockholders and boards of directors." Far more than private-sector managers, Simons argued, "the public official is subject to continuous scrutiny, accountability and recall, compared to which the corporate manager's life is an idyllic sanctuary." Others pointed out that the role of powerful pressure groups exerts "an impact similar to that which is produced by the operation of the profit motive in private industry."[59]

Here, the conception of worker empowerment as necessary only within a capitalistic private-sector context also shaped the view of left and liberal scholars who for many years omitted the struggles of public-sector workers from their examinations of labor. By approaching labor history from a "neo-Marxist conception of class," writes historian Joseph Slater, scholars from the 1960s to the 1980s emphasized relationships and conflicts created by the capitalist mode of production, that is, class as involving battles against capitalism and employers, rather than class as "the power and authority people have at work."[60]

Zeidler subscribed to the concept that a fundamental difference between union bargaining in the private sector and the public sector precluded public employees from gaining bargaining rights. "City government is unlike private management," he stated. "Private management bargains with its own funds. The city government bargains with the funds of others. If private management feels that too hard a bargain has been driven against it, it can fold up. The city government has no such alternative; it must carry on its functions and place the burdens on the citizens whether they can afford it or not."[61]

Zeidler viewed public-sector collective bargaining as creating two sides, and it was precisely this duality he opposed. He saw the strike as essential for any collective-bargaining arrangement and, as such, perceived the threat of a walkout as placing the union on a stronger footing than government. "In private industry, there is equality between unions and management in bargaining, for the unions' strongest weapon is the strike; the company's is the lockout," Zeidler asserted. "In government, however, the government cannot lock out the employees; in fact, the employees are already protected by civil service from discharge. Thus in a contract, the employees have a double advantage against the employers."[62]

Collective bargaining, with its essential strike component, meant "the union permits no similar challenge to its own authority, such as that it seeks from the government." When AFSCME's collective-bargaining bill came up for a vote, Zeidler made it clear in conversations with city hall reporters that he opposed collective bargaining for municipal workers. Or, as Zeidler put it bluntly in notes he compiled in 1958, "The existence of a union contract is prima facie evidence that the employer is an enemy and exploiter who cannot be trusted not to take advantage of the employee. The existence of continuous warfare between the union and the government is thus assured."[63]

The concept of sovereignty formed the philosophical core of the discussion surrounding collective-bargaining rights for public employees. The notion of sovereign authority involves the idea that "there must reside somewhere in the body politic an ultimate and final source of legal authority." The question then becomes "whether the possession of sovereign power by the state inherently precludes the possibility of collective bargaining between the state and its employees."[64]

Zeidler believed strongly that it did. As the sovereign authority, the government was not exercising power for its own sake but as the embodiment of the people. Collective bargaining would split government in two halves, one made up of traditional decision makers such as city council members and the mayor, and the other "chamber" composed of unionized public employees who have gained official recognition to negotiate. "The public business on wages and conditions of work, and therefore indirectly on policy, cannot be carried on without mutual agreement between these two chambers, much as the laws of Congress require the approval of both houses," he stated.[65]

Zeidler never questioned the need for public employees to be represented by unions. But the issue of collective-bargaining rights chafed against his conception of a government united with its residents in achieving the common good. Collective bargaining would cut apart that sacred unity. Strikes and arbitration were implicit in the collective-bargaining process, both of which took away from the government its ability to act in a paramount role as essence of the public. "The primary concern in employee-management relations in the public service is not that of the employee or of the public manager, but of the public," he stated. "The philosophy of employee relations must be based on the concern for the total public and the public good."[66]

Many typically wielded the sovereign state argument within a context that equated sovereignty with power, a construction antithetical to Zeidler. The vehemently anti-union lawyer Sylvester Petro lamented that state and local government, "already nearly incapacitated," would "become completely so if they had to yield their sovereign powers to public-employee unions." As Mire countered, "The idea that government has absolute powers and rights which must not be questioned is an absolutist doctrine which has no place in a democratic society."[67]

Others began from the same premise as Zeidler but reached a very different conclusion—one in which government had a duty as a sovereign state to assure its citizens the most liberal application of their rights. The secretary of the New Jersey State Board of Mediation asserted that the distinguishing characteristic of government should be its imperative not only to uphold constitutional principles but also to exceed them. "The public employee should have a voice respecting the conditions under which he works perhaps even to a greater degree than that enjoyed by his private counterpart, exactly because he is employed in the public service." Addressing fears that collective bargaining constituted a delegation of power incompatible with the concept of sovereign government, AFSCME president Zander said, "The question is not one of surrendering sovereignty: The problem does not involve giving up something which the government has but rather is to create something which we have not had but which we imperatively need in employer-employee relations in government."[68]

Zeidler: Public Interest or City Interest?

Zeidler's simultaneous support for the rights of working people and opposition to collective bargaining for public employees chafes against clear-cut liberal and conservative stereotypes. Superficially, such a stance resembles the arguments of economic conservatives seeking to limit the role of the public sector. Zeidler's record and history clearly indicate the opposite. But ironically, it was his strong belief in government as the instrument to achieve the greatest public good that, in his mind, necessitated that public-sector employees remain unified with the government that employed them. The collective bargaining process, he felt, would create a separate entity apart from the government and therefore from the public. His concept of government as inseparable from the people set it apart from midcentury conservative views of government as "other," a variation of classical liberalism in which the threat of an ever-expanding state made it a perpetual enemy.[69]

Zeidler's consciously developed philosophy of government and long-held views of public service made his stance qualitatively different from liberal employers whose support for collective bargaining expediently stopped at their doorstep. His concept of government service, formulated through the lens of socialist tenets, was an ongoing presence whose characteristics did not waver throughout his twelve years in office, even though his stance risked alienating the city's union movement, his largest base of political support. Yet in championing government sovereignty Zeidler did not embrace the more expansive notion of government setting the example by extending to public employees more rights than would be accorded in the private sector.

Writing in the 1960s, scholar W. B. Cunningham began from much the same premise as Zeidler but reached a very different conclusion—one in which government had a duty as a sovereign state to assure its citizens the most liberal application of their rights. The state "is all-important as a necessary condition for the achievement of the highest individual aspirations," Cunningham wrote. "It is surely this responsibility of the state that justifies its possession of sovereign power." Thus, the state as an employer "differs from all other employers not only because it possesses sovereign powers but also and more importantly, because it has different responsibilities." Yet Cunningham went on to describe those responsibilities as markedly different from those Zeidler envisioned. "In the democratic tradition the individual, not the state, is all important."[70]

Central to Zeidler's concept of government and underlying his stance on public-sector bargaining was his belief that interest-group politics were inimical to public service. This view in part was built on the tradition of

Milwaukee socialism which, while it "depended on the working class and the trade unions for political support at election time," did not allow any "section of the labor movement or the working class" to take precedence over city administration. Thus in rejecting a pluralist interpretation of public interest within the context of public-employee bargaining, Zeidler repudiated the argument that "the objectives of the state express values of no higher normative order than those embodied in other associations."[71]

He also saw AFSCME's attempts to secure through state legislation what it could not achieve when bargaining with city officials as proving the peril of public employees setting themselves apart as an interest group. In his role as a labor-relations consultant years after he left office, Zeidler warned government managers that such efforts were among the most pernicious actions of public-employee unions. There also likely was a sense of personal pride at stake. As a representative of liberal governance, he felt he would look out for the welfare of its workers without a third party involved.[72]

Zeidler had little patience with those who argued against a single public interest.

> The concept of "the public" is sometimes attacked by theoreticians for special interests, public employees, or other interests. The argument goes that there is no such thing as "the public"—only many "publics" each with its special set of interests. Under this argument, it is advanced that public employees are also a "public" who have higher claims against other "publics."

Such a view, Zeidler believed, contradicted the essence of democracy. "This argument is a fundamental assault on the democratic process by attacking the notion that there is or can be a total community of interest as against special interests. It is the democratic process which through its parliaments seeks to find this total community interest for the people as against special group interests." While seeing the concept as nearly synonymous with the common good, Zeidler also believed it to be the bedrock of governance. "I have always felt that if you lose the concept that there is such a thing as an overriding public interest, then you lose everything."[73]

Yet by the 1950s the notion of a unified public interest was receding, in large part because interest-group politics, which emerged as an influential force during the New Deal years, facilitated a pluralistic interpretation of American society, replacing the image of a coherent nation greater than the sum of its parts. A highly diverse public made up of ever-shifting individual and group interests spurned a unitary definition. And if the public interest was made up of the interests of many publics, democratic politics "must seek to reconcile them in all their diversity."[74]

A Perversion of the Public Spirit

The increasing number of public-sector workers fueled conservative fears of an expanding government. As early as 1954, Zeidler was discussing with concern "the attacks being made on governmental services and career public administration people," with an eye to determining what could be done to foster good public administration. As one scholar has speculated, the prestige of being a public employee declined "because of the perversion of public spirit." The principles of U.S. Lockean individualism, "without public spirit, are not sufficient." Public spirit is "discouraged by the traditional liberal emphasis on individual interest as the legitimate basis for creation of the state," a mantle picked up by the midcentury conservative movement. "Solving the problem of public unions depends upon rediscovering public spirit in liberal society; and that rediscovery must ultimately depend on the esteem in which the government is held by its citizens."[75]

Opposition to the rising number of public employees went hand in hand with a rejection of the expanding public sector. Even before the decade ended, Galbraith recognized that a key feature of the postwar years "was a remarkable attack on the notion of expanding and improving public services." In creating a "certain mystique" around the satisfaction of privately supplied demands, "all private wants, where the individual can choose, are inherently superior to all public desires which must be paid for by taxation and with an inevitable component of compulsion. . . . Public services, by comparison, are an incubus."[76]

Public-sector organizing bolstered union membership at a time when it had begun its inexorable decline in the private sector. Already between 1956 and 1961 the union movement lost more than 1 million members in the private sector. After President John Kennedy's 1962 Executive Order, which expanded a degree of collective-bargaining rights to public employees, union membership temporarily stabilized. Between 1956 and 1962 the number of public-employee union members increased by 33 percent, from 915,000 to 1.2 million.[77]

While it took decades more before public employees were awash in the opprobrium generated by conservative attacks on government, labor's ultimate failure to enact a "Wagner Act for public employees" found its roots in the anti-government foundation laid in the immediate postwar years. Historian Joseph McCartin found that public-sector unions in the 1970s were unable "to ignite a broad and enduring labor movement revival" like that after the rise of the CIO because of the ascendancy of anti-government conservatism.[78]

Zeidler was convinced that the way to change public opinion about government employees was to ensure the best possible service for taxpayers—but the day-to-day actions must be placed within a broader understanding of the public servant's larger mission. "The administrator—as well as man on the assembly line—must be interested not only in the work that immediately surrounds him and in his immediate objectives. He must also be concerned with the end uses to which his work is put."[79]

New municipal employees reading through the city's employee guide to orient them to their new jobs encountered a letter from the municipal personnel director who undoubtedly reflected Zeidler's views when he wrote, "The city expects enthusiasm and loyalty as well as a fair day's work from its employees.... [G]overnment is not an end in itself but that it exists to carry on services for its citizens."[80]

Zeidler believed public service made it a calling unique in the modern world, one that was a privilege and an honor to undertake. In putting the onus on the public servant to live up to a lofty ideal, he had faith that those they served would then raise their esteem of government.

> Public service must lead to the ennoblement and enrichment of the cultural heritage of mankind in the struggle against ignorance, squalor, want, disease and death. Where the public servant has this ideal, or the civil service body itself instills this ideal, public service will become a pleasure and a rewarding experience in a sense greater than a monetary sense. If this ideal is not attained, public service can become brutal and oppressive and wicked.[81]

Zeidler's emphasis on quality service paralleled his focus on making the public interest foremost in municipal governance. But his stance on extending collective bargaining to public employees also foreshadowed that of many urban officials who, in the ensuing years, resisted bargaining rights for teachers and other municipal employees, opposition countered by massive public-employee strikes that contributed to the upheavals of the 1960s. Attempts to maintain the status quo among public employees, as among people of color, ultimately failed in Milwaukee as elsewhere, but not without unnecessary trauma that contributed to divisions in the electorate and further shredded the nation's common purpose.

Conclusion

Milwaukee and Post-Liberal America

> It is about having a seat at the table in a system that is stacked against working people.
> —Jill Hopke, University of Wisconsin teaching assistant, 2012

On February 11, 2011, Wisconsin governor Scott Walker announced a proposed "budget repair bill," the goal of which was effectively to end collective bargaining for public employees at all levels of government throughout the state. In the ensuing weeks, hundreds of thousands of protestors defied the cold and snow to turn out for an ongoing series of rallies, packing the capitol building in Madison with mass sit-ins and garnering nationwide attention as the country watched to see if the first state to pass bargaining for public employees would now rescind the law.

The protests continued as the state's Finance Committee held hearings, where University of Wisconsin doctoral student and teaching assistant Jill Hopke was among public employees testifying against the bill. "I followed teachers and nurses pleading with the committee about the negative impacts the bill would have on this state and their livelihoods. Because state workers are taxpayers. I spoke about how my parents are teachers, about how proud I am to have been one, too. I thought that if enough of us spoke up they would listen."[1]

Democratic state lawmakers refused to return to the capitol for days, to forestall the quorum needed for a vote, and the tenacity of the protestors captured the imagination of people from across the country and from places as removed as Egypt, who faxed in orders to Madison-area pizzerias for deliveries to those encamped on the capitol grounds. Yet within weeks, the Wisconsin State Legislature voted in support of the governor's bill, and Wisconsin Act 10 went into effect June 29, 2011. Court challenges to the law failed, as did an effort in 2012 to recall Walker, who handily sidestepped the maneuver, retaining his office and, in the process, positioning himself as a potential contender for president.

To Hopke, the fight was about "the fundamental right to have a voice in determining our working conditions and the legal protections that come with union representation. It is about having a seat at the table in a system that is stacked against working people."[2]

Once again the trendsetter, Wisconsin offered state officials elsewhere an example to follow, this time with "history repeating itself, if in reverse."[3]

History in Reverse

The seemingly lightning-quick repeal of collective bargaining rights in Wisconsin stunned many commentators who pointed to the state's precedent-setting adoption of public-employee rights and long history of progressive politics. But the seeds had been planted decades before. In cities like Milwaukee, where Walker served as county executive for eight years, the postwar re-emergence of economic conservatism had laid the groundwork for actions unthinkable in an era shaped by notions forged during the New Deal.

In midcentury cities such as Milwaukee, which boasted both a strong labor movement and a liberal municipal government, continuation of the New Deal order had seemed a safe bet. The pugnacity of Milwaukee private- and public-sector workers in demanding a say at their workplaces, the overall acceptance of the social welfare state, and the repeated election of a liberal mayor who identified with socialism—this broader social and political environment easily obscured the undercurrents of conservative reaction simmering beneath the surface. The grassroots conservative movement was especially easy to underestimate in Milwaukee, where superficial impressions of socialist political dominance have detracted from an examination of the larger issues in play, especially postwar urban dilemmas and how those issues related to the nation's unfolding urban crisis.

Walker's career trajectory is illuminating. Failing in his attempt to win a seat on the State Assembly in a heavily Democratic Milwaukee district in his first run for public office, he moved to Wauwatosa when an assembly seat opened in the predominantly Republican suburb. There, he easily was elected state representative. The suburb that in the 1950s had emerged as the one of the staunchest opponents of achieving the greatest common good through broad-based public services provided the springboard for the launch of a governor whose bold action struck at the heart of employee rights and expansive government.[4]

Suburban conservatism did not emerge full blown in the upheaval of the 1960s but had its roots in the strong opposition to New Deal liberalism that resurfaced at the end of World War II, with its attacks on labor rights, affordable housing, and other public-sector initiatives. The decades-old formal and informal restrictions preventing African Americans and low-income residents from moving to suburbs such as Wauwatosa, and the suburbs' aggressive opposition to merging with the urban center in the 1950s, effectively consigned those with the fewest resources to the urban core. Unable to draw from the more abundant suburban tax base, Milwaukee struggled financially as did most U.S. cities in the latter half of the twentieth century.

With the city's dwindling tax base, the city in the 1960s turned to the federal government. Mayor Henry Maier, elected in 1960 after Zeidler left office, was instrumental in promoting the establishment of the federal revenue-sharing program, which brought much-needed financial support to Milwaukee and other cities in the 1960s. Maier, who became nationally known as president of both the United States Conference of Mayors and the National League of Cities, governed Milwaukee longer than any mayor. He used his twenty-eight years in office to amass political control over planning, housing, redevelopment, and the city budget, taking over appointments of boards and agencies. Maier, whose consolidation of power in the mayor's office was the antithesis of Zeidler's governing philosophy, moved quickly to reverse Milwaukee's longstanding strong-council–weak-mayor form of government. "He expected elected officials to be his vassals," observed one city lawmaker.[5]

Under Maier, the hard-edged divisiveness over race that materialized in the mid-1950s intensified, emerging most potently in the struggle by African Americans for fair housing. After the Common Council time and again voted nearly unanimously against fair housing bills introduced by Vel Phillips in the early 1960s—legislation that mirrored state law—civil rights leaders took to the streets in a series of high-profile marches in 1967. Led in part by a white Catholic priest, Father James Groppi, interracial groups of protestors pointedly marched from the north to the south side of Milwaukee, and over the city line to Wauwatosa, where white homeowners in both areas verbally and physically attacked the groups, which included priests and seminarians wearing white collars.

On the night of July 30, 1967, rioting broke out along the city's North Side. Maier responded by putting the city under a curfew, declared a state of emergency, and asked for help from the National Guard. Years later, Maier stated bluntly, "I would have forgiven Wisconsin Senator Joe McCarthy, whom I despised, as soon as forgiven Groppi."[6]

Maier, whose 1960 campaign against Democrat Henry Reuss turned in part on inferences that Reuss was "soft" on African Americans, shelved the 1960 report on the inner city when he took office, put a two-year freeze on public housing construction to "review" the situation, and warned his community-relations commission to go slow on civil rights, effectively ending the drive to rebuild the inner core. The housing plight of African American and low-income families was further heightened when the federally funded highway project that brought a knot of interconnected freeways into the heart of downtown in the early 1960s displaced some six thousand residents who were left with no recourse to housing assistance.[7]

Yet Maier was playing a politically winning hand. As a result of his response to the 1967 uprisings, his popularity soared. In the 1968 general elections, he received 86 percent of the vote, a mandate he saw as vindicating his hardline stance against civil rights and one that enabled him to push through fundamental changes in municipal governance. While electorally popular, his policies indelibly rent the city apart.[8]

By 2002 the situation had deteriorated to such an extent that a study cited racial disparities in Milwaukee as the worst in the nation. A *Los Angeles Times* report ticked off the list of inequities: black Milwaukeeans earned 49 cents for every dollar white workers earned, compared with 64 cents to the dollar nationwide. Some 44 percent of city's African American children lived in families with incomes below the poverty line, compared with 10 percent of white children. Middle-income African Americans were denied home loans three times as often as middle-income whites, and only 41 percent of black students finished high school—the lowest rate in the country.[9]

With African Americans making up only 1.6 percent of the suburban population at the start of the new millennium, the suburbs' efforts to prevent African Americans from taking up residence outside the city were more successful than just about anywhere else in the nation. As late as 1990, a study found that eleven suburbs participating in a $2 million Community Block Grant Development program were violating agreements in which they were required to take steps to promote fair housing. When Milwaukee offered to spend more than $2.17 million to buy fifty housing units for low-income families, with twenty-five located in suburbs to help address the disparity, only Shorewood agreed to take part.

As Zeidler left office in 1960, the number of Milwaukeeans reached its all-time high: more than seven hundred thousand residents. By 2010, the population stood at 594,832, a 15 percent drop. Shut out of the suburbs and trapped in the high-density urban core, African Americans increased in number even as the city's overall population declined. By 2010, African Americans represented nearly half of all Milwaukeeans.[10]

Suburban conservatism in the 1950s created the framework for Milwaukee's racial disparity, which a conservative Democratic mayor perpetuated in later decades, even after he was securely in office and had the leeway to act in the face of white voter resistance. The city's established black middle class, which had been satisfied with modest steps toward change, was replaced by younger and economically more marginal community members who took to the streets for immediate redress.

The opportunity existed in the 1950s to address festering civil-rights disparities before tensions erupted and positions hardened. Milwaukee's solid African American middle class had presented a potentially strong base of support that city officials could have more substantively tapped. This was especially the case in the early to middle part of the decade, before the increasing numbers of low-income black residents escalated the crisis over long-standing barriers to housing, jobs, and education. While robustly championing equality and deeply supportive of the rights of African Americans as citizens, Zeidler's response to the simmering discontent among the city's growing black community did not qualitatively address the issues of discrimination Milwaukee's African Americans faced.

The refusal of the Common Council to support fair housing signaled that deep changes likely could not have been made during Zeidler's terms in office. Yet in resting on solutions that depended on voluntary cooperation by the private sector to open doors to black residents, Zeidler provided no bold municipal vision. Without city leadership championing legislative redress, Common Council members could more easily reject out of hand any moves to expand civil rights. The inner-core report, with its emphasis on goodwill and voluntarism, reflected Zeidler's views as well as the opinions of the dozens of city residents, including African American clergy and civic leaders. Its conclusions signaled that if Zeidler was not ready to push for concrete measures, neither were even the most liberal segments of Milwaukee's urban base. Zeidler's shortcoming, then, was that of reflecting liberal Milwaukeeans all too well and failing to establish a dialogue about how African Americans could be brought into the mainstream.

The Post-Union World

José Gonzalez Davila, known by his co-workers as "José Union," was the first worker to publicly challenge management's treatment of workers at the Milwaukee-based Palermo's Pizza, and he quickly gained the trust of his Latino and Burmese co-workers. In 2013 he was also the first employee fired for trying to form a union. Before he was fired, Gonzalez was dogged by management, reprimanded if he was even one minute late from his break, and unfairly blamed for machinery that would break down on the production line, where frozen pizzas were packaged.

Workers at Palermo's first went on strike in June 2012, after several had experienced such serious job-related injuries as severed fingers. The company fiercely resisted negotiating with workers, who stayed on strike for more than a year. Organizing in part with the local Voces de la Frontera community group, the workers received substantial backing from the AFL-CIO, which sent staff to Milwaukee, supported a cross-country "Truth Tour" with Palermo's workers to build public support, and endorsed a nationwide boycott of Palermo's products. The online mobilization group, MoveOn.org, joined the campaign, sending e-mails to millions of members and asking them to sign support petitions. The company responded by firing nearly one hundred workers, most because they failed the company's "immigration audit."[11]

The NLRB ruled that nine workers, including Gonzalez, were illegally fired; the board directed Palermo's to provide back pay but found that the company did not use the immigration audit to retaliate for efforts to unionize the plant. In settling with the NLRB in late 2013, Palermo's agreed to allow a vote for the union. But workers contend the company continues to interfere with their efforts to unionize, and they remain without a union.[12]

The inability of two hundred workers to quickly form a union in a historically labor-friendly Midwest city and the sacrifices they made in trying to do so, even with the intervention and resources of national organizations and significant public support, illustrates the extent to which opponents of collectively expanded economic opportunity have come to prevail. Palermo's employees—immigrant and nonwhite, employed in the low-paid food-services sector—represent Milwaukee's, and the nation's, changing workforce and the city's evolution away from heavy industry. But unlike the blue-collar German and Polish laborers who preceded them, their opportunities for attaining the middle class in an environment hostile to unions are far more limited.

The Latino and Burmese pizza workers are struggling to support themselves and their families in a climate constructed over the decades by those who, like William Grede, saw the broadening of employee rights as a challenge to the essence of democratic freedoms, on a par with the expansion of government involvement in crafting the collective good. In successfully shifting the normative socioeconomic culture away from the broader sense of public good engendered by the New Deal, economic conservatives cultivated an atmosphere in which even workers' challenges to an employer who disregards fundamental safety practices are not guaranteed to succeed.

The plummeting numbers of union members in Milwaukee in the decades since the 1950s reflect a nationwide trend. By 2013, union membership in the Milwaukee-Racine-Waukesha area stood at 14.2 percent and the national rate at 11.3 percent. Following passage of Act 10, no public employee union was hit harder than the one representing Milwaukee city and county workers. In 2010, the year Walker was elected governor, AFSCME Council 48 represented more than nine thousand workers. By the end of 2012, membership dropped to fewer than thirty-five hundred workers, a loss of nearly two-thirds of the union's members. With no legal right to collectively bargain, the union has little to offer in return for monthly dues.[13]

Like the civil rights movement, the effort by public employees to gain collective-bargaining rights emerged in the 1950s after decades of groundwork. Yet as historian Joseph McCartin points out, "The labor question in general and the public-sector labor question in particular played a much more important role in the rise of the conservative revolution than the recent studies—which have emphasized race, religion, and social geography—have indicated." By not recognizing that the ascent of conservatism was indelibly tied to workers' challenge to management's authority, scholars have missed the extent to which the conservative movement has been fueled by perceived threats to its economic prerogative.[14]

While the nation's union movement notably contributed to its declining membership—through a "servicing" orientation that focused on gains for current members at the expense of organizing among new and growing sectors of the economy; top-heavy bureaucracies that often were out of touch with the workers they represented; and the slow recognition of women, people of color, and immigrants as central to the late-twentieth-century U.S. workforce—unions increasingly operated in a legislative and economic climate hostile to the interests of workers and those on the economic margins.

With fewer union members and diminished financial resources, Milwaukee unions, like their counterparts across the country, cut back on the number and frequency of labor publications, even as the consolidation of mainstream media accelerated. The 1995 merger of the *Milwaukee Journal* and the *Milwaukee Sentinel*, the continued vibrancy of conservative suburban weeklies, the spread of conservative talk radio, and the launch of the unabashedly conservative Fox News television network further limited working people's exposure to views supporting economic liberalism.

The turn away from a belief in a national consensus toward rights-based politics spawned in the public mind increasing suspicion of the labor movement. While Gilded Age barons and later corporate capitalists had never looked upon workers and their unions with favor, the shift in public attitude that began in the 1950s marked an irreversible move away from the long-held perception that labor represented all wage-earning Americans, not just a slice of the working and middle class. A perception of unions as special interests also helped pave the way for labor's demonization by advocates of free enterprise, who saw no room for compromise with workers as part of that vision.

The conservative movement, less recognized than the modern civil rights movement, had been a force since the closing years of World War II, and, after 1954, union membership began its inexorable decline from its peak, when nearly 35 percent of U.S. workers were union members.[15]

A Transitional Period for the Nation

When Zeidler decided not to run for re-election in 1960, he attributed the verbal assaults on him and threats to his family as among the reasons behind his decision. Less known is that Zeidler suffered from a physical illness at the time. And there was another key reason he did not run, according to Zeidler's daughter Anita, a lifelong Milwaukee resident: "He did believe, too, that in a democracy, that you shouldn't think that you are anointed to stay there forever." One factor that was not behind his decision to leave office was a fear of not being re-elected. Zeidler believed he could have been re-elected in 1960.[16]

Zeidler's annual $20,000 salary at the end of his three terms did not reflect a $2,400 annual midterm pay increase the Common Council approved in the early 1950s. He rejected the raise because he believed politicians should not benefit personally from decisions made during their terms. Similarly, although he approved a pension for city employees, he refused to take it for himself, a decision that meant he had no retirement income from his years as mayor.[17]

First and foremost, he saw himself as a public servant. "My father never referred to himself as a politician, always as a public servant," recalled Zeidler's youngest daughter, Jeanne, herself a multiterm mayor of Williamsburg, Virginia. Zeidler never separated his role as mayor from that of any other public employee, with all of the high standards he attributed to public service. So when municipal employees sought to assert their rights as distinct from those of their employer, the action created what he perceived to be a manufactured duality in public service, one at odds with the very essence of public service.[18]

After leaving office at age forty-seven, he became an arbitrator, mediating contract disputes between workers and their employers during the two decades when public employee unionization was at its peak, with strikes by teachers and postal workers filling the front pages. His daughter Anita often drove him to mediation sessions, where she witnessed the transformation his intervention worked on both sides in a dispute. "In the beginning, the people in that room, it would be labor and management and they would be so angry with each other that they could hardly look at each other," Anita said. But generally, Zeidler turned the situation around. "At the end, people would be talking again . . . and the thing would be settled." Zeidler showed them "where they could find commonalities."[19]

Influenced by his new role, at one point Zeidler seemed open to revising his views on public-sector collective bargaining, allowing the possibility that collective bargaining might offer a better solution to the problem of constructing a fair set of employment relations than civil service rules alone. "[I]n spite of all the disagreeableness that has and will occur in public-employee relations, the process of economic negotiations between public management and public employees may in the long run be a more efficient method for accomplishing the public's business than the older system was," he wrote in 1968, the year when striking sanitation workers in Memphis, Tennessee, successfully framed the issue of collective bargaining as one of fairness and equal treatment. "If the negotiating process continues over the years long enough for stable relations to develop between employees and administration, this condition, too, can accrue to the public benefit," Zeidler hoped.[20]

Yet twenty-five years later, when an interviewer asked him to list the untold stories that needed to be related, Zeidler listed "the evolution of public unions" as in the top two. "You have a government now that's a two-house government, the official elected government and then the employee union that says we won't work unless you work at the terms we agree on," he said. For Zeidler, the idea of a unitary public interest still transcended the demands of any group.[21]

Despite the impressive list of material accomplishments, Zeidler failed in his overarching goal: to plant the seeds for a political movement that would further democratic-socialism through a viable political vehicle. In the decades after his administration Zeidler went on to become a beloved Milwaukee icon, but the values he embodied and were recognized and admired by many residents had no expression in any viable political mechanism. The Public Enterprise Committee carried on through the decades and even into the twenty-first century, drawing a small and devoted following, but it was never the sustainable coalition of all "forward-looking and progressive citizens and voters" the coalition sought in its November 1947 founding call for members.[22]

The postwar era through the 1950s encompassed a key transitional period for the nation, in which foundational issues such as civil rights, the role of government, and the challenges of a pluralistic society confronted the postwar status quo. In struggling to respond while at the same time shaping the course of governance, Zeidler wrestled with issues, the resolutions of which would determine the course of the next decades. In championing affordable housing and the involvement of the public sector in job-creating projects like the St. Lawrence Seaway, Zeidler reflected a desire to continue and expand on the New Deal legacy. But his vision of capacious public service became highly contested ground as local opponents of government expansion dealt an enduring blow to Zeidler's original housing goals.

Similarly, Zeidler's attempts to expand the city's territory became instead a battle between supporters of government efforts to ensure housing opportunities for its citizens and those who asserted the priority of individual rights, as expressed through property ownership. Here, issues of class and taxpayer rights became inextricably tied in with those of race, as suburban leaders rejected the extension of quality housing options to black residents. The hostility Zeidler faced when attempting to put forward a plan for a city-operated public television station further demonstrated the antagonism of a small but active segment against such taxpayer expenditures. It also highlighted the extent to which the corporate-owned media was unwilling to cede any ground to noncommercial alternative voices.

Conservative Counterrevolution

While the immediate urban challenges in Milwaukee arguably arose from the less extreme side of the conservative spectrum, the radical right, operating in the background, was never far from the center of action. Although Grede's brand of conservatism differed from that of William Pieplow, both ideologies rested well within a corporate-created free-enterprise framework that privileged individual rights above a collective good.

Grede actively championed his vision throughout the 1960s and 1970s, urging the YMCA to reject federal support and blasting NAM in the 1970s when it sought to build bridges with the government. Such a stance, along with assertions like the one in 1966 in which he stated that all labor laws should be repealed, including those forbidding employment of children, kept him at the fringes of the political mainstream. Yet liberals dismissed Grede and his ideological allies at their peril: between 2011 and 2013, Idaho, Missouri, Maine, and, yes, Wisconsin rolled back child-labor laws. The unthinkable became the possible. In the late 1980s, Grede Foundries was one of the nation's largest independent foundries, with more than two thousand employees and plants in Wisconsin, Kansas, Kentucky, Michigan, and South Carolina. By the time he died in 1989 at age 92, Grede had lived long enough to witness the nation's first postwar embrace of conservatism, the early fruits of the conservative movement's fifty-year counterrevolution.[23]

Conservative opposition emerged in all the major issues facing Milwaukee in the postwar years. But while seemingly disparate, each challenged the New Deal order, and each is connected by a common conservative counterreaction that sought to stave off a perceived loss of individual rights as expressed through an economic vision that privileged unfettered free enterprise. The fundamental postwar challenge to the national narrative was one that rested firmly in an economic interpretation that sought to turn back acceptance of New Deal principles—expansive government involvement in social welfare, support for labor union rights, and the general notion of collective public good. While the origins of this opposition did not begin in the 1950s, it gained ground and furthered its agenda to an extent not possible in the immediate wake of the New Deal or during the war years. Uncovering the economic underpinnings of the conservative counterrevolution brings to light an often-overlooked aspect of its ascent. In doing so, it suggests research that must yet be undertaken to further flesh out how deeply conservatism is rooted in the American economic framework, one often manifested in an antigovernment animus.

Events in 1950s Milwaukee give credence to that decade as the launching point for postwar conservative reaction in the suburbs. In exploring this era, it is possible to perceive more clearly the role of economic issues before they became intertwined with, and overshadowed by, the backlash against civil rights and social liberalism. Suburban assertions of the precedence of free enterprise within a context of opposition to government expansion has, in fact, long formed the basis for the "flight to the suburbs." Yet such a rationale often has been lost in the focus on the 1960s.

Milwaukee in the 1950s illustrates the extent to which "consensus," long used to describe U.S. postwar history, in fact was as much a mirage as the corporate image making that reframed capitalism as free enterprise. On the one hand, mainstream corporations publicly played up their support for a consensus imbued with some acceptance of a Keynesian economic order. At the same time, some of these same major corporate players funded far-right organizations whose stated goals were well outside the accepted political and economic norms. By channeling their contributions through associations such as the National Association of Real Estate Boards, or by directly financing far-right conservative media, corporate leaders clearly signaled an antipathy to rather than an acceptance of the policies that governed the nation. Whether within a labor-management framework or through a broader lens that encompasses the entire political and economic spectrum of the 1950s, future studies of the interplay between and among business, labor, and government must go deeper than the public expressions of consensus in exploring this topic.

Further, examining the activism throughout the decade uncovers the means by which it sowed the seeds for its long-term growth. The wide reach of publications such as *Facts Forum News* and the broad corporate support for limiting union rights brings to light the extent to which far-right conservatives did not merely operate on the fringes but penetrated far more widely than studies of the era's conservative emergence have portrayed. The new scholarship on far-right conservatism must be expanded. By seriously examining the goals of such ideologues and by exploring fully the breadth of their outreach, future research can further uncover the role of far right in shaping the conservative movement that emerged in the twenty-first century.

A Lasting Government Built on Democracy and Justice

Initially excoriated by the *Milwaukee Journal* in his first run for office, Zeidler had, by the late 1970s, become an icon in the eyes of mainstream journalists and residents of all political stripes. He was revered for his knowledge and his experience but most of all for his integrity. When he died at age 93 in July 2006, hundreds of people packed Redeemer Lutheran Church for his funeral. As the *Journal-Sentinel* described the ceremony, "Mourners filled the twelve rows of pews, plus the thirty-six folding chairs set out in back. They squeezed in with the choir in the balcony and lined the brick walls and packed in the foyer, finally standing in the doorway and spilling down the stairs."[24]

Many of the mourners who gathered at the church where Zeidler worshipped throughout his life took part not only out of respect for him as a man of principle but also to honor the vision he championed. Two philosophies of government competed for precedence, he believed. One involves helping "the rich enterprisers grow richer, and hope that the crumbs which fall off their table can nourish their employees and . . . the people in the city." The other rests on the notion that "the purpose of a city is solely to advance human progress."[25]

By the time Zeidler was elected mayor, the "philosophy of government" he espoused was waning. Good government ideologists gave way to technocrats, while opponents of the New Deal society gained momentum with victories such as passage of the Taft-Hartley Act. Although significant expansion of the welfare state lay ahead, with Lyndon Johnson's Great Society, that expansion would soon be stalled by grassroots conservatives and aided by deep-pocketed corporations.

For all of the opposition he faced during his political career, Zeidler remained committed to a philosophy of governance that at times put him at odds with the direction in which modern liberalism was moving—evinced in his opposition to municipal workers' demands for collective bargaining. In rejecting a pluralistic understanding of the public interest, one that had gained momentum since the New Deal years, Zeidler professed an approach that proved unable to come to terms with the escalating rights-based demands. Milwaukee, like many cities, ultimately could not address the urban challenges of the postwar era and failed, in this key transitional decade, to take the far-reaching steps needed to ensure, as Zeidler put it, that "no part of the urban environment" is "deficient in meeting human needs." But its inability to do so rested not on the failure of a philosophy founded in the public interest but rather resulted from fundamental structural issues and a growing opposition that no single progressive urban leader, no matter how visionary, could address alone.[26]

Zeidler was unique among modern municipal leaders in his formulation of a philosophy of governance rooted in civic ideals. Describing Zeidler, his friend and socialist colleague Quinn Brisben said, "The words we have taken from ancient languages that are rooted in words meaning city: *urbanity, politeness, civility*, are losing their relevance. Frank did his best to stop this." Another Zeidler friend, Milwaukee historian John Gurda, explained Zeidler's approach to governance: "He believed with all his heart that government, in the end, is *all* of us, and we have lost that vision at our extreme peril. . . . He would say, and I can almost hear him, that the idea of citizenship he chose was a choice open to every one of us—and what are we waiting for?"[27]

In the long run, as Zeidler knew, no matter how many garden cities were created and no matter how many streets were paved, the ultimate test of a successful democracy was far more lasting. He defined that test in words that continue to resonate long after his death: "The many physical improvements we develop today will perish with time. The most magnificent building we can devise will decay. Lasting government therefore cannot be built with brick and stone. It must be built on faith in democracy, on justice, on vision, on honesty and respect for the dignity and rights of our fellow citizens."[28]

Notes

Abbreviations

AJK	Anthony J. King Papers, 1892–1965. Wisconsin Historical Society
CC	City Club of Milwaukee Records, 1909–1975. Wisconsin Historical Society
CFZ	Carl F. and Frank P. Zeidler Papers. Milwaukee Public Library
FZ	Frank Zeidler Collected Papers. Wisconsin Historical Society
HR	Henry Reuss Papers, 1839–1998. Wisconsin Historical Society
JF	John T. Flynn Collection. Special Collections and University Archives, University of Oregon
JWB	John W. Byrnes Papers, 1938–1972. Wisconsin Historical Society
LWVM	League of Women Voters of Greater Milwaukee, 1920–1981. Wisconsin Historical Society
MAC	Metropolitan Milwaukee Association of Commerce, 1870–1966. Wisconsin Historical Society
MU	Marquette University Department of Special Collections and University Archives
MUL	Milwaukee Urban League Records, 1919–1979. Wisconsin Historical Society
NAM	National Association of Manufacturers Records. Hagley Museum and Library

RL	Rubin Levin Papers, 1920–1981. Wisconsin Historical Society
RP	Richard Perrin. Unprocessed Collection. Milwaukee Public Library
WC	Wauwatosa Collection. Milwaukee County Historical Society
WGB	William George Bruce Papers, 1843–1960. Wisconsin Historical Society
WH	Walter Harnischfeger Papers. Milwaukee County Historical Society
WIAFL-CIO	Wisconsin State AFL-CIO Records, 1956–2000. Wisconsin Historical Society
WJG	William J. Grede Papers, 1909–1979. Wisconsin Historical Society
WLP	William L. Pieplow Collection, 1894–1959. Milwaukee County Historical Society
WMA	Wisconsin Manufacturers' Association Records, 1910–1975. Wisconsin Historical Society
WMSC	Wisconsin Metropolitan Study Commission Records, 1957–1961. Wisconsin Historical Society
ZFC	Zeidler Family Collection. Milwaukee County Historical Society

Introduction

1. William J. Grede, letter to J. R. Steelman, June 27, 1955, WJG, box 21, folder 3.

2. Chodorov, *Fifty-Year Project*; Chodorov, *Out of Step*.

3. Bowen, *Roots of Modern Conservatism*, 6; Phillips-Fein, "Conservatism," 3, 727; Ribuffo, "Rediscovering."

4. Rossiter, *Conservatism in America*, 170–75.

5. Ibid., 187.

6. Cowie and Salvatore, "Long Exception," 4–5.

7. The Christian American Association, for example, lobbied in the 1940s for antiunion "right-to-work" amendments in state constitutions. (Under "right-to-work" laws, made possible under the 1947 Taft-Hartley Act, employees are not required to join a union or pay fees as a condition of getting or retaining a job.) Lichtman, *White Protestant Nation*, 128.

8. McGirr, *Suburban Warriors*, 148.

9. Brinkley, *End of Reform*, 269. Housing expert Catherine Bauer is among those who argued that lack of interest by civic groups and others to press for more affordable housing was behind the stagnation of the federal housing acts. Bauer, "Dreary Deadlock."

10. Jackson, *Crabgrass Frontier*; Lassiter, *Silent Majority*; Kruse, *White Flight*; Self, *American Babylon*.

11. Kruse and Sugrue, *New Suburban History*, 3–5; Sugrue, *Origins of the Urban Crisis*.

12. See Sugrue, *Sweet Land of Liberty*, and Biondi, *To Stand and Fight*.

13. Examples include: Lowndes, *From the New Deal to the New Right*; Phillips-Fein, *Invisible Hands*; Edsell, *Chain Reaction*.

14. Nash, *Conservative Intellectual Movement*.

15. Burgin, *Great Persuasion*.

16. Bowen, *Roots of Modern Conservatism*.

17. Critchlow, *Phyllis Schlafly*.

18. Cowie and Salvatore, "Long Exception." Other scholars pointing to conservatism's long history in the United States include Allitt, *Conservatives*, and Schneider, *Conservative Century*.

19. Bell, *Radical Right*; Forester and Epstein, *Danger on the Right*; Thayer, *Farther Shores of Politics*.

20. Hurt, *Texas Rich*; Tuccille, *Kingdom*; Canning, *American Dreamers*; Moser, *Right Turn*.

21. Hendershot, *What's Fair on the Air?*

22. Griffith, "Selling of America"; Griffith, *Specter*; Wall, *Inventing the American Way*; Tedlow, *Keeping the Corporate Image*; Ewen, *PR!*

23. Fones-Wolf, *Selling Free Enterprise*, 5; Shermer, *Sunbelt Capitalism*; Phillips-Fein, *Invisible Hands*; Phillips-Fein, "Business Conservatism."

24. Kim Voss, in *The Making of American Exceptionalism: The Knights of Labor and Class Formation in the Nineteenth Century*, argues that employer resistance played a key factor in smashing solidarity between skilled and unskilled workers. Like Voss, David Brian Robertson (*Capital, Labor and State: The Battle for American Labor Markets from the Civil War to the New Deal*) sees the response of U.S. employers to workers' collective action as de-linking the development of the American labor movement from its European counterpart.

25. Commercial Keynesianism also features economic stability over the redistribution of income and the reallocation of resources, and a modicum of unemployment over a modicum of inflation. Collins, *Business Response to Keynes*, 17.

26. Morgan, "Inventing the 'Liberal Republican Mind.'"

27. "Iron ring" was frequently used by all sides of the annexation issue in the 1950s to describe suburbs resistant to incorporation within the city of Milwaukee.

28. U.S. Census, *Historical Census Statistics*.

29. Allen, *Big Change*, 214.

30. As Becky Nicolaides (*My Blue Heaven*) illustrates, the backlash had roots that went back to the 1920s.

Chapter 1. A Liberal in City Government

1. Foss-Mollan, *Hard Water*, 53; Peirce and Keefe, *Great Lakes States*, 147.

Notes to Chapter 1

2. Still, *Milwaukee*, 309–10.
3. Kenny and Hubka, "Surveying Milwaukee's Residential Landscapes," 235–36.
4. Still, *Milwaukee*, 453.
5. Pienkos, "Politics"; Gurda, *Making of Milwaukee*, 173–75; Schmandt, Goldbach, and Vogel, *Milwaukee*, 16.
6. Cutler, *Greater Milwaukee's Growing Pains*, 6.
7. McCarthy, *Making Milwaukee Mightier*, 68.
8. Peterson, *Day of the Mugwump*, 224.
9. Davis, "Milwaukee," 189–92.
10. Wells, *This Is Milwaukee*, 247; Davis, "Milwaukee," 189–92.
11. "Historic Preservation Study Report"; Davis, "Milwaukee," 192.
12. Geenen, *Shuster's and Gimbels*, 57; "Old Milwaukee."
13. Schmandt, Goldbach, and Vogel, *Milwaukee*, 21; Wells, *This Is Milwaukee*, 246.
14. Gurda, *Cream City Chronicles*, 186; Davis, "Milwaukee," 207–8.
15. "Milwaukee: More Than Beer"; Cutler, *Greater Milwaukee's Growing Pains*, 6–7; *Milwaukee Wisconsin Market*.
16. Peterson, *Day of the Mugwump*, 220–21; Davis, "Milwaukee," 189, 191.
17. Wells, *"Milwaukee Journal": An Informal Chronicle*, 359–61; Rast, "Governing the Regimeless City," 86–88; Fure-Slocum, *Contesting the Postwar City*.
18. Gurda, *Making of Milwaukee*, 347; "Milwaukee Plans to Make Postwar Dream Come True," *Providence [R.I.] Journal*, July 20, 1947, WGB, box 5, folder 4.
19. "Milwaukee Plans to Make Postwar Dream Come True"; U.S. Census Bureau, *Seventeenth Decennial Census*.
20. Beck, *Sewer Socialists*, 2:352–53; Austin, *Milwaukee Story*, 188–201; Gurda, *Making of Milwaukee*, 310. The SS La Salle, a merchant vessel from Mobile, Alabama, was torpedoed on November 7, 1942, at 10:50 P.M., by the German U-boat *U-159* under Kapitanleutnant Helmut Witte. The *La Salle*, under Captain Sillars, blew up in a massive explosion. Wells, *Milwaukee Journal*, 331.
21. Gurda, *Making of Milwaukee*, 310.
22. Frank Zeidler, letter to the author, June 18, 2000.
23. Years later, the house was torn down to build Marquette University's recreation center. Frank Zeidler, letter to the author, June 18, 2000.
24. "Mayoral Musings: Zeidler's Turning 90, but His Mind Is Going 100," *Milwaukee Journal*, July 15, 2002; "The Father and Mother of Two Mayors Believe Milwaukee Picked 'A Nice Fellow,'" *Milwaukee Journal*, April 7, 1948; Frank Zeidler, letter to the author, June 18, 2000; Frank Zeidler, letter to the author, October 9, 2005.
25. Zeidler, interview by the author, September 22, 2005.
26. Ibid.; Frank Zeidler, letter to the author, June 18, 2000; "Father and Mother of Two Mayors"; Mike McCallister, "A Renaissance Man," *Shepherd Express*, September 17, 1992; Bill Lueders, "Last of a Breed," *Milwaukee Magazine*, November 1985.
27. "Mayor Served the Public Welfare," *Milwaukee Journal-Sentinel*, July 9, 2006; Anita Zeidler, interview by the author, February 19, 2010; Frank Zeidler, letter to the

author, June 18, 2000; Zeidler, interview by the author, September 22, 2005; Beck, *Sewer Socialists*, 2:351.

28. Zeidler, letter to the author, June 14, 2000; "Mayor Served the Public Welfare."

29. Zeidler, interview by the author, September 22, 2005; see Page, *Social Evangelist*.

30. Addison, "Cold War Pacifist"; Allen, *Fight for Peace*, 525–56, 559.

31. Frank Zeidler, "Don't Fence Me In, October 8, 1952," speech to the American Society of Planning Officials, Boston, CFZ, box 107, folder 3.

32. Brisben, "Frank Zeidler's Legacy."

33. Shannon, *Socialist Party of America*, 24.

34. Miller, "Casting a Wide Net"; Schmandt and Standing, *Milwaukee Metropolitan Study Commission*, 17.

35. Gurda, *Making of Milwaukee*, 160; "Nonpartisan Vote Setup Is Outgrowth of Fusion," *Milwaukee Journal*, March 23, 1948; Miller, "Casting a Wide Net," 32.

36. "Wisconsin: Milwaukee's Mayor," *Time*, April 15, 1940; Hoan, *City Government*, 312; Zeidler, "Liberal in City Government," chap. 3, p. 2.

37. McGuinness, "Revolution Begins Here," 90; "Wisconsin: Marxist Mayor," *Time*, April 6, 1936.

38. Hoan, *City Government*, 220; "Wisconsin: Marxist Mayor."

39. "Wisconsin: Marxist Mayor"; Ettenheim, *How Milwaukee Voted*, 125–27.

40. Peirce and Keefe, *Great Lakes States*, 121; Trotter, *Black Milwaukee*, 149; Hauser, "Frank Zeidler."

41. Ettenheim, *How Milwaukee Voted*, 4; Polenberg, "Decline of the New Deal," 254.

42. Peterson, *Day of the Mugwump*, 223; Morris Hillquit, quoted by Frank Zeidler, "'Sewer Socialism': The Pragmatics of Running a Good City," speech, Society for Economic Anthropology, Milwaukee, April 27, 2001.

43. Stave, *Socialism and the Cities*, 5, 160, 170; Bucki, *Bridgeport's Socialist New Deal*.

44. Gurda, *Making of Milwaukee*, 204; Miller, *Victor Berger*, 27–28, 36.

45. Zeidler, "Liberal in City Government," chap. 1, p. 39. The name of the Municipal Enterprise Committee was later changed to the Public Enterprise Committee.

46. Schmitt, interview by the author, April 6, 2007; Zeidler, "Liberal in City Government," chap. 1, p. 34.

47. Discussion of Zeidler campaign: Zeidler, "Liberal in City Government," chap. 1.

48. "Father and Mother of Two Mayors"; "One of These Will Be Mayor, Here Are Close-Ups of Rivals," *Milwaukee Journal*, March 17, 1948. "He is no great shakes to look at . . ." cited in John Nichols, "Zeidler, Big Money Era Wouldn't Mix," *Milwaukee Journal-Sentinel*, July 10, 2006.

49. "One of These Will Be Mayor"; Hauser, *Public Enterprise Committee Record*.

50. Zeidler, "Liberal in City Government," chap. 1, pp. 91–93; Frank Zeidler, "'Sewer Socialism.'"

51. Zeidler, "Liberal in City Government," chap. 1, pp. 91–93.

52. Anita Zeidler, interview by the author; "Agnes Zeidler," *Milwaukee Labor Press*, October 29, 2009; "Zeidler Managed House, Husband's Mayoral Campaigns," *Milwaukee Journal-Sentinel*, September 25, 2009; "Frank Zeidler's Quiet Candidacy," *Milwaukee Journal*, October 24, 1976.

53. Zeidler, interview by Aims McGuinness; Zeidler, "Liberal in City Government," chap. 1, pp. 53–58; Zeidler, "'Sewer Socialism'"; Zeidler, interview by the author; Lueders, "Last of a Breed."

54. Zeidler, "Liberal in City Government," chap. 1, p. 51; Lueders, "Last of a Breed."

55. Bruce Murphy, "The Halo Effect," *Milwaukee Magazine*, September 2006; "A Simple Man, a Giant Life," *Milwaukee Journal-Sentinel*, July 13, 2006; Frank Zeidler, "So You Want to Be Mayor?" *American Magazine*, December 1954; "Frank Zeidler's Quiet Candidacy"; Lueders, "Last of a Breed"; Nichols, "Zeidler, Big Money Era Wouldn't Mix."

56. "A Midwest Mayor Revises the Bard: Milwaukee Troupe Stages 'Macbeth' by Shakespeare and Frank Zeidler," *New York Times*, June 7, 1959.

57. Three of the four translations were published, and all are available at the Milwaukee Public Library. *Macbeth, Translated to a More Modern Speech and Clarified by Frank P. Zeidler* (Milwaukee: Milwaukee Publishers, 1957); *A Midsummer Night's Dream, Translated to a More Modern Speech and Clarified by Frank P. Zeidler* (Milwaukee: Milwaukee Publishers, 1957); "Julius Caesar, Translated to a More Modern Speech and Clarified by Frank P. Zeidler" (unpublished, 1959); *The Tragedy of Hamlet, Prince of Denmark, Translated into Modern English by Frank P. Zeidler* (Fennimore, Wisc.: Westburg, 1979).

58. "Midwest Mayor Revises the Bard"; Zeidler, interview by Jane Hampden.

59. Zeidler, interview by the author.

60. Zeidler, "Liberal in City Government," chap. 1, p. 74.

61. Kessler, interview by the author.

62. Zeidler, interview by Jane Hampden; Zeidler, "Liberal in City Government," chap. 1, p. 30.

63. Zeidler, "Liberal in City Government," chap. 1, p. 50.

64. Ibid., chap. 1, pp. 62, 69.

65. Ibid. chap. 1, pp. 68–69, 96–97.

66. Liberals' failure to successfully push for expanded public housing is one example. Bauer, "Dreary Deadlock."

67. Zeidler, "Liberal in City Government," chap. 1, pp. 31–32, 91–93.

68. Ibid., chap. 1, p. 50.

69. Harold Alderfer to Zeidler, November 16, 1956, CFZ, box 197, folder 1; Alderfer, *American Local Government and Administration*.

Chapter 2. The Media Makes the Message

Epigraph. Griffith, "Forging America's Postwar Order."

1. "What's in a Label?" *Wisconsin CIO News*, April 2, 1948; Zeidler, "Liberal in City Government," chap. 1, p. 87.

2. Wells, *Milwaukee Journal*, 388; "No. 1," *Time*, October 2, 1950.
3. Wells, *Milwaukee Journal*, 352–53.
4. Ibid.
5. Zeidler, "Liberal in City Government," chap. 2, pp. 16–17.
6. Still, *Milwaukee*, 461–62.
7. Conrad, Wilson, and Wilson, *The Milwaukee Journal*, 72; "Nonpartisan Vote Setup Is Outgrowth of Fusion," *Milwaukee Journal*, March 3, 1948.
8. Zeidler, "Liberal in City Government," chap. 1, pp. 86–87; Zeidler, *Liberal in City Government*, 32–33.
9. Zeidler, "Liberal in City Government," chap. 1, p. 94; "Officials of City Deserve Re-Election, Have Good Records," *Milwaukee Journal*, March 31, 1952; "No Socialism in the City Hall under Zeidler Administration," *Milwaukee Journal*, March 22, 1956; Wells, *Milwaukee Journal*, 398–99.
10. A. J. Liebling, "The Press: How the News That Is Made in the Capital Gets from Washington to Your Breakfast Table Newspaper," *Holiday*, February 1950.
11. Dick Strout and Thomas Stokes, quoted in Liebling, "The Press."
12. Griffith, "Selling of America," 388.
13. "Business Is Still in Trouble," *Fortune*, May 1949; Tedlow, *Keeping the Corporate Image*, 152.
14. Whyte, *Is Anybody Listening?* 7; Lacey, *Truman Presidency*, 85.
15. Tedlow, *Keeping the Corporate Image*, xvi, 8; Ewen, *PR!*, 215–16.
16. Ewen, *PR!* 74–79.
17. Ibid., 349–52, 360.
18. Wall, *Inventing the American Way*, 5, 9.
19. Fones-Wolfe, *Selling Free Enterprise*, 286–87.
20. Shore, Fones-Wolf, and Danky, *German-American Radical Press*, 3–4.
21. Hoerder, "German-American Labor Press," 182–83.
22. Gavett, *Development*, 208; Still, *Milwaukee*, 453; see also, Conzen, *Immigrant Milwaukee*.
23. John R. Commons estimate, cited in Rubin Levin, "Labor Press, 1953," unpublished manuscript, n.d.; rev. March 1953, RL, box 2, folder 11.
24. Beck, *Sewer Socialists*, 1:36, 121, 144–52; Gurda, *Making of Milwaukee*, 217, 206; Miller, *Victor Berger*; Gavett, *Development*, 173; Beck, *Sewer Socialists*, 2:253.
25. McBride, "Progress," 325–48.
26. Beck, *Sewer Socialists*, 1:144–52; Gavett, *Development*, 173.
27. Fones-Wolf, *Waves of Opposition*, 17.
28. Ibid., 207.
29. George Addes, quoted in Fones-Wolf, *Waves of Opposition*, 59–60.
30. Ewen, *PR!* 179–80; Fones-Wolf, *Waves of Opposition*, 64–65.
31. Maier, *Career*, 31–33; Wells, *Milwaukee Journal*, 372. Former *Milwaukee Journal* reporter Robert Wells notes several instances when reporters saw McCarthy drinking heavily, including the time a reporter, meeting with McCarthy at a downtown hotel one Sunday morning, recognized that McCarthy was "already well into a bottle of

brandy." McCarthy "kept leaving to shake hands with parishioners, then going back to drink" (372).

32. William Grede biographical summary, WJG; "Grede Publishing Firm Completing First Year," *Wauwatosa News-Times*, June 28, 1956; "Who Runs This Country?" *Wauwatosa News-Times*, July 26, 1956.

33. "City Will Not Recognize Employees' Strike Call," *Wauwatosa News-Times*, January 3, 1957; "We Can Do Without," *Wauwatosa News-Times*, March 21, 1957; "The Probe Is Not Political," *Wauwatosa News-Times*, March 21, 1957; "Teachers Half the Price of Laborers," *Wauwatosa News-Times*, October 16, 1958.

34. "The Shoe Pinches," *Milwaukee Times*, November 18, 1954.

35. Pieplow, *History*, 62; "Stop Coddling the Minorities," *Milwaukee Times*, September 10, 1959.

36. "Who Owns U.S. Business?" *Wauwatosa News-Times*, June 6, 1957; "If Enterprise Is Free," *Wauwatosa News-Times*, May 31, 1956.

37. Canning, *American Dreamers*, 54–65.

38. "Never! Never! Never!" *Reader's Digest*, January 1950.

39. Phil Blank, interview by the author, January 10, 2010; "Goodbye to Faucet Drip," *Reader's Digest*, October 1951; "Every Dog Should Own a Man," *Reader's Digest*, April 1952; "What Became of the Man I Married?" an occasional series for women, condensed from *Better Homes and Gardens*, *Reader's Digest*, 1951–1952; "The 'Gimmies' Sap the Nation's Strength," *Reader's Digest*, March 1949 (article condensed from the *Pittsburgh Press*).

40. Allen, *Big Change*, 224; *Reader's Digest* full-page ad, *Milwaukee Journal*, October 21, 1952.

41. Thayer, *Farther Shores of Politics*, 149; H. L. Hunt, "Add Patriotism to Ads," *Facts Forum News*, March 1955; Tuccille, *Kingdom*, 216–17; Hurt, *Texas Rich*, 149–50.

42. Hurt, *Texas Rich*, 154.

43. Hurt, *Texas Rich*, 156; Forster and Epstein, *Danger on the Right*, 132–34; "Where One Texan's Money Goes: Oilman Hunt's Millions Keep Debate Forums on the Air," *U.S. News and World Report*, January 28, 1955.

44. "Will the Income Tax Destroy Capitalism?" teaser for July 1956, *Facts Forum News*, June 1956; "Should the Income Tax Be Repealed?" *Facts Forum News*, March 1955; Hurt, *Texas Rich*, 154–55.

45. Hurt, *Texas Rich*, 156–61; "Where One Texan's Money Goes"; A. C. Schmidt, Milwaukee School of Engineering librarian, letter to the editor, *Facts Forum News*, March 1955; "*Facts Forum News* Has 100,000 New Readers," *Facts Forum News*, February 1955.

46. "What They're Saying about *Facts Forum News*," *Facts Forum News*, April 1954; discussion of content based on examination of *Facts Forum News*, January 1954–November 1956; "*Facts Forum* Polling Results," *Facts Forum News*, October 1954.

47. "What They're Saying about Facts Forum," *Facts Forum News*, February 1954; "Facts about 'Facts Forum,'" *Facts Forum News*, November 1954; "Letters to the Editor of the Month Contest," *Facts Forum News*, November 1956.

48. *U.S. News and World Report* article quoted in "Facts Forum Featured in National Magazine," *Facts Forum News*, March 1955; "What They're Saying about Facts Forum," *Facts Forum News*, April 1954.

49. "Hunt, 'U.S. Richest,' Gives Cash and Time to Aid Facts Forum," *Washington Post*, February 16, 1954; reader survey, *Facts Forum News*, December 1956.

50. Hurt, *Texas Rich*, 161.

51. Hendershot, "God's Angriest Man," 376–77; Moser, *Right Turn*, 173.

52. Forster and Epstein, *Danger on the Right*, 138–39; Hendershot, "God's Angriest Man," 376.

53. "Drifting toward Doom," *Milwaukee Times*, February 17, 1955.

Chapter 3. Public or Private? The Battle over Channel 10

1. Golembiewski, *Milwaukee Television History*, 43–58.

2. Tony Weinlein, letter to Frank Zeidler, April 10, 1951, CFZ, box 162, folder 2; Anderson and Olson, *Milwaukee*, 160.

3. Zeidler, "Does Milwaukee Need a Noncommercial Educational Television Transmitter?" unpublished article, May 21, 1951, Milwaukee Public Library; Zeidler, statement to Common Council Committee on Public Utilities, May 7, 1951, *The Project Files, 1948–1960*, box 162, folder 2.

4. Golembiewski, *Milwaukee Television History*, 43–58; Zeidler, "Does Milwaukee Need . . . Transmitter?"; Maier, *Career*, 48.

5. Charles Lanphier, president, WFOX, letter to Frank Zeidler, carbon copies to Alderman Walter Koepke, Common Council chairman of the Public Utilities Committee, and Common Council president Milton J. McGuire, May 17, 1951; and Gaston Grignon, WISN general manager, letter to Alderman Walter Koepke, May 14, 1951, CFZ, box 162, folder 2; Zeidler, "Does Milwaukee Need . . . Transmitter?"

6. Frank Zeidler, letter to Alderman Fred Meyers, chairman of the Milwaukee Common Council, May 11, 1951, CFZ, box 162, folder 2, and "Information Sheet, Joint Committee on Educational Television," CFZ, box 162, folder 3; Golembiewski, *Milwaukee Television History*, 332–34.

7. Meaney, "Institution of Public Television," 406; Wayne Coy, "Additional Views of Commissioner Coy," *Extracts from the Commission's Third Notice of Further Proposed Rule Making Concerning the Reservation of Television Channels for Educational Purposes* (n.d.), CFZ, box 162, folder 3; Golembiewski, *Milwaukee Television History*, 334.

8. Gaston Grignon, WISN general manager, letter to Alderman Walter Koepke, chairman, Common Council Utilities Commission, May 14, 1951; and Charles Lanphier, WFOX president, letters to Frank Zeidler, May 17, 1951, and October 17, 1951, CFZ, box 162, folder 2.

9. Frank Zeidler, letter to Lanphier, October 23, 1952, CFZ, box 162, folder 2.

10. William Benton, "Television with a Conscience," *Saturday Review of Literature* (August 1951), in CFZ, box 162, folder 3; Frieda Hennock, "Separate Views of Commissioner Hennock," in *Extracts from the Commission's Third Notice of Further Proposed Rule Making Concerning the Reservation of Television Channels for Educational Purposes* (undated), CFZ, box 162, folder 3.

11. "Educational TV in Milwaukee," undated remarks, CFZ, box 162, folder 3; and Gerald Caffrey, letter to Milo Swanton, May 12, 1952, CFZ, box 162, folder 4; "Milwaukee Needs Educational Television," sworn statement of the Milwaukee Educators' Committee on Television, 1951, CFZ, box 162, folder 3.

12. "Milwaukee Needs Educational Television," sworn statement of the Milwaukee Educators' Committee on Television; Erina Romanik, president, Business and Professional Women's Club of Milwaukee, letter to Frank Zeidler, July 2, 1952; and Gerald Caffrey, "Educational TV in Milwaukee: A Chronological Report of Progress," undated article, CFZ, box 162, folder 4; Victor Leavens, recording secretary, IAM United Lodge 66, letter to Frank Zeidler, September 2, 1952, CFZ, box 162, folder 5; "Board Backs Video Plan," *Milwaukee Labor Press*, May 24, 1951.

13. Wesley Cox, coordinator, publicity, Community Chest Campaign, letter to Frank Zeidler, October 31, 1951, CFZ, box 162, folder 3; "Educators Are Urged to Explore Educational TV," *New York Times*, February 9, 1953.

14. Robert Riordan, "Milwaukee Can Have More Television," reprint *Milwaukee Sentinel*, August 1952 in CFZ, box 162, folder 4.

15. Webb, "Scooters, Skates, and Dolls," 7–12.

16. Golembiewski, *Milwaukee Television History*, 335–36.

17. Alma Bartell, secretary, Milwaukee County Property Owners' Association, letter to Frank Zeidler, November 26, 1951, CFZ, box 162, folder 3; "Educational TV," *Milwaukee Times*, October 21, 1954.

18. "City, County Voters Did Good Job at Polls on Tuesday," *Milwaukee Journal*, April 2, 1952; "At Last, Milwaukee's a None-Horse Town," *Milwaukee Journal*, April 18, 1952; "Council Overturns Veto 20–7," *Milwaukee Journal*, May 21, 1952; Sarah Ettenheim, *How Milwaukee Voted, 1848–1968*, 127–29.

19. Frank Zeidler, interview by John Johannes; "Council Overturns Veto 20–7."

20. Zeidler veto message to Milwaukee Common Council, May 12, 1952, CFZ, box 55, folder 9.

21. "Council Gets Protests," *Milwaukee Journal*, May 16, 1952; Walter Schmidt, business representative, International Brotherhood of Firemen and Oilers, letter to Alderman Charles Quirk, May 26, 1952, CFZ, box 162, folder 4.

22. Carl Kimmel, assistant city attorney, letter to the Milwaukee Common Council, July 25, 1952, CFZ, box 162, folder 4.

23. Maier, *Career*, 53–54.

24. D. L. Provost, letter to Frank Zeidler, May 12, 1952, CFZ, box 162, folder 4.

25. "Judge Curbs Action on TV," *Milwaukee Journal*, October 15, 1952; Golembiewski, *Milwaukee Television History*, 341–43; "Powerful Forces Seek to Block Channel for School Use, an FCC Member Says," *Milwaukee Journal*, October 26, 1952; "New TV Tower Sets Height Mark for State," *Milwaukee Journal*, October 17, 1952; "WTMJ-TV Tower," *Milwaukee Journal*, March 27, 1953.

26. F. R. Peterson, letter to Walter Mattison, city attorney, October 23, 1952, CFZ, box 162, folder 5; Frank Zeidler, letter to the Common Council, October 27, 1952, CFZ, box 162, folder 5; "Zeidler Veto Counters Ed TV Slap," *Milwaukee Journal*, October 26, 1952.

27. Frank Zeidler, letter to the Common Council, October 27, 1952, CFZ, box 162, folder 5; "Zeidler Veto Counters Ed TV Slap."

28. "School Video Station Here Seen in 1953," *Milwaukee Journal*, November 23, 1952; Golembiewski, *Milwaukee Television History*, 343.

29. Victor Leavens, recording secretary, IAM United Lodge 66, letter to Frank Zeidler, September 2, 1952, CFZ, box 162, folder 2; "Powerful Forces Seek to Block Channels for School Use, an FCC Member Says," *Milwaukee Journal*, October 26, 1952; Francis Hanson, director, Educational and Political Action, UAW/AFL, letter to Frank Zeidler, December 3, 1951, CFZ, box 162, folder 3.

30. "'Middle Way' Urged by Eisenhower," *Milwaukee Journal*, October 11, 1952.

31. David Lawrence, letter to Frank Zeidler, April 6, 1951, CFZ, box 162, folder 2.

32. For one example, see Lippmann, *Good Society*.

33. Walter Lippmann, quoted in Meaney, "Institution of Public Television," 407–8.

34. Golembiewski, *Milwaukee Television History*, 345, 352–56; Frank Zeidler, letter to John Hubel, trade journalist and technical writer, January 16, 1956, CFZ, box 163, folder 4.

35. Golembiewski, *Milwaukee Television History*, 352.

36. "McCarthy Says Complaint against FCC May Bring Probe," *Washington Post*, November 30, 1952; Golembiewski, *Milwaukee Television History*, 343–45; "M'Carthy Data Sought," *New York Times*, January 22, 1953.

37. "NAM Scores a Hit in Peddling Commercials," *Business Week*, April 19, 1952.

38. Ibid.

39. Prothro, "Public Interest Advertising," 173–76.

40. Miller and Nowak, *Fifties*, 7; Zenith television ad, *Milwaukee Times*, October 20, 1955; *Milwaukee Wisconsin Market*.

41. J. F. Friedrick, remarks at the Conference on Unemployment and Political Education, May 22–23, 1954, WIAFL-CIO, box 43, folder 8.

42. "The New Conservatism," *Time*, November 26, 1956.

43. Miller and Nowak, *Fifties*, 11; "The New Conservatism," *Time*, November 26, 1956.

Chapter 4. Let the People Vote

1. Frank Zeidler, statement to the Subcommittee of the U.S. Senate Committee on Banking and Currency, February 17, 1949, and "Description of Public Housing Projects," CFZ, box 175, folder 2; U.S. Census Bureau, *Historical Census Statistics*. The 232-unit Hillside project was not completed until May 1950. Zeidler, "Liberal in City Government," chap. 4, 179.

2. Housing Authority director Richard W. E. Perrin, letter to Frank Zeidler, citing a November 1948 survey by the Wisconsin Veterans' Housing Authority on the living conditions of World War II veterans, January 13, 1949, CFZ, box 175, folder 2; Trueman Farris (former *Milwaukee Sentinel* reporter and managing editor), interview by John R. Johannes, January 19, 1994, MU.

3. Housing Authority of the City of Milwaukee. *Milwaukee Housing Survey of 1949*, 1–11.

4. Housing Authority director Richard W. E. Perrin, letter to Frank Zeidler, January 13, 1949, CFZ, box 175, folder 2; Theresa Buller, letter to Frank Zeidler, n.d., CFZ, box 78, folder 5.

5. Stanley Budny, letter to Cornell Cinegin, July 20, 1949, CFZ, box 78, folder 6; Family Foundation, Inc., letter to Frank Zeidler, November 26, 1951, CFZ, box 78, folder 8; Richard Pearson, letter to Frank Zeidler, November 15, 1948, CFZ, box 78, folder 5.

6. Zeidler, "Liberal in City Government," chap. 4, pp. 112–13.

7. Davies, *Housing Reform*, 12–15, 111.

8. Rossiter, *Conservatism in America*, 32, 37–38.

9. "Man of the Month," ca. 1944, clipping of tribute likely printed in state or local U.S. Savings and Loan League publication, hand corrected by Pieplow, WLP, box 1, file 20.

10. William Bruce, quoted in "William Louis Pieplow, Honored by South Davison Civic Association, April 28, 1948, Sketch of the Man by Publishers of the *Milwaukee Times*," WLP, box 1, file 20.

11. "Man of the Month."

12. Pieplow, *Century Lessons*, 1, 32, 31; "Remarks" (n.d.), WLP, box 4, file 75.

13. "It's Milwaukee: The Modern, Hospitable Convention Center," *Savings and Loan News*, September 1946; Harry Conn, "Housing: A Vanishing Vision, the Real Estate Lobby Assumes Command," *New Republic*, July 23, 1951; "Annual publication of recommendations by USSLL Executive Committee for the 35,000 directors of member institutions," 1949, WLP, box 4, file 70.

14. "Government Public Housing Disastrous," address by William L. Pieplow to the Security Savings and Loan Association, January 24, 1949, WLP, box 3, file 47.

15. Webb, "Scooters, Skates, and Dolls," 7–12; Zeidler, "Liberal in City Government," chap. 4, pp. 153–64.

16. Pieplow, *History*, 51; Zeidler, "Liberal in City Government," chap. 4, pp. 153–64, 188–89; "Aldermen Hear Public Housing Branded Red," *Milwaukee Journal*, October 3, 1950.

17. Minutes of the Board of Directors' Meeting, March 24, 1950, and February 26, 1951, MAC, box 3, folder 1; D. J. McNally, letter to Frank Zeidler, February 13, 1950, CFZ, box 179, folder 1.

18. "'Canned' Campaign News Is . . . Bad and Good," *Journal of Housing*, August 1950; Zeidler, "Liberal in City Government," chap. 4, p. 155.

19. Milwaukee Common Council, Joint Committee on Judiciary Legislation and Public Buildings and Grounds, Office of the City Attorney, *Milwaukee Speaks on Housing and Blight Elimination*; Zeidler, "Liberal in City Government," chap. 4, p. 160.

20. William Pieplow, undated speech, ca. 1949, WLP, box 3, file 48; Beito, *Taxpayers in Revolt*, 22–23; Appendix: Affiliated Taxpayers Committee, March 4, 1950, Metropolitan Area Association of Commerce Minutes, 1915–1964, box 3, folder 1.

21. "Final Report: Public Housing Referendum Committee," WLP, box 3, folder 47; Public Housing Referendum Committee, memo to Team Captain and Members,

and Public Housing Referendum Committee, signed by William Pieplow, chairman, letter to Fellow American, CFZ, box 180, folder 1.

22. *Twenty-First Biennial Report.*

23. Walter Kirchuebel, letter to Frank Zeidler, February 16, 1951, CFZ, box 179, folder 2; Zeidler, "Liberal in City Government," chap. 4, pp. 186–91.

24. "Pickets Chase Anti-Housing Petitioners from City Hall," *Wisconsin CIO News*, January 12, 1951; "Final Report: Public Housing Referendum Committee," WLP, box 3, folder 47.

25. "Pickets Chase"; "Final Report."

26. Frank Zeidler, letter to members of the Public Housing Referendum Committee, January 22, 1951, Zeidler Collected Letters, CFZ, box 179, folder 1.

27. "Final Report: Public Housing Referendum Committee," WLP, box 3, folder 47; Zeidler, "Liberal in City Government," chap. 4, p. 205.

28. Federated Trades Council of Milwaukee, letter to affiliated unions, January 18, 1951; Alice Holz, recording secretary of the Women's Trade Union League, letter to the Common Council, January 23, 1951; Frank Zeidler, letter to the Democratic Organizing Committee of Milwaukee County, January 30, 1951, CFZ, box 179, folder 1; Zeidler, "Liberal in City Government," chap. 4, p. 181.

29. Zeidler, "Liberal in City Government," chap. 4, p. 186.

30. Ibid., chap. 4, pp. 80, 112–13; U.S. Congress, Senate Subcommittee, *General Housing Legislation*, 808.

31. "City Housing Vote Is Asked," *Milwaukee Journal,* August 26, 1949, cited in Zeidler, "Liberal in City Government," chap. 4, p. 143.

32. Anita Zeidler, interview by the author.

33. Frank Zeidler, letter to the author, October 9, 2005; Jacobs, *Death and Life*, 17; Leuchtenburg, "Keynote Address."

34. Frank Zeidler, letter to the author, October 9, 2005.

35. Gurda, *Making of Milwaukee*, 268–71.

36. Housing and Home Finance Agency, *Why and What of Title I*; U.S. Congress, House Select Committee, *Housing Lobby: Part 2*, 368.

37. "Digest of Public Opinion: Public Attitudes on Current Issues," May 1950, NAM, series I, Records, 1917–1970, box 6.

38. U.S. Congress, House Select Committee, *Housing Lobby: Part 2*, 351–362, 375, and Appendix.

39. Ibid., 375, 1,249–55, 1,261–62, and Appendix.

40. Conn, "Housing."

41. Minutes of the Board of Directors' Meeting, June 29, 1950, MAC, box 3, folder 1; Zeidler, "Liberal in City Government," chap. 4, p. 183.

42. "Final Report: Public Housing Referendum Committee," April 19, 1951, WLP, box 3, folder 47.

43. Ibid.; Zeidler, "Liberal in City Government," chap. 4, pp. 211–12; *Milwaukee Journal* and *Milwaukee Sentinel* advertisements and "Citizens' Committee Files Request for Referendum," Citizens' Committee press release, September 25, 1950, WLP, box 3, file 47.

44. "It's Your Money!" flier of the Public Housing Referendum Committee, CFZ, box 179, folder 1; Zeidler, "Liberal in City Government," chap. 4, pp. 181–86.

45. "Final Report"; Phone bank script; "Govt. Housing Costs YOU Money!" undated handbill, WLP, box 3, file 47; *The Property Owner* (Milwaukee: Milwaukee County Property Owners' Association, April 1951).

46. William Pieplow, letter to members of the Building-Savings and Loan Associations, December 7, 1950; William Pieplow, letter to organization leaders, n.d.; William Pieplow, letter to "Dear Pastor," January 9, 1951; William Pieplow, letter to "Dear Pastor," n.d.; WLP, box 3, file 47.

47. Richard Perrin, letter to Frank Zeidler, January 18, 1951, CFZ, box 179, folder 1.

48. "Final Report: Public Housing Referendum Committee," April 19, 1951; "Veterans Urge 'Yes' Vote on Referendum Number One," Housing Referendum Committee press release, March 19, 1951; and "Civic Groups Endorse Public Housing Referendum Petitions," Housing Referendum Committee press release, January 5, 1951, WLP, box 3, file 47. In 1985, Sen. Lloyd Bentsen (D-Texas) coined the term "Astroturf" to describe an orchestrated grassroots movement intended to appear spontaneous (Barrett, *Oxford Dictionary*, 34).

49. "Statement from the Public Housing Referendum Committee," January 18, 1951, CFZ, box 175, folder 5.

50. Reproductions of ads notated with placement; radio ad scripts for English and foreign language audiences, WLP, box 3, file 47.

51. *Twenty-First Biennial Report*. Public housing had helped frame the name of the Enterprise Committee. While debating what to call their new political vehicle, members rejected the word "public" because they recognized that even liberals equated "public housing" with socialism. Without the onerous word "public" to distract from their message, they could press for municipal ownership of housing and other services. (Zeidler, *Liberal in City Government*, 11–12.)

52. Conn, "Housing"; "'Canned' Campaign to Kill Public Housing Continues"; "Public Housing," *Milwaukee Labor Press*, January 25, 1951.

53. "Eagles Plan Award for Schoemann," *Milwaukee Labor Press,* April 15, 1948; "Schoemann Paired Union, Civic Leadership," *Milwaukee Sentinel*, July 15, 1957; Peter Schoemann obituary, *Milwaukee Journal*, August 8, 1976.

54. Zeidler, "Liberal in City Government," chap. 4, p. 283; "Schoemann Paired Union, Civic Leadership."

55. "Final Report."

56. "Committee Seeks Slum Clearance," *Referendum News*, Citizens' Anti-Slum Committee, n.d., RP, records carton 4, file Referendum-Housing-1951; "Final Report"; "Ask Milwaukee CIO Locals Contribute in Public Housing Fight," *Wisconsin CIO News*, February 16, 1951.

57. Zeidler, "Liberal in City Government," chap. 4, pp. 181–82; "So We Don't Need Public Housing?" *Milwaukee Labor Press*, March 15, 1951; Frank Zeidler, letter to A. E. Axtell, city manager, Kenosha, Wisconsin, February 7, 1951, CFZ, box 179, folder 2.

58. *Twenty-First Biennial Report*; "Final Report"; "Lose a Battle, Win a War," *Wisconsin CIO News*, April 6, 1951; "Housing Ban Winner; School Bonds Approved," *Milwaukee Labor Press*, April 5, 1951.

59. Zeidler, "Liberal in City Government," chap. 4, pp. 211–212; *Twenty-First Biennial Report*.

60. Zeidler, "Liberal in City Government," chap. 4, pp. 75, 216–69.

61. Pittsburgh mayor David Lawrence, letter to Frank Zeidler, January 29, 1951, CFZ, box 179, folder 1; Peterson, *Day of the Mugwump*, 91–95.

62. Hass, *DeLesseps S. Morrison*, 50–51; "Referendum Is Issue in Three Cities, Many States," *Journal of Housing*, February 1951.

63. Conn, "Housing"; "The Enduring Slums," *Fortune*, December 1957.

64. Smith, "From Socialism to Racism," 80; Zeidler, "Liberal in City Government," chap. 4, p. 229; Zeidler, interview by the author.

65. William Pieplow, undated speech, ca. 1949, WLP, box 3, file 48; U.S. Congress, Senate Subcommittee, *General Housing Legislation*, 807.

66. "'Go South First' Will Be Plea When Civic Group Meets," *Milwaukee Times*, July 25, 1957; Pieplow, *History*, 67–69, 143–44, 159; "Man of the Month"; see Zeidler and Koethe, *Reflections*.

67. "Pieplow Eulogies Planned by Group He Helped Organize," *Milwaukee Times*, September 24, 1959; Pieplow, *Century Lessons*, 8; William Pieplow, "Statement on Legislation," n.d., WLP, box 4, file 75.

68. William Pieplow, letter to Frank Zeidler, January 19, 1951, WLP, box 3, file 47.

69. "Government Public Housing Disastrous," undated speech, WLP, box 4, file 75.

70. Frank Zeidler, "Build Cities to Build Men, June 13, 1957," speech, in Wilke, "Selected Speeches," 156–57.

71. Zeidler, "First Inaugural Address," April 20, 1948, speech, in Wilke, "Selected Speeches"; William Pieplow, "Remarks," n.d., WLP, box 4, file 75.

72. As Foner notes, depictions of the nation's founders as embracing either liberalism (Hartz, Hofstadter) or republicanism (Wood, Pocock) and recent scholarship that has defined republicanism "as a shorthand for any political movement or ideology that seemed to reject the market capitalism of nineteenth and twentieth century America" have become reconciled so the strands are not so polarized. (Foner, *Tom Paine*, xviii–xix.) Frank Zeidler, "Greeting to the Conference of the Civil Service Assembly, May 28, 1956," in Wilke, "Selected Speeches," 90–92.

73. Zeidler, "Liberal in City Government," chap. 4, pp. 225–36.

74. "Continues at 80 as Active Head of Security S&L," *Milwaukee Sentinel*, April 7, 1956.

Chapter 5. Race, Class, Free Enterprise, and Suburbia

1. "The Negro Market," *Time*, July 5, 1954; "The U.S. Negro, 1953," *Time*, May 11, 1953.

2. Sugrue, *Sweet Land of Liberty*, 270–71, xv.

3. The "nonwhite" category in the 1950 U.S. Census included blacks, Native Americans, and Asians. Housing and Home Finance Agency, *Housing of the Nonwhite Population*, 10, 16, 18.

4. Ibid.; Abrams, *Forbidden Neighbors*, 28.

5. Zeidler, "Liberal in City Government," chap. 4, pp. 254–55, CFZ; Trotter, *Black Milwaukee*, 228; U.S. Census Bureau, *Historical Census Statistics*; League of Women Voters of Milwaukee, *Study of the Local Problems*.

6. "Nation Observes Negro History Week," *Milwaukee Defender*, February 14, 1957; "Housing Is Available If Nobody Wants It," *Milwaukee Journal*, June 2, 1960; "Halyards Go Far in City's Business Life," *Milwaukee Sentinel*, December 11, 1962.

7. Jones, *Selma*, 19.

8. Rueben Harpole, introduction to Geneen, *Images of Milwaukee's Bronzeville*; Cecil Brown Jr., "The Political Scene," *Milwaukee Defender*, May 29, 1957; Dougherty, "African Americans," 143; Jones, *Selma*, 25.

9. Holton quotation cited in Geneen, *Images of Milwaukee's Bronzeville*, 39, 9, 21; Shadd, *Negro Business Directory*; "The Pride of Ownership," *Milwaukee Defender*, August 10, 1957.

10. Andrew Kersten, "Fair Employment Practices Committee," in Arnesen, *Encyclopedia*, 1:428; "Negro Labor Gains Noted," *Milwaukee Journal*, June 22, 1952.

11. Geib, "From Mississippi to Milwaukee," 237; Minutes of the Board of Directors of the Milwaukee Urban League, January 21, 1955, MUL.

12. "'Fair Employment' Gains Shown in State in Past Year," *Milwaukee Journal*, October 5, 1952; Thompson, *History of Wisconsin*, 6:330; "Negro Labor Gains Noted."

13. Minutes of a Special Meeting of the Board of Directors of the Milwaukee Urban League, September 26, 1949, and Minutes of the Board of Directors of the Milwaukee Urban League, September 24, 1954, MUL; Rasche, "Need in Milwaukee."

14. Dougherty, *More than One Struggle*, 27, 34–36.

15. Trotter, *Black Milwaukee*, 184.

16. Thompson, *History of Wisconsin*, 6:334–35.

17. Citizens' Governmental Research Bureau, *Milwaukee's Negro Community*, 18; Loewen, *Sundown Towns*, 5–6; 414–15.

18. "Thinking of Selling. . . . Your Property?" flier, CFZ, box 175, folder 6.

19. League of Women Voters, *Study of the Local Problems*, part 4, p. 2.

20. "Block-Busting Sales Hinted," *Milwaukee Journal*, October 8, 1952; "Block-Busting Probe Likely," *Milwaukee Journal*, October 9, 1952; Zeidler, "Liberal in City Government," chap. 2, pp. 12, 28. The Common Council changed the name of the Mayor's Commission on Human Rights to the Milwaukee Commission on Human Rights in May 1954. Milwaukee Commission on Human Rights Newsletter, May–June 1954, CFZ, box 157, folder 2.

21. "Movement of Negroes Nothing New, Exciting," *Milwaukee Journal*, November 20, 1953; Zeidler, "Liberal in City Government," chap. 4, p. 144; Grover, "'All Things to Black Folk,'" 90; Minutes of the Regular Meeting of the Board of Directors of the Milwaukee Urban League, November 23, 1951, and December 21, 1951, MUL.

22. "Urge Housing for 6th Ward," *Milwaukee Journal*, November 23, 1952.

23. Davies, *Housing Reform*, 129–31; Hunt, "How Did Public Housing Survive the 1950s?"

24. Frank Zeidler, handwritten note, undated, ca. 1955, CFZ, box 101, folder 5; Zeidler, interview by the author; Zeidler, "Liberal in City Government," chap. 4, p. 247.

25. Milwaukee Public Library, *Milwaukee City and County: A Statistical History*; "Negro Group Suggests One of Its Members Be Given a Place on the Crime Commission," *Milwaukee Journal*, November 19, 1952; Zeidler, "Liberal in City Government," chap. 4, pp. 248–54.

26. Zeidler, "Liberal in City Government," chap. 4, pp. 248–56; "Movement of Negroes."

27. "Zeidler's Race Tension Statement Irks Realtors," *Milwaukee Journal*, November 19, 1952, "Realtors Deny Tension Role," *Milwaukee Journal*, November 25, 1952; "Urge Housing for 6th Ward," *Milwaukee Journal*, November 23, 1952; Zeidler, "Liberal in City Government," chap. 4, pp. 250–53.

28. Meyer, *As Long*, 7; Abrams, *Forbidden Neighbors*, 156–57; "Mayor Again Blasts Realtors," *Milwaukee Journal*, November 26, 1952.

29. Trotter, *Black Milwaukee*, 182–83.

30. Davies, *Housing Reform*, 125; Mayor's Study Committee, *Final Report*, "Fact-Finding Committee, Subcommittee on Housing Conditions and Availability, Study Committee on Social Problems in the Inner Core Area of the City," 20–21.

31. Mayor's Study Committee, *Final Report*, "Fact-Finding Committee, Subcommittee on Housing Conditions and Availability," 14–15; "Search for Housing Made as Test for Discrimination," *Milwaukee Journal*, May 25, 1960.

32. Frank Zeidler, "Occasion of the Opening of the Hillside Addition," speech, June 1, 1955, CFZ, box 107, folder 6.

33. Irwin Rinder, "The Housing of Negroes in Milwaukee," report of the Intercollegiate Council on Intergroup Relations, Milwaukee, 1955, MUL, box 22, folder 43; "Way to a Permanent Housing Boom," *Time*, February 7, 1955; Saffran, *Blight Elimination and Prevention*; Zeidler, "Liberal in City Government," chap. 4, p. 288.

34. Zeidler, "Liberal in City Government," chap. 4, p. 270–80.

35. Ibid., chap. 3, p. 32.

36. Geib, "From Mississippi to Milwaukee," 231.

37. "Zeidler's Race Tension Statement Irks Realtors," *Milwaukee Journal*, November 19, 1952; Frank Zeidler, "Talk by Mayor Zeidler before the Human Rights Commission," September 15, 1953, CFZ, box 107, folder 4; "Poor Political Fodder," *Milwaukee Times*, January 16, 1958.

38. "Thanks. . . . Help . . . Hope," *Milwaukee Defender*, January 3, 1957; "Discuss Crime in 6th Ward," *Milwaukee Journal*, March 9, 1953.

39. Trotter, *Black Milwaukee*, 109.

40. "Housing Woes Caused by a Variety of Factors," *Milwaukee Journal*, May 24, 1960; Mayor's Study Committee, *Final Report*; Fact-Finding Committee Subcommit-

tee on Availability of Community Facilities, "Report on Availability of Community Facilities in the Inner Core," February 1960, 2; Mayor's Study Committee, *Final Report*, 14.

41. Vel Phillips, interviews by the author.

42. "What Does the Future Hold for Us?" *Milwaukee Defender*, April 18, 1957. *The Globe*, published from 1946 to 1949, sought from its inception to seek out "the constructive, positive side of the news, still not ignoring the problems, the challenges, the unhealed tragedies of modern life." ("A Good Christmas," *The Globe*, December 25, 1948). The *Milwaukee Defender* and *The Globe* were the longest-lived of Milwaukee's African American newspapers in the 1940s and 1950s. The other papers included *The Milwaukee Sepian*, published from February 17, 1951, to April 10, 1951, and *The Rocket* and *The Beacon*, both published briefly in 1953.

43. Frank Zeidler, letter to the Milwaukee Common Council, December 23, 1951, CFZ, box 47, folder 11.

44. "Poor Political Fodder"; "A Welfare State?" *Milwaukee Times*, March 19, 1959; "Aid-For Strangers or Taxpayers?" *Wauwatosa News-Times*, February 20, 1958.

45. Minutes of the Board of Directors of the Milwaukee Urban League, February 15, 1957, and January 24, 1958, MUL.

46. Grover, "'All Things to Black Folk,'" 10, 18, 54, 92.

47. Cecil Brown Jr., "Political Scene," *Milwaukee Defender*, August 3, August 10, and August 24, 1957; "Preachers Help Us," *Milwaukee Defender*, October 5, 1957.

48. Geib, "From Mississippi to Milwaukee," 229, 232; Tilly, "Race and Migration," 143, 154, 156.

49. United States Commission on Civil Rights, *One Nation Under God*, 4:159.

50. For a history of city planning in Milwaukee with an emphasis supporting an approach that promotes compact urban neighborhoods, see McCarthy, *Making Milwaukee Mightier*.

51. Sugrue, *Sweet Land of Liberty*, 249; "Milwaukee's 'Growing Pains': A Series of Seven Articles Analyzing Milwaukee's Postwar Growth and Expansion," reprinted from the *Milwaukee Journal*, 1955; "Downtown Area Use Drops, Bruening Says," *Milwaukee Journal*, January 6, 1959; Zeidler, "Liberal in City Government," chap. 3, p. 23.

52. Zeidler, "Liberal in City Government," chap. 3, pp. 16–19, 52–56.

53. Ibid., chap. 3, p. 26; Milwaukee Commission on Human Rights, *Annual Report*, 1955, CFZ, box 156, folder 2.

54. United States Commission on Civil Rights, *One Nation Under God*, 4:143, 148.

55. Central Railroad of New Jersey magazine, cited in Abrams, *Forbidden Neighbors*, 144–45; McCarthy, *Making Milwaukee Mightier*, 68.

56. Zeidler, "A Liberal in City Government," chap. 3, pp. 48–52.

57. "Invitation to Consolidate Gets Pointed 'No,'" *West Allis Star*, July 5, 1956.

58. Zeidler, "Liberal in City Government," chap. 3, p. 13; "Vulnerability Is Fatal to Town Government," *Milwaukee Journal*, January 15, 1957; *Official Bulletin: Report by the City Government of Wauwatosa*, December 31, 1959, WC, box 2, folder 1.

59. McCarthy, *Making Milwaukee Mightier*, 69.

60. "Over My Dead Body," *Wauwatosa News-Times*, June 14, 1956; *Official Bulletin: A Report by the City Government of Wauwatosa*, December 31, 1954, WC, box 2, folder 1.

61. "Alderman Opposes Water Request for Wauwatosa People," *Wauwatosa News-Times*, June 7, 1956; "City Files Water Petition in Madison," *Wauwatosa News-Times*, November 15, 1956; "Over My Dead Body," *Wauwatosa News-Times*, June 14, 1956.

62. "Construction of Water Reservoir Approved Here," *West Allis Star*, October 25, 1956, "Water Rate Boost Not Felt Here," *West Allis Star*, July 19, 1956.

63. Zeidler, "Liberal in City Government," chap. 3, pp. 102–4; "They've Earned Bitterness," *West Allis Star*, October 25, 1956.

64. Zeidler, "Liberal in City Government," chap. 3, pp. 61–62.

65. Banfield, *Government and Housing*, 142–43; Zeidler, "The Metropolitan Area," speech to the U.S. Conference of Mayors, July 1959, CFZ, box 332, folder 3; Zeidler, "Liberal in City Government," chap. 3, pp. 8–10.

66. "Invitation to Consolidate Gets Pointed 'No'"; "Racial Issue Is a Moral One–Not Legislative," *West Allis Star*, April 5, 1956.

67. "Aren't We the 'Villains'?" *West Allis Star*, July 26, 1956; "Time to Crack Down," *Wauwatosa News-Times*, October 5, 1956; "Prosperity and Poverty Still," *Wauwatosa News-Times*, October 24, 1957.

68. Zeidler, "Liberal in City Government," chap. 3, pp. 32–33, 36; Sol Ackerman, letter to the editor, *Wauwatosa News-Times*, May 23, 1957.

69. "Mr. Zeidler's 'One World,'" *West Allis Star*, May 24, 1956.

70. "Bread First, Then Culture," *West Allis Star*, August 2, 1956; "Touch of Socialism," *Wauwatosa News-Times*, February 14, 1957.

71. "PSC Orders Milwaukee to Sell Us Water," *Wauwatosa News-Times*, April 3, 1958, "Common Sense Scores a Victory," *Wauwatosa News-Times*, April 10, 1958.

72. "The Whys of the Iron Ring," *Wauwatosa News-Times*, February 6, 1958.

73. Zeidler, "Liberal in City Government," chap. 3, p. 211.

74. Zeidler, interview by the author; "Here's Proof of 'Billboard' Falsehoods," *Milwaukee Labor Press*, March 15, 1956, CFZ, box 48, folder 1; "Labor Group Finds 'No Billboard Ads for Negroes,'" *Milwaukee Journal*, March 14, 1956.

75. Arndorfer, "Cream City Confidential," 75; Murray Kempton, "Designed for Export?" *New York Post*, March 15, 1956, clipping, CFZ, box 47, folder 11; "'Vicious' Race Rumors in Mayor's Fight Decried," *Milwaukee Journal*, March 10, 1956; "The Shame of Milwaukee," *Time*, April 2, 1956.

76. "Shifts Made by McGuire Campaign," *Milwaukee Journal*, March 30, 1956; "The Smear That Failed," *Time*, April 16, 1956.

77. Zeidler, "Milwaukee's Racial Tension: The Problem of the New Negro Migration," *The Socialist*, March 1954, CFZ, box 331, folder 2.

78. "Zeidler, McGuire, Stage Lively Debate," *Milwaukee Journal*, March 29, 1956; "Union Faction Aids McGuire," *Milwaukee Journal*, March 2, 1956.

79. Perlstein, *Before the Storm*, 11–12; "'For America' Plans a Drive," *Milwaukee Journal*, March 3, 1956, "Mayor Asks McGuire to Deny Group," *Milwaukee Journal*, March 14, 1956; J. J. Woerfel, letter to employees, March 20, 1956, CFZ, box 48, folder 2.

80. "'For America' Group Support OK'd by McGuire," *Milwaukee Journal*, March 16, 1956; "A Disappointed Taxpayer," letter to Zeidler, received in the mayor's office March 21, 1956, CFZ, box 47, folder 11.

81. "No Socialism in City Hall under Zeidler Administration," *Milwaukee Journal*, March 22, 1956; Gavett, *Development*, 209.

82. "McGuire Has Been in a Position to Lead; Look at Record," *Milwaukee Journal*, March 19, 1956; "No Socialism in City Hall under Zeidler Administration," *Milwaukee Journal*, March 22, 1956.

83. "No Socialism in City Hall"; "New Strength in City Hall," *Fortune*, November 1957; "The Voter's Review," Zeidler for Mayor Committee, March 1952, FZ, box 3, folder 4.

84. "'Vicious' Race Rumors"; "Pastor Hits 'Whispers' Raised against Zeidler," *Milwaukee Journal*, March 19, 1956; Anita Zeidler, interview by the author.

85. "Shame of Milwaukee"; "The Vote in Wisconsin," *Toledo Blade*, April 5, 1956; "Milwaukee Voters Rebuke a Campaign of Bigotry," *St. Paul Pioneer-Press*, April 6, 1956, clippings, CFZ, box 48, folder 1; "Indecisive Wisconsin," *Washington Post and Times Herald*, April 5, 1956; "Smear That Failed."

86. Vel Phillips, interview by the author, October 18, 2009; Barbara Miner, "Valiant Lady Vel," *Milwaukee Magazine*, January 1, 2005.

87. Vel Phillips, interview by the author, October 18, 2009; "Council Race Hard Fought," *Milwaukee Journal*, April 1, 1956.

88. Jones, *Selma of the North*, 32–35, 38.

89. Ibid., 38 and 270n1; Dougherty, "African Americans," 143.

90. Mayor's Study Committee, *Final Report*, 23.

91. Frank Zeidler, statement at a meeting on the Social Problems of the Core of the City, September 3, 1959, in Mayor's Study Committee, *Final Report*; Arndorfer, "Cream City Confidential," 75–76; Maier, *Mayor*, 38–39; Jones, *Selma of the North*, 25; Vel Phillips, interview by the author, October 18, 2009.

92. "The Mayor, the Press, and a Stormy Era," *Milwaukee Journal*, April 10, 1988; "An Era of Achievement and Neglect," editorial, *Milwaukee Journal*, April 17, 1988; Stephanie Simon, "The Old South up North: Milwaukee Is the Most Segregated Metro Area, Data Show," *Los Angeles Times*, December 30, 2002.

93. "Shame of Milwaukee"; Zeidler, "Liberal in City Government," chap. 4, p. 246; Arndorfer, "Cream City Confidential," 75–76.

94. Zeidler, interview by John Johannes.

95. "Commission Report," *Time*, September 14, 1959.

Chapter 6. Collective Action and the Threat to Free Enterprise

1. "Foundry Workers!" display ad, *Milwaukee Journal*, September 3, 1946.
2. Miner, *Grede of Milwaukee*, 90–100.
3. Ibid., 13, 23–26, 31–35.
4. Ibid., 56, 75–79, 90–94, 238–39.
5. Ibid., 53–54, 61–69.

Notes to Chapter 6

6. Ibid., 99; Miner, *Grede of Milwaukee*, 79–87, 99, 110; Miner, "New Wave," 248; William Grede Biographical Summary, WJG.

7. Miner, *Grede of Milwaukee*, 171–72; Miner, "New Wave," 248.

8. Harris, *Right to Manage*, 43.

9. Ibid., 67–71.

10. Gavett, *Development*, 190–92; Seidman, *American Labor*, 221.

11. *Fortune* poll cited in Harris, *Right to Manage*, 40.

12. Collins, *Business Response to Keynes*, 15–17, 205; Harris, *Right to Manage*, 118–19.

13. Phillips-Fein, *Invisible Hands*, 325; Vogel, *Kindred Strangers*, 268.

14. *Fortune* editors, *USA*, 7, 191–92; Lichtenstein, "Corporatism to Collective Bargaining," 126; Lichtenstein, *State of the Union*, 136; Harris, *Right to Manage*, 71.

15. Anthony J. King papers, box 7, folder 4, AJK.

16. Frank Zeidler, letter to Walter Reuther, April 23, 1948, CFZ, box 84, folder 3.

17. For two examples of such intervention, one involving a strike at International Harvester and another at Heil, see Assistant City Attorney Arthur Saltzstein, letters to Frank Zeidler, August 26, 1948, and August 30, 1948; Frank Zeidler, letter to John E. Cudahy, president of International Harvester Federal Labor Union, August 30, 1948; Frank Zeidler, letter to the Wisconsin State Employment Office, August 10, 1949; Willett S. Main, Manager, Milwaukee Wisconsin State Employment Office, letter to Frank Zeidler, August 11, 1949, CFZ, box 181, folder 10.

18. Frank Zeidler, memorandum to himself, January 5, 1949, CFZ, box 181, folder 10.

19. "Block Wins First Round by 3–2 Vote," *Milwaukee Labor Press*, June 30, 1949.

20. For instance, see Walter J. Burke, director of Steelworkers District 32, letter to Frank Zeidler regarding Zeidler's instrumental intervention in settlement of a strike at Heil, October 17, 1949, CFZ, box 181; Cigar Makers Local 25, letter to Frank Zeidler with Zeidler's handwritten response, undated, ca. 1950, CFZ, box 182, folder 1.

21. Harris, *Right to Manage*, 127; NAM, Public Relations Department, "Public Opinion Digest," February 28, 1949, citing a Gallup survey, NAM, box 6, Series I, Record, 1917–1970.

22. "Equipment Maker Sets Two Records: Harnischfeger Corp. Sales and Profits Were Highest Yet in Fiscal Year," *New York Times*, December 30, 1953; loose pages from a Harnischfeger company booklet, WH, box 1, folder 8; Miner, *Grede of Milwaukee*, 129–30.

23. Harnischfeger biographical information, WH; "Taft-Hartley Situation Calls for Immediate Action," Public Affairs Bulletin, MAC, March 28, 1948, CFZ, box 37, folder 1.

24. Walter Burke, Steelworkers District 32 Director, letter to George Haberman, October 9, 1958, and George Haberman, letter to all affiliates, November 4, 1958, WIAFL-CIO, box 5, folder 46.

25. Shefferman, *Man in the Middle*, 13, 152; Pearson, "What's So New," 4–5.

26. Phillips-Fein, "Business Conservatism," 12, 15–16; Jacoby, *Modern Manors*, 204–5; Lee, *Eisenhower*, 41.

27. Study of business journals by Marver Bernstein cited in Vogel, *Kindred Strangers*, 31–38.

28. "Freedom Forum Fascist Front" and "Show Talks Tied Up with Fascist Groups," *Wisconsin CIO News*, January 6, 1950; "'Freedom Forum Hokkum,' Union Reporter Finds," *Wisconsin CIO News*, February 3, 1950; Max Raskin, "Is Freedom Forum Legal?" *Wisconsin CIO News*, June 23, 1950.

29. Fones-Wolf, *Selling Free Enterprise*, 53.

30. Minutes of the Board of Directors' Meeting, January 30, 1956, and March 28, 1956, MAC, box 3, folder 7.

31. Minutes of the Board of Directors' Meeting, January 25, 1951, MAC, box 3, folder 2; Miner, *Grede of Milwaukee*, 163.

32. Wisconsin Manufacturers' Association, *Bulletin*, December 6, 1951; Wisconsin Manufacturers' Association, *Wisconsin Manufacturers' Association and You!*; Wisconsin Manufacturers' Association, *Behind the Headlines*.

33. Miner, *Grede of Milwaukee*, 100; William J. Grede, letter to E. J. Ellis, March 27, 1952, WJG, box 25, folder 1.

34. Goldfield, *Decline of Organized Labor*, 90–91, 10–11.

35. Uphoff, *Kohler on Strike*, 275–76.

36. Ibid., 55–65, 382–83; "Business: Unhappy Birthday," *Time*, April 18, 1955.

37. "CIO Will Call a City-Wide Strike in Milwaukee if Kohler Clay Is Unloaded; Meet with Mayor Friday," *Wisconsin CIO News*, July 8, 1955; "Kohler Negotiations Are Resumed; Wisconsin State CIO Reaffirms Its Support," *CIO News*, July 29, 1955.

38. "CIO Will Call"; "CIO Wins Objective: Ike Orders Kohler Peace Talks; No Council Guarantee to Unload," *CIO News*, July 15, 1955; Zeidler, interview by John Johannes; Frank Zeidler, letter to the Milwaukee Common Council July 15, 1955, CFZ, box 106, folder 5; Uphoff, *Kohler on Strike*, 236.

39. A Group of Milwaukee Taxpayers, letter to S. Douglas Brian, President, Papermakers Importing Company, Easton, PA, July 11, 1955, CFZ, box 106, folder 4.

40. J. F. Friedrich, testimony, "Proceedings of Public Hearing Held by the Board of Harbor Commissioners of the City of Milwaukee, at the City Hall Annex Board Room, in the City of Milwaukee, on the 13th day of September 1955, commencing at 2:00 o'clock pm," CFZ, box 106, folder 5; Uphoff, *Kohler on Strike*, 243.

41. "A Keystone of the Free World," *Time*, January 4, 1954; *Milwaukee Wisconsin Market*; "Higher High Life," *Time*, January 12, 1953.

42. Allen, *Big Change*, 214; "Have the Very Wealthy Achieved Their Victory in the Class War?" *Dollars and Sense*, November 11, 2009; Galbraith, *Affluent Society*, 86.

43. NAM, series I, Records, 1917–1970, box 105, Positions/St. Lawrence Seaway.

44. Julius Barnes, President, National St. Lawrence Association, letter to "My dear St. Lawrence Advocate," July 31, 1948, CFZ, box 132, folder 7.

45. NAM, series I, Records, 1917–1970, box 105, Positions/St. Lawrence Seaway; Frank Zeidler, Letter to George Hampel Jr., Director, Publicity and Research, Wisconsin State Federation of Labor, 1950, and Louis Quarles, letter to Frank Zeidler, April 11, 1951, CFZ, box 132, folder 8; "Wisconsin Urges Seaway Project: State Leaders Press Drive in Congress for Waterway-Labor Aids in Campaign," *New York Times*, April 6, 1952.

46. Walter Harnischfeger, Testimony before the Public Works Committee of the U.S. House of Representatives, April 24, 1951, CFZ, box 132, folder 8.

47. Ibid.

48. Editorial, *Federationist*, May 1951, vol. 5, CFZ, box 26, folder 7.

49. "Hearings Stop; Leave Action for Next Year," *Federationist*, June 1950, CFZ, box 132, folder 8.

50. Eisenhower, *Mandate for Change*, 301; Frank Zeidler, letter to Senator John Kennedy, February 1, 1954, CFZ, box 133, folder 4.

51. Thompson, *History of Wisconsin*, 6:663–65.

52. Cornell, "Collective Bargaining," 46; "Referendum Chance Is Slim," *Wauwatosa News-Times*, June 13, 1958; Thompson, *History of Wisconsin*, 6:672.

53. Lee, *Eisenhower*, 62. McNamara cited in Kennedy, *Enemy Within*, 301.

54. Perlstein, *Before the Storm*, 22, 37.

55. Gallup poll cited in Lichtenstein, *State of the Union*, 163–64; Lee, *Eisenhower*, 73; "Labor Hits Bias in Probe Report," *AFL-CIO News*, March 29, 1958.

56. "Unions Eye Municipal Employees," March 21, 1958, *Business Week*.

57. "Organized Labor–The Dwindling Minority?" *Fortune*, November 1958.

58. Milwaukee Public Library, *Milwaukee City and County*; Anderson and Olson, *Milwaukee*, 138; "10% of Industry Growth Is Going to Other States," *Milwaukee Journal*, March 31, 1953; Crabb, *Milwaukee's Industrial Growth*.

59. "State Tax Climate under Fire at Annual Meeting," *Milwaukee Commerce*, November 25, 1958, CFZ, box 37, folder 1; *The Property Owner* [newsletter of Milwaukee County Property Association], September 1957, Frank Zeidler, letter to Milwaukee County Property Owners' Association, August 15, 1957, and Arthur Buenger, vice-chairman, Affiliated Taxpayers Committee, letter to Frank Zeidler, August 23, 1957, all CFZ, box 193, folder 6.

60. William J. Grede, address before the Grocery Manufacturers Association, November 21, 1952, Milwaukee, WJG, box 25, folder 1.

61. Harnischfeger biographical information, WH, box 1, folder 8; Herbert Hoover, letter to Harnischfeger, August 22, 1954, box 1, folder 8a.

62. William Lawson, memo to William Grede, December 19, 1952, WJG, box 25, folder 1; Miner, *Grede of Milwaukee*, 127.

63. Zeidler, "Liberal in City Government," chap. 4, p. 416.

64. Forster and Epstein, *Danger on the Right*, 279; Dore Schary, foreword to Forster and Epstein, *Danger on the Right*, xii.

65. Forster and Epstein, *Danger on the Right*, 8, 10, 191. For Grede's fundraising efforts on behalf of Manion, see WJG, box 21, folder 3.

66. William Grede, letter to Board of Directors, Grede Foundries Inc., July 21, 1958, WJG, box 9.

67. William Grede, generic fundraising letter, May 13, 1960, and Robert LeFevre, letter to C. W. Anderson, Executive Director, Employers' Association of Milwaukee, November 29, 1958, WJG, box 7, folder 6; Report on the Phrontistery, Robert LeFevre, June 1964, WJG, box 45, folder 2; LeFevre, *Way to Be Free*, 2:405–6, 429–30.

68. "The Assault on Representative Government by Mr. Grede, Mr. Buckley, and the Communists," editorial, *Capital Times*, March 25, 1953; for Grede's Republican

Party activities, see WJG, box 28, folders 8 and 9; "A Report to Members," 1956, NAM, series I, Records, 1917–1970, box 115.

Chapter 7. Public Interest vs. Public Employees

1. "Strike Vote Is Approved by AFSCME," *Milwaukee Labor Press*, December 4, 1958; "Meeting Set on City Strike," *Milwaukee Journal*, December 4, 1958.

2. "Milwaukee: Mayor, Council Heads Deserve Backing on Strike Attitude," *Milwaukee Journal*, December 4, 1958; "City Strikes Alarm Mayors–Zeidler," *Milwaukee Sentinel*, December 2, 1958.

3. "City Workers to Weigh Offer," *Milwaukee Labor Press*, November 25, 1958; "Union Demand Cost Put Near $375,000," *Milwaukee Journal*, December 30, 1958; "Mayor, Aldermen Rip Strike Vote," *Milwaukee Sentinel*, December 3, 1958.

4. "No Appeal to Zinos Union, Zeidler Says," *Milwaukee Journal*, December 2, 1958.

5. "Tough but Dedicated, Zinos Helped Shape Public-Sector Labor Union Law," *Milwaukee Journal-Sentinel*, December 17, 2006.

6. Germanson, interview by the author; Zeidler, "Liberal in City Government," chap. 2, p. 32.

7. "No Appeal to Zinos Union, Zeidler Says," *Milwaukee Journal*, December 2, 1958; Cling, "Industrial Labor Relations," 577–78.

8. "Map Steps to Solve City Strike Issues," *Milwaukee Journal*, December 8, 1958; "Mercury Plummets to −10; 5 Below Is Forecast Tonight," *Milwaukee Journal*, December 9, 1958; "This Figures," *Milwaukee Labor Press*, December 11, 1958.

9. "City Union Drops Demand," *Milwaukee Labor Press*, December 23, 1958.

10. Kramer, *Labor's Paradox*, 37; Slater, *Public Workers*, 75–76; Cunningham, "Public Employment," 409.

11. Kramer, *Labor's Paradox*, 37; Arnold Zander, "How Can Strikes by Municipal Employees Be Avoided? Avoid Delays or Condescension, Urges Labor Leader," *American City*, February 1947, 84.

12. "Unions Eye Municipal Employees," *Business Week*, March 21, 1959.

13. Kramer, *Labor's Paradox*, 1–3, 32.

14. Mire, "Collective Bargaining," 350; Slater, *Public Workers*, 173.

15. Slater, *Public Workers*, 183–91; "Strike Threat against City Gets Support," *Milwaukee Journal*, December 8, 1958; Wisconsin Education Association Council, "WEAC History Book, Chapter 2."

16. "Strike Threat against City Gets Support," *Milwaukee Journal*, December 8, 1958.

17. "City Employees Organize," *Milwaukee Journal*, August 8, 1919; "City Firemen's Union Is Non Strike Body," *Milwaukee Journal*, April 6, 1920; White, *Trends in Public Administration*, 307; Cling, "Industrial Labor Relations," 389–90, 413.

18. "Milwaukee Reports to the People," *Milwaukee Sentinel*, supplement to Sunday paper authorized by resolution adopted by the Milwaukee Common Council, May 17, 1955, and prepared by the Municipal Reference Library, published October 9, 1955; Cling, "Industrial Labor Relations," 447–51, 458, 471–72; "AFSCME: 75 Years of

History," http://www.afscme.org/union/history/afscme-75-years-of-history (accessed May 10, 2014); "City and County Union, Packing House Workers Swing 1,530 into CIO," *Wisconsin CIO News*, August 14, 1937.

19. Cling, "Industrial Labor Relations," 629–74; "City Workers Out on Strike Face Ouster," *Milwaukee Journal*, November 5, 1943; "City 'Ousters' Sent Strikers," *Milwaukee Journal*, November 8, 1943; CIO Economic Outlook, quoted in Seidman, *American Labor*, 221. Roosevelt's much-cited quote was part of a letter to Luther Steward, the president of the National Federation of Federal Employees, and reads in part, "All government employees should realize that the process of collective bargaining, as usually understood, cannot be transplanted into the public service. It has its distinct and insurmountable limitations when applied to public personnel management. The very nature and purposes of government make it impossible for administrative officials to represent fully or to bind the employer in mutual discussions with government employee organizations. The employer is the whole people, who speak by means of laws enacted by their representatives in Congress. Accordingly, administrative officials and employees alike are governed and guided, and in many instances restricted, by laws which establish policies, procedures, or rules in personnel matters" (Cornell, "Collective Bargaining," 48).

20. Friedrich et al., *Problems*, 172, 226.

21. Cornell, "Collective Bargaining," 55; Mire, "Collective Bargaining," 349–50; H. Eliot Kaplan, "How Can Strikes by Municipal Employees Be Avoided? Adequate Machinery Needed to Handle Public Employee Grievances," *American City*, February 1947, 83; Meany, "Union Leaders," 165.

22. "Employees Organize in Growing Numbers in Cities," *American City*, July 1949; "AFSCME: 75 Years of History."

23. "Court Backs Strike Right! Utility Act Is Killed by High Court," *Milwaukee Labor Press*, March 1, 1951; Cling, "Industrial Labor Relations," 334–36.

24. Zinos, "American City," 112; Germanson interviews by Michael Gordon.

25. "Pay Boosts Opposed in Council Unit," January 6, 1959, and "Aldermen, Union Split on Settling Rifts," *Milwaukee Journal*, December 29, 1958.

26. "Meeting Set on City Strike," *Milwaukee Journal*, December 4, 1958; "Strike Threat against City Gets Support," *Milwaukee Journal*, December 8, 1958.

27. Frank Zeidler, letter to Walter Swietlik, October 31, 1951, CFZ, box 182, folder 5; Zeidler, *A Liberal in City Government*, 18.

28. "Right to Strike," *Milwaukee Times*, December 11, 1958.

29. Notes compiled by Frank Zeidler, fall of 1958, "Relating to Collective Bargaining and Contracts between City and Labor Organizations," CFZ, box 182, folder 5.

30. Paul Gauer, Gauer, Buer, and Murray, Attorneys at Law (Milwaukee), letter to Frank Zeidler, December 16, 1958, and Frank Zeidler, letter to Paul Gauer, December 17, 1958, CFZ, box 182, folder 5.

31. Edward Jeffries, "How Can Strikes by Municipal Employees Be Avoided? Peaceful Settlement Advocated," *American City*, February 1947, 85.

32. Zander, "Union View," 314.

33. Cornell, citing American Bar Association's Committee on Labor Relations of Government Employes report in the 1955 Proceedings of the ABA Section of Labor Relations Law, in "Collective Bargaining," 57; Anderson, "American City," 92.

34. Meany, "Union Leaders," 173; Wurf, "Union Leaders," 180.

35. Frank Zeidler, letter to Joseph Mire, May 15, 1951, CFZ, box 182, folder 1; Zeidler, "Public Servants," 9.

36. Frank Zeidler, letter to Richard Humphreys, ACLU, Milwaukee, April 21, 1959, CFZ, box 182, folder 3.

37. Murphy, *Blackboard Unions*, 209–10, 226–27.

38. Blank interview; Murphy, *Blackboard Unions*, 226.

39. Ibid.; Murphy, *Blackboard Unions*, 216; Wisconsin Education Association Council, "WEAC History Book, Chapter 2."

40. "Local Unions Plan to Merge," *Milwaukee Journal*, February 5, 1956; "CIO and AFL Pledge Fight against Chamber Attack; Legislative Battle Looms for Our Union's Future," *Wisconsin City and County Union News*, October 1956.

41. League of Wisconsin Municipalities survey cited in Cling, "Industrial Labor Relations," 353–54.

42. "Map Steps to Solve City Strike Issues," *Milwaukee Journal*, December 8, 1958; "Opposition Builds Up to Union Shop in City," *Milwaukee Journal*, November 2, 1956.

43. "Orderly Collective Bargaining the Issue," *Wisconsin CIO News*, November 15, 1957.

44. Cornell, "Collective Bargaining," 57–58; Cunningham, "Public Employment," 413.

45. Cling, "Industrial Labor Relations," 471, 472; "Opposition Builds Up to Union Shop in City," *Milwaukee Journal*, November 2, 1956; Folke Peterson, letter to Elmer Riemann, CFZ, box 182, folder 1.

46. Hansen, "Milwaukee City Employees." Hansen was counsel for the journal.

47. "No Appeal to Zinos Union, Zeidler Says," *Milwaukee Journal*, December 2, 1958; "Meeting Set on City Strike," *Milwaukee Journal*, December 4, 1958; "Council Group Pushes Benefits for City Union," *Milwaukee Journal*, January 3, 1959; Captain Leroy Bach, letter to Frank Zeidler, December 3, 1958, CFZ, box 182, folder 5.

48. "Opposition Builds Up to Union Shop in City," *Milwaukee Journal*, November 2, 1956.

49. "Meeting Set on City Strike," *Milwaukee Journal*, December 4, 1958, "City Will Get Pact Demands," *Milwaukee Journal*, November 12, 1956.

50. Frank Zeidler, letter to Walter Mattison, February 19, 1959; Harry Slater, letter to Frank Zeidler, February 20, 1959; Frank Zeidler, letter to Common Council, February 25, 1959, CFZ, box 182, folder 5.

51. Notes compiled by Frank Zeidler, fall 1958, "Relating to Collective Bargaining and Contracts between City and Labor Organizations"; Frank Zeidler, letter to F. W. Krueger, January 6, 1959, CFZ box 182, folder 5; Frank Zeidler, letter to Richard Humphreys, April 29, 1959; Frank Zeidler, letter to Bob Repas, November 27, 1957, CFZ, box 182, folder 3; Zeidler, "Public Servants," 11.

52. Cornell, citing 1955 American Bar Association report, in "Collective Bargaining," 56–57.
53. Mire, "Collective Bargaining," 348–49; Mire, "Unions."
54. Frank Zeidler, "Greeting to the Conference of the Civil Service Assembly," May 28, 1956, in Wilke, "Selected Speeches," 78–80.
55. Weisenfeld, "Philosophy of Bargaining," 42.
56. Rains, "Collective Bargaining," 548.
57. Galbraith, *Affluent Society*, 265; Weisenfeld, "Philosophy of Bargaining," 42.
58. Godine, *Labor Problem*, 26; Simons, "American City," 106.
59. Godine, *Labor Problem*, 26; Simons, "American City," 106.
60. Slater, *Public Workers*, 4, also quoting historian Michael Zwieg.
61. Notes compiled by Frank Zeidler, fall 1958, "Relating to Collective Bargaining and Contracts between City and Labor Organizations," CFZ, box 182, folder 5.
62. Ibid.
63. Ibid.
64. Cunningham, "Public Employment," 406–9.
65. Zeidler, "Public Servants"; Zeidler et al., "Rethinking," 2.
66. Zeidler, "Public Servants"; Zeidler et al., "Rethinking," 6.
67. Petro, "Sovereignty," 358.
68. Weisenfeld, "Philosophy of Bargaining," 46; Zander, "Union View," 314–15.
69. Nash, *Conservative Intellectual Movement*, xv.
70. Cunningham, "Public Employment" 424.
71. Devinatz, "Zeidler's Views," 329–30; Cunningham, "Public Employment," 424.
72. Zeidler et al., "New Roles."
73. Zeidler et al., "Rethinking," 9; John Nichols, "Zeidler Keeps the Old Red Flag Flying," *Madison Capital Times*, June 6, 1996.
74. Frankel, "Employer-Employee Relations," 223.
75. Zeidler, "Administrator," 180; Mansfield, "Prestige of Public Employment," 35–49.
76. Galbraith, *Affluent Society*, 133, 266–67.
77. Weisenfeld, "Collective Bargaining," 1–2.
78. McCartin, "Wagner Act," 124, 148.
79. Zeidler, "Administrator," 182.
80. "Your Work in Milwaukee City Service," published by the authority of the Milwaukee Common Council, 1955.
81. Zeidler, "Greeting to the Conference of the Civil Service Assembly," May 28, 1956, in Wilke, "Selected Speeches," 90–92.

Conclusion

1. Jill Hopke, "Remembering: As We Move Wisconsin Forward," *Defend Wisconsin*, February 11, 2012, available at http://www.defendwisconsin.org/?s=hopke (accessed May 10, 2014); link has expired but has been cross-posted to the following site: http://www.aflcio.org/Blog/Organizing-Bargaining/Remembering.-As-We-Move-Wisconsin-Forward (accessed July 31, 2015).
2. Ibid.

3. "Wisconsin's Legacy for Unions," *New York Times*, February 22, 2014. For detailed coverage of the protests, see the [Madison] *Capitol Times*, beginning February 14, 2011.

4. "Preacher's Kid Was Drawn to Politics Early in Life," *Milwaukee Journal-Sentinel*, March 29, 2002.

5. "Milwaukeeans Say Farewell to Their Longest-Reigning Mayor," *Milwaukee Sentinel*, July 22, 1994; "Maier Leaves a Mixed Legacy," *Milwaukee Sentinel*, July 18, 1994; "An Era of Achievement and Neglect," *Milwaukee Journal*, April 17, 1988.

6. For a detailed examination of the struggle for civil rights in 1960s Milwaukee, see Jones, *Selma of the North*; Maier, *Mayor*, 269.

7. "Housing Is Available–If Nobody Wants It," *Milwaukee Journal*, June 2, 1960; Jim Arndorfer, "Cream City Confidential: The Black-Baiting of Milwaukee's Last Pink Mayor," *The Baffler* (Winter 1999, no. 13), 75–76; Frank Zeidler, interview by author, September 22, 2005.

8. "Maier Leaves a Mixed Legacy.".

9. "The Old South, Up North: Milwaukee Is the Most Segregated Metro Area, Data Show; Its Black Residents Face Glaring Inequities in Income, Schools, and Home Loans," *Los Angeles Times*, December 30, 2002.

10. Ibid.; "Study Says Suburbs Violate Agreement on Fair Housing," *Milwaukee Journal*, July 11, 1990; "So You're Going to Vote for Mayor?" press release, February 17, 1960, CFZ, box 107, folder 7; "Population and Hispanic and Non-Hispanic Data, Wisconsin Municipalities, Census 2000 and 2010 Comparisons," based on Census 2010 Geography, U.S. Census Bureau, C2000 Summary File 1 and C2010 Redistricting Data File, Wisconsin Department of Administration.

11. "Palermo Cited by OSHA: Employee Loses Three Fingers in Accident," *Milwaukee Business Journal*, May 22, 2013; "Fight over Immigrant Firings," *New York Times*, July 27, 2012; "Taking the Truth About Palermo's Pizza to Costco," AFL-CIO *Now*, November 16, 2012; "AFL-CIO Endorses National Boycott of Palermo's," *Milwaukee Journal-Sentinel*, August 9, 2012; "Tell Palermo's Pizza–Stop the Harassment!" Online petition, MoveOn.org, http://petitions.moveon.org/sign/tell-palermos-pizza-stop (accessed March 30, 2014); "Union Files New Complaint Against Palermo's Pizza in Milwaukee," *Milwaukee Journal-Sentinel*, October 24, 2013.

12. "NLRB Ruling Mostly Sides with Palermo's Pizza in Labor Dispute," *Milwaukee Journal-Sentinel*, November 21, 2012.

13. "Metropolitan Area: Union Membership, Coverage, Density and Employment by Metropolitan Area and Sector, 1986–2013," *Union Membership Coverage Database from the CPS*, Union Stats, www.unionstats.com (accessed April 5, 2014); "American Union Membership Declines as Public Support Fluctuates," February 24, 2014, Pew Research Center, http://www.pewresearch.org/fact-tank/2014/02/20/for-american-unions-membership-trails-far-behind-public-support (accessed March 30, 2014); "Membership in Public Worker Unions Takes a Hit under Act 10," *Milwaukee Journal-Sentinel*, July 20, 2013.

14. McCartin, "Public Employee Union," 3.

15. MacLean, *Freedom Is Not Enough*, 35–37. MacLean argues that both the civil rights movement and conservative movement began in 1955. Gerald Mayer, "Union Membership Trends in the United States," August 31, 2004, *Congressional Research Service*.

16. Zeidler, "Liberal in City Government," chap. 4, pp. 643–44; Anita Zeidler interview.

17. "The Halo Effect," *Milwaukee Magazine*, September 2006; "So You're Going to Vote for Mayor?" press release, February 17, 1960, CFZ, box 107, folder 7; "Zeidler, Big Money Era Wouldn't Mix," *Milwaukee Journal-Sentinel*, July 10, 2006; Bill Lueders, "The Last of a Breed," *Milwaukee Magazine*, November 1985.

18. Jeanne Zeidler, "Frank Zeidler: 90th Birthday Tribute" (Tribute, Interfaith Conference of Greater Milwaukee, Sept. 18, 2002).

19. Anita Zeidler interview.

20. Zeidler et al., "Rethinking," 5.

21. Zeidler, interview by John Johannes.

22. "Why a Municipal Enterprise Committee?" pamphlet, 1947, CFZ, box 2, folder 10.

23. "Maine's Governor Wants to Make It Easier for Children to Work," *Washington Post*, January 8, 2014; Miner, *Grede of Milwaukee*, 237, 243, 248; "Industrialist Grede Dies at Age 92," *Milwaukee Journal*, June 5, 1989.

24. "It's Still Zeidler's City," *Milwaukee Journal-Sentinel*, September 16, 1999; "A Simple Man, A Giant Life," *Milwaukee Journal-Sentinel*, July 13, 2006.

25. Zeidler, "Liberal in City Government," chap. 2, pp. 61–62.

26. Zeidler, *Essays*, 32. Essays extracted from Zeidler, *Making Urban Renewal More Effective*.

27. Brisben, "Frank Zeidler's Legacy"; John Gurda, "A Model Milwaukeean," *Milwaukee Journal-Sentinel*, August 6, 2006.

28. Frank Zeidler, "Message to Common Council," April 18, 1950, CFZ, box 55, folder 7.

Bibliography

Abrams, Charles. *Forbidden Neighbors: A Study of Prejudice in Housing*. New York: Harper, 1955.
Addison, Barbara. "Cold War Pacifist: Devere Allen and the Postwar Peace Movement, 1946–1955." *Peace and Change* 32, no. 3 (July 2007): 391–414.
Alderfer, Harold Frederick. *American Local Government and Administration*. New York: Macmillan, 1956.
Allen, Devere. *The Fight for Peace*. New York: Macmillan, 1930.
Allen, Frederick Lewis. *The Big Change: America Transforms Itself: 1900–1950*. New York: Harper, 1952.
Allen, Robert S., ed. *Our Fair City*. New York: Vanguard, 1947.
Allitt, Patrick. *The Conservatives: Ideas and Personalities throughout American History*. New Haven, Conn.: Yale University Press, 2009.
American Federation of State, County, and Municipal Employees. "AFSCME: 75 Years of History." Available at http://www.afscme.org/about/1028.cfm (accessed June 15, 2015).
Anderson, Arvid. "The American City and Its Public Employee Unions Discussion." In Somers, *Collective Bargaining*, 91–96.
Anderson, Harry, and Frederick Olson. *Milwaukee: At the Gathering of the Waters*. Tulsa, Okla.: Continental Heritage, 1981.
Anderson, Margo, and Victor Greene, eds. *Perspectives on Milwaukee's Past*. Champaign: University of Illinois Press, 2009.
Arndorfer, Jim. "Cream City Confidential: The Black-Baiting of Milwaukee's Last Pink Mayor." *Baffler* 13 (Winter 1999): 69–77.
Arnesen, Eric, ed. *Encyclopedia of Labor and Working Class History*. Vol. 1. New York: Routledge, 2007.
Austin, H. Russell. *The Milwaukee Story: The Making of an American City*. Milwaukee: Milwaukee Journal, 1946.

Banfield, Edward. *Government and Housing in Metropolitan Areas.* New York: McGraw Hill, 1958.

Barrett, Grant, ed. *Oxford Dictionary of American Political Slang.* Oxford: Oxford University Press, 2004.

Bauer, Catherine. "The Dreary Deadlock of Public Housing." *Architectural Forum,* May 1957.

Beck, Elmer. *The Sewer Socialists: A History of the Socialist Party of Wisconsin, 1897–1940.* Vol. 1, *Socialist Trinity of the Party, the Union, and the Press.* Vol. 2, *The 1920s and 1930s.* Fennimore, Wis.: Westburg, 1982.

Beito, David. *Taxpayers in Revolt: Tax Resistance during the Great Depression.* Auburn, Ala.: Ludwig von Mises Institute, 2009.

Bell, Daniel. *Marxian Socialism in the United States.* Ithaca, N.Y.: Cornell University Press, 1952.

———. *The Radical Right: The New American Right.* Expanded and updated. New York: Doubleday, 1963.

Berlau, A. Joseph. *The German Social Democratic Party, 1914–1921.* New York: Columbia University Press, 1949.

Bernard, Richard, ed. *Snowbelt Cities: Metropolitan Politics in the Northeast and Midwest since World War II.* Bloomington: Indiana University Press, 1990.

Bertlet, Chip, and Matthew Lyons. *Right-Wing Populism in America: Too Close for Comfort.* New York: Guilford, 2000.

Biondi, Martha. *To Stand and Fight: The Struggle for Civil Rights in Postwar New York City.* Cambridge, Mass.: Harvard University Press, 2003.

Blank, Phil. Interview by the author, January 10, 2010.

Booth, Douglas E. "Municipal Socialism and City Government Reform: The Milwaukee Experience, 1910–1940." *Journal of Urban History* 12 (1985): 51–74.

Bowen, Michael. *The Roots of Modern Conservatism: Dewey, Taft, and the Battle for the Soul of the Republican Party.* Chapel Hill: University of North Carolina Press, 2011.

Boyle, Kevin. *The UAW and the Heyday of American Liberalism, 1945–1968.* Ithaca, N.Y.: Cornell University Press, 1995.

Braeman, John, Robert Bremner, and David Brody, eds. *The New Deal: The National Level.* Columbus: Ohio State University Press, 1975.

Brinkley, Alan. *The End of Reform: New Deal Liberalism in Recession and War.* New York: Knopf, 1995.

———. *Voices of Protest: Father Coughlin and the Great Depression.* New York: Knopf, 1982.

Brisben, J. Quinn. "Frank Zeidler's Legacy." Presentation. Public Enterprise Committee, Milwaukee, November, 24, 2006.

Bucki, Cecelia. *Bridgeport's Socialist New Deal, 1915–36.* Champaign: University of Illinois Press, 2001.

Burgin, Angus. *The Great Persuasion: Reinventing Free Markets since the Depression.* Cambridge, Mass.: Harvard University Press, 2012.

Canning, Peter. *American Dreamers: The Wallaces and Reader's Digest; An Insider's Story.* New York: Simon and Shuster, 1997.

Chickering, A. Lawrence, ed. *Public Employee Unions: A Study of the Crisis in Public Sector Labor Relations*. Richmond, Calif.: Institute for Contemporary Studies, 1976.
Chodorov, Frank. *A Fifty-Year Project: To Combat Socialism on the Campus*. N.p.: Intercollegiate Society of Individualists, 1950.
———. *Out of Step: The Autobiography of an Individualist*. Introduction by E. Victor Milione. New York: Devin-Adair, 1962.
Citizens' Governmental Research Bureau. *Milwaukee's Negro Community*. Milwaukee: Bureau, 1946.
Cling, Edwin Layne. "Industrial Labor Relations Policies and Practices in Municipal Government, Milwaukee, Wisconsin." Dissertation. Northwestern University, 1957.
Collins, Robert. *The Business Response to Keynes, 1929–1964*. New York: Columbia University Press, 1981.
Conrad, Will, Kathleen Wilson, and Dale Wilson. *The* Milwaukee Journal: *The First Eighty Years*. Madison: University of Wisconsin Press, 1964.
Conzen, Kathleen. *Immigrant Milwaukee, 1836–1860: Accommodation and Community in a Frontier City*. Cambridge, Mass.: Harvard University Press, 1976.
Cornell, Herbert W. "Collective Bargaining by Public Employee Groups." *University of Pennsylvania Law Review* 107, no. 1 (November 1958): 43–64.
Cowie, Jefferson, and Nick Salvatore. "The Long Exception: Rethinking the Place of the New Deal in American History." *International Labor and Working-Class History* (Fall 2008): 3–32.
Crabb, Charles. *Milwaukee's Industrial Growth during the Last Decade*. Milwaukee: Milwaukee Association of Commerce, September 1959.
Critchlow, Donald. *Phyllis Schlafly and Grassroots Conservatism: A Woman's Crusade*. Princeton, N.J.: Princeton University Press, 2008.
———, ed. *Socialism in the Heartland: The Midwestern Experience, 1900–1925*. Notre Dame, Ind.: University of Notre Dame Press, 1986.
Cunningham, W. B. "Public Employment, Collective Bargaining, and the Collective Wisdom: USA and Canada." *Industrial Relations* 21, no. 3 (1966): 406–33.
Cutler, Richard. *Greater Milwaukee's Growing Pains, 1940–2000: An Insider's View*. Milwaukee: Milwaukee County Historical Society, 2001.
Davies, Richard O. *Housing Reform during the Truman Administration*. Columbia: University of Missouri Press, 1966.
Davis, Richard. "Milwaukee: Old Lady Thrift." In Allen, *Our Fair City*, 189–210.
Devinatz, Victor. "Frank P. Zeidler's Views on Public Sector Labor Relations as Milwaukee's Last Socialist Mayor, 1948–1960." *Journal of Collective Negotiations* 31, no. 4 (2007): 319–32.
Donald J. Curran. *Metropolitan Financing: The Milwaukee Experience, 1920–1970*. Madison: University of Wisconsin Press, 1973.
Dougherty, Jack. "African Americans, Civil Rights, and Race-Making in Milwaukee." In Anderson and Greene, *Perspectives on Milwaukee's Past*, 131–61.
———. *More than One Struggle: The Evolution of Black School Reform in Milwaukee*. Chapel Hill: University of North Carolina Press, 2004.

Drucker, Peter. "Labor in Industrial Society." *Annals of the American Academy of Political and Social Science* 274 (March 1951): 145–51.
Edsell, Thomas. With Mary Edsell. *Chain Reaction: The Impact of Race, Rights, and Taxes on American Politics.* New York: Norton, 1991.
Eisenhower, Dwight D. *Mandate for Change, 1951–1956.* Garden City, N.Y.: Doubleday, 1963.
Ettenheim, Sarah. *How Milwaukee Voted, 1848–1968.* Milwaukee: Institute of Governmental Affairs, University Extension, University of Wisconsin, 1970.
Ewen, Stuart. *PR! A Social History of Spin.* New York: Basic, 1996.
Farley, Reynolds. "The Changing Distribution of Negroes within Metropolitan Areas: The Emergence of Black Suburbs." *American Journal of Sociology* 75, no. 4 (January 1970): 512–29.
Farris, Trueman. Interview by John R. Johannes, January 19, 1994. Marquette University Department of Special Collections and University Archives.
Flynn, John T. *The Road Ahead: America's Creeping Socialist Revolution.* New York: Devin-Adair, 1949.
Foner, Eric. *Tom Paine and Revolutionary America.* Updated edition. Oxford: Oxford University Press, 2005.
Fones-Wolf, Elizabeth. "Media Democracy—Who Owns the Media?" Lecture. Labor's Voices 3 Conference, New York City, April 27, 2007.
———. *Selling Free Enterprise: The Business Assault on Labor and Liberalism, 1945–1960.* Champaign: University of Illinois Press, 1994.
———. *Waves of Opposition: Labor and the Struggle for Democratic Radio.* Champaign: University of Illinois Press, 2006.
Forester, Arnold, and Benjamin Epstein. *Danger on the Right.* New York: Random House, 1964.
Fortune, editors of, in collaboration with Russell W. Davenport. *USA: The Permanent Revolution.* New York: Prentice Hall, 1951.
Foss-Mollan, Kate. *Hard Water: Politics and Water Supply in Milwaukee, 1870–1995.* West Lafayette, Ind.: Purdue University Press, 2001.
Frankel, Saul. "Employer-Employee Relations in the Public Service." *Public Personnel Review* (October 1964): 220–24.
Fraser, Steven, and Gary Gerstle, eds. *The Rise and Fall of the New Deal Order, 1930–1980.* Princeton, N.J.: Princeton University Press, 1989.
Freund, David. *Colored Property: State Policy and White Racial Politics in Suburban America.* Chicago: University of Chicago Press, 2007.
Friedrich, Carl, et al. *Problems of the American Public Service.* New York: McGraw Hill, 1935.
Fure-Slocum, Eric. "Cities with Class? Growth Politics, the Working-Class City, and Debt in Milwaukee During the 1940s." *Social Science History* 24, no. 1 (2000): 258–305.
———. *Contesting the Postwar City: Working-Class and Growth Politics in 1940s Milwaukee.* Cambridge: Cambridge University Press, 2013.
Gable, Richard. "NAM: Influential Lobby or Kiss of Death?" *Journal of Politics* 15, no. 2 (May 1953): 254–73.

Galbraith, John Kenneth. *The Affluent Society.* Cambridge: Riverside / Boston: Houghton Mifflin, 1958.
Gavett, Thomas. *Development of the Labor Movement in Milwaukee.* Madison: University of Wisconsin Press, 1965.
Geib, Paul. "From Mississippi to Milwaukee: A Case Study of Southern Black Migration to Milwaukee, 1940–1970." *Journal of Negro History* 83, no. 4 (Autumn 1998): 229–48.
Geneen, Paul. *Images of Milwaukee's Bronzeville, 1900–1950.* Introduction by Rueben Harpole. Charleston, S.C.: Arcadia, 2006.
———. *Shuster's and Gimbels: Milwaukee's Beloved Department Stores.* Charleston, S.C.: History Press, 2012.
Germanson, Ken. Interview by the author, February 16, 2007.
———. Interview by Michael Gordon, July 9, 16, and 22, 2009. Milwaukee Labor History Society.
Godine, Morton. *The Labor Problem in Public Service: A Study in Political Pluralism.* Cambridge, Mass.: Harvard University Press, 1951.
Goldfield, Michael. *The Decline of Organized Labor in the United States.* Chicago: University of Chicago, 1987.
Golembiewski, Dick. *Milwaukee Television History: The Analog Years.* Milwaukee: Marquette University Press, 2008.
Griffith, Robert. "Dwight D. Eisenhower and the Corporate Commonwealth." *American Historical Review* 87, no. 1 (February 1982): 87–122.
———. "Forging America's Postwar Order: Politics and Political Economy in the Age of Truman." In Lacey, *Truman Presidency*, 57–88.
———. "The Selling of America: The Advertising Council and American Politics, 1942–1960." *Business History Review* (Autumn 1983): 388–412.
———, ed. *The Specter: Original Essays on the Cold War and the Origins of McCarthyism.* New York: New Viewpoints, 1974.
Grover, Michael Ross. "'All Things to Black Folk': A History of the Milwaukee Urban League, 1919–1980." Master's thesis. University of Wisconsin–Milwaukee, 1994.
Gurda, John. *Cream City Chronicles: Stories of Milwaukee's Past.* Milwaukee: Wisconsin Historical Society Press, 2007.
———. *The Making of Milwaukee.* Milwaukee: Milwaukee County Historical Society, 1999.
Hansen, Robert. "Milwaukee City Employees Launch Educational Campaign." *Public Management* (April 1936): 119.
Harris, Howell. *The Right to Manage: Industrial Relations Policies of American Business in the 1940s.* Madison: University of Wisconsin Press, 1982.
Hass, Edward. *DeLesseps S. Morrison and the Image of Reform: New Orleans Politics, 1946–1961.* Baton Rouge: Louisiana State University Press, 1974.
Hauser, Stephen K. "Frank Zeidler, Milwaukee's Presidential Candidate." *Milwaukee History* 3, no. 2 (Summer 1980): 47–58.
———. *Public Enterprise Committee Record.* Milwaukee: Public Enterprise Committee, July 2006.

Hayek, F. I. *The Road to Serfdom*. Chicago: University of Chicago Press, 1944, 1974, 1994.

Heath, Frederick. "Labor and the Progressive Movement in Connecticut." *Labor History* 12, no. 1 (Winter 1971): 52–67.

Heisel, W. D. "The American City and Its Public Employee Unions." In Somers, *Collective Bargaining*, 96–98.

Hendershot, Heather. "God's Angriest Man: Carl McIntire, Cold War Fundamentalism, and Right-Wing Broadcasting." *American Quarterly* (June 2007): 373–98.

———. *What's Fair on the Air? Cold War Right-Wing Broadcasting and the Public Interest*. Chicago: University of Chicago Press, 2011.

"Historic Preservation Study Report: Milwaukee City Hall." City of Milwaukee, Spring 1982. Available at http://www.city.milwaukee.gov/ImageLibrary/sGroups/cityHPC/DesignatedReports/vticnf/CityHall.pdf (accessed May 10, 2014).

Hoan, Daniel W. *City Government: The Record of the Milwaukee Experiment*. New York: Harcourt, Brace, 1936. Reprint, Westport, Conn.: Greenwood, 1974.

Hoerder, Dirk. "The German-American Labor Press and Its Views of the Political Institutions of the United States." In Shore, Fones-Wolf, and Danky, *German-American Radical Press*, 182–98.

Holter, Darryl. *Workers and Unions in Wisconsin: A Labor History Anthology*. Madison: State Historical Society of Wisconsin, 1999.

Housing and Home Finance Agency. *Housing of the Nonwhite Population, 1940–1950*. Washington, D.C.: GPO, July 1952.

———. *The Negro in Public Housing, 1933–1953: Problems and Accomplishments*. Unpublished report. Washington, D.C., May 1954.

———. *The 1950 Housing Situation in Charts: Based on Preliminary Results of the 1950 Census of Housing*. Washington, D.C.: GPO, 1951.

———. *A Summary of the Evolution of Housing Activities in the Federal Government*. Washington, D.C.: GPO, 1950.

———. *The Why and What of Title I Housing Act of 1949*. Washington, DC: GPO, 1951.

Housing Authority of the City of Milwaukee. *Milwaukee Housing Survey of 1949*. Milwaukee: n.p., n.d.

———. *Milwaukee Project No. 2, Lower Third Ward Redevelopment, Title I, Slum Clearance and Urban Redevelopment Program*. Milwaukee: n.p., 1952.

Hunt, D. Bradford. "How Did Public Housing Survive the 1950s?" *Journal of Policy History* 17, no. 2 (2005): 193–216.

Hurt, Harry, III. *Texas Rich: The Hunt Dynasty from the Early Oil Days through the Silver Crash*. New York: Norton, 1981.

Jackson, Kenneth. *Crabgrass Frontier: The Suburbanization of the United States*. New York: Oxford University Press, 1985.

Jacobs, Jane. *The Death and Life of Great American Cities*. New York: Random House, 1961.

Jacoby, Sanford. *Modern Manors: Welfare Capitalism Since the New Deal*. Princeton, N.J.: Princeton University Press, 1997.

Johnson, Lee F. "The Housing Act of 1949—and Your Community." In *Two-Thirds of a Nation: A Housing Program*, edited by Nathan Straus. New York: Knopf, 1952.

Jones, Patrick. *The Selma of the North: Civil Rights Insurgency in Milwaukee*. Cambridge, Mass.: Harvard University Press, 2009.

Kennedy, Robert F. *The Enemy Within*. New York: Harper, 1960.

Kenny, Judith, and Thomas Hubka. "Surveying Milwaukee's Residential Landscapes: Prospects for Research." In Anderson and Greene, *Perspectives on Milwaukee's Past*, 223–55.

Kessler, Fred. Interview by the author, December 21, 2009.

Kramer, Leo. *Labor's Paradox—The American Federation of State, County, and Municipal Employees, AFL-CIO*. New York: Wiley, 1962.

Kruse, Kevin. *White Flight: Atlanta and the Making of Modern Conservatism*. Princeton, N.J.: Princeton University Press, 2005.

Kruse, Kevin, and Thomas Sugrue, eds. *The New Suburban History*. Chicago: University of Chicago Press, 2006.

Lacey, Michael J. *The Truman Presidency*. Cambridge: Press Syndicate of the University of Cambridge, 1989.

Laidler, Harry. *Concentration of Control in American Industry*. New York: Crowell, 1931.

Lassiter, Matthew. *The Silent Majority: Suburban Politics in the Sunbelt South*. Princeton, N.J.: Princeton University Press, 2006.

League of Women Voters of Milwaukee. *A Study of the Local Problems of Human Relations with Emphasis on Equal Opportunities in Housing*. Milwaukee: League of Women Voters, November 1962.

Lee, R. Alton. *Eisenhower and Landrum-Griffin: A Study in Labor-Management Politics*. Lexington: University Press of Kentucky, 1990.

LeFevre, Robert. *A Way to Be Free: The Autobiography of Robert LeFevre*. Vol. 2, *The Making of a Modern American Revolution*. Culver City, Calif.: Pulplesspress.com, 1999.

Leuchtenburg, William. "Keynote Address: The Greenbelt Conference." George Mason University, Fairfax, Va., May 2, 1987.

Lichtenstein, Nelson. "From Corporatism to Collective Bargaining." In Fraser and Gerstle, *Rise and Fall*, 122–52.

———. "Labor in the Truman Era: Origins of the 'Private Welfare State.'" In Lacey, *Truman Presidency*, 128–55.

———. *State of the Union: A Century of American Labor*. Princeton, N.J.: Princeton University Press, 2002.

———. *Walter Reuther: The Most Dangerous Man in Detroit*. New York: Basic, 1995.

Lichtenstein, Nelson, and Elizabeth Tandy Shermer, eds. *The Right and Labor in America: Politics, Ideology and Imagination*. Philadelphia: University of Pennsylvania Press, 2012.

Lichtman, Allan. *White Protestant Nation: The Rise of the American Conservative Movement*. New York: Atlantic Monthly Press, 2008.

Lippmann, Walter. *The Good Society*. New York: Grosset and Dunlap, 1936.
Loewen, James. *Sundown Towns: A Hidden Dimension of American Racism*. New York: New Press, 2005.
Lowndes, Joseph. *From the New Deal to the New Right: Race and the Southern Origins of Modern Conservatism*. New Haven, Conn.: Yale University Press, 2008.
MacLean, Nancy. *Freedom Is Not Enough: The Opening of the American Workplace*. Cambridge, Mass.: Harvard University Press, 2006.
Maier, Henry. *The Mayor Who Made Milwaukee Famous: An Autobiography*. Lanham, Md.: Madison, 1993.
Maier, Irwin. *A Career in Newspapers and Broadcasting*. Milwaukee: Journal Company, 1981.
Mansfield, Harvey, Jr. "The Prestige of Public Employment." In Chickering, *Public Employee Unions*, 35–49.
Mayor's Study Committee on Social Problems in the Inner Core Area of the City, Fact-Finding Committee, Subcommittee on Housing Conditions and Availability. *Final Report to the Honorable Frank P. Zeidler, Mayor*. Milwaukee, April 15, 1960.
McBride, Genevieve. "The Progress of 'Race Men' and 'Colored Women' in the Black Press in Wisconsin, 1892–1985." In *The Black Press in the Middle West, 1865–1995*, edited by Henry Louis Suggs, 325–48. Westport, Conn.: Greenwood, 1996.
McBride, Genevieve, and Stephen Byers. "The First Mayor of Black Milwaukee: J. Anthony Josey." *Wisconsin Magazine of History* 91, no. 2 (Winter 2007–2008): 2–15.
McCarthy, John. *Making Milwaukee Mightier: Planning and the Politics of Growth, 1910–1960*. DeKalb: Northern Illinois University Press, 2009.
McCartin, Joseph. "The Public Employee Union Upsurge and the Making of the Reagan Revolution, 1968–1981." Presentation. Historical Society Conference, Johns Hopkins University, Baltimore, Md., June 7, 2008.
———. "'A Wagner Act for Public Employees': Labor's Dream Deferred and the Rise of Conservatism, 1970–1976." *Journal of American History* (June 2008): 123–48.
McGirr, Lisa. *Suburban Warriors: The Origins of the New American Right*. Princeton, N.J.: Princeton University Press, 2001.
McGuinness, Aims. "The Revolution Begins Here: Milwaukee and the History of Socialism." In Anderson and Greene, *Perspectives on Milwaukee's Past*, 79–108.
Meaney, John W. "The Institution of Public Television." *Review of Politics* 30, no. 4 (October 1968): 403–14.
Meany, George. "Union Leaders and Public-Sector Unions—AFL-CIO." In Chickering, *Public Employee Unions*, 165–74.
Meyer, Stephen. *"Stalin over Wisconsin": The Making and Unmaking of Militant Unionism, 1900–1950*. New Brunswick, N.J.: Rutgers University Press, 1992.
Meyer, Stephen Grant. *As Long as They Don't Move Next Door: Segregation and Racial Conflict in American Neighborhoods*. New York: Rowman and Littlefield, 2000.
Miller, Douglas, and Marion Nowak. *The Fifties: The Way We Really Were*. New York: Doubleday, 1977.
Miller, Sally. "Casting a Wide Net: The Milwaukee Movement to 1920." In Critchlow, *Socialism in the Heartland*, 18–45.

———. *Victor Berger and the Promise of Constructive Socialism: 1910–1920*. Westport, Conn.: Greenwood, 1973.
Milwaukee Common Council. Joint Committee on Judiciary Legislation and Public Buildings and Grounds. Office of the City Attorney. *Milwaukee Speaks on Housing and Blight Elimination*. Milwaukee, February 1945.
"Milwaukee: More Than Beer Makes It Famous." *Business Week*, November 8, 1952.
Milwaukee Public Library in cooperation with Research Clearing House of Milwaukee. *Milwaukee City and County: A Statistical History*. Milwaukee, 1958.
The Milwaukee Wisconsin Market, Population, Homes, Income, Employment, Retail Sales by Counties, Cities, Marketing Areas. Milwaukee: Milwaukee Journal, 1959.
Miner, Craig. *Grede of Milwaukee*. Wichita, Kan.: Watermark, 1989.
———. "The New Wave, the Old Guard, and the Bank Committee: William J. Grede at J. I. Case Company, 1953–1961." *Business History Review* 61, no. 2 (Summer 1987): 243–90.
Mire, Joseph. "Collective Bargaining in the Public Service." *American Economic Review* (May 1946): 347–58.
———. "Unions in the Public Service." *Labor and Nation* (September–October 1947): 41–42.
Morgan, Edmund. "Inventing the 'Liberal Republican Mind.'" Review of *Dangerous Nation*, by Robert Kagan. *New York Review of Books*, November 16, 2006, 30–32.
Moser, John. *Right Turn: John T. Flynn and the Transformation of American Liberalism*. New York: New York University Press, 2005.
Muller, Jerry, ed. *Conservatism: An Anthology of Social and Political Thought from David Hume to the Present*. Princeton, N.J.: Princeton University Press, 1997.
Mumford, Lewis. *The Culture of Cities*. New York: Harcourt, Brace, 1938.
Murphy, Marjorie. *Blackboard Unions: The AFT and the NEA, 1900–1980*. Ithaca, N.Y.: Cornell University Press, 1992.
Nash, George. *The Conservative Intellectual Movement in America since 1945*. Wilmington, Del.: Intercollegiate Studies Institute, 1976, 1996.
Nesbit, Robert C. *Wisconsin: A History*. Madison: University of Wisconsin Press, 1973.
Nicolaides, Becky. *My Blue Heaven: Life and Politics in the Working-Class Suburbs of Los Angeles*. Chicago: University of Chicago Press, 2002.
"Old Milwaukee." Available at http://oldmilwaukee.net/query-basic-yeard.php (accessed May 10, 2014).
Olson, Frederick I. "Socialists and Labor." In Paul and Paul, *Badger State*, 376–79.
Ozanne, Robert. *The Labor Movement in Wisconsin: A History*. Madison: State Historical Society of Wisconsin, 1984.
Page, Kirby. *Kirby Page, Social Evangelist: The Autobiography of a 20th Century Prophet for Peace*. Edited by Harold Fey. Nyack, N.Y.: Fellowship, 1975.
Paul, Barbara, and Justus Paul, eds. *The Badger State: A Documentary History of Wisconsin*. Grand Rapids, Mich.: Eerdmans, 1979.
Pearson, Chad. "What's So New about the 'New Right'? Rethinking the Origins of Postwar Anti-Unionism." Unpublished paper. Presented at the Organization of American Historians Conference, Washington, D.C., April 9, 2010.

Peirce, Neal, and John Keefe. *The Great Lake States of America: People, Politics, and Power in the Five Great Lakes States*. New York: Norton, 1980.

Perlstein, Rick. *Before the Storm: Barry Goldwater and the Unmaking of the American Consensus*. New York: Hill and Wang, 2001.

Peterson, Lorin. *The Day of the Mugwamp*. New York: Random House, 1961.

Petro, Sylvester. *The Kohler Strike: Union Violence and Administrative Law*. Chicago: Regnery, 1961.

———. "Sovereignty and Compulsory Public-Sector Bargaining." *Wake Forest Law Review* (March 1974): 25–166.

Phillips-Fein, Kim. "Business Conservatism on the Shop Floor: Anti-Union Campaigns in the 1950s." *Labor* (Summer 2010): 9–26.

———. "Conservatism: A State of the Field." *Journal of American History* (December 2011): 723–43.

———. *Invisible Hands: The Making of the Conservative Movement from the New Deal to Reagan*. New York: Norton, 2009.

Phillips, Vel. Interview by Katherine Shannon, February 12, 1968, Transcript, Ralph J. Bunche Oral History Collection, Howard University.

———. Interviews by the author, October 3, 2009, and October 18, 2009.

Pienkos, Donald. "Politics, Religion, and Change in Polish Milwaukee, 1900–1930." *Wisconsin Historical Magazine* 61, no. 3 (Spring 1978): 178–209.

Pieplow, William. *Century Lessons: Commemorating One Hundred Years of Building and Loan Associations*. Appleton, Wis.: Nelson, 1931.

———. *History of the South Division Civic Association, Milwaukee: Oldest Civic Association in the United States*. Milwaukee: Milwaukee Times, 1947.

Polenberg, Richard. "The Decline of the New Deal, 1937–1940." In Braeman, Bremner, and Brody, *New Deal*.

"Postwar Anti-Unionism." Unpublished paper. Presented at the Organization of American Historians Conference, Washington, D.C., April 9, 2010.

Prothro, James. "Public Interest Advertising—Hucksterism or Conservatism? *Social Studies* 45 (May 1954): 172–78.

Rains, Harry. "Collective Bargaining in Public Employment." *Labor Law Journal* (August 1957): 548–50.

Rasche, William. "The Need in Milwaukee for Extending Employment of Negroes." Speech to Employers Association of Milwaukee, January 22, 1946, Wisconsin Historical Society, Madison. Available at http://www.wisconsinhistory.org/turningpoints/search.asp?id=1097 (accessed April 27, 2014).

Rast, Joel. "Annexation Policy in Milwaukee: An Historical Institutionalist Approach." *Polity* 39, no. 1 (January 2007): 55–78.

———. "Governing the Regimeless City: The Frank Zeidler Administration in Milwaukee, 1948–1960." *Urban Affairs Review* 42, no. 81 (2006): 81–112.

Ribuffo, Leo. "The Discovery and Rediscovery of American Conservatism Broadly Conceived." *Magazine of History* (January 2003): 5–10.

———. *The Old Christian Right: The Protestant Far-Right from the Great Depression to the Cold War*. Philadelphia: Temple University Press, 1983.

———. "Rediscovering American Conservatism Again." *History News Network*. Available at http://hnn.us/article/38415 (accessed April 12, 2014).

Robertson, David Brian. *Capital, Labor, and State: The Battle for American Labor Markets from the Civil War to the New Deal*. Rowman and Littlefield, 2000.

Rock, Eli. "Municipal Collective Bargaining: New Areas for Research." In Somers, *Collective Bargaining*, 70–80.

Rossiter, Clinton. *Conservatism in America: The Thankless Persuasion*. 2nd ed., rev. New York: Knopf, 1968 (1955).

Saffran, George C. *Blight Elimination and Prevention: A Study of Milwaukee's Blight Elimination and Prevention Process and Improvement Thereof, Prepared for the Honorable Frank Zeidler, Mayor, City of Milwaukee*. Milwaukee, July 1954.

Saltzstein, Arthur. Interview by John Johannes, January 5, 1994. Marquette University Department of Special Collections and University Archives.

Schmandt, Henry, John Goldbach, and Donald Vogel. *Milwaukee: A Contemporary Urban Profile*. New York: Praeger, 1971.

Schmandt, Henry, and William Standing. *The Milwaukee Metropolitan Study Commission*. Bloomington: Indiana University Press, 1965.

Schmitt, John W. Interview by the author, April 6, 2007.

Schneider, Gregory. *The Conservative Century: From Reaction to Revolution*. Lanham, Md.: Rowman and Littlefield, 2009.

Seidman, Joel. *American Labor from Defense to Reconversion*. Chicago: University of Chicago Press, 1953.

Self, Robert O. *American Babylon: Race and the Struggle for Postwar Oakland*. Princeton, N.J.: Princeton University Press, 2003.

Shadd, Mary Ellen. *Negro Business Directory of the State of Wisconsin, 1950–1951*. Milwaukee, 1950. Available at http://www.wisconsinhistory.org/turningpoints/search.asp?id=1254 (accessed June 15, 2015).

Shannon, David. *The Socialist Party of America: A History*. New York: Macmillan, 1955.

Shefferman, Nathan. With Dale Kramer. *The Man in the Middle*. New York: Doubleday, 1961.

Shermer, Elizabeth Tandy. "Origins of the Conservative Ascendancy: Barry Goldwater's Early Senate Career and the De-legitimization of Organized Labor." *Journal of American History* 95 (December 2008): 678–709.

———. *Sunbelt Capitalism: Phoenix and the Transformation of American Politics*. Philadelphia: University of Pennsylvania Press, 2013.

Shore, Elliott, Ken Fones-Wolf, and James P. Danky, eds. *The German-American Radical Press: The Shaping of a Left Political Culture, 1850–1940*. Champaign, Ill.: University of Illinois Press, 1992.

Simons, Jesse. "The American City and Its Public Employee Unions, Discussion." In Somers, *Collective Bargaining*, 104–11.

Slater, Joseph E. *Public Workers: Government Employee Unions, the Law, and the State, 1900–1962*. Ithaca, N.Y.: ILR / Cornell University Press, 2004.

Smith, Kevin. "From Socialism to Racism: The Politics of Class and Identity in Milwaukee." *Michigan Historical Review* 29, no. 1 (Spring 2003): 71–95.

Somers, Gerald, ed. *Collective Bargaining in the Public Service*. Proceedings of the 1966 Annual Spring Meeting. Champaign, Ill.: Industrial Relations Research Association, May 6–7, 1966.

Stave, Bruce M. *Socialism and the Cities*. Port Washington, N.Y.: Kennikat, 1975.

Stetler, Henry Gruber. *Socialist Movement in Reading, Pennsylvania, 1896–1936: A Study in Social Change*. Storrs, Conn.: self-published, 1943.

Still, Bayrd. *Milwaukee: A History of a City*. Madison: State Historical Society of Wisconsin, 1948.

Sugrue, Thomas. *The Origins of the Urban Crisis: Race and Inequality in Postwar Detroit*. Princeton, N.J.: Princeton University Press, 1977.

———. *Sweet Land of Liberty: The Forgotten Struggle for Civil Rights in the North*. New York: Random House, 2008.

Tedlow, Richard. *Keeping the Corporate Image: Public Relations and Business, 1900–1950*. Greenwich, Conn.: JAI, 1979.

Thayer, George. *The Farther Shores of Politics: The American Political Fringe Today*. New York: Simon and Schuster, 1967.

Thomas, Norman. *Human Exploitation in the United States*. New York: Stokes, 1934.

Thompson, William F. *The History of Wisconsin*. Vol. 6, *Continuity and Change, 1940–1965*. Madison: State Historical Society of Wisconsin, 1988.

Tilly, Charles. "Race and Migration to the American City." In Wilson, *Metropolitan Enigma*, 135–57.

Trotter, Joe, Jr. *Black Milwaukee: The Making of an Industrial Proletariat, 1915–1945*. Champaign, Ill.: University of Illinois Press, 1985.

Tuccille, Jerome. *Kingdom: The Story of the Hunt Family of Texas*. Ottawa, Ill.: Jameson, 1984.

Twenty-First Biennial Report of the Board of Election Commissioners of the City of Milwaukee, Report 21, 1951, for the Years 1950–1951. Milwaukee, 1951.

United States Commission on Civil Rights. *One Nation under God, Indivisible, with Liberty and Justice for All: An Abridgement of the Report of the United States Commission on Civil Rights*. Washington, D.C.: GPO, 1959.

Uphoff, Walter H. *Kohler on Strike: Thirty Years of Conflict*. Boston: Beacon, 1966.

U.S. Bureau of Labor Statistics. *Average Weekly Earnings of Production Workers, 1947–2003*.

U.S. Census Bureau. *Average Income of Families, 1949–1954 (Current Yearly Prices)*.

———. *Historical Census Statistics on Population Totals by Race, 1790 to 1990, and by Hispanic Origin, 1970 to 1990, for Large Cities and Other Urban Places in the United States*. Table 50, "Wisconsin—Race and Hispanic Origin for Selected Large Cities and Other Places: Earliest Census to 1990." Available at http://www.census.gov/population/www/documentation/twps0076/WItab.pdf (accessed June 15, 2105).

———. *A Report of the Seventeenth Decennial Census of the United States Census of Population:1950*. Vol.1, *Number of Inhabitants*. Washington, D.C.: GPO, 1952.
U.S. Congress. House Select Committee on Lobbying Activities. *Expenditures by Corporations to Influence Legislation*. 81st Congress, 2d Session. H.R. Rep. No. 3238, 1951.
———. *General Interim Report on Lobbying*. 81st Congress, 2d Session. 1950.
———. *Housing Lobby: Part 2 of Hearings before the Select Committee on Lobbying*. 81st Congress, 2d Session. April 19, 21, 25, 26, 27, and 28, 1950; May 3, 5, and 17, 1950.
———. *Lobbying, Direct and Indirect: Committee for Constitutional Government*. Part 5. 81st Congress, 2d Session. June 27–29, August 25, 1950.
———. *Lobbying, Direct and Indirect: National Economic Council*. Part 4. 81st Congress, 2d Session. June 6, 20, 21, and 28, 1950.
———. *Report Citing Edward A. Rumely*. 81st Congress, 2d Session. 1950, H.R. Rep. No. 3024, 1949.
———. *Report of the House Select Committee on Lobbying Activities*. 81st Congress, 2d Session. October 31, 1950.
U.S. Congress. Senate Subcommittee on Housing and Rents, Committee on Banking and Currency Committee. *General Housing Legislation*. 81st Congress, 1st Session. February 17, 1949.
U.S. President's [Eisenhower's] Advisory Committee on Government Housing. *Report of the Subcommittee on Urban Redevelopment, Rehabilitation, and Conservation. Recommendations on Government Housing Policies and Programs*. December 1953.
Vick, William. "From Walnut Street to No Street: Milwaukee's Afro-American Businesses, 1945–1967." Master's thesis. University of Milwaukee, 1993.
Vogel, David. *Kindred Strangers: The Uneasy Relationship between Politics and Business in America*. Princeton, N.J.: Princeton University Press, 1996.
Voss, Kim. *The Making of American Exceptionalism: The Knights of Labor and Class Formation in the Nineteenth Century*. Ithaca, N.Y.: Cornell University Press, 1993.
Wall, Wendy. *Inventing the American Way: The Politics of Consensus from the New Deal to the Civil Rights Movement*. New York: Oxford University Press, 2008.
Webb, Daryl. "Scooters, Skates, and Dolls: Toys against Delinquency in Milwaukee." *Wisconsin Magazine of History* 87, no. 4 (Summer 2004): 2–13.
Weems, Robert, Jr. "Black Working Class, 1915–1925." *Milwaukee History* 6, no. 4 (Winter 1983): 107–14.
Weisenfeld, Allan. *Collective Bargaining by Public Employees in the U.S.* In Somers, *Collective Bargaining*, 1–9.
Weisenfeld, Allan. "The Philosophy of Bargaining for Municipal Employees." *American Arbitration Association* 22, no. 1 (1967): 40–47.
Wells, Robert. *The Milwaukee Journal: An Informal Chronicle of Its First 100 Years*. Milwaukee: Milwaukee Journal, 1981.
———. *This Is Milwaukee*. Milwaukee: Renaissance, 1970.
White, Leonard. *Trends in Public Administration*. New York: McGraw-Hill, 1933.

Whyte, William, and the editors of *Fortune*. *Is Anybody Listening? How and Why U.S. Business Fumbles When It Talks to Human Beings*. New York: Simon and Schuster, 1952.

Wilke, Raymond G. "Selected Speeches of Frank Zeidler." Master's thesis. University of Wisconsin, 1962.

Wilson, James Q., ed. *The Metropolitan Enigma: Inquiries into the Nature and Dimensions of America's "Urban Crisis."* Cambridge, Mass.: Harvard University Press, 1968.

Wisconsin Education Association Council. "WEAC History Book, Chapter 2." Previously available at http://www.weac.org/About_WEAC/history/history_book_chp2-1.aspx.

Wisconsin Manufacturers' Association. *Behind the Headlines with the Wisconsin Manufacturers' Association*. Booklet. Madison, 1949.

———. *The Wisconsin Manufacturers' Association and You!* Pamphlet. Madison, 1947.

Wurf, Jerry. "Union Leaders and Public-Sector Unions—AFSCME." In Chickering, *Public Employee Unions*, 174–82.

Zander, Arnold. "A Union View of Collective Bargaining in the Public Service." *Public Administration Review* (Winter 1962): 310–20.

Zeidler, Anita. Interview by the author, February 19, 2010.

Zeidler, Frank. "The Administrator and Public Policy." *Public Administration Review* (Summer 1954): 180–82.

———. *Essays in More Effective Urban Renewal*. Madison: Institute of Governmental Affairs, University Extension Division, University of Wisconsin, 1964.

———. Interview by Aims McGuinness, May 13, 2006. Wisconsin Labor History Society.

———. Interview by the author, September 22, 2005.

———. Interview by Jane Hampden, September 7, 2005. WUWM, *At 10*, Milwaukee.

———. Interview by John Johannes, December 9, 1993. Marquette University Department of Special Collections and University Archives.

———. Interview by John Miller, November 3, 1972. Wisconsin Historical Society.

———. *A Liberal in City Government: My Experiences as Mayor of Milwaukee*. Milwaukee: Milwaukee Pub., 2005.

———. "A Liberal in City Government: My Experiences as Mayor of Milwaukee." Unpublished manuscript. Chapter 1, "A Campaign for Public Office on a Liberal Platform." Chapter 2, "Some City Problems of 1948 to 1960 and Related Administrative Problems in the Mayor's Office." Chapter 3, "The Expansion of the City of Milwaukee from 1940 to 1960 and Some Related Issues." Chapter 4, "The Struggle for Public Housing and Redevelopment." CFZ.

———. *Making Urban Renewal More Effective*. Washington, D.C.: American Institute for Municipal Research, Education, and Training, 1960–1961.

———. "Management's Rights under Public Sector Collective Bargaining Agreements." *Public Employee Relations Library* 59, International Personnel Management Association (1980): 1–35.

---. "Public Servants as Organized Labor." *Municipality* (February 1972): 1–12. Reprint, University of the State of New York, State Education Department, New York State Library Legislative Research Service, Albany, February 1974.

---. *The Spirit of American Socialism*. New York: Socialist Party, 1970.

Zeidler, Frank, and John Koethe. *Reflections: The Poetry of a Young Frank Zeidler*. Milwaukee: Milwaukee Public Library, 2002.

Zeidler, Frank, et al. "New Roles for Public Officials in Labor Relations." *Public Employee Relations Library* 23, Public Personnel Association (1970): 1–31.

---. "Rethinking the Philosophy of Employee Relations in the Public Service." *Public Employee Relations Library* 1, Public Personnel Association (1968): 1–29.

Zeidler, Jeanne. "Frank Zeidler: 90th Birthday Tribute." Interfaith Conference of Greater Milwaukee, September 18, 2002.

Zinos, John. "The American City and Its Public Employee Unions, Discussion." In Somers, *Collective Bargaining*, 68–111.

Index

Ackerman, Sol, 117
Addes, George, 46
Affiliated Taxpayers' Committee (Milwaukee): anti-tax campaign, 144; opposition to county museums, 117; in public housing debate, 79–82; in public television debate, 63, 64, 67; real estate delegates in, 77–78; "Watching Your Taxes" motto, 77
Affiliated Taxpayers' Public Housing Referendum Committee: on CIO, 80; economic conservatism of, 94; grassroots outreach of, 84, 93; media advertising by, 87; petition on public housing, 78–82, 85; public relations campaign, 85, 86, 88; targeting of resources, 94; and Veterans against Public Housing committee, 87
AFL: in Clay Boat incident, 138; Firemen and Oilers Local 125-B, 164; political conservatism of, 100; political mobilization campaigns of, 30; on public housing referenda, 90; public-sector unions, 155; on St. Lawrence Seaway, 141; support for housing legislation, 88; use of radio, 46
AFL-CIO, work with AFSCME, 161–62
African American community, Milwaukee, 11, 15; on civil rights strategies, 125; class divisions in, 108–9; growth of, 98; in inner core, 106, 108, 113, 178; leaders of, 98, 111; living conditions of, 106; neighborhoods of, 98–99; newspapers of, 45; press of, 107–8, 109, 206n42; and public housing debate, 94; public services for, 126; racism facing, 118–19; southern migrants to, 101, 107–11, 116–17; Zeidler's relationship with, 23, 118–19, 125, 179
African Americans: migration to North, 97, 107; in radio audience, 97
African Americans, Milwaukee: civil rights of, 109; educational opportunities for, 109; employment discrimination against, 99–100, 101; housing discrimination against, 96, 101–3, 178; income of, 178; job training opportunities for, 61; middle-class, 96–99, 108, 179; migrants from South, 101, 107–11, 116–17; in municipal politics, 125; police discrimination against, 125; racial disparity of, 178–79; racially mixed interactions of, 101; racial profiling of, 125; registered voters, 110–11, 123; in suburbs, 178
AFSCME: civil service goals of, 152; local unions of, 152; membership of, 155; national strategy of, 151–54; on public-sector strikes, 158–59; successes of, 151–52; of Wisconsin, 152–53; work with AFL-CIO, 161–62
AFSCME District Council 33 (Philadelphia), 162
AFSCME District Council 48 (Milwaukee): bargaining rights for, 161–65; and building trades, 164; collective bargaining strategy of, 151–54, 162; and Common Council, 162; constituents of, 163; dues checkoff system of, 150; formation of, 153; membership of, 153–54, 181; relationship with other organizations, 163–66; standoff with city, 156–57; strike (1957), 165; strike threats by, 148–50, 158

Allegheny Conference on Community Development, 90
Allen, Devere: *The Fight for Peace*, 24
Allen-Bradley company, segregation at, 100
Allis-Chalmers company, 129, 140; compulsory lectures at, 135; strike (1946), 130; union at, 35, 130, 135
America First (political organization), 126
American Citizens League, 87
American Dream, individualist-centered, 56
American Federation of State, County, and Municipal Employees. *See* AFSCME
American Federation of Teachers Local 212 (Milwaukee), 160, 161
"Americanism," employers' lectures on, 135–36
American Legion, 27; opposition to public housing, 87; in public housing debate, 87
American Local Government and Administration (1956), 38
American Municipal Association, on public-sector strikes, 155
Americans for Constitutional Action, 146
Anderson, Arvid, 159
annexation, Milwaukee, 81, 184; protection from, 112–13; suburban opposition to, 11, 95, 112–16, 177; tax base and, 113
Answers for Americans (radio program), 54
Anti-Defamation League, 6
anti-unionism, 2; in business messages, 135–36; challenges to New Deal, 11; conservatives,' 4, 8; grassroots, 144; of McClellan Committee, 142–43; of mid-twentieth century, 3–4; in Milwaukee, 9
A. O. Smith company, 136; segregation at, 99
arbitration, 159–60; for public-sector employees, 159
Arizona, right-to-work law of, 143
Association of Commerce: opposition to St. Lawrence Seaway, 140; resources for business, 136

baby boom, Milwaukee, 97
Banfield, Edward, 38
Basile, Anthony, 115
Bauer, Catherine, 190n9, 194n66
The Beacon (African American newspaper), 206n42
Behind the Headlines (radio program), 54; corporate sponsorship of, 55
Bell, Daniel (shooting victim), 123
Bell, Daniel: *The Radical Right*, 6

Benton, William, 61
Bentsen, Lloyd, 202n48
Berger, Meta, 25
Berger, Victor, 5, 29, 158; founding of *Milwaukee Leader*, 45; founding of Socialist Party, 25
Bitker, Bruno, 97, 103
black-and-tan clubs, Milwaukee, 101
Blank, Phil, 51; AFT leadership of, 160–61
Block, Richard, 133
blockbusting, 102, 103, 104, 105, 125
Bohn, John, 154, 157; mayoralty of, 21, 22
Boncel Ordinance (Milwaukee), 27
Boston police strike (1919), 154–55
Brawley, George, 102–3
breweries, Milwaukee, 17, 18, 19, 33
Brinkley, Alan, 4, 5
Brisben, Quinn, 187
Bronzeville (Milwaukee), 98–99, 101
Brown, Cecil, Jr., 110–11
Brown, John, 129
Brown, W. E., 153
Brown v. Board of Education, 100, 101
Bruce, William George, 75–76
Buckley, William F.: *National Review*, 7
Budny, Stanley, 133
Budzien, John, 156
Buller, Theresa, 74
Busby, Allen, 114
Busby, Bert, 114
business community, Milwaukee: African American, 99; opposition to labor, 8–9, 130–32; relationship with Zeidler, 37; vision for Milwaukee, 20
business district, Milwaukee, 17–18
businesses: anti-union messaging by, 135–36; captive-audience speeches by, 135–36; challenge to workplace rights, 137; in conservative movement, 131; opposition to NLRA, 130–31; promotion of free enterprise, 39, 135; view of socialism, 42. *See also* corporations
Business Weekly, on union weakness, 143–44
busing, suburban-urban dialectic on, 11

Caitlin Act (Wisconsin), 142
capitalism: as free enterprise, 185; relationships/conflicts of, 168
Census, U.S. (1950), "nonwhite" category of, 204n3
channel 10 (Milwaukee): commercial interest in, 62; debate over, 61–62; Hearst application for, 67; licensing to Milwaukee

Vocational School, 68; potential value of, 59; transmitter for, 67. *See also* public television, Milwaukee

Chicago: public housing in, 91; southern migrants to, 111

Chicago Defender (African American newspaper), 45

Chodorov, Frank, 2

Christian American Association, right-to-work advocacy of, 190n7

CIO: Civic and Government Employees Union (CGEU), 157, 161; in Clay Boat incident, 138; political mobilization by, 30, 93; political mobilization campaigns of, 30; and public housing, 80, 89, 90; public-sector unions of, 155

CIO News, 45–46

cities, U.S.: economic conservatism in, 6; liberal-conservative interplay in, 2; migration into, 97, 107; postwar crises of, 176; postwar ideals of, 2

Citizens' Anti-Slum Committee (Milwaukee), 89

Citizens' Free Enterprise Committee, 94

City Hall, Milwaukee, 17–18

city planning, Milwaukee, 20–21, 206n50. *See also* urban renewal

civic center, Milwaukee, 38

civil defense program, Milwaukee, 38

civil rights movement: in Milwaukee, 177, 179, 216n6; origins of, 217n15

civil service: AFSCME goals for, 152; collective bargaining under, 165–66; reforms, 156. *See also* public employees

Coggs, Isaac, 99, 123

Cohen, Oscar, 6

collective bargaining: conservative opposition to, 132; versus free enterprise, 136; private versus public, 168; strike components of, 168; in Wisconsin, 162

collective bargaining, public-sector, 149; backlash against, 155; for civil service system, 165–66; in conservative counterrevolution, 181; delegation of power in, 169; judicial rulings on, 151; Kennedy's Executive Order on, 172; opponents of, 154, 167; proponents of, 166–67; repeal in Wisconsin, 175–76; sovereign authority in, 168–69; state laws on, 155; supporters of, 158; for teachers, 160–61. *See also* AFSCME District Council 48 (Milwaukee)

collective bargaining, public-sector (Milwaukee), 148–60, 183; Common Council and, 149, 162, 163, 164; representatives for, 161–65; rulings against, 152

Collins, Robert M., 9

commerce, promotion of virtue, 93

Commission on Civil Rights, federal, 125–26

Committee for Economic Development (CED), 131

common good: in democratic process, 171; union support for, 140; Zeidler's belief in, 92

Commons, John R., 45

Communications Act (1934), 47

Communism, Zeidler's dissociation from, 34–35

conservatism: in American history, 8, 191n18; anti-unionism of, 8; benevolent, 72; of Eisenhower era, 72; free-market, 2, 3; historiography of, 6–7; in media, 7–8; motivations for, 147; origins of, 217n15; race-based, 4; religious, 4; resurgence of, 2–3, 6; rise of, 5–9; sociocultural issues of, 5, 6; suburban, 5, 6, 176–77; temporal character of, 3; twenty-first century, 186

conservatism, economic, 4; among middle class, 126; of mainstream media, 42; opposition to collective action, 132; in postwar cities, 6; postwar re-emergence of, 176; race and, 119, 126

conservatism, Milwaukee: economic, 11, 19, 21; grassroots, 20, 176; in suburbs, 5, 126, 179, 185

conservatives: biographies of, 7; liberal, 3; opposition to labor movement, 127; resilience of, 4

conservatives, far right, 3; corporate funding for, 55–56; influence of, 7; scholarship on, 6, 186

conservatives, moderate, 3; anti-unionism of, 4; far right and, 7

consumers, African American, 96–97

Coolidge, Calvin, 155

Cornell, 159, 165

corporations, postwar: antipathy to government policy, 185–86; anti-union tactics of, 4, 43; employee-relations expenditures of, 43; far-right sponsorships of, 55–57; free enterprise campaigns of, 42–43; funding of conservative organizations, 43; liberal support for, 43–44; public-interest advertising of, 70–71; public relations campaigns of, 42, 43–44, 55–57; shaping of public opinion, 39. *See also* businesses

Cortright, Frank, 84

Cory, Jack, 117
Coughlin, Father Charles, 136
Council of State Governments, public services report of, 116
Cowie, Jefferson, 6
Coy, Wayne, 60
crime, Milwaukee: and residential overcrowding, 104; rumors concerning, 119
Cunningham, W. B., 170

D'Angelo, Harry, 157
Dan Smoots Reports (radio program), 55
Davila, José Gonzalez, 179–80
Davis, Richard, 17
Davisk, Dick, 40
deindustrialization: in Milwaukee, 13, 180; in Wisconsin, 144
Democratic Organizing Committee, in public housing debate, 87
department stores, Milwaukee, 18
Divina, M.S.: union action against, 137, 138

economics, Austrian School of, 7
Edsall, Thomas B. and Mary, 6
education, public: corporate opposition to, 67
Eisenhower, Dwight D.: election of, 68; moderate policies of, 1; on St. Lawrence Seaway, 141
electric power system, Milwaukee: private ownership of, 27
Employers' Association of Milwaukee, 147
Epstein, Benjamin: *Danger on the Right*, 6
Erchul, Fred, 80
Ewen, Stuart, 8

factories, Milwaukee, 19. *See also* deindustrialization
Facts Forum News, 7, 141, 186; audience interaction with, 53; broadcasts of, 53, 54; contributions to, 52, 53; groups associated with, 53–54; readers of, 54
Facts Forum State of the Nation (radio program), 54
Fair Employment Practices Commission (FEPC), 99
FCC: educational television proposal, 59–60; freeze on television permits, 58–59; on public programming, 61. *See also* public television; television
Federal Housing Administration (FHA), racial restrictions of, 105
Federated Press, 45

Federated Trades Council of Milwaukee: disputes committee of, 150; publications of, 46; in public housing debate, 81
fish fries, 19
Flynn, John, 7; *Behind the Headlines* program of, 54–55
Foner, Eric, 203n72
Fones-Wolf, Elizabeth, 8; *Selling Free enterprise*, 44
Forester, Arnold: *Danger on the Right*, 6
"For America" (political organization), 119. *See also* Milwaukee for America
Fortune magazine, 42; on Milwaukee government, 121; on NLRA, 130; "Organized Labor-The Dwindling Minority?," 144; on public housing, 91
Fossum, M.S.: union action against, 137, 138
Fox News, 181
Freedom School, Grede's support of, 147
free enterprise, 5; in American conservatism, 3; business promotion of, 39, 135; capitalism as, 185; versus collective action, 136; conservative media on, 50; corporate campaigns for, 42–43; demonization of unions, 182; freedom from regulation, 4; versus individual rights, 185; versus labor movements, 126; NAM tv series on, 70; in postwar media, 8; unions and, 134
free enterprise, Milwaukee, 14; worker challenges to, 137–39
Friedman, Milton, 147
Friedrick, J. F., 71–72; on Clay Boat incident, 138–39

Galbraith, John Kenneth, 166, 172
Gant, Harry, 40
Garden City Movement (Great Britain), 82, 112, 187
Gau, Harvey, 157
Gauer, Paul, 158
Geib, Paul, 111
German community, Milwaukee, 15–16; press of, 44; during World War I, 23, 24
German language, teaching in Milwaukee, 41
Gimbels Department store, 18
The Globe (African American paper), 109, 206n42
Goldwater, Barry, 143
Goss, Edna, 54
governance: ideals of, 187; pluralist approach to, 158; public interest in, 172
government: collectivist incursions in, 68; duty to citizens, 169; employee unity

with, 170; expansion of, 64, 73, 140; fear of, 126; ideological war against, 72; as not-for-profit employer, 167; postwar public support for, 55; role in public life, 13; role in social programs, 8, 43; unity with residents, 169
grassroots movements, 20, 176; Affiliated Taxpayers, 84, 93; "astroturf," 87, 202n48; opposing public housing, 86
Great Depression, Milwaukee during, 26
Greater Milwaukee Committee, 20, 47
Great Lakes District, steel supply for, 141
Grede, Arthur, 49
Grede, William, 7; anti-strike advertising of, 127–28; anti-unionism of, 12, 127–30, 145, 180; challenge to government, 145; death of, 185; divide-and-conquer tactics of, 128–29; early life of, 128; far-right conservatism of, 75, 145, 184; on federal government, 184; individualist worldview of, 2, 134; NAM presidency of, 145–46; newspaper interests of, 49, 56; opposition to collective bargaining, 129, 130; political contributions of, 146–47, 211n65; positions held by, 129, 136–37; proselytizing of employees, 1–2, 128; public influence of, 145–47; and Robert Welch, 50; *The Virtue of Selfishness*, 145
Grede Foundries: anti-union policies of, 127–28; growth of, 184–85
Greenbelt suburbs, U.S., 82
Greendale (Milwaukee), segregation in, 102
green spaces, Milwaukee, 19, 83
Griffith, Robert, 8
Gromacki, Matt, 103
Groppi, Father James: activism of, 177
Group Research (liberal organization), 55
Gurden, John, 187

Haberman, George, 134, 141
Halyard, Wilbur and Ardie, 98
Hambley, Genevieve, 81
Hannah, John, 125–26
Harnischfeger, Walter, 12, 137; anti-unionism of, 145; opposition to St. Lawrence Seaway, 140–41, 147; public influence of, 145; strikers and, 134; testimony before Congress, 134; in Wisconsin Manufacturers' Association, 136
Hartsfield, William Berry, 37
Hass, Alfred, 66, 81; on collective bargaining, 152
Hearst, William Randolph, 48

Hearst Corporation: in educational television debate, 63, 64–67, 65; interest in channel 10, 62, 67; petition to FCC, 69; support for McCarthy, 69
Heinz, H. J., 90
Hendershot, Heather, 7–8
Hennock, Frieda: on commercial radio interests, 67; educational tv advocacy, 59, 60, 61, 66
Herzfeld, Richard, 21
Hesburgh, Theodore, 97
highways, construction of, 20, 124, 178
Hillside Terrace housing complex (Milwaukee), 73, 74; completion of, 199n1; taxes paid in, 86
Hilquit, Morris, 28
Hoan, Daniel Webster: annexation under, 112; anti-graft efforts of, 47; election campaigns of, 27; liberalism of, 24; mayoralty of, 9, 22, 26–27, 28–29; and Milwaukee Common Council, 26–27; in 1948 election, 21
Holton, Chuck, 99
homeownership, role in economic freedom, 84
homicide rates, Milwaukee, 104
Hopke, Jill, 175, 176
housing: affordable, 10, 74, 82–83, 117, 190n9; federal funding for, 75, 77, 90. *See also* public housing; segregation, racial
housing, Milwaukee: government expansion of, 73; overcrowding in, 103, 104; racial discrimination in, 96, 101–3, 178; restrictive covenants in, 101–2; substandard, 74, 81, 89; for veterans, 73–74, 77, 78, 88, 93
Housing Act (1937), 74–75
Housing Act (1949), 11, 74–75, 78; opponents of, 76, 83; Pieplow on, 91; private enterprise in, 83; U.S. Savings and Loan League on, 79
Housing and Home Finance Agency (HHFA), 105
housing reform, national proponents of, 75
housing shortage, Milwaukee: postwar crisis in, 73–74, 89, 94–95, 97, 179
Howard, Ebenezer, 82, 112
Humphreys, Richard, 160
Hunt, H. L. (Haroldson Lafayette), 56; political views of, 52. *See also Facts Forum News*

income equality, postwar, 139–40
individualism, Lockean, 172

individual rights: economic, 12; versus free enterprise, 185; versus public good, 2, 5, 11, 72, 73
industrialists, Milwaukee, 17. *See also* deindustrialization
industry, public ownership of, 26–27
International Association of Firefighters (IAFF), 162
International City Managers' Association, 155
International Harvester (Milwaukee), strike at, 209n17
International Labor News Services, 45

Jackson, Kenneth, 5
Jeffries, Edward, Jr., 158
Jewish population, Milwaukee, 15
Joers, Stanley, 162
John Birch Society, 50
Johnson, Lyndon: Great Society of, 187
Joint Action Committee for Better Housing, 81
Joint Committee on Educational Television, national, 60
Juneau Town (Milwaukee), 15

Kelley, William, 100, 101, 110
Kennan, George, 5
Kennedy, John F., 141; Executive Order on public employees, 172; support for St. Lawrence Seaway project, 141
Kersten, Charles, 69
Kessler, Fred, 35
Keynesianism, 46, 185; commercial, 9, 10, 131, 191n25
Kilbourn Town (Milwaukee), 15
King, Anthony, 62, 132
King, Martin Luther, Jr.: visit to Milwaukee, 111
Kinnickinnic River, 14
Kirchuebel, Walter, 79–80
Koch, Fred, 50
Koch, Gerda, 54
Kohler, Herbert: anti-unionism of, 137–38, 143; lockout of employees, 150
Kohler, Walter, 92
Kohler, Walter, Jr., 142; mediation efforts of, 137–38; veto of collective bargaining, 152
Kohler industry: lockout at, 150; proposed boycott of, 49; union action against, 137–38
Kramer, Leo, 151
Kruse, Kevin, 5

labor: corporatist vision of, 131–32; reform, 45. *See also* unions; working class
labor, Milwaukee: business's opposition to, 8–9, 130–32; in public housing debate, 88; support for St. Lawrence Seaway, 141
labor laws, conservative challenges to, 11–12
labor movements, U.S.: bureaucracies of, 181; business opposition to, 8; capitalist competitors of, 46; delegitimization of, 72; de-linking from European labor, 191n24; economic conservatives' opposition to, 127; versus free enterprise, 126; lack of diversity in, 181; of mid-twentieth century, 3–4; and municipal socialism, 29; national support for, 84; postwar momentum of, 127; press of, 45; public opinion on, 128, 181–82; radio programs of, 46–47; *Reader's Digest* on, 51; support for public programs, 127; weakening of, 144. *See also* collective bargaining; unions
Labor Press (Milwaukee), 46
Labor Press Associated, 45
labor reform, in foreign language press, 45
LaFollette, Philip, 27
LaFollette, Robert, 27, 28; progressivism of, 5
Lake Michigan, deep-water port of, 19
Lanphier, Charles, 60
La Salle, SS: torpedoing of, 192n20
Lassiter, Matthew, 5
Latino community, Milwaukee: housing problems of, 110
Laubach, Guy, 87
Lawrence, David, 37, 68; in public housing debate, 90
Lawton, John, 156–57
League of Milwaukee County Municipalities, 118
League of Wisconsin Municipalities, 112; Green Bay meeting, 115
Lee, Ivey, 43
LeFevre, Robert, 147
Lewis, Dallas Bedford, 55
liberalism: early American, 203n72; New Deal, 131
liberalism, Milwaukee: conservative challenge to, 9–13; domestic agenda of, 36; postwar, 5, 10
liberalism, postwar, 3–5; business opposition to, 8; complacency in, 5; consensus in, 72; limits of, 2, 4; in Milwaukee, 5; social agenda of, 4
Liebling, A. J., 41–42, 44; on political elite, 47

Lippmann, Walter, 68
Lowndes, Joseph, 6
Ludlow massacre (1914), 43

MacLean, Nancy, 217n15
Maier, Henry, 21, 37; accomplishments of, 177; campaign against Reuss (1960), 178; consolidation of power, 177; and "Covenant of Open Occupancy," 124; popularity of, 178; and public housing, 88, 91
Maier, Irwin, 47
Manion, Clarence, 1, 56, 119; Grede's support of, 211n65; radio program of, 55
Manion Forum, 138, 146
Marx, John, 80
Mattison, Walter, 133
mayors, socialist, 28–29; of Milwaukee, 25, 30, 120
Mayor's Commission on Human Rights (Milwaukee), 97, 101, 125, 204n20
McCarthy, Joseph, 5, 28; alcohol abuse by, 48, 195n31; Hearst's support of, 69; in 1952 elections, 68, 69; in public television debate, 69
McCartin, Joseph, 172, 181
McClellan Committee, 49; anti-unionism of, 142–43
McGirr, Lisa, 4; *Suburban Warriors*, 5
McGuire, Milton, 64, 66; in 1956 mayoral race, 118–22; presidency of Common Council, 121; race-baiting by, 118–19, 120, 121, 122, 126; real estate's endorsement of, 91; Red-baiting by, 119; supporters of, 119
McLevy, Jasper, 25, 28–29
McLin, W. J. G., 89, 108
McNamara, Patrick, 143
Meany, George, 71, 143; on arbitration, 159; on public employees, 155
media: challenge to authority, 41–42; consolidation of, 39, 42, 44–47, 56; corporate-owned, 40, 184; publicity releases of, 43
media, broadcast: privatization of, 57; union use of, 46–47. *See also* radio; television
media, conservative, 7–8, 42; business interests in, 49; corporate sponsorship of, 55–56; far-right, 10, 56–57, 185; on free enterprise, 50; nationwide reach of, 50–55; working-class audience of, 8
media, Milwaukee: African American, 45; assault on New Deal, 38; conservative, 10, 47–55; consolidation of, 39; corporatized, 38; far-right, 39; labor newspapers of, 45–46; mainstream, 39

Meet the Press, 70, 71
Mellon, Richard, 90
Memphis, sanitation workers' strike in, 183
Menomonee River, 14
Menomonee River valley, 15, 16
Mercury Proving Grounds (Nevada), atomic explosion at, 25
Meyers, Fred, 103, 104, 152
middle class, Milwaukee: African American, 96–99, 108, 179; liberal, 125
middle class, under New Deal, 127
migrants, African American (Milwaukee), 101, 107–11; diversity among, 111; suburban hostility to, 116–17
Miller, Sally, 25–26
Milwaukee: Civil Service Law, 153; commercial decentralization in, 18; cross-boundary traditions of, 18–19; early settlements of, 15; ethnic enclaves of, 15–16, 18, 98–99; during Great Depression, 26; Magnificent Mile, 38; mansions of, 16–17; in post-liberal era, 175–86; rivers of, 14–15; toy loan program, 63; wealthy population of, 17–18; work-relief program, 26
Milwaukee, postwar: bond rating of, 121; challenges of, 14; "Clay Boat" incident, 137–39; competing visions for, 20; conflict with suburbs, 6, 41; consensus in, 185–86; conservative counterrevolution in, 2, 184–86; decline of socialism in, 27; deindustrialization in, 13, 180; demographic change in, 124–25; economic power of, 14; finances of, 9, 19–20, 177; income levels in, 19, 139, 178; inner core of, 106, 107, 108, 124, 178, 179; labor-management conflict in, 8–9; liberal leadership of, 145; low-income residents of, 11; modernization of municipal services, 64; municipal consolidation efforts in, 116–17; parkway around, 83; population of, 178; race riots (1967), 124; residency laws of, 109–10; and rise of conservatism, 5
Milwaukee Area Technical College (MATC), 160, 161
Milwaukee Association of Commerce, and public housing debate, 78
Milwaukee Board of Realtors, 84; on urban renewal, 105
Milwaukee Board of Vocational and Adult Education, support for public television, 66, 69
Milwaukee Building and Trades Council, 20

Milwaukee Catholic Archdiocese: and collective bargaining, 162; in public television debate, 65; and sanitation workers' strike, 154
Milwaukee City and County Public Service Employees Union, CIO affiliation of, 153
Milwaukee Common Council, 12; and African American rights, 109; and AFSCME District 49, 162; anti-labor actions, 133; closed-door sessions, 121; composition of, 34, 36–37; conservative Democrats of, 36, 37; Finance Committee, 150, 162; Hoan and, 26–27; Joint Committee on Housing and Finance, 81; Judiciary Committee, 69; liberal Republicans of, 36, 37; on metropolitan consolidation, 116; in 1952 election, 91; price gouging issues before, 102–3; and public employee bargaining, 149, 162, 163, 164; in public housing debate, 73, 77, 81, 86, 88, 179; in public television debate, 58, 59, 62, 63, 64–67, 69; Public Utilities Committee, 65, 115, 133; and residential segregation, 102–3, 109–10, 125; Special Committee on Radio, 59; Zeidler and, 37–38
Milwaukee County: Home for Dependent Children, 74; manufacturing losses, 144; Park Commission, 83
Milwaukee County Board of Supervisors, Committee on Suburban Services, 113–14
Milwaukee County Property Owners' Association, 144; "Captain's Group," 79, 80–81, 86; public relations campaign of, 86; in public television debate, 63, 64; Zeidler on, 84
Milwaukee County Republican Party, 1, 12, 146, 147
Milwaukee Defender (African American newspaper), 45, 206n42
Milwaukee Educators' Committee on Television, 61; report to FCC, 62
Milwaukee Election Committee, 80
Milwaukee Federated Trades Council, 28, 29
"Milwaukee flats," 22
Milwaukee For America (political organization), 120. See also "For America"
Milwaukee Government Service League, 153, 163–64
Milwaukee Harbor Commission, 138
Milwaukee Housing Authority, 106; affordable housing proposal, 74; creation of, 73; public relations messages of, 85; reports on housing shortage, 89; on substandard housing, 74; tax study of, 85–86; veterans' housing plan, 74
Milwaukee Housing Commission, African American members of, 109
Milwaukee Human Rights Commission, 102, 103, 109
Milwaukee Journal: on African American housing, 106; business ties of, 47; circulation of, 48; corporate liberalism of, 47; coverage of McCarthy, 48; coverage of 1948 elections, 39, 40; focus on clean government, 47; housing referendum in, 85, 87; influence of, 40–41; manipulation of information, 41; merger with *Sentinel*, 181; nationwide reputation of, 39–40; in 1956 election, 41, 119–20; on nonpartisan elections, 41; on public-sector bargaining, 149; on public television debate, 66–67; Pulitzer Prize of, 41; on southern migrants, 107; support for Reuss, 39, 40; women readers of, 48; Zeidler's relationship with, 41
Milwaukee Journal Company, television station of, 58
Milwaukee Journal-Sentinel, 186
Milwaukee Junior Chamber of Commerce, 121
Milwaukee Labor Press (AFL publication), 45–46, 133
Milwaukee Leader, 45
Milwaukee League of Women Voters, 81, 102; in public housing debate, 87
Milwaukee River, 14–15; closure to navigation, 144
Milwaukee Security Savings and Loan Association, 76; on public-sector bargaining, 150
Milwaukee Sentinel, 47; anti-communism of, 40, 48; far-right conservatism of, 48; Hearst subsidization of, 65; housing referendum in, 85, 87; merger with *Journal*, 181; in public television debate, 63, 65
The Milwaukee Sepian (African American newspaper), 206n42
Milwaukee Steel, strikes at, 128
Milwaukee Times: on AFL-CIO merger, 56; economic conservatism of, 48; on educational television, 63; on Latino community, 110; on public-sector strikes, 157; readers of, 56; on southern migrants, 107
Milwaukee Urban League: on employment segregation, 100; on southern migrants, 110

Index

Milwaukee Vocational and Adult Schools, 61; licensing of channel 10, 68; in public television debate, 63, 64, 65; restraining order against, 66, 67; training for African Americans, 61
Mire, Joseph, 166, 167, 169
Mises, Ludwig von, 130, 136, 147
Missouri Supreme Court, on public-sector bargaining, 151
Morrison, DeLesseps, 37, 90
Morrison Advertising Agency (Milwaukee), 128
mortgages, racial restrictions on, 105, 106
Mortier, James, 149
MoveOn.org, in Palermo Pizza strike, 180
movies, business-sponsored, 136
municipal debt, Milwaukee: avoidance of, 19, 21, 92; Hoan's abhorrence of, 26; nonpartisan, 36; referendum of 1948 on, 20–21; Zeidler's opposition to, 35, 92
municipal elections, Milwaukee: of 1912, 26; of 1936, 27; of 1948, 9, 14, 21–22, 85; of 1952, 64, 68, 91; of 1956, 96, 118–22, 146; of 1960, 178; of 1968, 178
municipal elections, Wisconsin: nonpartisan, 26
Municipal Enterprise Committee (MEC), 30, 32; coalition platform of, 29; on consolidation, 116; Zeidler and, 30, 32, 33, 35–36, 37. *See also* Public Enterprise Committee

NAACP (Milwaukee), 98
Nash, George, 6
National Association of Home Builders (NAHB): "Public Housing on the Community Level," 83–84; public relations by, 84
National Association of Manufacturers (NAM), 135; *Industry on Parade* series, 70; opposition to St. Lawrence Seaway, 140; resources for business, 136; and Taft-Hartley Act, 132
National Association of Real Estate Boards (NAREB), 76, 185–86; racial criteria of, 105
National Education Association (NEA), on collective bargaining, 160–61
National Institute of Municipal Law Officers, 155
National Labor Relations Act (NLRA), 129; backlash against, 4, 27; business opposition to, 130–31, 132; employer free speech ruling of, 135; Palermo Pizza ruling, 180; protection of unions, 130; workers omitted from, 151, 155
National Recovery Act (NRA), 129
Nazi Friends of New Germany, 27
Near Northside Businessmen's Association (Milwaukee), 99
Negro Business Directory of the State of Wisconsin, 99, 109
Nelson, Gaylord, 152
New Deal: anti-union challenges to, 11; backlash against, 10; challenges to, 185; challenge to corporate preeminence, 131; collectivism of, 2; conservative resistance to, 13, 126; corporate opposition to, 10, 56; domesticated, 3; interest-group politics in, 171; labor under, 131; Milwaukee views on, 13; opposition to, 2–3, 186; postwar rollbacks to, 36, 145, 176; public good under, 38, 144, 180; suburban opposition to, 95
New Jersey, State Board of Mediation, 169
New Orleans, public housing in, 90–91
newspapers: consolidation of, 56; labor, 45–46; working-class readers of, 46
newspapers, foreign-language: decline of, 47; German, 44; of Milwaukee, 44–45; unions,' 45
New Urbanism, 112
New York World, 42
1948 Corporation, 47, 89; improvements agenda of, 20–21
Norris, William, 48
North: African American migration to, 97, 107; residential segregation in, 97
North Shore (Milwaukee), mansions of, 16–17
North Side (Milwaukee): blockbusting tactics in, 103; crime in, 104; racially mixed, 102; rioting (1967), 177
November Folk Fair (Milwaukee), 19
Nunn, Henry, 89
Nymeyer, Frederick, 129

Oak Creek (Milwaukee), anti-annexation struggle of, 112, 115
O'Baird, J. T., 23–24
Opinion Research Corporation, 42
Organization to Repeal Federal Income Taxes, 55
Our Way of Living (film), 136

Pabst, Frederick, 17
Page, Kirby, 24
Palermo's Pizza (Milwaukee), 179; strike against, 180
peace movement (1930s), 24
Pendleton Act (1883), 166
People's Party, 26
periodicals, conservative, 7
Perrin, Richard, 81, 85, 86
Petro, Sylvester, 169
Phillips, Dale, 122
Phillips, Vel Rogers, 108–9; Common Council campaign, 122–23; fair housing bills of, 177
Phillips-Fein, Kim, 6, 8
Pieplow, William: in Affiliated Taxpayers' Committee, 77; anti-Socialist remarks of, 87; chairmanship of Referendum Committee, 78; challenge to government, 145; conservatism of, 10–11, 75; on home ownership, 76; and Housing Act of 1949, 76, 91; on individual initiative, 91, 92; interest in the arts, 92; offices held by, 75; in public housing debate, 50, 74–76, 77; religious identity of, 92; republican/liberal synthesis of, 93; in savings and loan industry, 76, 94; view of government, 92, 93; views on citizenship, 76
Pittsburgh, public housing in, 90
Plantz, Edward, 86
Polcyn, John, 119
Polenberg, Richard, 28
Polish community, Milwaukee, 15, 16; *Milwaukee Times* readers, 56
politics: backlash narrative of, 6; interest-group, 170–71; right-based, 181
politics, Milwaukee: liberal, 5; religion in, 16; temperament of, 19
politics, prewar: conflicts shaping, 2
Prasser, Josephine, 103
private enterprise, corporate advertising on, 43
Progressive era: city beautification of, 112; employee rights in, 153
Progressive Party (Wisconsin), 28
The Property Owner (newsletter), 86
property rights, under free enterprise, 4
Prothro, James, 70–71
Proxmire, William, 142
Prussian Turnverein movement, 31
public employees: arbitration for, 159; conditions of employment for, 165–69; job security for, 166; numbers of, 172; prestige of, 172; relationship with management, 169; unity with government, 170; wages of, 166–67; Wisconsin, 176. *See also* collective bargaining, public-sector
public employees, Milwaukee: bargaining rights of, 12; in City Hall, 153; expectations of, 172; numbers of, 148; rights of, 148–49, 150, 153; strikes by, 154, 157; unions of, 153; workplace rights of, 147
Public Enterprise Committee, 81, 88, 183, 202n51. *See also* Municipal Enterprise Committee
public good: versus corporate interests, 57; versus individual rights, 2, 5, 11, 72, 73; Milwaukee proponents of, 14; move away from, 36; under New Deal, 38, 144, 180; tax base for, 94; through annexation, 94
public housing: local consensuses on, 75; local referenda on, 91; nationwide fights for, 90–91; public support for, 83; real estate industry's opposition to, 75, 76, 77–78, 79, 81–82, 83, 90; states' enabling of, 75
public housing, Milwaukee, 178; aldermen's opposition to, 77, 88, 94; conservative campaign against, 10–11; debates over, 74–90, 93–95; delaying tactics for, 77; economic conservatives on, 73; federal funding for, 77; individual rights and, 11; lack of interest in, 194n66; opponents of, 74, 77–78, 84; proponents of, 77, 81, 83; and redevelopment, 103; savings and loan associations' opposition to, 84; women's support for, 81; Zeidler and, 34, 80, 81–82, 84, 87, 106
public housing referenda, Milwaukee (1951), 72, 73, 77, 85–90, 93; Affiliated Taxpayers' petition for, 78–82, 85; CIO and, 80; outcomes of, 89–90; suburbs in, 118
public interest: advertising, 70; housing in, 75; and individual rights, 5; labor and, 158; Milwaukeeans' vision of, 21; Pieplow and, 11; public television in, 58–64; unified, 171, 183; Zeidler's conception of, 9, 32, 36, 61, 93, 157, 158, 165, 170–73, 183, 187
public library, Milwaukee, 38
public opinion: corporate involvement in, 39; media shaping of, 39, 40
public parks, Milwaukee, 82, 83
public service: for African American community, 126; Council of State Governments on, 116; duality in, 182; ideals of,

172; interest-group politics and, 170–71; in postwar era, 172
public spirit, in liberal society, 172
public television: commercial radio opposition to, 67; debates over, 68; FCC proposal on, 59–60; in government expansion debate, 64; nationwide implementation of, 69. *See also* television
public television, Milwaukee, 10, 38; aldermen's opposition to, 69; Common Council on, 58, 59; as community resource, 62; debate over, 58–71; opponents of, 62–67, 68–69; public demand for, 62; public-relations campaign for, 62; role in community well-being, 61; supporters of, 61–62, 68, 72; tax increases for, 63–64

race: in crime incidents, 104; and economic conservatism, 119, 126; in 1956 elections, 96, 118–19, 120, 126; as political weapon, 11; in public housing debate, 94
racial violence, Milwaukee, 101, 123, 124
radicalism: of 1960s, 6; worker, 8
radio: African American listeners, 97; educational programs on, 61; labor movement's use of, 46–47; pro-business messages on, 137
radio, conservative, 52, 54; expansion into television, 55; talk, 181
Rains, Harry, 166
Reader's Digest, 7; audience of, 51, 52; conservatism of, 51
real estate industry: opposition to public housing, 75, 76, 77–78, 79, 81–82, 83, 90; public relations campaigns, 83–84, 93; segregation tactics of, 102–4; targeting of Zeidler, 103–4
Reap, Howard, 53, 54
Red Cross Housing Bureau (Milwaukee), 74
religion, in Milwaukee politics, 16
religious leaders, Milwaukee: civil rights record of, 119
republicanism, early American, 203n72
Republican Party, Milwaukee, 1; Common Council members in, 36, 37; Grede's involvement in, 146, 147; Pieplow's involvement in, 92
restaurants, Milwaukee, 19
Reuss, Henry, 30, 35–36; campaign against Maier (1960), 178; in 1947 primary, 22; in 1948 elections, 39, 40, 85; press support for, 32

Reuther, Walter, 35, 49; before McClellan Committee, 143
revenue sharing, federal, 177
right-to-work laws, postwar, 142, 143
Roache, John, 105
The Rocket (African American newspaper), 206n42
Roosevelt, Franklin: liberal tradition of, 9, 10; on public-sector bargaining, 154, 213n19; social-welfare vision of, 12–13
Rossiter, Clinton, 3
Rotary Club, Milwaukee, 47

Saltzstein, Arthur, 33
Salvatore, Nick, 6
savings and loan associations, Milwaukee, 76; opposition to public housing, 78, 84
Saxton, H. Ellis, 78
Schimenz, Matt, 115
Schlesinger, Arthur, Jr., 72
Schmitt, John, 29, 30, 138
Schoemann, Peter, 20, 59; criticism of Eisenhower, 89; offices held by, 88; in public housing debate, 81, 88–89
Schultz, Elton, 78
Schurz, Carl, 166
Scott, Fitzhugh, Jr., 50
The Secret of Selling the Negro (film), 96
segregation, racial: federal policy on, 105, 106; in North, 97, 99–101
segregation, racial (Milwaukee), 97–98, 101–3; blockbusting tactics in, 102, 103, 104, 105, 125; in education, 100–101; in employment, 99–100; law on, 109–10; tactics of, 102–4; transitional areas in, 105; in twenty-first century, 124; Zeidler and, 102, 103–6, 110
Seidel, Emil, 41, 83; anti-graft efforts of, 47; founding of Vocational School, 64; mayoralty of, 26
Select Committee on Improper Activities in the Labor and Management Field, 49, 142–43
Self, Robert O., 5
Shadd, Mary Ellen, 109, 111
Shefferman, Nathaniel, 135
Shermer, Elizabeth Tandy, 8
Shinners, Joseph, 27
Shister, Joseph, 135
Simons, Jesse, 167
Sinclair, John S., 44
Slater, Harry, 164

Slater, Joseph, 167–68
slum clearance, Milwaukee, 77; bond issue for, 85, 106; displacement following, 103, 124; under federal law, 82; Zeidler on, 94. *See also* housing, Milwaukee; urban renewal
slum clearance, national: public support for, 83
Smith, A. O., 136
Smith, Kate, 22
Smith, Lawrence, 69
Smith Steel (Milwaukee), strike at, 127, 128
Smoot, Dan, 56; *Dan Smoot Reports*, 55; *Facts Forum* work, 52–53; television debates of, 54
Socialism: postwar businesses on, 42; practical, 28
Socialism, Milwaukee, 170–71; aspirational, 34; decline of, 27; of mayors, 25, 30, 120; sewer, 28, 166; working class support for, 35
Socialist Party of America: in Milwaukee, 25–27, 29, 45, 79, 120; schisms in, 25; Zeidler in, 24
The Socialist Quarter Hour (radio program), 45
social programs, government role in, 8
social welfare: acceptance in Milwaukee, 176; expansion of, 186–87; media attacks on, 42
states: right-to-work provisions of, 190n7; sovereign power of, 170
Stevenson, Adlai, 68
St. Josaphat, Basilica of, 16
St. Lawrence Seaway: Milwaukee workers' support for, 12; opponents of, 140–41, 147
St. Louis, civil service system of, 166
Stocking, Lewis, 78
Stokes, Thomas, 2, 42
strikes, Milwaukee: AFSCME's, 165; AFSCME threats, 148–50; conveyance of materials through, 137–39; of postwar period, 127–28, 130, 134, 137–39, 148–50; by public employees, 154, 157–58; sanitation workers,' 154, 157; twenty-first century, 180; unrest in, 133; violence in, 137; during World War II, 156; Zeidler and, 132–33, 209n17
strikes, public-sector, 154–55; alternatives to, 159; legislation prohibiting, 155; teachers,' 155, 161; worker empowerment through, 155–57

Strout, Dick, 42
St. Stanislaus Catholic Church (Milwaukee), 16
Study Committee on Social Problems in the Inner Core Area of the City (Milwaukee), 124
suburbanization: class-consciousness in, 113; Milwaukee challenge to, 94
suburbs, Milwaukee: affordable housing in, 117; African Americans in, 178; autonomy of, 95; community participation in, 117; conflict with metropolitan area, 6, 41; conservatism in, 5, 126, 179, 185; conservative press of, 10, 181; economic conservatism of, 116, 117; "flight to," 185; growth of, 112; "iron ring" of, 11, 95, 112, 113, 118, 191n27; opposition to annexation, 11, 95, 112–16, 177; race/class issues in, 116–17, 118; tax base in, 111–13; water services for, 112, 113–16, 117–18; zoning restrictions in, 113
Sugrue, Thomas, 6, 97
sundown towns, 101
Supreme Court, U.S.: on public-utilities law, 156; on racial covenants, 105; on urban decay, 106
Swietlik, Walter, 154, 157

Taft-Hartley Act (1947), 137, 186, 190n7; corporate lobbying for, 132; free-speech provision of, 135; repeal efforts against, 134; value to businesses, 133–34
taxes, postwar reductions in, 9
taxes, Milwaukee: geographic base for, 96, 118; increase in base, 112; suburban base for, 111–13
Taxpayers' Advisory Council (Milwaukee), 78–79
teachers: strikes by, 155, 161; workplace rights for, 160–61
Technical Engineers Association Local 54, Zeidler in, 30
technocrats, government, 186
Tedlow, Richard, 8
television: commercial, 58–59; nonprofit access to, 58; public-private struggle over, 56–57; public programming on, 61, 66; right-wing broadcasts on, 55; UHF, 60; unions' use of, 47; VHF, 60. *See also* public television
television sets, number of, 71
television viewership, union membership and, 71

Teske, Roland, 82
Thayer, George: *The Farther Shores of Politics*, 6–7
35th Street Advancement Association (Milwaukee), 23
Thomas, Norman, 24
Till, Emmett, 123
Time magazine: on African American consumers, 97; on postwar prosperity, 139
Toliver, Bernard, 104
Towell, Harold and Henry, 50, 56, 157
Trotter, Joe, 108
Tugwell, Rexford: Greenbelt New Town Program of, 82
Typographical Union (Milwaukee), 29

unions: anti-individualism of, 134; conservative attacks on, 142–43; corporate attacks on, 43; craft, 143; discrediting by business, 133–37; economic opportunity through, 7, 43; federal recognition of, 137; foreign-language papers of, 45; and free enterprise, 134; funding of Democratic candidates, 142; media attacks on, 49–50; New Deal laws on, 11; personal freedom and, 12; postwar membership in, 137, 144; power in manufacturing, 130; public opinion on, 134, 143; role in income equality, 139–40; as special interest, 182; support for common good, 140; televised outreach by, 71; urban support for, 132–33; use of broadcast media, 46–47; weakening of, 143–44. *See also* collective bargaining; labor movements, U.S.
unions, Milwaukee, 9; at Allis-Chalmers, 35, 130, 135; apprentice training programs of, 100; attacks on, 126; business responses to, 1; members in city government, 133; public opinion on, 138; racial discrimination in, 100; radicalism of, 130; support for Zeidler, 29–30, 132–33; in twenty-first century, 179–81; worker rights of, 147; Zeidler and, 12, 36
unions, public-sector: AFL affiliations, 155; anti-government conservatism and, 172; CIO affiliations, 155; memoranda of agreement for, 151; supporters of, 158. *See also* AFSCME; collective bargaining, public sector
unions, Wisconsin: politically active members of, 142
United Auto Workers, Local 248, 130, 135

United Steelworkers strike, 134
urban decay: 1948 Corporation on, 21; postwar, 14, 17; Supreme Court on, 106
urban renewal: national, 20; of Progressive era, 112. *See also* city planning; slum clearance
urban renewal, Milwaukee, 103, 105; cost of, 107
U.S. Chamber of Commerce, 132; "American Opportunity Program," 136
U.S. Savings and Loan League, 76; anti-public-housing materials, 78; on 1949 Housing Act, 79

veterans, World War II: housing bond referendum (1949), 77, 85; housing shortage for, 73–74, 97; living conditions of, 199n2
Veterans against Public Housing committee, 87
Voces de la Frontera (community group), 180

Walker, Scott, 181; "budget repair bill" of, 175; public career of, 176; recall movement against, 175–76
Wall, Wendy, 8, 43–44
Wallace, DeWitt, 7; conservatism of, 51
Wallace, Lila Bell, 7
Washington, Booker T., 98, 109
Wauwatosa (Milwaukee): anti-annexation struggle of, 114; anti-unionism in, 142; conservatism of, 176; housing restrictions in, 177; water services for, 114–15, 117–18
Wauwatosa News-Times: attack on unions, 49–50; defense of business, 50; on housing, 110; on welfare recipients, 116, 117
WBAL (Baltimore), 66
Weeks, Sinclair, 96
Weinlein, Tony, 59
Weisenfeld, Allen, 166–67
Welch, Robert, 50
Wells, Robert, 195n31
WEMP radio (Milwaukee), 59; transmitter of, 67
West Allis (Milwaukee): anti-annexation struggle of, 114; Common Council, 114, 116
West Allis Star (Milwaukee), 48; on annexation, 115; on municipal consolidation, 117
WFOX radio (Milwaukee), 59, 60
white flight, suburban-urban dialectic on, 11
Whitnall, Charles B., 82, 83

Wigren, Harold, 62
Wiley, Alexander, 69
Wilson, Charles, 146
Wisconsin: Act 10, 175, 181; AFL-CIO of, 29; child-labor laws of, 184; collective-bargaining bill (1959), 152–53, 161, 168; collective bargaining in, 162, 175–76; Corrupt Practices Act, 80; deindustrialization of, 144; Employment Relations Board, 152; Fair Employment Practices Law, 100; Finance Committee, 175; public employees of, 12; repeal of public-sector collective bargaining, 175–76; right-to-work legislation in, 142; savings and loan associations in, 76; State Federation of Labor, 162
Wisconsin Employers' Association, 118
Wisconsin Manufacturers' Association, free-enterprise campaigns of, 136–37
Wisconsin Progressive Party, 27–28
Wisconsin Public Services Commission, on water services, 117, 118
Wisconsin Republican Party, 69, 147
Wisconsin State Federation of Labor, 27, 28, 162
Wisconsin State Legislature, on Milwaukee expansion, 112
WISN radio (Milwaukee), 48, 59, 69; conservative ideology of, 62–63; *Facts Forum* on, 54; interest in channel 10, 62–63; television application of, 60
WMVS-TV. *See* channel 10 (Milwaukee)
Woerfel Corporation (Milwaukee), in 1956 election, 119
Women's Civic Group, 87
Women's Trade Union League, 81
workers, in economic decision making, 127
worker solidarity, employer resistance to, 191n24
working class, under New Deal, 127
working class, Milwaukee, 14, 15–16; activism of, 12; support for Socialism, 35; in twenty-first century, 180; unionization of, 19; vision for Milwaukee, 20
World War I, Milwaukee during, 23, 24
World War II: strikes during, 156; U.S. economic policy during, 129. *See also* veterans, World War II
WTMJ-TV (Milwaukee), 58; advertising revenue of, 59

Zablocki, Clement, 69
Zancanaro, John, 164
Zander, Arnold: AFSCME leadership of, 151, 152; on sovereign authority, 169; on strikes, 159
Zedler, Edwin, 66, 67; in public housing debate, 78
Zeidler, Agnes Reinke, 29, 121; affordable housing experiences, 82; *Journal* photograph of, 40; in 1948 campaign, 32
Zeidler, Anita, 182, 183
Zeidler, Carl: comparison with Frank, 31, 32; conservative government of, 22; death of, 22, 24, 192n20; mayoralty of, 21–22, 28; World War II service of, 21, 22
Zeidler, Clara (daughter of Frank), 33
Zeidler, Clara (mother of Frank), 22, 31
Zeidler, Frank: accomplishments as mayor, 38, 183; affordable housing philosophy, 82–83; AFSCME and, 171; aid to strikers, 132–33, 209n17; anti-nuclear activism of, 25; on anti-tax campaign, 144; on arbitration, 159; belief in common good, 92; childhood home of, 22, 192n23; civic ideals of, 187; on civil-service system, 166; in Clay Boat incident, 138; and Common Council, 37–38, 66–67; comparison with Carl, 31, 32; conception of public interest, 9, 32, 36, 61, 93, 157, 158, 165, 170–73, 183, 187; death of, 186; on democratic process, 171; dissociation from Communism, 34–35; early life of, 22–24; education of, 23; elected offices of, 25; family of birth, 22, 23; fluency in German, 44; in Greendale, 82; hands-on approach, 33; horror of war, 24; illness of, 182; inner core study of, 105, 108, 124, 179; interest in the arts, 92; *Journal* photograph of, 40; as labor relations consultant, 171, 182–83; learning of, 31; liberal coalition of, 1, 35; *A Liberal in City Government*, 34; liberalism of, 13, 35–36; long-term goals of, 33, 34; marriage to Agnes, 32; mayoralties of, 9–10, 32–36; and MEC, 30, 32, 33, 35–36, 37; media opposition to, 10; meeting with Hearst representatives, 65; memorial service for, 186; *Milwaukee Sentinel* on, 39; and Milwaukee unions, 12, 36; in municipal consolidation debate, 117–18; municipal governance of, 37, 38, 150; in 1948 elections, 29–32, 39–41, 85; in 1952 election, 64, 94; in 1956 elections, 41, 118–22, 146; objectives for Milwaukee, 35; opposition to debt, 35; opposition to public-sector

bargaining, 148, 157–58, 159–60, 164–65, 168–69, 170–71, 173, 182, 187; personalist approach of, 34; personality of, 31, 33–34; philosophy of governance, 186–87; philosophy of public housing, 91; philosophy of service, 32–33, 36, 93, 170–71, 173, 177, 186; physical demeanor of, 31; popularity of, 183; pragmatism of, 37; on Progressive Party ticket, 28; public good under, 38; public housing accomplishments, 90; in public housing debate, 34, 80, 81–82, 84, 87, 106; as public servant, 182; in public television debate, 59, 60–61, 64–68, 184; race-based attacks on, 94; on race relations, 124; and real estate industry, 103–5; rejection of capitalism, 37; relationship with AFSCME, 149–50; relationship with *Milwaukee Journal*, 41; relations with business community, 37; religious identity of, 92; and residential segregation, 102, 103–6, 110; retirement from public office, 182; rumors spread about, 118; salary of, 182; school board duties of, 30; socialism of, 1, 24–25, 34, 119, 170, 176; in South Division Civic Association, 92; on southern migrants, 107; and strike of 1957, 165; and suburban annexation, 11, 112, 115–16, 184; support for integration, 11; support for St. Lawrence Seaway, 140, 184; support from labor, 29–30; threats against, 121; translations of Shakespeare, 33, 194n57; union support for, 29–30, 132–33; view of government, 92–93; visionary approach of, 33

Zeidler, Frank (uncle of Frank), 103–4
Zeidler, Jeanne, 182
Zeidler, Michael, 22, 31
Zinos, John, 153, 161, 164; early life of, 150; leadership of AFSCME, 149–50, 162–63; on municipal governance, 150; strategy of, 151; and strike of 1957, 165; strike threats by, 156

TULA A. CONNELL is a labor writer and historian living in Washington, D.C.

The Working Class in American History

Worker City, Company Town: Iron and Cotton-Worker Protest in Troy
  and Cohoes, New York, 1855–84   *Daniel J. Walkowitz*
Life, Work, and Rebellion in the Coal Fields: The Southern
  West Virginia Miners, 1880–1922   *David Alan Corbin*
Women and American Socialism, 1870–1920   *Mari Jo Buhle*
Lives of Their Own: Blacks, Italians, and Poles in Pittsburgh, 1900–1960
  John Bodnar, Roger Simon, and Michael P. Weber
Working-Class America: Essays on Labor, Community, and
  American Society   *Edited by Michael H. Frisch and Daniel J. Walkowitz*
Eugene V. Debs: Citizen and Socialist   *Nick Salvatore*
American Labor and Immigration History, 1877–1920s:
  Recent European Research   *Edited by Dirk Hoerder*
Workingmen's Democracy: The Knights of Labor and American Politics
  Leon Fink
The Electrical Workers: A History of Labor at General Electric
  and Westinghouse, 1923–60   *Ronald W. Schatz*
The Mechanics of Baltimore: Workers and Politics
  in the Age of Revolution, 1763–1812   *Charles G. Steffen*
The Practice of Solidarity: American Hat Finishers
  in the Nineteenth Century   *David Bensman*
The Labor History Reader   *Edited by Daniel J. Leab*
Solidarity and Fragmentation: Working People and Class Consciousness
  in Detroit, 1875–1900   *Richard Oestreicher*
Counter Cultures: Saleswomen, Managers, and Customers
  in American Department Stores, 1890–1940   *Susan Porter Benson*
The New England Working Class and the New Labor History
  Edited by Herbert G. Gutman and Donald H. Bell
Labor Leaders in America   *Edited by Melvyn Dubofsky and Warren Van Tine*
Barons of Labor: The San Francisco Building Trades and Union Power
  in the Progressive Era   *Michael Kazin*
Gender at Work: The Dynamics of Job Segregation by Sex
  during World War II   *Ruth Milkman*
Once a Cigar Maker: Men, Women, and Work Culture
  in American Cigar Factories, 1900–1919   *Patricia A. Cooper*
A Generation of Boomers: The Pattern of Railroad Labor Conflict in Nineteenth-
  Century America   *Shelton Stromquist*
Work and Community in the Jungle: Chicago's Packinghouse
  Workers, 1894–1922   *James R. Barrett*
Workers, Managers, and Welfare Capitalism: The Shoeworkers
  and Tanners of Endicott Johnson, 1890–1950   *Gerald Zahavi*
Men, Women, and Work: Class, Gender, and Protest in the New England
  Shoe Industry, 1780–1910   *Mary Blewett*

Workers on the Waterfront: Seamen, Longshoremen, and Unionism
   in the 1930s   *Bruce Nelson*
German Workers in Chicago: A Documentary History of Working-Class
   Culture from 1850 to World War I   *Edited by Hartmut Keil and John B. Jentz*
On the Line: Essays in the History of Auto Work   *Edited by Nelson Lichtenstein
   and Stephen Meyer III*
Labor's Flaming Youth: Telephone Operators and Worker
   Militancy, 1878–1923   *Stephen H. Norwood*
Another Civil War: Labor, Capital, and the State in the Anthracite Regions
   of Pennsylvania, 1840–68   *Grace Palladino*
Coal, Class, and Color: Blacks in Southern West Virginia, 1915–32
   Joe William Trotter Jr.
For Democracy, Workers, and God: Labor Song-Poems and
   Labor Protest, 1865–95   *Clark D. Halker*
Dishing It Out: Waitresses and Their Unions in the
   Twentieth Century   *Dorothy Sue Cobble*
The Spirit of 1848: German Immigrants, Labor Conflict,
   and the Coming of the Civil War   *Bruce Levine*
Working Women of Collar City: Gender, Class, and Community
   in Troy, New York, 1864–86   *Carole Turbin*
Southern Labor and Black Civil Rights: Organizing
   Memphis Workers   *Michael K. Honey*
Radicals of the Worst Sort: Laboring Women in Lawrence,
   Massachusetts, 1860–1912   *Ardis Cameron*
Producers, Proletarians, and Politicians: Workers and Party Politics
   in Evansville and New Albany, Indiana, 1850–87   *Lawrence M. Lipin*
The New Left and Labor in the 1960s   *Peter B. Levy*
The Making of Western Labor Radicalism: Denver's
   Organized Workers, 1878–1905   *David Brundage*
In Search of the Working Class: Essays in American Labor History
   and Political Culture   *Leon Fink*
Lawyers against Labor: From Individual Rights
   to Corporate Liberalism   *Daniel R. Ernst*
"We Are All Leaders": The Alternative Unionism of the Early 1930s
   Edited by Staughton Lynd
The Female Economy: The Millinery and Dressmaking
   Trades, 1860–1930   *Wendy Gamber*
"Negro and White, Unite and Fight!": A Social History of Industrial
   Unionism in Meatpacking, 1930–90   *Roger Horowitz*
Power at Odds: The 1922 National Railroad Shopmen's Strike   *Colin J. Davis*
The Common Ground of Womanhood: Class, Gender,
   and Working Girls' Clubs, 1884–1928   *Priscilla Murolo*
Marching Together: Women of the Brotherhood
   of Sleeping Car Porters   *Melinda Chateauvert*

Down on the Killing Floor: Black and White Workers
   in Chicago's Packinghouses, 1904–54   *Rick Halpern*
Labor and Urban Politics: Class Conflict and the Origins of Modern Liberalism
   in Chicago, 1864–97   *Richard Schneirov*
All That Glitters: Class, Conflict, and Community
   in Cripple Creek   *Elizabeth Jameson*
Waterfront Workers: New Perspectives on Race and Class
   Edited by Calvin Winslow
Labor Histories: Class, Politics, and the Working-Class Experience
   Edited by Eric Arnesen, Julie Greene, and Bruce Laurie
The Pullman Strike and the Crisis of the 1890s: Essays
   on Labor and Politics   *Edited by Richard Schneirov,
   Shelton Stromquist, and Nick Salvatore*
AlabamaNorth: African-American Migrants, Community,
   and Working-Class Activism in Cleveland, 1914–45   *Kimberley L. Phillips*
Imagining Internationalism in American and British
   Labor, 1939–49   *Victor Silverman*
William Z. Foster and the Tragedy of American Radicalism   *James R. Barrett*
Colliers across the Sea: A Comparative Study of Class Formation
   in Scotland and the American Midwest, 1830–1924   *John H. M. Laslett*
"Rights, Not Roses": Unions and the Rise of Working-Class
   Feminism, 1945–80   *Dennis A. Deslippe*
Testing the New Deal: The General Textile Strike of 1934
   in the American South   *Janet Irons*
Hard Work: The Making of Labor History   *Melvyn Dubofsky*
Southern Workers and the Search for Community:
   Spartanburg County, South Carolina   *G. C. Waldrep III*
We Shall Be All: A History of the Industrial Workers of the World
   (abridged edition)   *Melvyn Dubofsky, ed. Joseph A. McCartin*
Race, Class, and Power in the Alabama Coalfields, 1908–21   *Brian Kelly*
Duquesne and the Rise of Steel Unionism   *James D. Rose*
Anaconda: Labor, Community, and Culture in Montana's
   Smelter City   *Laurie Mercier*
Bridgeport's Socialist New Deal, 1915–36   *Cecelia Bucki*
Indispensable Outcasts: Hobo Workers and Community
   in the American Midwest, 1880–1930   *Frank Tobias Higbie*
After the Strike: A Century of Labor Struggle at Pullman   *Susan Eleanor Hirsch*
Corruption and Reform in the Teamsters Union   *David Witwer*
Waterfront Revolts: New York and London Dockworkers, 1946–61   *Colin J. Davis*
Black Workers' Struggle for Equality in Birmingham
   Horace Huntley and David Montgomery
The Tribe of Black Ulysses: African American Men
   in the Industrial South   *William P. Jones*
City of Clerks: Office and Sales Workers in Philadelphia, 1870–1920
   Jerome P. Bjelopera

Reinventing "The People": The Progressive Movement, the Class Problem,
  and the Origins of Modern Liberalism   *Shelton Stromquist*
Radical Unionism in the Midwest, 1900–1950   *Rosemary Feurer*
Gendering Labor History   *Alice Kessler-Harris*
James P. Cannon and the Origins of the American
  Revolutionary Left, 1890–1928   *Bryan D. Palmer*
Glass Towns: Industry, Labor, and Political Economy
  in Appalachia, 1890–1930s   *Ken Fones-Wolf*
Workers and the Wild: Conservation, Consumerism, and Labor
  in Oregon, 1910–30   *Lawrence M. Lipin*
Wobblies on the Waterfront: Interracial Unionism
  in Progressive-Era Philadelphia   *Peter Cole*
Red Chicago: American Communism at Its Grassroots, 1928–35   *Randi Storch*
Labor's Cold War: Local Politics in a Global Context
  Edited by Shelton Stromquist
Bessie Abramowitz Hillman and the Making of the Amalgamated
  Clothing Workers of America   *Karen Pastorello*
The Great Strikes of 1877   *Edited by David O. Stowell*
Union-Free America: Workers and Antiunion Culture   *Lawrence Richards*
Race against Liberalism: Black Workers and the UAW in Detroit
  David M. Lewis-Colman
Teachers and Reform: Chicago Public Education, 1929–70   *John F. Lyons*
Upheaval in the Quiet Zone: 1199/SEIU and the Politics
  of Healthcare Unionism   *Leon Fink and Brian Greenberg*
Shadow of the Racketeer: Scandal in Organized Labor   *David Witwer*
Sweet Tyranny: Migrant Labor, Industrial Agriculture,
  and Imperial Politics   *Kathleen Mapes*
Staley: The Fight for a New American Labor Movement
  Steven K. Ashby and C. J. Hawking
On the Ground: Labor Struggles in the American Airline Industry
  Liesl Miller Orenic
NAFTA and Labor in North America   *Norman Caulfield*
Making Capitalism Safe: Work Safety and Health Regulation
  in America, 1880–1940   *Donald W. Rogers*
Good, Reliable, White Men: Railroad Brotherhoods, 1877–1917
  Paul Michel Taillon
Spirit of Rebellion: Labor and Religion in the New Cotton South   *Jarod Roll*
The Labor Question in America: Economic Democracy
  in the Gilded Age   *Rosanne Currarino*
Banded Together: Economic Democratization
  in the Brass Valley   *Jeremy Brecher*
The Gospel of the Working Class: Labor's Southern Prophets
  in New Deal America   *Erik Gellman and Jarod Roll*
Guest Workers and Resistance to U.S. Corporate Despotism
  Immanuel Ness

Gleanings of Freedom: Free and Slave Labor along the
    Mason-Dixon Line, 1790–1860   *Max Grivno*
Chicago in the Age of Capital: Class, Politics, and Democracy
    during the Civil War and Reconstruction   *John B. Jentz and Richard Schneirov*
Child Care in Black and White: Working Parents and the History
    of Orphanages   *Jessie B. Ramey*
The Haymarket Conspiracy: Transatlantic Anarchist Networks
    Timothy Messer-Kruse
Detroit's Cold War: The Origins of Postwar Conservatism   *Colleen Doody*
A Renegade Union: Interracial Organizing and Labor Radicalism   *Lisa Phillips*
Palomino: Clinton Jencks and Mexican-American Unionism
    in the American Southwest   *James J. Lorence*
Latin American Migrations to the U.S. Heartland: Changing Cultural Landscapes
    in Middle America   *Edited by Linda Allegro and Andrew Grant Wood*
Man of Fire: Selected Writings   *Ernesto Galarza, ed. Armando Ibarra
    and Rodolfo D. Torres*
A Contest of Ideas: Capital, Politics, and Labor   *Nelson Lichtenstein*
Making the World Safe for Workers: Labor, the Left, and Wilsonian
    Internationalism   *Elizabeth McKillen*
The Rise of the Chicago Police Department: Class and Conflict,
    1850–1894   *Sam Mitrani*
Workers in Hard Times: A Long View of Economic Crises
    Edited by Leon Fink, Joseph A. McCartin, and Joan Sangster
Redeeming Time: Protestantism and Chicago's Eight-Hour Movement,
    1866–1912   *William A. Mirola*
Struggle for the Soul of the Postwar South: White Evangelical Protestants
    and Operation Dixie   *Elizabeth Fones-Wolf and Ken Fones-Wolf*
Free Labor: The Civil War and the Making of an American
    Working Class   *Mark A. Lause*
Death and Dying in the Working Class, 1865–1920   *Michael K. Rosenow*
Immigrants against the State: Yiddish and Italian Anarchism in America
    Kenyon Zimmer
Fighting for Total Person Unionism: Harold Gibbons, Ernest Calloway,
    and Working-Class Citizenship   *Robert Bussel*
Smokestacks in the Hills: Rural-Industrial Workers
    in West Virginia   *Louis Martin*
Disaster Citizenship: Survivors, Solidarity, and Power
    in the Progressive Era   *Jacob A. C. Remes*
The Pew and the Picket Line: Christianity and the American
    Working Class   *Edited by Christopher D. Cantwell, Heath W. Carter, and Janine
    Giordano Drake*
Conservative Counterrevolution: Challenging Liberalism
    in 1950s Milwaukee   *Tula A. Connell*

The University of Illinois Press
is a founding member of the
Association of American University Presses.

University of Illinois Press
1325 South Oak Street
Champaign, IL 61820-6903
www.press.uillinois.edu